ADVANCE PRAISE FOR

Six Lenses for Anti-Oppressive Education

"I read this book in one sitting because each of the chapters within the six parts is intellectually illuminating. The authors provide powerful teaching insights based upon authentic classroom knowledge and understanding of schooling that is valuable learning for educators and students. Each chapter provides a critical analysis of how oppression operates in classrooms, and how anti-oppressive education can combat these conditions. The six lenses for anti-oppressive education (authoritative discourses, hidden curriculum, learning to read critically, addressing resistance, complicating race and racism, and situating anti-oppressive education) examined in the book are key areas that teacher-candidates need to understand in order to be successful teachers of all students. With this publication, Kumashiro and Ngo have greatly advanced the anti-oppressive education discourse within the discussions of transformative education."

Carl C. Grant, Professor, Department of Curriculum and Instruction,
University of Wisconsin-Madison

Six Lenses for
Anti-Oppressive Education

Scotty —
With best
wishes in this
important work —

Studies in the
Postmodern Theory of Education

Joe L. Kincheloe and Shirley R. Steinberg
General Editors

Vol. 315

PETER LANG
New York • Washington, D.C./Baltimore • Bern
Frankfurt am Main • Berlin • Brussels • Vienna • Oxford

Six Lenses for
Anti-Oppressive Education

Partial Stories, Improbable Conversations

Kevin K. Kumashiro and Bic Ngo, Editors

PETER LANG
New York • Washington, D.C./Baltimore • Bern
Frankfurt am Main • Berlin • Brussels • Vienna • Oxford

Library of Congress Cataloging-in-Publication Data

Six lenses for anti-oppressive education: partial stories, improbable conversations /
edited by Kevin K. Kumashiro, Bic Ngo.
p. cm. — (Counterpoints; 315)
Includes bibliographical references.
1. Discrimination in education—United States.
2. Teaching—United States.
I. Kumashiro, Kevin K. II. Ngo, Bic.
LC212.2.S58   370.11'5—dc22   2006024522
ISBN 978-1-4331-0040-6 (hardcover)
ISBN 978-0-8204-8849-3 (paperback)
ISSN 1058-1634

Bibliographic information published by **Die Deutsche Bibliothek**.
Die Deutsche Bibliothek lists this publication in the "Deutsche
Nationalbibliografie"; detailed bibliographic data is available
on the Internet at http://dnb.ddb.de/.

Cover design by Lisa Barfield

© 2007 Peter Lang Publishing, Inc., New York
29 Broadway, 18th floor, New York, NY 10006
www.peterlang.com

Printed in the United States of America

Contents

Part I: Contesting Authoritative Discourses in Education: "Tradition," "Nature," and "Academic"

Part II: Unearthing Hidden Curriculums: Standards, Socialization, and Silences

Part III: Learning to Read Critically: From High School to College to Teacher Education

Part IV: Addressing Resistance: Uncertainties in Learning to Teach

Part V: Complicating Race: Engaging Anti-Racist Educational Theory and Practice

Part VI: Situating Anti-Oppressive Education: In Times of War and Globalization

Foreword

ALLAN LUKE & BENJI CHANG

No one said a critical approach to education, state and culture in mainstream educational systems was going to be easy. Its development and realization in schools, universities and communities has now spanned over four decades in North America, the UK, Australia and New Zealand. Much of this work has occurred under the radar of the official curriculum, relying on the ongoing efforts of three generations of educators since Freire. This volume brings together a tapestry of the artifacts and work of committed teachers and scholars, learners and students. As a text, it is multi-voiced in design and authorship. The chapters and dialogues focus on the education of particular communities marginalized on the basis of race and culture, social class, gender, sexual preference, age, 'disability' and location. They travel through a range of local cultures and identities, enlisting diverse theoretical models of culture, discourse, and political economy. They all land squarely where they should: in the everyday efforts by teachers, learners, researchers and intellectuals to make sense of and change a dynamic and vexed moral, economic and social order.

There is a necessary instability here. In their piece on Canadian universities, Proma Tagore and Fairn Herising live and write what they term the "contradictions and tensions" of critical education. These contradictions are not simply the result of inevitable clashes with the authority of state institutions and ideologies. Current conditions require something more than a simple binary divide of 'us' and 'them', dominant/marginal, centre/margin, or, indeed, oppressor/oppressed. Where these binaries hold, as they did for Freire and still do for others at the point of decolonisation, the development of strategic and practical direction is more straightforward. But education in "hypercapitalist" contexts (Graham, 2006) requires more nuanced and multiple theories and practices.

The contradictions and tensions that run across this volume are legacies from the materialist and textualist foundations of critical and cultural theory. *Where pedagogy is taken as material, institutional praxis*—it will run into the everyday contradictions of structure and agency, large scale macro politics and face-to-face classroom social relations. In their decisions about who should speak, when, about what, about which texts and discourses should be foregrounded, and which analytic approaches—critical educators are faced with everyday weaving back and forth between foci on identity, voice and position of individual learners and their own locations in place, space and history.

Where pedagogy is taken as text and discourse—it self-reflexively opens its texts and face-to-face exchanges to the same kinds of critique and deconstruction that it desires for its participants. What this means is that critical teachers and scholars are ethically obliged to subject their own stances, practices and assumptions to the kind of scrutiny that they set out engender in their teaching (Luke & Gore, 1991).

The volatility and uncertainty of new historical conditions, student cultures, and forms of knowledge and communication requires purposive but mindful responses to contradiction and self-reflexivity. We would argue that all "truth claims" are put up for grabs in dialogue, including the very foundational assumptions about the "power" of the "critical", "critical consciousness" and critical pedagogies (Luke, 1996). How and to what ends we might approach this without falling prey to a paralyzing relativism and pedagogical introspection is the focus of our brief comments here. And because we live in the intrinsically normative and political world of teaching and classrooms, there is no space or time—as there might be for academics and theorists—to endlessly defer interpretation and decisions about what is to be done.

Feminist, postcolonial and psychoanalytic work on standpoint has taught us that the critical educator is always a materially located, raced, and gendered human subject—and that there is no singular grand narrative that will provide unproblematic or non-contradictory grounds for our teaching. There's no formula here. Accordingly, each teacher necessarily is always at a crossroads (or, potentially, a roundabout), faced with everyday choices and agency, often in muddy institutional waters, typically in intercultural contact with new and unfamiliar signs and communities. What we like about this volume is how Ngo, Kumashiro and colleagues here have captured that moment on the page–that moment where the 'critical' is being made and unmade, a moment fraught with moral and political contradiction, locality and indeterminacy of events, demographics and cultures that we just haven't lived before. It couldn't be any other way.

During our recent work together in Australia, we read Bic and Kevin's book together. We used it as a jumping off point for our own cross-generational exchange, the reconsideration of our own histories, and the development of own takes on what is to be done in the current geopolitical and lived contexts of education, schooling and kids' lives. We thank the editors and authors here for the chance to share our narrative interaction over the issues.

The two of us grew up in the Asian-American communities of Los Angeles several decades apart. Allan is a second generation Chinese-American, descended from Cantonese grandparents who migrated around 1900. He started school in Echo Park in the mid-1950s—before the Civil Rights Acts, before *Brown vs. Board of Education*. Benji is also a second generation son of more recent Chinese immigrants from the diaspora of northern and southern China, Hong Kong, Vietnam, and Taiwan. He was schooled in the minority communities of LA's outer suburbs, and began his teaching in the very Chinatown community where Allan began school. Both of us cut it in public schools, got to university, taught school and became working teacher educators and researchers.

Through very different routes, we've wound up in a common space. Allan is a teacher educator, researcher and policymaker in Australia for the last two decades. He has worked with Aboriginal and Torres Strait Islander educators, and across Asian and South Pacific educational systems—where colonization and globalisation have established difficult community and educational conditions. Benji works as a teacher, community activist, researcher and moonlighting DJ in Los Angeles, where current educational policies show little signs of shifting longstanding patterns of discrimination and inequality. We share a commitment to the critical project that features in this volume: that of a socially just and equitable education for children who are relative outsiders to dominant cultural institutions, economic privilege and, indeed, dominant cultural and institutional narratives. Our standpoints remain connected to the generational struggles of our parents and grandparents.

But our longstanding commitments and practices in critical education haven't brought with them a methodological or moral certainty. Quite the contrary. For with the territory comes a commitment to face "contradiction and tension", each time with a freshness and openness to new readings of political, economic and institutional worlds. The shunting between our experiences of educational work in our two contexts, California and Queensland, has been enough to teach us once again about the idiosyncrasy and locality of different national and regional political economic, cultural contexts, Foucault's (1972) "discontinuity of discourse" principle at work. For Benji, as for many readers of this book, the key decisions now reside in whether to focus on school-based critical teaching and community-activism, and/or whether to formally make the move into the academy. For Allan, the key decisions now reside in how and where to engage with governments to try to build and shape critical educational policy. As for many of the writers here, there are tradeoffs, personal and psychological costs involved.

The authors here work through the wide array of strategies for changing the subject of pedagogy, for shifting and remaking the relations of exchange and value in the classroom. There is a strong focus on practical curriculum strategies. These range from the teaching of critical discourse analysis, to undergraduate training in postcolonial and postmodern theories of knowledge, from teacher-based action research and activism on curriculum and dialogue, to community-based intergenerational "memory work". They outline ways of building new curriculum around print, visual and digital texts, around popular and community cultures.

One of the offhand dismissals of critical education is that it is impractical within state schools, in conditions of high-stakes accountability environments, an already crowded curriculum and the intensification of teachers' work. This is simply not the case. Some of the pedagogical approaches and their affiliated theories here are relatively new to schools and classrooms (e.g. critical discourse analysis, standpoint epistemology, multi-literacies). Yet many others have been longstanding curriculum histories. These include: service learning, the use of autobiographical narrative (Holmes), the study of non-canonical texts (Wilson), portfolio-based assessment (Hirsch), and critical literary study (Hines). Consider, for example, Mary Beth Hines (Chapter 6) work with student teachers in the setting of university literature study. There she and her students draw upon Marxist cultural studies to begin unpacking the assumptions underlying many liberal, student-centered approaches to teaching. Her student Richard comments: " . . . the liberal humanist way of teaching literature is to just throw out ideas, and students would pick them up or bring in their own . . . like a free market. . . . the best ideas, the best products will win out". He goes on to show us how a traditional pedagogical approach to a longstanding canonical text, a "close reading" of *The Great Gatsby*, can open out into a more broadly critical, interpretive and grounded analysis of social relations.

As Hines suggests—these strategies need strong self-critical and self-analytic work. Simple axioms about "child-centeredness" and "dialogue", or even "resistance" and "critical consciousness" in themselves cannot ground or sustain practice. Critical education begins from embodied disposition and standpoint on 'otherness' (Luke, 2003), rearticulated via a critical reading of the world. The consequence is not 'a' singular method, formula or approach, as Ngo and Kumashiro here point out. It involves ways of seeing and seizing opportunities to transform and remake available elements and new pedagogic and curricular resources. Hines' use of the literary canon and Hirsch's engagement with mathematics curriculum are but two models for how we can translate dominant curriculum into a reoriented and redirected "curriculum in use". In other instances teachers here deliberately bring the 'strange' into the classroom: standpoints, discourses and texts, popular and community knowledges and the problems of everyday life repressed by official curriculum.

Our view is that we can't proceed simply on the grounds of assumed ideological consensus or political solidarity, since our translations of these things into practice are locally contingent and necessarily idiosyncratic, dependent on each of our pedagogic repertoires and on the contingent ethical and moral decisions made by the teachers described here. This local indeterminacy of pedagogy, discourse and teachers' and students' work was recently described by Erickson and colleagues (in press/2007) as only enabling a "paper-thin hegemony" in classrooms, rather than a seamless reproduction. And it is in this instability of local practice that we find the possibilities for undoing and redoing dominant ideologies and institutional practices. Neoliberal policy makers have learned, at their peril, hard lessons about the ultimate uncontrollability of teachers and students.

How, then, can we gauge the moment-by-moment decisions we make in the shaping of the critical? Nancy Fraser's (1996) landmark work on social justice offers two related educational approaches, focusing on "recognitive" and "redistributive" social justice. In education, the focus of recognitive approaches to social justice in education is upon the inclusion of alterior and non-dominant knowledges, 'other' voices, and the critique, denaturalization and revision of dominant curricular knowledges. Redistributive justice refers to an alteration of social and economic relations of exchange, aiming towards more equal distribution of cognitive, discourse and material resources. Many of the chapters here focus on social exchange in classrooms to effect different distributions of discourses, texts and critical analytic capacities, to shape other, critical and self-critical kinds of habitus and identity.

But what is *redistributed* in many of the projects described here is 'critique'. It is often the critique of state, institutional and media power, ideologies and practices, but it remains as a redistribution of a certain species of knowledge: knowledge about the structures, mechanisms and effects of oppression and repression of difference. The supposition of critical education, including our own, has been that this mode of critique, once experienced, transforms standpoints and experience, world view and lives.

To work towards redistributive justice, we need to know more about the longitudinal effects and diachronic durability of the critical dispositions, knowledges and practices achieved here. How durable is the 'critical' across life pathways and social fields? What do the subjects/objects of critical education actually do and take from their experiences in these classrooms? Both of us have used various approaches described by the teachers here, with what appeared to us and our students to be significant, life changing consequences. Benji is working with a cohort of LA Chinatown students who he has taught over the past 6 years, as they move from an early experience of critical education in the elementary classroom and local community groups. His current work involves following these students, as they move to other 'critical' and acritical classrooms, through community lives and risky situations, across fences of ethnicity and class, race and gender, through tough material conditions, institutional access and denial, to secondary schools, further education and employment, and, hopefully, into gainful, meaningful *and* critical lives.

We ask: What are the redistributive consequences of critical education? If we are committed to the redress of material inequality, and indeed if pedagogy and curriculum are to have both discourse and material effects–we are not only interested in how Benji's students use discourse in all of its forms, but as well whether and how their critical education has impacted on their ability to access, exchange and transform other forms of capital. To return to Fraser's point, the aim of the project of social justice can be both more inclusive discourses of schooling, and at the same time, the redistribution of educational resources and material pathways.

In this regard, the ideas of 'outcomes' and 'accountability'—however they have been fatally appropriated and compromised by Neoliberal and Neoconservative educational projects, are worth rethinking. Committed to a social justice based upon substantive change in our students' lives and life pathways, we need to hold ourselves and critical education more generally 'accountable' to understand and explain the material and life consequences of classroom practice, as these are remediated and influenced by other social, economic and political contexts (Luke, 2003/2007). This may seem ironic in light of *Reading First* and a corporate model of schooling based on an obsessive "countability" (Rose, 1997). But we welcome the challenge to define the grounds for which we are accountable: for changed material life contexts for those who we teach and work with, for agentive and influential pathways to and through other social fields of education, work, civic and cultural life.

Significant work is being done across a host of educational sites to achieve recognitive justice. This volume provides a practicable, substantial starting point for teachers to begin shaping and reshaping their own practice. Encouraged by this, our response is to begin documenting on whether, how, when and in what contexts curriculum and pedagogy based on principles of recognitive justice translates into different formations of cultural, economic and social capital. Our concern is with how a critical educational experience can lead to materially better educational outcomes, broadly defined, and the opening and expanding of life chances and pathways, and improved economic and cultural conditions for marginalized learners.

Allan Luke
Queensland University of Technology

Benji Chang
University of California, Los Angeles

References

Erickson, F., Bagrodia, r., Cook-Sather, A., Espinoza, M, Jurow, S, Shultz, J & Spencer, J. (in press/2007) Students' Experience of Curriculum: In-School and Out-of-School. In M. Connolly, Ed., *Sage Handbook of Curriculum*. London: Sage.

Foucault, M. (1972) *The Archaeology of Knowledge and the Discourse on Language*. Trans. A. Sheridan Smith. New York: Harper & Row.

Fraser, N. (1996). *Justice Interruptus*. London: Routledge.

Graham, P. (2006) *Hypercapitalism*. New York: Peter Lang.

Luke, A. (1996) Genres of power: Literacy education and the production of capital. In Hasan, R. & Williams, G. (Eds) *Literacy in society* (pp. 308–338). London: Longmans.

Luke, A. (2003) Two takes on the critical. In B. Norton & K. Toohey, Eds. *Language Learning and Critical Pedagogy* (pp. 21–31). Cambridge: Cambridge University Press.

Luke, A. (2003/2007) After the marketplace: Evidence, social science and educational research. *Australian Educational Researcher* 9(3), 43–78. Reprinted in J. Ozga & R. Lingard, Eds., *The Routledge Educational Policy Reader*. London: Routledge.

Luke, C. & Gore, J. Eds. (1991) *Feminism and Critical Pedagogy*. New York: Routledge.

Rose, N. (1997) *The Powers of Freedom*. London: Routledge.

1

Introduction

KEVIN K. KUMASHIRO AND BIC NGO

It was almost ten years ago that we met as graduate students in education at the University of Wisconsin-Madison. Although neither of us entered graduate school expecting to make "oppression" and "activism" central in our work, we constantly found ourselves in conversations where the personal could not help but to be political. As a person of color, a woman, a person who is queer, a person who is disabled, or a close friend and ally to one, we found that our experiences in and perspectives at the margins gave us profoundly troubling lenses through which to engage with what we were learning about education, injustice, and their intersections.

Of course, in many of our graduate courses, we found ourselves engaged in conversations about injustice, difference, or the personal and the political. As often happens in critical work, we found ourselves "mired in critique," as one friend put it, where we not only read many critical studies, but also learned to critique them, often to a point where classroom conversations seemed to focus only on what was problematic with the studies, and not on how they advanced the field of research or practice. While we believe such critical knowledge and critical thinking are necessary steps in disrupting the status quo, we also believe that any study, perspective, or practice cannot help but to be partial (i.e., it has both strengths and weaknesses). Thus, we were often struck by the ways in which "conversations" (whether they were in the classroom or in print) seemed not really to be about having a conversation about the partial perspectives inherent in any study.

As students, as commentators, as researchers, and even as teachers, we often "converse" with researchers by discussing their strengths and weaknesses, such as when discussing a study in class, or writing a book review, or serving as a discussant at a conference. When reading or observing such situations, we were struck by the degree to which the discussant seemed to speak as much about their own work as about the work under review. This happened not necessarily in direct or explicit ways, but because the analysis of strengths and weaknesses could only happen through a lens (of what makes something strong/weak) that the discussant brings to the conversation, the analysis had to be about more than the study under review. In other words, discussing strengths and weaknesses involves discussing how the study maps onto how the discussant already thinks about strengths and weaknesses, making the conversation more of a repetition of the discussant's lens, and less a conversation that explores different lenses (or that disrupts the lenses we already have). We were particularly struck by the contradictions of scholars and educators who spoke passionately of being "critical," "self-reflexive," or "nonnormative," but who would nonetheless resist critiques not only of their own work (which is perhaps understandable), but also of their field of study or of the canonical perspectives of their field.

As mentioned earlier, we believe that any perspective is partial: every perspective has strengths and weaknesses; every perspective makes some learning and change possible, and others, impossible. For this reason, we have become more interested in seeing conversations that really grapple with the partialities of various perspectives, including our own, and including at our intersections. Over the past few years, we have come across theories and practices of curriculum, instruction, and teacher preparation that promise new insights for multicultural, feminist, critical, queer, and postcolonial education. Particularly when juxtaposed with one another, we believe these studies can take the field of education research in new and innovative directions. This is why we have assembled this book.

This book offers a range of conceptual and curricular resources for elementary and secondary educators and teacher educators interested in exploring new and innovative ways to challenge racism, classism, sexism, heterosexism, and other forms of oppression in the classroom (i.e., new and innovative approaches to anti-oppressive education). It blends analyses of and recommendations for K-12 education and teacher education, and focuses on the barriers we often confront when teaching, learning, and learning to teach toward social justice. In an effort to be as concrete as possible, this volume includes "Teaching Stories" that delve, in much detail, into how anti-oppressive education played out in the classroom. The authors work in K-12 schools and teacher education programs across North America, and advocate perspectives and practices that, when combined, promise to take the field of anti-oppressive education in helpful, groundbreaking directions.

Of course, none of the chapters purport to present a perspective on anti-oppressive education that is without its share of problems. As we experienced when in graduate school, the field of anti-oppressive education includes multiple theoretical traditions, with no consensus on how to teach in anti-oppressive ways. This book affirms this multiplicity of perspectives on anti-oppressive education, and illustrates the value of a field that contains complex, incongruous, even conflicting perspectives. We believe that anti-oppressive education requires us to be continuously reflexive about how any of our perspectives on teaching and learning are partial, and necessarily so.

As we discussed earlier, anti-oppressive education is best served when educators engage in collaborative conversation about their perspectives and work. Toward this end, we have asked the contributors of this book to converse with one another about their chapters. Thus, the unique feature of this book is the "Conversation" in each of the six parts in which authors collaboratively respond to and engage with one another's chapters. These conversations model the types of insights and collaborative movements made possible when educators and researchers with very different experiences and knowledge speak with, question, and learn from one another. The conversations are not places to do the strengths-and-weaknesses type of reviews that are all too prevalent in academia. Rather, they are places to explore ways of responding to one another that challenge or trouble one's own knowledge and take us in new directions. And, they are places that invite the reader to imagine multiple ways of reading and engaging with these chapters beyond how you would have normally read them.

The goal is to explore how the juxtaposition of different writings invites readers (and authors) to look beyond the chapters. That is, we hope that the conversations invite readers to reflect on ways that different routes of reading both enable and hinder the reader in engaging with the ideas articulated in the chapters. Such reflection on *how* you read is important, given the controversial and uncomfortable nature of anti-oppressive education research that often generates much emotion and even resistance to thinking and talking about these issues. In the spirit of the book, we suggest that readers reflect on not only what we are saying, but also how we are saying it, how others are responding to it, and why our different ways of researching/responding/learning need to be examined.

The chapters are grouped around six themes of anti-oppressive education, what we call six "lenses" for observing and analyzing education and its relation to oppression and anti-oppressive change. Each grouping consists of at least two chapters and a "Conversation." Some groupings also include chapters that are called "Teaching Stories," which go into detail about how some educators are addressing that theme in the classroom. The chapters and teaching stories reflect a range of content areas (social studies, English language arts, "foreign" languages, natural sciences, and mathematics) in both K-12 education and teacher education; student and teacher populations (elementary, secondary, university); social differences and oppressions (based on race, culture, social class, gender, sexual orientation, language, age, disability); activities (simulations, service learning, book clubs, lesson planning); and research methods (historiography, curriculum analysis, discourse analysis, case study, self-study).

Part I, "Contesting Authoritative Discourses in Education," disrupts authoritative discourses in education by exploring how popular notions of "tradition," "nature," and "academic" significantly influence the ways we think about what and how we are supposed to be teaching and learning, and who we are supposed to be. The chapters by Linda Fernsten, Jane L. Lehr, and Charlotte Lichter examine ways in which such popular discourses play out in education both historically and today, and what it might look like to challenge the authority of these discourses.

Part II, "Unearthing Hidden Curriculums," examines unintended teachings about differences and oppression that occur in and out of schools, particularly teachings that reinforce inequities and bias based on social class, age, culture, and ability. The chapters by Mark R. Davies, Judi Hirsch, and Gloria Graves Holmes shed light on the contradictions of curriculum standards, as well as the silences in classrooms, to show how hidden curriculums operate and ways we might challenge them through social studies, mathematics, and other disciplines.

Part III, "Learning to Read Critically," argues that anti-oppressive education within the English language arts requires changing not only what students read, but also how they read. Unlike the other sections in this book, which bring together chapters from multiple theoretical lenses and disciplines, Part III brings together chapters that focus on the lens of critical literacy and the discipline of English language arts. The chapters by Jocelyn Anne Glazier, Mary Beth Hines, and Carol Ricker-Wilson analyze critical literacy in the high school, college, and teacher preparation classroom.

Part IV, "Addressing Resistance," describes activities (i.e., service learning, book clubs, and simulations) that were conducted within teacher education courses and that aimed to raise awareness of inequities and bias regarding social class, gender, language, culture, and race. The chapters by Ann Berlak, Mary Curran, Rita M. Kissen, and Sekani Moyenda not only examine the tensions between goals and unintended outcomes, but also highlight the resistances that learners (including teachers-in-training) express toward inwardly acknowledging privilege or outwardly challenging bias, and ways to address such resistances.

Part V, "Complicating Race and Racism in Theory and Practice," raises questions about how race, culture, cultural bias, and racism in teaching and learning are often conceptualized, particularly regarding how some ideologies of race and racism become taken-for-granted as "common sense." The chapters by Connie North and

Thomas M. Philip examine strategies for, and highlight resistances to, teaching against racism, particularly when looking at the language we use to do this work.

Part VI, "Situating Anti-Oppressive Education in Our Times," examines the broader social and political contexts for doing anti-oppressive education today. The chapters by George Lipsitz, Proma Tagore, and Fairn Herising reflect on what it means to teach in times of war, of globalization, and of conflicts between national priorities and international identities. Unique to Part VI is the inclusion on an additional voice in the conversation, namely, Jocelyn Anne Glazier, a contributor from earlier in the book whose "Teaching Story" on critical literacy for teacher educators helps us think about the implications of these chapters for teaching and teacher education.

Throughout the process of producing this book, the contributors and editors grappled with the challenges of having fruitful conversations that would (and that, in fact, do) model the kind of anti-oppressive movement that we envision. The challenges were not only logistical (e.g., conflicting schedules of authors, short timelines, and limitations of e-mail as a primary form of conversing), but also interpersonal (e.g., trying to communicate disagreements in a professional or cordial manner; feeling misunderstood or unheard; and not having clear guidance from the editors or sample models of how this conversation should or could "look"). Indeed, the production of this book was a messy process, but rather than caution against future attempts, we believe it reflects the need not only for more conversations like these in our classrooms and in our publications, but also for more conversations among researchers and educators about how to have productive conversations. We hope that this book pushes the field of education research in this direction, and we look forward to seeing the changes that result.

Part I

Contesting Authoritative Discourses in Education

"Tradition," "Nature," and "Academic"

1

Manners, Intellect, and Potential

A Historiography on the Underachievement of Boys in Literacy

CHARLOTTE LICHTER

Recently, growing concerns over the academic underachievement of boys in literacy have become rife in educational and media domains (Alloway and Gilbert, 1997; Cohen, 1998; Connell, 1996; Gilbert and Gilbert, 1998). Results of various educational studies and surveys from numerous industrialized countries have indicated that girls were making gains in all academic disciplines while boys were lagging behind, specifically in the areas of literacy and languages. Consequently, a torrent of articles, news headlines, and backlash politics has sounded the alarm on this seemingly "new" phenomenon of why boys are *now* underachieving and has positioned a dichotomous paradigm of boys versus girls, with the new outcry being "What about the boys?"

Boys have been portrayed by the media and by some researchers as an educationally disadvantaged group. Girls' achievements have somehow become correlated with boys' underachievements. This mindset creates a dichotomy of winners and losers, a battle between boys and girls, a zero–sum game in which success is attained and measured by one gender at the expense of the other.

Current public debates and publications have permeated the media and educational forums in Australia, the United States, the United Kingdom, New Zealand, and Canada (Alloway and Gilbert, 1997; Connell, 1996; Mahony, 1998). A plethora of analyses has flooded both the public and pedagogical terrain, mooting explanations and recommendations for the underachievement of boys in education. As a result, various camps with variant and opposing viewpoints have developed and are presenting and recommending suggestions for changes.

Quick-fix solutions and reforms are being made to curriculum, pedagogical practices, tools of assessment, and educational policies that coalesce and reestablish hegemonic depictions of masculinity (Mahony, 1998; Reed, 1998). Remediation, as cited by Mahony and Reed, includes adoption of programs that are more pertinent to and of interest to boys; narrowly focused curriculums; masculinization of teaching styles to include technical, rule-bound methodologies and phonics-based methods; and revisions of teacher-appraisal systems. Other simple remedies include initiating more male teachers into schools as positive male role models, replacement of classroom storybooks with more boy-orientated books, and a call for reexamining the allocation of resources along gender lines (Epstein et al., 1998; Reed, 1998). Numerous scholars have suggested that many of these quick-fix solutions could be and are detrimental to the education of girls (Epstein et al., 1998) as well as to the education of boys (Gilbert and Gilbert, 1998).

Reports of performance differentials, media hysteria, and a global sense of crisis have led copious authors to theorize about the interconnectedness between literacy education and gender. Issues of male identity and the social construction of literacy as a feminized practice are key factors in this contemporary discourse. The historical and social practices of gender and of literacy are critical in our comprehension and discernment of the underachievement of boys, which is inextricably linked to the complex sociological conception of masculinity.

What about the boys? Cohen (1998) implies that the current focus on boys' underachievement stems from the implicit assumption that until recently, boys have always surpassed girls. How concerned should we be over this seemingly new phenomenon of boys' underachievement in literacy? By examining this issue through a historical perspective, it becomes palpable that this is *not* new and that until recently, boys' underachievement, although a concern, has never been considered problematic (Cohen, 1998).

I want to argue that in order to critically analyze the current viewpoints and debates that are emerging in North America about underachieving boys, it is pivotal that such issues be located within a British historical perspective. Such an approach will illuminate how the construction of this present-day concern, which is embedded in a historical fabric, has resurfaced and re-formed and is being replayed in the present.

As a British colony, Canada, as well as Australia, New Zealand and the United States, was influenced by British ideas, traditions, and practices. The English model of education was passed down to the colonies in America and continued to function as a guideline even after the American Revolution (MacNaughton, 1947). "An understanding of the English conception of education is therefore of importance"

(MacNaughton, 1947, p. 5). As the North American education system is a derivative of its English model, this chapter primarily focuses on and traces the British educational system as a basis for its historical trajectory of the underachievement of North American boys.

The British Education System

Katherine MacNaughton (1947) articulates how in an aristocratic social organization, the policies and decrees of a government are fashioned by the vested interests and desires of the ruling class, which seek to perpetuate and maintain the existing social and economic order. In pre- and post-Reformation England, education was virtually in the hands of the church. Education was a vehicle for engendering aristocratic leadership, authority, and status for church and state. Apart from enactments pertaining to workhouse schools, the British Parliament did not pass any laws regarding education throughout the eighteenth century. "Secular instruction for the masses was considered unnecessary, even unwise" (MacNaughton, 1947, p. 6).

After the Reformation, the Church of England was in control of education and its strategic agenda was to teach its particular faith and doctrines (Hans, 1967; MacNaughton, 1947). Schools for the working class were organized in the early 1700s and focused on the inculcation of morals and religion as well as impressing upon their students "habits of labour and industry and . . . proper humility towards the ruling class" (Hans, 1967, p. 132). The Sunday schools that started in 1780 included reading, writing, and simple arithmetic, in addition to moral and religious instruction. Between 1780 and 1870, all elementary schools were voluntary and were set up and maintained by religious or charitable organizations, private enterprise, or by individuals (Taft, 1999).

Grammar Schools including nine boarding schools known as Public schools were initially intended for poor-class boys; however, because of the high fees, only boys from wealthy or from the rising middle-class families could afford to attend. These endowed nine "public" schools—Eton, Winchester, Harrow, St. Paul's, Rugby, Charterhouse, Westminster, Shrewsbury, and Merchant Taylors—were actually private schools founded by wealthy donors and "through the patronage of the aristocracy became in the eighteenth century the nurseries of the ruling class" (Hans, 1967, p. 264). In 1833, the state assumed a small measure of responsibility for the working-class schools and annual grants toward education commenced.

As the primary purpose of the working-class schools was the indoctrination of morals and religious doctrine, I, for the most part, examine the education of British upper-class boys up until the Education Act of 1870 when the state assumed responsibility for public education and asserted compulsory elementary education.

British Culture of Politeness: Manners, Conversation, and the English Gentleman

The emergence of a polite society in Britain in the late seventeenth century gave rise to new forms of manliness as an alternative to existing standards, which were condemned by many critics as boorish. As French culture dominated much of Europe during the seventeenth and eighteenth centuries (Mizukoshi, 1999), English gentlemen tenaciously adapted an analogous code of conduct (politeness and conversation) fashioned on French practices of sociability and politesse. In 1747, Lord Chesterfield wrote in a letter to his son: "A Frenchman, who, with a fund of virtue, learning and good sense, has the manners and good-breeding of his country, is the perfection of human nature" (1917, p. 10). By mid-eighteenth century, new forms of social refinement began to emerge, which embraced expositions of overt emotional sensitivity and compassion as an indication of true politeness.

During the seventeenth and eighteenth centuries, a moiety of education focused on the refinement of the English tongue. Genteel manners and elegant conversation skills were essential, as a socially defining practice, for an English gentleman. His manner of expression and display of polite decorum served as a marker of his identity and distinguished him from the commoner. Therefore, it was imperative that he was properly schooled. Around the turn of the eighteenth century, the apex of a young gentleman's education was cultured by foreign travel known as the Grand Tour that not only educated him in matters of foreign policies and affairs, but also facilitated social and political success.

In this age of politeness, the eighteenth-century English gentleman's manliness was characterized by self-presentation, polite sociability, and polished modes of conduct. Chesterfield imbues the perspicuity of an English gentleman:

> I hope you received that mark of distinction with respect and with steadiness, which is the proper behavior of a man of fashion. People of a low, obscure education cannot stand the rays of greatness . . . whereas, *les honnêtes gens* [people of breeding] are not dazzled by superior rank . . . and can converse just as easily with a king as with any one of his subjects. . . . The characteristic of a well-bred man is to converse with his inferiors without insolence, and with his superiors with respect, and with ease. (1917, p. 74)

To develop the English gentlemen and to refine his manners, politeness, and social success, males were encouraged to practice social intercourse through conversation. Such politeness and vivacity of conversation was perfected through conversation with women who were deemed central agents of refinement. John Locke (1693) commented:

Persons of quality of the softer sex, and such of them as have spent their time in well-bred company, show us that . . . without the least study or knowledge of grammar, can carry them to a great degree of elegance and politeness in their language: and there are ladies who, without knowing what tenses and participles, adverbs and prepositions are, speak as properly, and as correctly . . . as most gentlemen who have bred up in the ordinary methods of grammar-schools. (§168: Grammar, para. 2)

Interestingly, while women's expressive and fluent oral skills were noted, concerns were being expressed over boys' difficulties to master fluency and diction.

Locke addressed his concerns for boys' failure to master Latin and their difficulties to perfect written and oral English. He questioned and criticized the current methods (grammar rules) by which upper-class boys were being taught Latin. Noting that girls seemed to learn conversational French with ease, he hence assumed that it was *the method* that assured success and thus, endorsed the "conversational method" for teaching boys Latin:

Latin is no more unknown to a child, when he comes into the world, than English: and yet he learns English without master, rule, or grammar: and so might he Latin too . . . And when we so often see a French woman teaching an English girl to speak and read French perfectly in a year or two, without any rule of grammar, or anything else, but prattling to her, I cannot but wonder, how gentlemen have overseen this way for their sons, and thought them more dull or incapable than their daughters. If therefore a man could be got who himself speaks good Latin, who would be always about your son and talk constantly to him and make him read Latin, that would be the true, genuine and easy way of teaching him Latin. (Locke, 1693, §165–166: Latin)

It is interesting to note that Locke appropriated boys' failure to learn Latin to the pedagogical method being used to teach the boys and not to boys themselves. This very thought is again mirrored when Locke expressed concern over their ability to master English:

There can scarce be a greater defect in a gentleman than not to express himself well, either in writing or speaking. But yet . . . a great many, who . . . should have the qualities of gentlemen, who cannot so much as tell a story as they should, much less speak clearly and persuasively in any business? This I think not to be so much their fault, as the fault of their education. (Locke, 1693, p. 189: Rhetoric-Logic, para. 2)

Locke was not the only writer to impugn education as the basis for men's inarticulateness and hampered fluency. Eighteenth-century conduct writer James Fordyce blamed their perceived ineptness on the study of the classics; renowned essayist Joseph Addison and writer Thomas Wilson condemned taciturnity (Cohen, 1998).

Throughout much of the eighteenth century, the focus continued to be on cultivating conversational skills and fluency. Conversely, there emanated concern that overexposure to female company would engender effeminacy. Various tracts, periodicals, and pamphlets began to publicly emerge criticizing and expressing concern over the feminization of English men (Kimmel, 1992; Norton, 2000). By mid-eighteenth century, attitudes toward the French model of gentlemanliness vitiated as profound anxieties about the emasculation of men emerged. Kimmel (1992) purports that France was imputed for gender discombobulation and that feminization was linked to sedition even as conventional masculinity was emblematized by patriotism.

Perceptions of the effeminizing influence of education, the Grand Tour, excessive luxury, and French culture contributed to the trepidation of effeminacy, which became perpetually woven into notions of masculinity. Young boys' schooling, and more often the women who ran the nursery and early schools, were often blamed for the effeminacy of the English youths (Norton, 2000). From an educational standpoint, the Grand Tour, resulting in pretentious and false refinement, was perceived as a failure. Concerns were raised that young English gentlemen who were sent to France frequently turned into over-refined Frenchified fops instead of polished gentlemen (Kimmel, 1992; Mizukoshi, 1999).

Embedded within the paradigm of eighteenth-century politeness was the imperative ability to also converse in French, as this defined the gentleman and was the universal language of the European courts at that juncture. In the latter part of the eighteenth century, a paramount shift occurred whereby the focus on cultivating conversation, oral, and fluency skills in the definition of the gentleman was replaced by a focus on developing reason and intellectual abilities, the basis for the new style of British manliness. Some scholars suggest that a moribund interest in Parisian education and the wars with France engendered the shift in attitude toward the employment of conversational French in the fashioning of English gentlemen and in the forging of a British national identity (Colley, 1992). French language was now viewed as flowery and seductive and seen as a female accomplishment in contrast to the English language, which was viewed as manly and taciturn. Men were expected to divert more of their time to developing and honing mental abilities and to spend less time cultivating their oral skills through conversation. The learning of foreign languages and the study of grammar were now inaugurated in Public schools (rather than through foreign travel) as a method of developing mental faculties and training the mind. The persona of the English gentleman was now characterized through a "manly" education.

"Politeness and manliness were incompatible desires, for the former could only be acquired and polished in the company of the other sex" (Mizukoshi, 1999, II para. 6). Henceforth, the English gentleman was no longer fashioned and defined by the eloquent and fluent dialectical English tongue, but by his reticence, which had been previously deemed as an emblematic fault and had now become a confirmation of his intellectual capacity, self-restraint, and manliness. Furthermore, adept and loquacious expression and fluency associated with women and the French now became verification of a feeble and superficial intellect. Consequently, a correlation linking masculinity, taciturnity, and strength of intellect was unveiled (Cohen, 1998).

The Birth of Gender: Dichotomizing the Sexes

Prior to the eighteenth century, men and women—although recognized as different—were not seen as being two distinct genders, but rather perceived as one sex in which women possessed the inferior or deficient constituent of the same attribute (McKeon, 1995). In the eighteenth century, a new climate of thought emerged as Newton's scientific theories revolutionized beliefs about nature and the laws of nature. McKeon (1995) explains that "England acquired the modern wisdom that there are not one but two sexes; that they are biologically distinct and therefore incommensurable; and that they are defined not by behavior, which is variable, but by nature, which is not" (p. 301). As a result of this rethinking of the body, difference became embedded in the biological and not the social. This was strengthened by the shift in scientific ideology and translated into prescriptive codes for behavior.

"In this new discourse of difference, male and female bodies were believed to be homologous with their minds" (Cohen, 1998, p. 25) and hence, the emergence of pseudoscientific evidence of gendered abilities. Weak bodies meant weak minds. Therefore, women's physical weakness was considered a sign of and indeed proof of their intellectual inferiority. John Bennett wrote: "Women's outward frame is marked with a physical inferiority. It appears not to be calculated for such efforts of thinking as the more abstracted sciences require" (Bennett, 1778, as cited in Cohen, 1998, p. 25). Bennett argued that although boys did not seem to be as perspicuous as girls, they were actually much brighter. Their "dullness," he concluded, was indicative of reflective and deep thinking (Cohen, 1998).

Thus, by the end of the eighteenth century, English language and skills had become gendered in that vivaciousness of conversational skills became considered babble and feminine while taciturnity became construed as reserved and masculine. Gendered identities were being polarized by purportedly inherent and distinctive feminine and masculine characteristics. "Girls' brightness, construed as inferiority, and boys' dullness construed as *potential* [emphasis added], were woven into the fabric of gender difference" (Cohen, 1998, p. 25). Hence, femininity and masculinity were depicted in opposition to each other. Intellectuality and rationality had thus become couched as masculine attributes, obtuseness and irrationality as feminine characteristics.

Throughout the nineteenth century, the focus continued on training and cultivating the inherent male intellect. With the development of a mass schooling system in the late nineteenth century, English as a subject was seen as a means of regaining social stability and for controlling and civilizing the working class and humanizing the new middle class. Cohen (1998) interestingly noted that, although training and disciplining the mind was an important principle, the academic achievement and underperformance of boys were not considered as essential as the development of moral fiber and character. "The public school system aimed to produce . . . 'manly gentlemen' (Vance 1975: 23) not 'effeminate, enfeebled bookworms' (Mangan 1981: 189)" (Cohen, 1998, p. 28).

Subject English was considered an important principle underpinning national solidarity. According to Cohen (1997), the moral fiber of English national identity was linked to masculinity. The construction and the inculcation of masculinity remained at the forefront, given the ongoing fears of effeminacy and its accompanying din of anxieties. Numerous manuals and books were published by physicians and writers apprising proper socialization skills for boys in order to avoid feminization. Others advised against the use of featherbeds for boys, dancing, fraternities, and *book learning*.

In 1864, Lord Taunton's School Enquiry Commission began evaluating the array of curricula and the system of secondary education, including proprietary and grammar schools and the education of girls. In its 1868 report, it revealed that girls up until the age of twelve outperformed boys (Cohen, 1998; Taft, 1999). John Henry Newman wrote:

> Not one boy in a hundred does avail himself of this assistance; your boy is not solitary in his inaccuracy; all boys are more or less inaccurate, *because* they are boys; boyishness of mind means inaccuracy. Boys cannot deliver a message, or execute an order, or relate an occurrence, without a blunder. They do not rouse up their attention and reflect: they do not like the trouble of it: they cannot look at anything steadily; and, when they attempt to write, off they go in a rigmarole of words, which does them no good, and never would, though they scribbled themes till they wrote their fingers off. (1873/1907, p. 358)

Boys' underperformance was attributed as a natural essence of boyhood and masculinity, a sign of his deep and profound thinking, and indicative of his potential (Cohen, 1998). According to Bob Powell, boys' underachievement "becomes transformed into a healthy . . . rebellion against ineffectual teaching techniques" (Cohen, 1998, p. 21). By the turn of the nineteenth century, this "dullness," which had been written about a century earlier, was viewed as an indicator of the upper-class boy's potential that separated and differentiated him from astute and raucous lower-class boys and from *all* girls (Cohen, 1998).

Erudition of Women, Medical Hypotheses, and the Theory of Overstrain

Male power, control, and privilege were threatened by opportunities for women to access higher education. Women were deemed as intellectually inferior to men and, therefore, did not need the same mode of education. In the late nineteenth century, social anxiety and escalating tension sanctioned an urgent rationale for keeping women in the home. Herbert Spencer alleged that higher education for women was responsible for the differentiation between men and women's roles (Morantz-Sanchez, 1985). Women were discouraged from developing their own potential and from attaining higher education. Hence, with the rise in medical knowledge during this century, many myths and "medical" theories burgeoned to thwart and prevent women's further educational pursuits; and to sustain the "man-made" doctrine of the alleged inferiority of women.

Efforts were made by physicians, anthropologists, psychologists, and physiologists to scientifically prove this "inferiority" assumption by attributing women's inferior intelligence to their smaller skull and brain size. Paul Broca, neuroanatomist, conceded that "the relatively small size of the female brain depends in part upon her physical inferiority and in part upon her intellectual inferiority" (Broca, 1861, as cited in Sommers, 2000, p. 91). Gustave Le Bon, social psychologist, claimed, "There are a large number of women whose brains are closer in size to those of gorillas than to the most developed male brains. This inferiority is so obvious that one cannot contest it for a moment" (Le Bon, 1879, as cited in Sommers, 2000, p. 92). Doctors warned that higher forms of education would result in afflictions such as pelvic distortions, infertility, sickness and disease, inability to breastfeed, induced psychiatric disorders, growth of chest hair, explosion of female brains, and overstrain or mental fatigue (Morantz-Sanchez, 1985; Spender, 1982). As Morantz-Sanchez (1985) points out,

> According to Spencer, the human body was a closed energy system in which any abnormal demands made on one part would inevitably deplete the healthy development of some other part. This theory was often applied to men, particularly when physicians discussed sexuality, but historians have discovered an even greater willingness among medical thinkers to appeal to variations of the closed energy theory when discussing women. (Morantz-Sanchez, 1985, pp. 205–206)

Based on Spencer's closed energy theory, the "medical theory" of overstrain or mental fatigue, the primary assertion of Dr. Edward Clarke and his medical supporters, soon became a common premise across Europe and North America that "anything above a minimum level of intellectual effort would overstrain the constitution of the average woman" (Spender, 1982, p. 22). This belief permeated the discourse on education, and girls' enthusiasm for learning, and assiduousness became encapsulated in the discourse of overstrain. How does this relate to boys' underachievement? Cohen (1998) points out that when the Taunton Commission noted in their report "girls' eagerness to learn and the female mind's tendency to develop more rapidly than the males" (p. 26), concern developed about overstrain for girls.

The perception of overstrain continued into the twentieth century whereby girls' achievement, and not boys' underachievement, became the main area of concern. What about the boys? Why was their underperformance not considered problematic? Boys' underachievement was considered a manifestation of their inherent boyishness and as depicted by the 1923 Board of Education report, "a habit of healthy idleness" (Cohen, 1998, p. 27). Similarly, this same perspective was reemphasized by Brereton when he penned, "Girls on the whole are more conscientious in their attitude toward their work. Many girls will work at a subject they dislike. No healthy boy ever does" (Brereton, 1930, as cited in Cohen, 1998, p. 27). Cohen (1998) declared: "'Overstrain' is thus a critical construct for a history of boys' underachievement, because it is contributed to producing the underperformance of boys as an index of their mental health" (p. 27). This mindset of boy's natural superior intellect was always presupposed and never questioned. Idleness, indifference, and underachievement were viewed not only as normal constructs of boyishness, but also as symbols of "potential."

Throughout the twentieth century, this position of "males are superior" continued. Their "natural" superiority became a taken-for-granted assumption and underpinned the discourse of education. Within the parameters of schooling and society, the aristocratic philosophy continued to inform the model of the true gentleman, the ideal of what it meant to be masculine. The true "manly gentlemen" did not have to work at "achieving," as it was the development of the masculine character that was most important (Cohen, 1998). It is interesting to note that even in the 1970s, R. R. Dale reinforced the analogical notion that "high academic attainment is not the most important aim of a school . . . good character, right attitudes and a healthy emotional development are of far more value" (Dale, 1971, as cited in Cohen, 1998, pp. 28–29).

Conclusion

If, from an historical perspective, boys' academic performance has not been a major area of concern, then why has it become one now? Media reports have illuminated the perceived underachievement of boys and have kindled the mounting back-lash against girls' achievement. The influence of feminist educational discourses cannot be omitted as it has been pinpointed as a contributing factor of boys' academic failures. In the 1970s and 1980s, feminists fought for changes and reforms in educational policy aimed at improving equality, opportunity, and education for girls and women. As a result, improvements and successes were reported in girls' performance. Have these affirmative action policies and programs disadvantaged boys as has been suggested by some?

It is not my intention to decry concerns over boys' poor academic performance in literacy, but rather to suggest a framework for thinking and rethinking about gender issues (and more specifically about the construction of masculinity) in the education of boys. The historical and social practices of gender are critical in our comprehension and discernment of the discourse of the underachieving boy. The backlash against women teachers, mothers, and feminism as the dissenters in a war against boys has positioned the boys as victims. The media has been rife with blaming gender differences and the feminization of education as the source of boys' plight. Significant factors such as race and class have been disregarded. Boys who are already disadvantaged by social class and ethnic positioning become all the more marginalized when pressured to conform with dominant forms of masculinity, which run counter to academic success.

Explanations for differences between girls' and boys' performance in literacy are multifaceted and diverse. Rather than assume a position with a simplistic focus on achievement levels, this chapter has examined boys' underachievement from a historical perspective in an attempt to raise critical awareness of the correlation of literacy with feminized practice. The underlying causes of boys' underachievement are complex and problematic as they are inextricably interconnected to sociological issues of masculine identity. Schoolwork and, more particularly, English and the humanities have been poised as feminine and, as such, positioned against the norms of masculinity. It seems paradoxical that on one hand there stems this impetus to fix boys' problems and yet on the other hand, boys who do well in school are labeled as wimps, nerds, geeks, and so forth.

The issues of boys and masculinities are indeed complex and thus defy simple and hasty solutions to fix the problem. Are we going to ameliorate boys' performance by providing more male role models or by changing curriculum or by adopting programs and teaching methodologies that are more structured, competitive, and rule-bound? These are Band-Aid solutions that are fixating on symptoms and not the root of the problem. Such simplistic solutions neglect to allow for the complexities and diversity of different versions of masculinity within schools.

Educational agenda should include a critical reassessment of the gendered practice and perception of literacy. Critical literacy discourses provide a forum for critical inquiry and interrogation into the ways in which language positions boys. Problematizing the social construction of masculinity is critical in understanding boys' underachievements. Analyzing this problem from a historical context sheds light on the current debate and the way that it has been framed. Cohen (1998) reminds readers that if

> the discourse on achievement is structured so that practices have the achievement of boys as their main object, then the call for a new focus on boys not only is not "new," but is likely to perpetuate the historical process which has worked for so long to produce the fiction of boys' potential and has protected boys' underachievement from scrutiny. (p. 30)

References

Alloway, N., and Gilbert, P. (1997). Boys and literacy: Lessons from Australia. *Gender and Education, 9*(1), 49–58.

Chesterfield, P. D., Earl of (1917). *Letters to his son on the art of becoming a man of the world and a gentleman 1694–1773* (Vol. 1). New York: The Chesterfield Press.

Cohen, M. (1997). Author's response: Dr. Michelle Cohen. [Response to Review of the book *Fashioning masculinity: National identity and language in the eighteenth century*] Retrieved January 20, 2003, from http://www.history.ac.uk/reviews/paper/shomaker.html

Cohen, M. (1998). "A habit of Healthy idleness" boys' underachievement in historical perspective. In D. Epstein, J. Elwood, V. Hey, and J. Maw (Eds.), *Failing boys? Issues in gender and achievement* (pp. 19–34). Buckingham, England: Open University Press.

Colley, L. (1992). *Britons: Forging the nation 1707–1837.* London: Yale University Press.

Connell, R. W. (1996). Teaching the boys: New research on masculinity, and gender strategies for schools. *Teachers College Record, 98*(2), 206–235.

Epstein, D., Elwood, J., Hey, V., and Maw, J. (1998). Schoolboy frictions feminism and "failing" boys. In D. Epstein, J. Elwood, V. Hey, and J. Maw (Eds.), *Failing boys? Issues in gender and achievement* (pp. 3–18). Buckingham, England: Open University Press.

Gilbert, R., and Gilbert, P. (1998). *Masculinity goes to school.* London: Routledge.

Hans, N. (1967). *Comparative education.* London: Routledge.

Kimmel, M. (1992). The contemporary "crisis" of masculinity in historical perspective. In H. Brod (Ed.), *The making of masculinities* (4th ed., pp. 121–153). New York: Routledge.

Locke, J. (1693). *Some thoughts concerning education.* Retrieved January 20, 2003, from http://www.socsci.kun.nl/ped/whp/histeduc/locke/

MacNaughton, K. F. (1947). *The development of the theory and practice of education in New Brunswick 1784–1900: A study in historical background.* Fredericton, Canada: University of New Brunswick.

Mahony, P. (1998). Girls will be girls and boys will be first. In D. Epstein, J. Elwood, V. Hey, and J. Maw (Eds.), *Failing boys? Issues in gender and achievement* (pp. 37–55). Buckingham, England: Open University Press.

McKeon, M. (1995). Historicizing patriarchy: The emergence of gender difference in England, 1660–1760. *Eighteenth-Century Studies, 29*(3), 295–322.

Mizukoshi, A. (1999). The Cockney politics of gender—the cases of Hunt and Keats. *Romanticism On the Net*. Retrieved on December 30, 2002, from http://users.ox.ac.uk/~scat0385/cockneygender.html

Morantz-Sanchez, R. M. (1985). *Science and sympathy: Women physicians in American medicine* (pp. 203–231). Oxford: Oxford University Press.

Newman, J. H. (1907). *The idea of a university: Defined and illustrated* [Electronic version]. London: Longmans, Green & Co. (Original work published 1873) Retrieved December 30, 2002, from http://www.newmanreader.org/works/idea/index.html

Norton, R. (2000). Plain reasons for the growth of Sodomy, 1728. In R. Norton (Ed.), Homosexuality in eighteenth-century England: A sourcebook. Retrieved December 30, 2002, from http://www.infopt.demon.co.uk/1749grow.htm

Reed, L. R. (1998). "Zero tolerance": gender performance and school failure. In D. Epstein, J. Elwood, V. Hey, and J. Maw (Eds.), *Failing boys? Issues in gender and achievement* (pp. 56–76). Buckingham, England: Open University Press.

Sommers, C. H. (2000). *The war against boys: How misguided feminism is harming our young men.* New York: Simon & Schuster.

Spender, D. (1982). *Invisible women-the schooling scandal.* London: Writers and Readers Publishing.

Taft, D. (1999). *The Victorian education*. Retrieved December 30, 2002, from http://www.gober.net/victorian/reports/schools.html

2

Why Social Justice Educators Must Engage Science in All of Our Classrooms*

JANE L. LEHR

On Monday March 31 at 11 A.M., a woman was sexually assaulted in a parking lot on the Virginia Tech campus—my campus since 1998. That day, in response to the reported sexual assault, the university issued a statement to the Virginia Tech community, "encourag[ing] prudence and vigilance on- and off-campus." Further, all recipients were instructed: "When possible, walk with another individual and be aware of your surroundings. In addition, be mindful of campus emergency phones marked with blue lights." While this message was sent to the entire campus, the aim was clear to me as a feminist and social justice activist, educator, and scholar—to socially control Virginia Tech women through fear. I see the use of fear to control the actions of women as part of a pattern of "blaming the victim" so common in sexual assault discourses, which seek to protect women from sexual assault by limiting their mobility, but in no way challenge the dominant discourses of masculinity and femininity that produce a "rape culture" on our university campuses, in K-12 educational contexts, and in our broader social environment.

Further, this type of response perpetuates the "rape myth" that a woman is too weak or helpless to challenge would-be assailants. This "rape myth" tells a woman that she must avoid all situations in which she could be attacked, thus severely limiting her basic freedom to move around in the world. This makes self-defense invisible as a valid response to the threat of rape and sexual assault. Further, this response perpetuates the dangerous fallacy that rapists are unknown men and that rapes occur primarily in unknown or unusual places. On the contrary, at least 80 percent of sexual assaults are committed by someone the victim knows and about 50 percent of sexual assaults occur in either the victim's or assailant's home. Most other assaults occur in public places like grocery store parking lots, libraries, jogging trails, laundry rooms—in other words wherever women must be on a daily basis (McCaughey 1997; Fisher et al., 2000).

As a social justice educator at Virginia Tech, I was compelled to address this dangerous and oppressive response by the Virginia Tech police to the reported sexual assault. On the following day, my Spring 2003 Social Foundations of Education class, a required course for undergraduate preservice teachers at Virginia Tech, was scheduled to begin a discussion of gender, gender roles, and sexism in U.S. educational contexts. The goals for the class, as a whole, include the examination of historical examples, different contemporary contexts, and ourselves as sites to explore:

> Our personal values and beliefs as they shape our teaching practices,
> Our personal identities and cultural histories of race, class, gender, and sexuality as these affect our teaching philosophies,
> The popular myths and histories we have learned in our own schooling, families, and social experiences,
> Forms of truth and fiction portrayed by popular sources such as school textbooks and media (e.g., from popular culture to news and advertising) as these shape our values and beliefs.

At the beginning of this class, the day after the sexual assault, we mapped dominant discourses of masculinity and femininity, drawn from the assigned readings and my students' everyday lives, as well as their teaching experiences: men are rational, women are emotional; men are strong and tough, women are weak; men are active, women are passive; and so forth. We then explored what kind of interactions these social norms create. Some of my students noted how these dominant discourses of masculinity and femininity work together to provide what is necessary for a family to function well—paraphrasing the Victorian (white, middle-to-upper class) argument for the necessity of public and private spheres. In the context of the recent on-campus sexual assault and the university's response to it, I pushed them: "What other kinds of interaction do these dominant discourses of masculinity and femininity naturalize?" In further discussion, we concluded as a class that the dominant discourses of masculinity and femininity make rape and other forms of sexual assault "natural." They continually re-create what I called the "rape culture" above—an everyday situation in which women must continually fear being attacked and one in which any man could rape any woman at any moment.

At this point, I began to discuss how to challenge the dominant discourses of masculinity and femininity and through this critique the university's response to the sexual assault. However, some of my students overtly resisted. They linked these dominant discourses with a biological determinism that then made it impossible (from their perspective) to challenge the discourses because they just *are*, they are *natural*. The students supported this claim by pointing to recent sociobiological and genetic research: "If it's in our genes, we can't escape it."

As a social justice educator, I faced a significant challenge: I must critically engage that scientific knowledge, both its legitimacy as objective and its status as the ultimate authority within our society, and hence our classrooms. Otherwise, I would not succeed in my goal of encouraging these future educators to most effectively challenge sexual assault and everyday violence against women and girls. They will not succeed because they won't be able to challenge the dominant discourses of masculinity and femininity. This chapter starts in the space of that challenge and with these questions: *What happens if we all, as social justice educators, remain silent and do not accept the challenge to critically engage scientific knowledge? How will we create a more just and equitable world if our teaching is always already nullified by the authority and legitimacy of scientific knowledge at its most critical juncture—In this case when I seek to challenge the naturalness of sexual assault? What will happen?* I believe that we will not succeed in meeting our social justice goals.

Social Justice Pedagogies and Scientific Knowledge

As social justice educators, we teach, in many ways, against the curriculum of our colleagues, against what counts as knowledge in their classrooms, and against the ways of knowing that they sanction. We challenge accepted truths by mapping and exploring power relationships amongst actors at the locations in which truth is created—both those actors typically recognized in the curriculum and those who are most often silenced and made invisible. We identify inequities and seek to address them and in this way encourage our students to act. In my classroom, I pointedly teach against the liberal multiculturalism available in my students' other education courses and at Virginia Tech more broadly. Liberal multiculturalism addresses issues related to social diversity by celebrating differences, for instance, including non-Anglo-American foods, holidays, or cultural traditions within the educational space. However, liberal multiculturalism ignores the social inequalities attached to these cultural differences, marginalizing the difference that matters—who has power and who does not? On the second day of my Fall 2002 class, my students admitted that in all their other education classes at Virginia Tech that have discussed diversity, they have never talked about power differentials. Proponents of liberal multiculturalism such as the teacher education curriculum at Virginia Tech do not (choose to) perceive institutional and systematic inequalities. They "take for granted that if individuals are taught to give up their individual prejudices and treat everyone the same, we will 'all get along,' and any remaining limits to equal opportunity will simply disappear" (Berlak and Moyenda, 2001, p. 94). I understand my class as working directly against this liberal multiculturalism embedded in the university and the education program and in it I critique this approach to diversity education. I push my students to acknowledge ongoing inequalities, and look for explanations that move from "blaming the individual" to interrogating our society, and more specifically, the U.S. education system for its role in creating and maintaining these inequities.

Beyond challenging liberal multiculturalism, social justice pedagogies differ from "good teaching practices" in a number of related ways. First, social justice pedagogies recognize that teaching is a political act. How we educate and are educated shapes not only the ways with which we and our students interact with the world, but also the world itself. From this position, choices in pedagogical approaches are read as value-laden and as embodying different understandings of knowledge, knowledge production, authority, and expertise. These understandings then enable or limit what knowledge, knowledge production practices, authority, and expertise can be contested or challenged by ourselves and our students, and what is off-limits (i.e., what counts as "natural" or "normal," what is privileged, and what is not). Because teaching is a political project, it is never neutral and any perceived neutrality is a political achievement. For social justice educators, this neutrality is not an accurate representation of the position of the instructor, the politics of the curriculum, or the ideology embedded within specific educational models.

Critically, social justice pedagogies mean locating the politics of pedagogy in the space of real classrooms. Bob Peterson, a fifth-grade teacher at La Escuela in Milwaukee, and editor of *Rethinking Schools*, writes: "Most teachers believe that politics should be kept out of the classroom. But it never is. Even a teacher who consciously attempts to be politically 'neutral' makes hundreds of political decisions—from the posters on the wall to attitudes toward holidays" (Peterson, 1994, p. 40). For Peterson, what a teacher *does not* do in the classroom is just as important as what the teacher does: What voices are silenced in the curriculum? What histories and practices are marginalized? Are controversies recognized or made invisible? Peterson argues that ignoring the political nature of education in the classroom and pretending to have no opinion on controversial subjects as a teacher "is not only unbelievable, but sends a message that it's OK to be opinionless and apathetic toward key social issues" (Peterson, 1994, p. 40). This encourages students to accept the knowledge, knowledge production practices, authority, and expertise of the dominant culture(s). It thus limits their ability to critically analyze and potentially disrupt or transform (or even consciously choose to support) the practices legitimized by the status quo narratives inside and outside of the classroom.

Second, from this politicized and situated position, social justice approaches to education begin with a recognition of inequality and multiple forms of oppression in our world today—for example, oppressions based on intersecting differences of race, class, gender, sexual orientation, physical and mental ability, and other social factors. Social justice pedagogies "agree that oppression is a dynamic in which certain ways of being (or having certain identifications) are privileged in a society while others are marginalized" (Kumashiro, 2002, p. 31). Part of the educational project of social justice pedagogies, then, as I see it, is to challenge inequality both inside and outside of the classroom by examining the creation and maintenance of systems of oppressions and privileges. Further, social justice pedagogies encourage students to challenge the silences and omissions that Peterson (1994) identifies: "Whose voices? Which stories? What meanings? Who benefits? Why?"

But to return now to my crisis: the challenge of scientific knowledge (brought in by my students) within my social justice classroom. What resources are available to all social justice educators to challenge the legitimacy and authority of science? How can we include the detailed analysis of scientific truths within our curriculum? How can we challenge the dominant discourses legitimated by science that create and maintain inequality and oppression? What tools can we use in our classrooms and in our communities? What tools can we provide our students? Returning to Bob Peterson's (1994) idea that what a teacher *does not* do in the classroom is just as important as what the teacher does, we must locate these tools to break our silence about science. I needed them here. You need them. Where and what are they?

Within the various social justice-oriented syllabi that I inherited from other instructors at Virginia Tech who teach the Social Foundations of Education class against the grain of dominant discourses, and within the books I reviewed and then selected for my course, I found a pervasive silence about science in the teacher education curriculum (e.g., Adams et al., 1997, 2000; Berlak and Moyenda 2001; Bigelow et al., 1994, 2001; and Loewen 1996). With the exception of some discussion of the historical role of eugenics in creating a contemporary school system that includes IQ tests, standardized testing, and tracking (Berlak 2001; Bigelow 1994; Stoskepf 1999), few teachers and educational theorists engaged the role that scientific knowledge—its legitimacy as objective and its authority as truth—plays in shaping our world, our educational experiences, and systemic patterns of haves and have-nots. In the first semester I taught the Social Foundations of Education course (Fall 2002); I struggled with the texts I had assigned and the student resistance based on the legitimacy and authority of science—like that described earlier. At these different crisis points (e.g., the unnaturalness of homosexuality, the biological determinism of race) I turned to research within Science and Technology Studies to place a critique of science within the official curriculum. So can you.

Science and Technology Studies: Resources and Tools for Social Justice Educators

What is Science and Technology Studies (STS)? How can it serve as a resource for all social justice educators? STS research over the past two decades provides alternative models of science and scientific knowledge production. What I am calling STS research in this essay includes work by scholars in cultural studies, ethnic studies, and women's studies, among other disciplines, that critically engages science, technology, and medicine, as well as work on these topics in anthropology, history, sociology, philosophy, and policy studies. By STS research, I mean more the critical interrogation of science, technology, and medicine rather than any specific institutional affiliation of the researcher. STS case studies produced from these different vantage points show that all sciences and technologies do have a politics, and thus provide a way of introducing an analysis of science into social justice pedagogies. In his introduction to the field, David Hess writes that STS provides

> a conceptual tool kit for thinking about technical expertise in more sophisticated ways. Science Studies tracks the history of disciplines, the dynamics of science as a social institution, and the philosophical basis of scientific knowledge. It teaches, for example, that there are ways of developing sound criteria for evaluating opposing theories and interpretations, but also that there are ways of finding the agendas sometimes hidden behind a rhetoric of objectivity. In the process, Science Studies makes it easier for laypeople to question the authority of experts and their claims. It teaches how to look for biases, and it holds out a vision of greater public participation in technical policy issues. (Hess, 1997, p. 1)

Research in STS, as well as the example I provided at the beginning of this essay, points to the special and unique role that science plays in Western culture today. Scientific knowledge, knowledge production practices, authority, and expertise function as ultimate truth in our society—science speaks *for* nature. Scientific knowledge can then be used to achieve closure in public and private debates, in most cases silencing alternative knowledge systems and knowledge producers—including non-Western indigenous knowledge systems. Thus, through the lens of STS research, we can see that how we are trained to think about science—or not think about science—embodies different understandings of the status of its knowledge, knowledge production practices, authority, and expertise. These understandings then shape our ability (or lack of ability) to challenge science.

Most importantly, STS research allows us to challenge the authority and legitimacy of scientific research, and the use of scientific research to support racist, sexist, classist, and homophobic agendas (cf. Haraway, 1991, 1996; Harding, 1993). This ability is integral to the success of the social justice pedagogies and the creation of a more just and equitable world.

I now describe some of the possibilities for social justice pedagogies that choose to engage science through research and case studies in STS—to pick up the tools that are available to us as social justice educators. By choosing to critically engage science in our classrooms—we can challenge the following:

Objectivity: Research in STS shows that scientific knowledge is situated (i.e., context-specific and historically located in relationship to factors including race, class, gender, sexual orientation, physical and mental ability, and religion) and negotiated rather than objective. These biases (which cannot be removed or escaped but must be recognized and made visible to all) enter the production of scientific knowledge at all levels—from the ways scientists make sense of what they see in the lab or in the field to the types of projects that are funded. Making these biases or cultural imprints visible opens up ways for social justice educators and their students to actively engage science, and claims backed by science, without having to produce bigger or better science of their own. Debates previously closed by the authority of objective scientific claims are reopened and decisions legitimated by science can now be understood as illegitimate, or at least worthy of continued discussion and analysis. Donna Haraway's work on primatology (1990) and biotechnology (1996) deconstructs what she refers to as the god-trick of infinite vision, of objectivity, of the positionless position that allows scientists to speak and do with no accountability. In its place, she offers what she sees as a better account of the world, suggesting that instead of the god-trick of objectivity, we can insist "metaphorically on the particularity and embodiment of all vision" (Haraway, 1991, p. 189). For Haraway, "feminist objectivity means quite simply *situated knowledges*" (Haraway, 1991, p. 188). She concludes as follows:

> So, not so perversely, objectivity turns out to be about particular and specific embodiment, and definitely not about the false vision promising transcendence of all limits and responsibility. The moral is simple: only partial perspective promises objective vision. This is an objective vision that initiates, rather than closes off, the problem of responsibility for the generativity of all visual practices. Partial perspectives can be held accountable for both its promising and its destructive monsters. (Haraway, 1991, p. 190)

Haraway's "situated knowledges" and other research in STS on objectivity offers social justice educators new ways to talk about truth, authority, legitimacy, and expertise—and to hold science, scientists, and those who use the discourse of science accountable.

Embedded Values: Challenging objectivity by locating the production of scientific knowledge within specific local contexts begins to blur the distinction between scientific knowledge and other forms of knowledge. Scientific knowledge must then be understood as value-laden, rather than value-free. Recognizing the values already at work within scientific knowledge production practices provides us with an opportunity to ask whose values are present and why. We can then push to change these values to ones more consistent with a more socially just world. Vandana Shiva's critical analysis of genetically modified organisms (1997, 1999, 2001b/1995) and large-scale dam projects in India (2001a), in combination with her political organizing, does just that. She asks scientists, policymakers, and the public to choose values that benefit humanity as a whole, rather than specific elite segments of the population and multinational corporations. She specifically challenges the supremacy of Western values and argues for a return to knowledge production rooted in indigenous values.

Scientific Progress: The dominant image of science is one of linear progress. Research in STS (Bijker et al., 1997/1987; Callon, 1999/1986; Hughes, 1983; Latour, 1987), however, shows that broadly defined social factors often play a critical role in determining the success or failure of specific theories and projects. Further, other research (see, e.g., Fleck, 1981/1935; Kuhn, 1996/1962) point to the disconnect between consecutive and simultaneous scientific research programs drawing into question, again, the idea of scientific progress. As social justice educators, what could happen if the notion of scientific progress is removed as a valid reason for pursuing certain scientific projects? What will happen if we consciously choose to define progress in new ways?

What Counts as Natural: In the example detailed at the beginning of this chapter, I described how notions of the "natural" limited my ability to challenge the dominant discourses of masculinity and femininity. Much work in STS challenges this idea of an ahistorical and universal "nature" by recovering histories of supposedly natural ideas such as gender (e.g., Haraway, 1990, 1991, 1996; Harding, 1993, 1998; Keller, 1988; Schiebinger, 1993), sexuality (e.g., Dreger, 1997; Foucault, 1990/1986; Terry, 1995), and race (e.g., Fausto-Sterling, 1995; Nelkin and Lindee, 1995; Schiebinger, 1993). Often, as this research describes, what counts as natural is determined by the specific historical lens of the observer. This lens is positioned, often along lines of race, class, gender, sexual orientation, physical and mental ability, and other social characteristics. By making these histories visible, we can draw into question the natural knowledge of today and ask the following question: What context is being disappeared from today's scientific claims? Again, whose lens is science using and why?

All of these arenas of research, all of these tools available to us, challenge processes of classification: both the classification of what counts as scientific knowledge and what does not. In doing so, we challenge what determines who has a voice in our society, as well as social classifications supported by scientific knowledge. Other ongoing and intersecting oppressions based on categories such as gender, race, physical and mental ability, and sexual orientation function, in part, because of the historical and contemporary scientific classifications of these "differences." STS work allows us to ask, "How would the world be different if we had the power to name and classify ourselves?"

Most important for social justice educators, all of these challenges to science open up space for nonscientists (i.e., social justice educators, students, community members, and others) to participate in scientific knowledge production and decision making. We cannot be dismissed as political and then excluded from scientific debates because science is just as political as we are. This can change what counts as authority and expertise in our communities. Our experiences can count and scientific knowledge no longer will be able to create instant debate closure. Further, these challenges to the legitimacy of objectivity and the authoritative role of science expand the dominant image of who can become a scientist and who can succeed, as well as what it means to succeed in science. Finally, recognizing the social nature of science creates an opportunity to set different aims for science and for our future. We can challenge and change all dominant discourses—even those that are most *scientific* and *natural*.

Challenging Gendered Scientific Truths in My Classroom

Let us return to my classroom. How did I challenge the assertion that the dominant discourses of masculinity and femininity are *natural*, and thus inescapable? In this section, I describe in detail the strategy I used to explicitly challenge science in my nonscience classroom from the first day of class the second time I taught the Social Foundations of Education (Spring 2003), which prepared me to deal with "naturalness" of gender discourses later in the semester. Here, I make the social and historical nature of scientific knowledge (specifically, knowledge about reproduction and fertilization) explicit, using the work of STS scholar Emily Martin (1991) to highlight the gendered context in which scientific knowledge is produced. While Martin's article may not be accessible to students of all ages, this lesson can be adapted for a variety of age levels across the curriculum.

The Romance of the Egg and the Sperm

On the very first day of the second semester that I taught the Social Foundations of Education (after the first semester, the one in which I began to notice and examine the silence about science within the context of social justice pedagogies, and my resulting inability to most effectively challenge social inequities with my students), we immediately began to engage gender and science through an analysis of what Emily Martin refers to as the "romance between the egg and the sperm" (1991). Using the blackboard, we mapped the process of fertilization, paying special attention to the activities of the egg and the activities of the sperm. Students told the story of a passive egg and active, autonomous sperm—very similar to what Martin found in her examination of typical descriptions of reproduction in science textbooks:

> The egg is seen as large and passive. It does not *move* or *journey*, but passively "is transported," "is swept," or even "drifts" along the fallopian tube. In utter contrast, sperm are small, "streamlined," and invariably active. They "deliver" their genes to the egg, "activate the developmental program of the egg," and have a "velocity" that is often remarked upon. Their tails are "strong" and efficiently powered. Together with the forces of ejaculation, they can "propel the semen into the deepest recesses of the vagina." For this they need "energy," "fuel," so that with a "whiplash-like motion and strong lurches" they can "burrow through the egg coat," and "penetrate" it. (Martin, 1991, p. 489)

Following our mapping of the relationship between the egg and the sperm, the class then watched the opening minutes of *Look Who's Talking*—the 1989 film with John Travolta, Kirstie Alley, and Bruce Willis as the voice of the "Mikey." At the beginning of the film, the viewer sees fertilization happen—much in the same way as we and Martin described: the egg floats to the uterus where it rests; the ejaculated sperm are on a mission, in competition with each other to get to the egg first. What I particularly like about this film is that the voice of the sperm (Bruce Willis) then becomes the voice of the fertilized egg, and then finally the voice of the child ("Mikey"). The egg's agency—if it ever had any—completely disappears.

After we watched the film, I asked the students whether they wanted to add anything to our map of the fertilization process. The answer was "No." They were satisfied that we had a true, biologically accurate, objective representation. At this point I began to pose some of the questions Martin raises in her STS research on the fertilization process: What is the relationship between our knowledge of the egg and the sperm and our cultural understandings of femininity and masculinity? Why do we know the egg as a "damsel in distress" and the sperm as the "heroic warrior to the rescue"? Is it possible that our dominant discourses of masculinity and femininity have shaped these "facts"? Is it credible to examine this aspect of the reproduction process and tell a different story if we were to look through different cultural lenses, with different discourses in mind?

Pointing to recent research on fertilization, Martin argues that it is possible to understand the interactions between the egg and the sperm differently. For instance, she describes how researchers at Johns Hopkins, while trying to develop a contraceptive that would work topically on sperm, found that "the forward thrust of sperm is extremely weak," contradicting the "assumption that sperm are forceful penetrators" (p. 492). Martin further explains:

> Rather than thrusting forward, the sperm's head was now seen to move mostly back and forth. The sideways motion of the sperm's tail makes the head move sideways with a force that is ten times stronger than its forward movement. So even if the overall force of the sperm were strong enough to mechanically break the [egg's] zona, most of its force would be directed sideways rather than forward. In fact, its strongest tendency, by tenfold, is to escape by attempting to pry itself off the egg. Sperm, then, must be exceptionally efficient at *escaping* from any cell surface they contact. And the surface of the egg must be designated to trap the sperm and prevent their escape. Otherwise, few if any sperm would reach the egg. (Martin, 1991, pp. 492–493)

Despite research like this pointing to the necessary agency of the egg, Martin then describes how scientists continue to use gender stereotypes (e.g., the "aggressive male," the "damsel in distress," and then the introduction of the egg as the "femme fatale") to make sense of new findings. As Martin points out, "These revisionist accounts of egg and sperm cannot seem to escape the hierarchical imagery of older accounts" (Martin, 1991, p. 498). However, waking these "sleeping metaphors in science" (Martin, 1991, p. 501) offers us, as social justice educators, many opportunities to challenge gendered discourses in our classrooms and in our everyday lives.

Martin's work challenges science by drawing our attention to the situatedness of scientific researchers, the way the gendered values embedded in their cultural frame shape the scientific knowledge production processes in their laboratories. In this case, the scientists *produce what counts as natural*, rather than objectively reading the natural world. Notably, what is classified as "natural" mirrors the unequal gender relations of their everyday lives. Even when "scientific progress" is made, as Martin describes in the article, it is limited by the gendered expectations of the researchers: they resist alternative explanations of fertilization. From this vantage point, we can ask the following: How do our biology textbooks and curricula reinforce oppressive gender discourses? What are our students learning about gender and gender relations in science classrooms? How do other metaphors—metaphors about race, gender, sexual orientation, physical or mental ability, or other social factors—shape scientific knowledge today? *Further, and most importantly for this study, we must ask, what happens when we challenge gender oppression in our nonscience class-*

rooms and our everyday lives at the same time we allow gendered stereotypes in science to "act natural"?

Conclusion

So, again—What happened in my classroom on the day after the sexual assault? Oh, the suspense! How did I respond to my students' support of the naturalness of dominant discourses of masculinity and femininity? As we left it, I was in crisis. My pedagogical goals were challenged by scientific truths. Was this challenge successful or had the groundwork done on the first day of class prepared us to critically engage what counts as natural?

My immediate response to it was, "Well, if it's natural (and thus legitimate) for men to rape and sexually assault women, what is the one solution to ending rape and sexual assault? [Dramatic pause] We have to kill all the men!" While this caused many of my students to laugh, this rather unrealistic solution pushed them to reconsider the naturalness of gender discourses, and the question of whether or not we can intervene in its dominant discourses. We could then continue the discussion. One of my students then said, "Wait, this all goes back to the first day of class and the egg and the sperm. Is that intentional?" After I said, "Yes," he continued: "You set the whole class up for this discussion." While I had not, of course, intended for the sexual assault that occurred the previous day, I did very intentionally foreground a challenge to the authority and legitimacy of scientific knowledge within our classroom, which then created the space for us to challenge genetic determinism and sociobiology. At this point, I encouraged him to tell the rest of the class what he had posted on the discussion board 24 hours previously:

> "Gender, however, is how your sex is portrayed socially." I must say I think that is an awesome line that Tiffany brought up. I mean, think about it . . . on Day 1 of this class what was the topic about? "The Sperm vs. The Egg." I think it is rather interesting to put it all together now, because at first I thought we were just trying to "b.s." the first day of class. We organized our thoughts of men versus women on day one, and it makes more sense now. Lorber on page 204 of RDSJ writes, "Gender is one of the major ways that human beings organize their lives." Is that not exactly what we did on the first day of class?? Although I feel a part of the first day was a "get-to-know-you" session, I do think we fell into the pattern talked about by Lorber.

My discussion of Martin's article then became the context for our continued discussion about the dominant discourses of masculinity and femininity—a challenge to the legitimacy and authority of science had been made. Science, naturalness, genetic determinism, sociobiology, masculinity, and femininity were at least now in question.

For the next class (our second day and last day examining gender, gender roles, and sexism in U.S. educational contexts), I assigned two groups of students to research sociobiology. First, what is sociobiology and what does it say about gender? And second, what critiques of sociobiology exist? After the presentation of this research to the rest of the class, we continued our discussion about the naturalness (or unnaturalness) of the gender discourses with which we are so familiar. Critically, we were able to have this discussion whether or not all of my students were convinced. This was a major contribution of my social justice teaching practices.

I know for certain that not all of the students walked away from this discussion or from my class convinced that a social justice approach to education is the best pedagogical choice or that the objectivity, authority, and legitimacy of science can be challenged or even that we can talk a different way about the interaction between the egg and the sperm. However, I do feel that the combination of social justice pedagogies and the critical analysis of science provided students with access to the right tools to create greater equity and justice in their classrooms, their schools, and their communities if they choose to do so. They could now more effectively challenge sexual assault. They could also have this discussion in their future classrooms. One of my students even was interviewed later for a critical article on the university's response to the sexual assault. She brought this up on the last day of class, indicating that she would never have critiqued Virginia Tech's sexual assault prevention policy before this class and would never, never have spoken up about it, signed a petition that critiqued it, and then talked to the college newspaper. In her evaluation of herself at the end of class, she wrote: "I learned that one voice CAN make a difference. What a mind-opener!" For me, her change in perspective throughout the course counts very much as a success. I see the challenge to the legitimacy and authority of scientific knowledge that we undertook in our classroom as a key feature in her transformation.

The tools to challenge the legitimacy and authority of science—tools that situate and position objectivity; draw attention to its embedded values; reopen for discussion what counts as scientific progress and as natural—position us as social justice educators to critically engage science and to demand its accountability for the inequalities it creates and maintains. To most effectively challenge oppression, all social justice educators across the curriculum must expand our available resources to include the critical analysis of science as part of our ongoing projects to create a more just and equitable world. Without these new tools, we will not succeed—and we must.

Note

*Special thanks is extended to Megan Boler for serving as an inspiration to the author and to everyone who wishes to take social justice seriously in their classrooms and in their lives.

References

Adams, M., Bell, L. A., and Griffin P. (1997). *Teaching for diversity and social justice: A sourcebook.* London and New York: Routledge.

Adams, M., Blumenfeld, W., Castaneda, R., Hackman, H., Peters, M., and Zuniga, X. (2000). *Readings for diversity and social justice: An anthology on racism, antisemitism, sexism, heterosexism, ableism, and classism.* London and New York: Routledge.

Berlak, A., and Moyenda, S. (2001). *Taking it personally: Racism in the classroom from kindergarten to college.* Philadelphia, PA: Temple University Press.

Berlak, H. (2001). Race and the achievement gap: Using standardized tests to measure achievement perpetuates a system of institutionalized racism and lends the cloak of science to discriminatory practices. *Rethinking Schools, 15*(4), 10–11.

Bigelow, B. (1994). Testing, tracking, and toeing the line: A role play on the origins of the modern high school. In B. Bigelow (Ed.), *Rethinking our classrooms: Teaching for equity and justice, volume 1* (pp. 117–123). Milwaukee, WI: Rethinking Schools, Ltd.

Bigelow, B., Christensen, L., Karp, S., Miner, B., and Petersen, B. (1994). *Rethinking our classrooms: Teaching for equity and justice, volume 1.* Milwaukee, WI: Rethinking Schools, Ltd.

Bigelow, B., Harvey, B., Karp, S., and Miller, L. (2001). *Rethinking our classrooms: Teaching for equity and justice, volume 2.* Williston, VT: Rethinking Schools, Ltd.

Bijker, W., Hughes, T. P., and Pinch, T. (Eds.). (1997). *The Social Construction of Technological System: New Directions in the Sociology and History of Technology.* Cambridge: MIT Press. (Originally published 1987)

Callon, M. (1999). Some elements of a sociology of translation: Domestication of the scallops and the fishermen of Saint Brieuc Bay. In M. Biagoli (Ed.), *The science studies reader* (pp. 67–83). New York and London: Routledge. (Reprinted from J. Law (Ed.). (1986). *Power, action, and belief: A new sociology of knowledge?* (pp. 196–233). London: Routledge and Kegan Paul.)

Dreger, A. (1997). *Hermaphrodites and the medical invention of sex.* Cambridge: Harvard University Press.

Fausto-Sterling, A. (1995). Gender, race, and nation: The comparative anatomy of "hottentot" women in Europe, 1815–1817. In J. Terry and J. Ursula (Eds.), *Deviant bodies: Critical perspectives on difference in science and popular culture* (pp. 19–48). Bloomington and Indianapolis: Indiana University Press.

Fisher, B. S., Cullen, F. T., and Turner, M. G. (2000). *The sexual victimization of college women.* Washington, DC: National Institute of Justice.

Fleck, Ludwick (1981). *Genesis and development of scientific fact.* Chicago and London: University of Chicago Press. (Originally published 1935)

Foucault, M. (1990). *The history of sexuality: An introduction, volume 1*. New York: Vintage Books. (Originally published 1986)

Haraway, D. (1990). *Primate visions: Gender, race, and nature in the world of modern science*. New York and London: Routledge.

Haraway, D. (1991). Situated knowledges: The science question in feminism and the privilege of partial perspective. In D. Haraway (Ed.), *Simians, cyborgs, and women: The reinvention of nature* (pp. 183–203). New York: Routledge.

Haraway, D. (1996). *Modest_Witness@Second_Millenium. Femaleman_ Meets_Oncomouse: Feminism and technoscience*. London and New York: Routledge.

Harding, S. (Ed.). (1993). *The racial economy of science*. Bloomington and Indianapolis: Indiana University Press.

Harding, S. (1998). *Is science multicultural? Postcolonialisms, epistemologies*. Bloomington and Indianapolis: Indiana University Press.

Hess, D. (1997). *Science studies: An advanced introduction*. (New York: New York University Press).

Hughes, T. P. (1983). *Networks of power: Electrification in western society, 1880–1930*. Baltimore: Johns Hopkins University Press.

Keller, E. F. (1988). *Reflections on gender and science*. New Haven: Yale University Press.

Kuhn, T.S. (1996). *The Structure of scientific revolutions* (3rd ed.). Chicago and London: University of Chicago Press. (Originally published 1962).

Kumashiro, K. (2002). *Troubling education: Queer activism and anti-oppressive pedagogy*. London: RoutledgeFalmer.

Latour, B. (1987). *Science in action*. Milton Keynes: Open University Press.

Loewen, J. (1996). *Lies my teacher told me: Everything your American history textbook got wrong*. New York: Simon & Schuster.

Martin, E. (1991). The eggs and the sperm: How science has created a romance based on stereotypical male-female roles. *Signs: Journal of Women in Culture and Society, 16*, 485–501.

McCaughey, M. (1997). *Real knockouts: The physical feminism of women's self-defense*. New York: New York University Press.

Nelkin, D., and Lindee, M. S. (1995). The mediated gene: Stories of gender and race. In J. Terry and J. Ursula (Eds.), *Deviant bodies: Critical perspectives on difference in science and popular culture* (pp. 387–402). Bloomington and Indianapolis: Indiana University Press.

Peterson, B. (1994). The complexities of encouraging social action. In B. Bigelow (Ed.), *Rethinking our classrooms: Teaching for equity and justice, volume 1* (pp. 40–42). Milwaukee, WI: Rethinking Schools, Ltd.

Schiebinger, L. (1993). *Nature's body: Gender in the making of modern science*. Boston: Beacon.

Shiva, V. (1997). *Biopiracy: The plunder of nature and knowledge*. Cambridge: South End Press.

Shiva, V. (1999). *Stolen harvest: The hijacking of the global food supply*. Cambridge: South End Press.

Shiva, V. (2001a). *Water wars, vol. 1*. Cambridge: South End Press.

Shiva, V. (2001b). Democractizing biology: Reinventing biology from a feminist, ecological, and third world perspective. In M. Lederman and I. Bartsch (Eds.), *The gender and science reader* (pp. 447–465). London and New York: Routledge. (Reprinted from Lynda Birke and Ruth

Hubbard (Eds.), *Reinventing biology* (1995). Bloomington and Indianapolis: Indiana University Press.)

Stoskepf, A. (1999). The forgotten history of eugenics: High stakes testing has its origins in the eugenics movement and racist assumptions about IQ. *Rethinking Schools, 13*(3), 12–13.

Terry, J. (1995). Anxious slippages between "us" and "them": A brief history of the scientific search for homosexual bodies. In J. Terry and J. Ursula (Eds.), *Deviant bodies: Critical perspectives on difference in science and popular culture* (pp. 129–169). Bloomington and Indianapolis: Indiana University Press.

Teaching Story

Academic Writing and the Silence of Oppression

LINDA FERNSTEN

Educators in schools across the United States are being asked to consider equity issues regarding increasingly heterogeneous student populations. The results have produced tensions between official language use (traditional formal academic discourses) and a variety of "minority" discourses (Luke, 1995–1996), especially in written language. A "minority" discourse in the academy may be viewed as one infused with language patterns associated with certain ethnicities, races, classes, and regions that differ from traditional practices utilized in schools.

Many students struggling to become more skillful users of the discourses expected in secondary and college-level written work become convinced they are simply "bad writers." They have entered the world of teachers and college professors who often valorize academic discourses and marginalize or devalue other discourses that are a part of students' lives. At both levels, the efforts of well-intentioned gatekeepers to critique and "fix" the language differences they find have resulted in some students becoming fearful of writing and academic writing tasks. In large part, this story emerged from my own experience of watching young writers struggle within the academy to find a voice and gain acceptance of their writing. Sometimes silenced in ways they do not understand, many have come to see their writing practices as inferior or incompetent receiving the negative responses of others more as a "truth" than a social construction.

They live these "truths," unaware that the social and political negotiations that reinforce this labeling and sustain these hegemonic practices may stifle them as students who are expected/required to write. They have become powerfully silenced, believing their writing to be "inferior" when, in fact, "difference" may be the issue. It is my contention that, as educators, we must examine both the social and political forces that have created, perpetuated, and supported the oppressive situation that exists for some student writers and help them find avenues to more positive writer identities.

Background

Over the last three decades, researchers began studying in earnest what composition theorists were calling "basic writers." Harris (1997) found three central metaphors used to typify these diverse students who many in the academy have deemed "problem writers." While "problem writers" have been identified for decades, this population seemed to increase considerably when post–World War II college opportunities were presented to ever-wider groups of students. Difference from the norms and expectations of what had been the traditional college student became of increasing concern.

Additionally, the acceptance of students with more varied ethnic, racial, and class backgrounds in the Open Admissions movement of the 1960s refocused higher education's attention to writing issues. In the 1970s and into the 1980s these writers were seen as "deficient in growth" or as immature users of the language. This stunted growth metaphor emphasized the need for students' improved mental conceptions regarding writing and frequently saw practitioners offering sequential steps to help students become better writers (Harris, 1997).

This view was later replaced by an initiation metaphor, strongly influenced by Bartholomae (1986). It characterized writers who did not measure up to the academic standard as "uninitiated" into the discourse community of the university. It encompassed the concept that entering the university was not just an intellectual step, but a social and political step as well, which involved accepting new value systems and cultural practices (Rose, 1985). Both of these earlier models regarded writers who did not conform to the university standards as somehow immature as writers or outsiders to the still unquestioned standard of academic discourse. By the 1990s, however, a major shift took place when that standard began to be questioned in earnest.

Conflict, the latest metaphor to be embraced by composition theorists, is best articulated by Lu (1991) in her discussion of the political dimensions of language choice. The emphasis changed from unquestioned acceptance of dominant discourses to discourses as political choice. Writer identity came to be viewed as related to issues of race, class, and gender and include the social and political considerations of language. Lu believes that students often feel marginalized, or like outsiders to academic discourse, because of the way their own discourses have been received in the academy. Marginal writer identities can evolve when students are unable to disrupt the practices of the academy that have made them outsiders. The situation cannot improve if they remain without access to conversations that provide building blocks to a more emancipating understanding of their situation and the factors influencing it.

This new understanding of student conflict with writing has not, for the most part, reached our state testing boards. While composition scholars are familiar with the concept, it has not become embedded in practitioners' literature or the teaching vocabularies of many college and high school instructors.

Writer Profile

This teaching story involves the study of Len, one of the students in my college writing class. Through him, I discovered how the more prevalent "stunted growth" discourse of our classrooms can negatively impact writer identity today. Len was in my required junior year writing class for education majors at a large public university in the Northeast. He was Haitian American, in his senior year, and planned to enter the field of education, but still unsure in which capacity.

I selected Len to study because he had an uneasy relationship, stated and observed, with aspects of the academic discourses he had been required to adopt. His concerns about peer response further reflected his fragile relationship with academic writing. Of particular interest to me, as researcher and instructor of this course, was the surprisingly positive relationship to writing I discovered when Len participated in expressivist as opposed to traditional formal writing. Information about his difficult earlier life in another country, his language history, and fragmented early schooling cast a light on how difference pays a price in the academy. He had put off, until his senior year, this required course and was a frequent "resister," advising me that his papers were too incomplete to discuss or "forgotten" at home, though his attendance was excellent. Len's class journal revealed a strongly held view that learning another language should not make one forget his/her native tongue, whatever it may be, though he commented that this is not easy to do in America.

Because of his classroom silence, many students did not realize Len was bilingual or Haitian, assuming he was African American. Even when other bilingual students shared personal experiences, he did not openly reveal those aspects of his identity until the end of the semester. Whatever had silenced him was powerful. In conversation one day, when I told him how important it was for others to hear his voice of experience, he told me solemnly that many did not want to hear opinions very different from their own.

Using a technique called Critical Discourse Analysis (CDA) I examined the language Len (and other students) brought to the classroom in an effort to unpack the social, cultural, and political influences that were at work in it. Norman Fairclough's CDA (1995) approach requires examining segments of language (a sentence or a phrase at a time, for example) in order to determine embedded ideologies. By combining this method with classroom assignments that had students describing who they were as writers, what they believed had influenced that writer identity, and best or worst experiences with writing, I was able to search out the different discourses at work in their language, an arduous though enlightening task. For example, linking Len's ideas such as "I enjoy telling stories about my adolescence" to expressivist philosophy is easy in retrospect, but initially coming to understand and interpret which different philosophies were at work took some time.

Once I realized, however, that Len did not dislike *all* writing, and in fact, enjoyed more personal assignments, that pattern became easy to spot in my other students. Len's dislike of formal academic writing was another pattern repeated in other students who, like Len, felt confined by the rigors of formal language and uncomfortable with genres whose required discourse felt unfamiliar and awkward. One African American student talked about how writing in a way that was different from his normal speech felt pretentious and phony. I began to notice that quite a few of my students identified as "bad writers," dreading or detesting writing when confined to formal academic discourses. Far easier to find in Len's language was the more typical ideology of today's test-driven schools and the push for homogeneity in writing. Len wrote that he felt "different from other students" and was quick to label himself a poor writer. He also feared the judgment of his peers, which had made him feel "low" and incompetent.

I would like to report that by the end of my class Len had gained confidence in his ability to write. Unfortunately, I do not believe that is the case. In his final class-assigned letter to me, he reiterated many of the themes you will find in the microanalyses that follow. These include the idea that he is "different" from others, still fears the comments of those who read his writing and despite the fact that peer response may help him complete a better paper, he would choose not to do it. This was the discourse he came with, and despite discussions on the complexities and politics of language, it is the discourse with which he left. I am left wondering whether the ideas of social and cultural influence and the power of academic discourse to both free and oppress had touched him and realize, as is usual with my students, I will probably never know. Len's history, set beside the microanalysis that follows, tells a story of identity that could be missed in an instructor's need to "get through curriculum" and prepare students for writing in the "real world."

Len's Words

While I analyzed a number of Len's texts, I have combined a few of the pieces in order to demonstrate how discourse analysis can work. The following integrates Len's discussion of writer identity, influences, and his worst experiences with writing.

1. I never thought of myself as a good writer.
2. But there are times that I enjoyed writing certain topics that cash (catch) my interest and most important my readers.
3. I like writing about things that happened to me as a young adolescent.
4. My worst experience with writing is the remarks that I get from people evaluating, correcting my writing.
5. The first evaluation is always full with numerous remarks on how to improve the writing.
6. I hate watching someone evaluating my writing because of the remarks and comments that I expect to see.
7. I'd rather have them correct it without me being present.
8. Many times I get response back from people who evaluate my writing like how to make my writing more accurate, need more details and they always tell me that I have unnecessary information in the paper.
9. I only ask people that know me first, and my writing to read my writing because they have better understanding of my writing.
10. They are more likely to understand the structure of my writing than those that do not know my writing or me.
11. It makes me feel unsecured about my work based on people's reactions to the writing.
12. I am a student that needs serious help writing a paper of any subject.
13. I am an individual that has strong feeling for my writing.
14. I decided to start ahead of times because of the numerous corrections that I feel that I might have to do to do an accurate writing assignment.
15. Through out the semester I like to improve my writing abilities so I can be a better writer.
16. I look forward to quitting the weakness that I have in papers.
17. I also know that all the problems and weaknesses may not be taken care of at once.
18. But I feel I can improve those weaknesses.

Discourse Analysis

In line 1, Len makes his claim that he has never thought of himself as a good writer, probably drawing his identity from the stunted growth discourse he has faced in his academic endeavors. In lines 2 and 3, he attempts to explain, however, that there are some kinds of writing he actually enjoys. Embedded in his words is expressivist philosophy, that is, writing that values personal voice and story and holds meaning and interest for the writer. As a writing teacher of many years, I was surprised how easy it was for me to miss the enjoyment that personal writing can hold for even the most reluctant college writers! I came to realize that when Len shared his personal experiences, his audience was able to focus on his ideas, whereas in academic papers, they seemed to focus on issues of grammar, structure, and spelling. Through his words, we witness Len's tremendous struggle and clear awareness that writing in the academy was a landmine of problems for him. Academic writing created frustration as he discovered that no matter how much time and effort he put in, he felt very little success.

In line 4, Len makes the decision to focus on the "worst" writing experiences, telling his story in a way that again reflects the stunted growth discourse so familiar in classrooms. In the past, others have positioned him as an immature writer with grammatical difficulties, and here we see he both accepts and subtly resists that identity. The worst thing, he says, are "the remarks" of those who read his work. The fact that the "first evaluation is always full with numerous remarks on how to improve the writing" (line 5) is problematic for him. Though it demonstrates a lack of access to the idea that writers, novice and professional alike, are commonly dissatisfied with early drafts, we can see he also personalizes the responders' comments and seems to interpret them as a reflection on his personhood, perhaps tying it to his familiarity with institutionalized racism. The fact that he hates being present during response (lines 6, 7) calls attention to the complexity of his writer identity. Is it oppression he feels? What social situations has he faced that make this student feel fearful and powerless when it comes to a discussion of his writing? Because he realizes another indictment of deficiency awaits him, he would choose to be elsewhere (line 4).

In line 8, Len reveals the types of critique he has received. The work needs to be more "accurate" and have more "details," and he needs to eliminate "unnecessary information." In a process classroom these would not be untypical or harsh responses. For Len, who seems to feel battered by the responses of others, however, they are crushing. Convinced that his writing is "deficient" and feeling positioned as an "outsider" after trying long and hard to improve, he appears to conclude that nothing works to the satisfaction of those judging his work. His peers and professors, perhaps familiar with the initiation model discussed earlier, continually focus on "fixing" his language so he can "enter the university" (i.e., write a paper that meets the "standard").

Len never takes up a discourse that emphasizes how second-language speakers often struggle with the grammar of their adopted language. He does not mention that being unable to articulate ideas "well" in the academic discourse of a second language is a common struggle. He does not even say that appropriating the conventions of academic discourse may be difficult for anyone who has not had much access to them in the past. Without access to classroom discussion on that topic, he would, of course, lack a political discourse to do so.

Lines 9 and 10 hit home hard for me. He says it takes people who know him to understand his writing. Here his ideas border on the political as he hints that second-language speakers may be in conflict with the system. While constantly correcting the spoken English of non-native speakers is something most of us would not do, ironically, we feel comfortable red-lining their papers in our classes. Len looks for those who understand the patterns of his English and who will not judge him, as he feels native English-speaking classmates do. He seeks those who will just help him adjust his written discourse to one that the professor seeks. Len's words reinforce the idea that, in practice, initial readings of papers may best be read with a focus on ideas, not language constructions.

Additionally, Len's resistance to peer response groups tells a story of negative judgments that he seems to assume extend beyond the writing to his personhood. Len feared peer responders in the classroom but did embrace his own version of process, shaping it to his needs. He told me he found people he trusted, people who really knew *him*, and would help make his papers fit class requirements. He found comfort in the fact that they would not judge him as incompetent. In our quest to have students work cooperatively in our classrooms, do we subject them to a situation where they may not feel helped at all, but pushed even further into the margins? Students like Len have taught me that we do, despite our best intentions.

In line 13, Len says he cares deeply for his writing, as if a reader might assume that someone who writes as he does must not care. How many times in the traditional classroom have teachers made the assumption that "errors" indicate carelessness, laziness, or a lack of effort? He refutes this by saying he spends much time writing and starts "ahead of times" (line 14) to make sure he completes an accurate assignment. No matter how hard he pulls on those bootstraps, however, he has not felt like a successful writer. He appears to trust that the problem is *within* him and looks forward to "improving his writing abilities" and "quitting the weakness" (lines 15–16), as if it were a choice and a matter of self-control. In lines 17–18, though, he says he knows that all the weaknesses may not be taken care of at once, but "he can improve," another possible echo of teachers' bootstraps discourse. Len typically blames himself for being a poor writer, appearing to accept the ideology of stunted growth. The discourses of so many classroom writing instructors, including myself, reverberated painfully as I analyzed his reflections.

What I Learned

I studied a number of Len's portfolio papers, learning more about him, writing classes in general, and even about my own teaching as I dug deeper and examined which discourses could have a negative effect on the writer identities of students. Len's struggle with academic discourses demonstrates the thinking that can lurk behind a strong negative writer identity in the classroom. His case also reflects the complexity of writing in the academy for students whose first language is not English and for whom race and/or class have been marginalizing factors. While there are discourses that could help him (and others) better understand his writing patterns and help alleviate his writing anxiety Len, like most of my students, remained unable to access them as that political conversation is so seldom a part of our classrooms.

Len's story also points out how certain uses of the process writing method can be a source of great trepidation and embarrassment for students already feeling the effects of marginalization. When he takes up process discourse, his resistance is evident. He demonstrates how traditional formal discourse's emphasis on language structures and form contribute to a silencing of voices and a need to find trusted responders who understand that there is more to a person than the writing structures they see on the page.

The teaching of formal academic discourse and oppression are linked in subtle ways. First, there are multiple aspects of writer identity and even those who may at first appear to dislike writing may be ardently seeking a discourse that allows their voices to be heard. Second, without access to liberating discourses, students tend to blame themselves for being "different," and accept the marginalized position of stunted or uninitiated offered to them in many classrooms. While microanalysis of Len's words gave some evidence of resistance to the hegemonic influences of certain educational discourses, he clearly lacked access to other discourses that may have better explained his struggles in the academy. The academy has shaped and limited his writer identity, and his words demonstrate how much he has been influenced by that judgment—and how difficult it is to understand the complexity of his situation in it.

Do not hear me saying that we should not teach Standard English. Do hear the following as my message. The teaching of writing and language is a political act. By explicitly teaching writing as such, we help demystify the power of institutions to define and label what is "good" and what is "correct." By redefining the variety of dialects as different ways to communicate, and by explicitly saying that use of particular dialects in certain situations has social and political implications, we help students understand that difference does not have to equate with "less than" or "ignorant."

Unfortunately, my class did not offer a strong enough sociopolitical discourse to help Len construct a more positive and productive writer identity. We had talked about the politics of language, but, in retrospect, what I offered was enough to help him map substantial change. Clearly, the road to empowerment is not straight, steady, or uncomplicated, and coming to see oneself through a new lens is a process, not an overnight conversion. Additionally, the power of judgment in institutions silences and maintains the status quo in many nuanced ways. As a writing teacher in the academy, fulfilling the required curriculum tasks often seems overwhelming. Despite that, I have come to believe a discussion of language politics and how and why some students may be in conflict with them is an educational responsibility. Writing instructors and workshop coordinators operate in the modes we were taught, often convinced that our quest to create "good writers" involves transformation of the writer rather than redefinition of the issue.

When we teach formal academic discourse, if that is a goal, we can learn to do it in ways that do not leave second-language students (and others) feeling colonized or marginal to the discourse. Wider acceptance of more multicultural discourses and more freedom of presentation in academic writing tasks may help students move more effectively through academic writing tasks. Gaining meta-knowledge regarding how dominant discourses affect us in society may allow students like Len to feel less marginalized and compliant. Conflict in the institution, as Lu (1991) presents it, allows for struggle and uncertainty as it deals with issues of diversity. Though struggle can be discomforting, it can eventually provide for a more empowered view of the world of writing and one's position in it.

I find it helpful to focus on the idea that it is the discourse used to interpret the experience rather than the experience itself that is at the heart of identity for our students. How they and we discuss, respond to, and react to writing can move us to a critical dialogue about relevant history, culture, language, and writing. Knowledge and power create and re-create themselves through curriculum, so it becomes the responsibility of educators to find ways to successfully include those students who have been systematically excluded. By explicitly teaching how discourses operate and work to give or deny access in society, we can be part of a process of liberation rather than contributors to a world of oppressive silence.

We can also shift away from an emphasis on a standardized product and give students access to a more epistemological discussion of writing models. This is not to say we should eliminate all classical modes of rhetoric, only that we can also make room for more expressivist forms. Furthermore, by explicitly discussing competing ways of writing we can help students come to understand why they prefer writing in a certain way and why they identify negatively when required to adopt certain discourses.

Most of us strive for a pedagogical approach that encourages students to write while allowing them wider avenues for success. We can do this by helping to eliminate the fears and negativity so often associated with the red pen and responses like the one a devastated student told me about, "This paper is an embarrassment. Take a writing course!" Hybrid discourses, that is, discourses that combine the formality of academic discourse with more personalized writing genres, may help students achieve a more balanced view of themselves as writers, tackle writing tasks with more confidence, and further understanding of effective writing for all.

References

Bartholomae, D. (1986). Inventing the university. *Journal of Basic Writing, 5,* 4–23.

Fairclough, N. (1995). Critical discourse analysis: The critical study of language. New York: Longman.

Harris, J. (1997). *A teaching subject: Composition since 1966.* New Jersey: Prentice.

Lu, M. (1991). Redefining the legacy of Mina Shaughnessy: A critique of the politics of linguistic innocence. *Journal of Basic Writing, 10,* 26–40.

Luke, A. (1995–1996). Text and discourse in education: an introduction to critical discourse analysis. In M. Apple (Ed.), *Review of research in education* (pp. 1–48). Washington, DC: American Education Association.

Rose, M. (1985). The language of exclusion: Writing instruction at the university. *College English, 47,* 341–359.

Conversation

Contesting Authoritative Discourses in Education

LINDA FERNSTEN, JANE L. LEHR, CHARLOTTE LICHTER

Linda: Charlotte, as I read your chapter, I was struck by some disquieting albeit interesting parallels to my own. First, I'll address MacNaughton's concept "that policies and decrees of a government are fashioned on the vested interests and desires of the ruling class, which seek to perpetuate and maintain the existing social and economic order" (Lichter, chapter 1, this volume). The unquestioned acceptance of formal, stylized academic writing discourses as the only way to conduct business in college courses across the curriculum attests to some of those same vested literacy interests that you discuss. Up until the late 1980s, few writing theorists even questioned the use of that writing tradition, just accepting it as a requirement for all who, as Bartholomae (1986) noted, hoped to enter the University. Even in the twenty-first century, with America's increasingly multicultural society, traditional academic discourses remain, for the most part, the "correct" or "proper" way to express oneself in academia.

   The power of that hegemonic thinking is evident in a number of the high-stakes writing tests now popular as graduation requirements in many states. These typically penalize students who lack more privileged language backgrounds. Under the guise of a promise to "Leave No Child Behind," we have created "outsiders" of certain children, punished those whose language is judged to "not meet the standard," and labeled as deficient those who differ from America's "ruling class." Like those in your chapter, we, too, uphold the social status of the "haves," equating the use of a specialized discourse with intelligence and achievement rather than exposure and access.

Charlotte: The concern of unequal access and social justice for those students who have been marginalized and silenced is indeed a common thread throughout our chapters. It is through classes like yours, Linda, and Jane's that education students can become cognizant of dominant hegemonic discourses and learn to critically examine and challenge such discourses.

Academia practices are historically and socially embedded in patriarchal and hegemonic privilege. Literacy education, in Western society, pivots around the dissemination of cultural knowledge, values, and social power. Literacy practices are constructed and established as neutral and natural and as a result, left virtually uncontested. Grant (1986) says, "Literacy exists as a set of social practices, the significance of which is never 'autonomous' or 'neutral' but rather embedded in social institutions and contexts" (p. 12). In order to make visible and critically examine and deconstruct those taken-for-granted, natural, "common sense" assumptions, it is imperative that we acknowledge literacy as a gendered social practice.

The theoretical framework that I have adopted encompasses a critical–social analysis of gender relations framed within a historical perspective. Gender as a principal category of analysis encompasses notions of sexism, power relationships, and inequality. As Patti Lather (1984) articulates, "Adopting gender as a basic analytic tool will enable critical theory to see what is right under its nose" (p. 52). As gendering does not occur in a vacuity, but rather through social and historical contexts, drawing upon a historical framework helps to analyze commonsense issues from a different perspective. Hilary Janks (1997) claims:

> All social practices are tied to specific historical contexts and are means by which existing social relations are reproduced or contested and different interests are served. It is the questions pertaining to interests that relate discourse to relations of power. How is the text positioned or positioning? Whose interests are served by this positioning? Whose interests are negated? What are the consequences of this positioning? (p. 329)

Gender categories, laden with stereotypical assumptions, are constructed as taken-for-granted, natural conceptions, which permeate every facet of society. It is without question that many students—both male and female—would resist any challenge to the usurpation of that which is considered natural and normal. Jane, how did you respond to some of the overt forms of resistance when challenging the dominant discourses of gender? I would imagine that you met with some hostility.

Jane: Yes, I did (grin). However, social justice approaches to education necessitate an implicit critique of the myth of the neutral instructor and a simultaneous recognition that teaching and learning can be dangerous and uncomfortable—for both the instructor and the students. Megan Boler (1999) describes this type of education as a "pedagogy of discomfort," which aims to invite "educators and students to engage in critical inquiry regarding values and cherished beliefs, and to examine constructed self-images in relation to how one has learned to perceive others" (pp. 176–177; see also Kumashiro, 2002). Critically, social justice educators seek to make visible taken-for-granted assumptions about the everyday world and to examine how our commitments—both emotional and political—"define how and what one chooses to see, and conversely, not to see" (p. 177). Students (and instructors) do often react to this project with what Boler calls "defensive anger"—which she sees as a very understandable "defense of one's investments in the values of the dominant culture" (p. 191). The question then becomes "How can I as an instructor respond productively to this (defensive) resistance?" Further: "How can I respond in a way that does not reinforce the idea that my political analysis is 'right' and other positions are 'wrong'?"

Like you, Charlotte, I believe that it is necessary to employ a theoretical framework that grounds explorations and critiques of today's gender systems and educational practices within historical analyses. Thus, to better position ourselves as educators to understand and critically engage acts of student resistance—what Herbert Kohl calls "willed not-learning"—I believe that we need to unpack the historical and contemporary links between the "tough guise" of masculinity (Katz et al., 1999) and student resistance in the classroom. What intersection do you see between the gendering of literacy and of student resistance?

Finally, Linda's essay pushes us both to examine how race intersects with the gendering of literacy and student resistance. Charlotte, in your essay, you wrote, "Significant factors [in literacy] such as race and class have been disregarded. Boys who are already disadvantaged by social class and ethnic positioning become all the more marginalized when impacted with dominant forms of masculinity, which run counter to academic success." Charlotte and I must ask ourselves: How would using race as the primary lens—rather than gender— open new paths in our analyses and, in fact, how does race intersect with gender in the narratives we have developed? Further, how do we, as researchers and teachers, navigate the simultaneous need to address these intersections (and others along the lines of sexual orientation, class, age, dis/ability, and so forth) at the same time that we craft coherent narratives for publications like this and put into practice specific pedagogical interventions?

Charlotte: Jane, I agree that in order to critically analyze and to respond to acts of resistance in the classroom, we must uncover the nexus between masculinity and student resistance. Schools, as institutional structures in society, are constructed not only by the actors within, but also by the social forces enveloping them. While legitimizing a particular way of life, they disconfirm and marginalize the voices of those from subordinate groups who are not English-speaking, white, middle-class, heterosexual males. Educational institutions are more than mere instructional sites for the transmittal of knowledge, but are in fact, cultural sites, which sanction and embody specific forms of values, knowledge, interests, practices, and experiences that epitomize that of the dominant culture.

Academic subjects are gendered and stereotyped in that the sciences, mathematics, technology, physical education, and shop are considered masculinized while English, music, drama, art, family studies, and the humanities are feminized (Connell, 2000; Gilbert and Gilbert, 1998). Many males tend to eschew subjects they view as categorically feminine. Hence, hegemonic constructions of masculinity are seen to be incompatible with literacy and English literature, both within elementary and secondary classrooms. Alloway and Gilbert (1997) suggest that antipathy toward school-based literacy tasks starts in the early elementary years whereby boys read and write less. They contend that school-based literacy practices that typically pivot around discourses of emotion, phenomenological reflexivity, aesthetics, and personalized, empathetic, and creative responses and expression contradict and gainsay dominant constructions of masculinity.

It seems that resistance is indeed tied to a wider set of social practices through which a particular gender regime operates. Luke (1993) contends that, historically, schools have played a role in the production and procreation of "stratified social systems." Linda's essay certainly brings to light the marginalizing and oppressing effects that dominant academic discourses can have on people of color and of different ethnic and cultural backgrounds. Factors such as race, social class, sexual orientation, disability, and ethnicity intersect with gender and thus complicate and trouble the way that gender regimes impact the lived experiences of students. This challenges us to further investigate the convoluted ways that gender, race, and class affect academic success. Gender cannot be looked upon as a monolithic homogeneous construct; social and cultural backgrounds, race, sexuality, and class cannot be ignored. Even within specific groups, there are differences and diversities that further problematize the seemingly unproblematic, taken-for-granted category of gender. This unearths the magnitude and the complexity of masculinity, underachievement, and gender.

I acknowledge the limitations of my own "gendered" viewpoints and biases and question my ability, as a white middle-class female, to truly see the world through the lens of people of color or those from a specific class or ethnic group who are oppressed and marginalized by the dominant culture. This leads me to push for a greater understanding of the diversities and differences within the various subcultures and further question which groups of boys and girls are at risk and which groups are more privileged. This would call for educational programs, agenda, and policies to be targeted where most needed. Knowing that we all are shaped by race, class, ethnicity, gender, and other social practices and perspectives, I too believe that it is through critical dialogue and self-reflection that we can make visible the invisible as we strive toward a greater social justice for all.

Linda: Charlotte, your piece definitely pushes me to remember the importance of a historical view and to review who wins and who loses when policies and agendas are pushed for what is touted as the greater good. The power of privilege and the invisible push to accept hegemonic thinking as "common sense" are certainly subtexts of both our pieces.

In the section on dichotomizing the sexes we could replace the word gender with race and the facts would still fit. When I was conducting research on writer identity, one of the most useful books I read was by Chris Weedon (1987), titled *Feminist Practice and Poststructural Theory*. While she focused on feminist thinking, almost all of her major points paralleled marginalization issues related to race, class, and ethnicity as well. As you wrote about how women were discouraged "from developing their own potential and from attaining higher education," I was pushed to consider how often we continue to do this for second-language learners, those who speak a nondominant dialect, those who look different, and those who learn differently.

Conducting research helped me think differently about young writers in the classroom, though I cannot honestly say my practice was magically or quickly transformed. As Jane intimated, living into a practice that halts marginalization and encourages transformation is the challenge, especially when teachers and professors are, in most cases, the gatekeepers of the existing system. Changes have been made, and it can be painful at times to shine a light on past practices, but living into Freire's world is more easily imagined than lived on a daily basis.

Jane: Linda, your chapter opened up space for me to consider how the ways in which students are trained to literally "write science" plays an important role in the construction of specific forms of science literacy and citizenship. By disciplining their thoughts and bodies in the production of "objectivity," "rationality," and, indeed, laboratory reports, science students are trained to "practice citizenship" in a way that limits the types of knowledge that can count—or even become visible—in decision-making processes and scientific practices in an a priori manner. In your chapter, you wrote:

Many students struggling to become more skillful users of the discourses expected in secondary and college-level written work become convinced they are simply "bad writers." They have entered the world of teachers and college professors who often valorize academic discourses and marginalize or devalue other discourses that are a part of students' lives. At both levels, the efforts of well-intentioned gatekeepers to critique and "fix" the language differences they find have resulted in some students becoming fearful of writing and academic writing tasks.

In effect, this interaction with "official discourses" produces students who disengage from civic and professional arenas as their voices are "written out" of these contexts. I think that this concept of "gate-keeping" may be extremely useful when we think about science education and the privileging of scientific literacy as a way of knowing the world. In both cases, bodies and perspectives that do not fit into "official discourses" are silenced. Education, in this sense, produces what Foucault describes as "docile bodies," disciplined to accept scientific knowledge and other dominant discourses as truth with few tools to challenge ongoing inequalities.

Linda: Jane, your chapter, alongside my own, certainly focuses on the question of how we go about challenging oppressive dominant discourses. While you concentrate on those legitimated by science and I center on writing, your piece pushed me to consider that educators across the curriculum concerned about social justice issues face the same hurdles. While the privilege of formal academic and science discourses goes almost unchallenged, there have been other social/educational discourses that, disturbingly, have been met with blind acceptance. It was in my lifetime that children were universally excluded in mainstream facilities because of the color of their skin or the nature of their disability. When Len (my case study) talks about enjoying writing when he can tell the story of his life and what is important in it, he is calling out for recognition of the importance and significance of a story that does not mesh with traditional success tales or bootstraps mythology. Expressivists have long touted the importance of individual voices, but their call is being silenced in the so-called standards movement. Whose standards are unquestioningly privileged and why?

Your piece, Jane, also reminds me how difficult it can be for us as educators to challenge what many have come to believe are the best practices of our educational system. The nature of power is to hold onto that power. "Throw away" students, those we decided were unskilled, inept, cognitively delayed, the wrong color, class, among others have always been "losers" in a system that judges, categorizes, and belittles. Well meaning as we may be, we are a part of the gate-keeping system; so fostering as well as enacting a more critical consciousness remains a daily challenge. The expressivists of the 1960s—those who called out for freedom of expression as well as appreciation and acceptance of individual voices—were criticized as naïve and faulted for encouraging substandard work. Inroads have been made and continue to be made, however. For example, the idea of including real teacher conversations in an academic book is an example of a hybrid text, one that mixes the traditional research voice with the more personal. It may be trite to say that change comes slowly, but the hardest lesson for this impatient person to remember is that teaching for social justice is an organic and dynamic process rather than a fait accompli.

References

Alloway, N., and Gilbert, P. (1997). Boys and literacy: Lessons from Australia. *Gender and Education, 9*(1), 49–58.

Bartholomae, D. (1986). Inventing the university. *Journal of Basic Writing, 5*, 4–23.

Boler, M. (1999). *Feeling power: Emotions and education.* New York and London: Routledge

Connell, R. (2000). *The Men and the boys.* Berkeley, CA: University of California Press.

Gilbert, R., and Gilbert, P. (1998). *Masculinity goes to school.* London: Routledge.

Grant, A. (1986). Defining literacy: Common myths and alternative readings. *Australian Review of Applied Linguistics, 9*(2), 1–22.

Janks, H. (1997). Critical discourse analysis as a research tool. *Discourse: Studies in the Cultural Politics of Education, 18*(3), 329–342

Katz, J., Earp, J., and Jhally, S. [director] (1999). *Tough guise: Violence, media, and the crisis in masculinity* [motion picture]. Media Education Foundation.

Kumashiro, K. (2002) "Against Repetition: Addressing Resistance to Anti-Oppressive Change in the Practices of Learning, Teaching, Supervising, and Researching." *Harvard Educational Review, 72*(1), 67–92.

Lather, P. (1984). Critical theory, curricular transformation and feminist mainstreaming. *Journal of Education, 166*(1), 49–62.

Luke, A. (1993). The social construction of literacy in the primary classroom. In Unsworth (Ed.), *Literacy learning and teaching: Language as social practice in the primary school* (pp. 1–55). Melbourne, Australia: MacMillan.

Weedon, C. (1987) *Feminist practice and poststructural theory.* Cambridge, UK: Blackwell.

Part II

Unearthing Hidden Curriculums

Standards, Socialization, and Silences

3

Curriculum for [Dis]Empowerment

Uncovering Hegemony within the *New Jersey Social Studies Curriculum Framework*

MARK R. DAVIES

New social studies standards have influenced curriculum in many schools and have become the driving force behind much of the local curricular reform and has influenced the way that many teachers shape their lessons. Educators are attending in-service workshops en masse to learn how to link the standards to everyday practice. Many teachers object to being told how and what to teach, seeing this process as the latest in a long line of directives they must begrudgingly work to implement. Resistance to these directives, unfortunately, is not based on what I contend is the predominantly oppressive messages that are embedded into the standards as well as the learning activities that accompany them.

My examination of the language within the *New Jersey Curriculum Framework* attempts to lift out of these documents examples of language that attempt to perpetuate the control of particular socioeconomic groups. This occurs through the teaching of what is expressed as common values—values that reflect those of more powerful individuals that are generally wealthier, white, and often male, while subordinating people of color and poorer, less powerful classes in an attempt to shape or construct a view of the world that mirrors the values and experiences of more powerful groups. The standards thus present a moral and intellectual view that is not consistent with that of many students and works to undercut their lived experiences and future expectations. Uncovering hidden beliefs and values within the standards will help teachers and teacher educators to see this form of oppression more clearly.

As this chapter illustrates, the standards give students little alternatives but to go along with and accept dominant practices even when they undermine and negatively influence one's concept of self, in regard to class, race, and social and political practice. Ironically many politicians and educators claim the standards are empowering, even emancipatory. They believe that the standards "embody a vision of the skills and understanding all of New Jersey's children need to step forward into the twenty-first century and to be successful in their careers and daily lives" (NJDOE, 1996). But what exactly are the skills and understandings the Framework believes are important?

The New Jersey curriculum standards believe it is important "to educate citizens who will be competitive in the international marketplace of the future, since the goals of public education is to prepare students for the world of work" (NJDOE, 1996). The *New Jersey Curriculum Framework* also presents values that are expressed as a society of common experiences, values, and democratic practices and are representative of the understanding that students should have in the twenty-first century.

This new curricular reform simply reinforces existing dominant values and practices within society, a practice referred to as hegemony. Hegemony can be described as the "moral and intellectual leadership of a dominant class over a subordinate class" wherein "[h]egemony is not a process of active domination as much as an active structuring of the culture and experiences of the subordinate class by the dominant class" (McLaren, 1989, p. 174). Essentially hegemony works through the unspoken, the embedded, and the taken-for-granted. Thus, the standards are a setting in which dominant ideology is structured and arranged in order to appear as morally correct and status quo.

Much of the language within the standards reflects a concept of reality that can be considered oppressive when considering the perspective of those who have historically been dominated. John B. Thompson (1987) recognizes the need to place language within its proper ideological, social, and historical context. He states, "One cannot 'understand the meaning of an expression' without investigating the social-historical conditions in which it is produced as well as the conditions—historically specific and socially differentiated—in which it is received" (p. 520). This is an important distinction, which pushes me to develop an understanding of how social knowledge is represented and accepted by all people in order to shed light on the social conditions that produce, reproduce, maintain, and further domination and oppression.

In order to understand the hidden messages within the standards, the text must be examined and placed in its proper social and historical context, and then interpreted. Thompson (1987) stresses the importance of interpreting knowledge claims. The claim of objective truth, or what we will refer to as a "truth or knowledge claim," he states, is "an expression which claims to say something about something; and it is this claim, understood in terms of what is asserted by an expression and what that expression is about, which must be grasped by interpretation" (pp. 520–521). However, interpreting oppressive power masked within knowledge and language presents a problem, because it depends upon the contextual framework of the individual examining the knowledge. Accordingly, any claims to objective truth or fact need to be evaluated, arrived at, and developed through interpretation and discussion by many groups. But often claims are made without alternative interpretations or input and represent claims that may not be accepted by all people and are imposed by the group with the power to make and implement the claim. This chapter illustrates such truth claims embedded within the learning standards and accompanying progress indicator made clear through the conceptual framework provided by Thompson's four modalities for the operation of ideology.

Legitimation: The Right View

The process of legitimation sustains a system of domination by representing this system as legitimate. It also establishes the ideology of a particular group as the logically correct or right view of reality, a view that is to be accepted by all people. As Thompson (1987) notes, within the process of legitimation, "Stories are told which seek to justify the exercise of power by those who posses it and strive to reconcile others to the fact that they do not" (p. 527). These stories establish a distorted lens through which one views the world and one's place in the world and it degrades and devalues the experiences of some groups—undermining their conceptions of self, personal experiences, histories, languages, and knowledge. The ideology imposed upon students presents a view of the world that is easy to accept because it is seen as right or correct and so it becomes the dominant knowledge.

The standards use legitimation by crafting a narrative of American society and history that characterizes knowledge of history, civics, and geography as basic to what all students must know in order to be part of a democracy. The standards state, "Social studies education . . . is key to developing every student's appreciation of our American heritage. This knowledge and appreciation will enable students to participate in the great public dialogue" (NJDOE, 1999, p. 9). There is an amount of "telling" going on here in order to legitimate oppression, in the flawed idea that a student needs only to acquire the core knowledge in order to participate in the great public dialogue. The implications are that people who do not learn the core knowledge or possess it already will not be able to participate in democratic life. The entire system of inequality is legitimated as citizens are divided into those who have knowledge and appreciation of American heritage and those who do not.

The standards also present dissimilar ideologies that are fused together as legitimate dominant practices. The capitalistic system uses democratic concepts for the legitimation of an oppressive system. It does this through cloaking itself in the democratic words of equality (equal opportunity) and freedom (free markets). The standards present a system based on the accumulation of capital as legitimate while limited access to capital, and the degraded and devalued labor for many, is presented as unproblematic. In this way the capitalist system is sustained as it is presented as a legitimate economic system and an extension of democracy that is consistent with democratic practices, even when these practices come at the expense of many.

The introduction to the Framework tells us a story of capitalist urgency and need: "The new demands of the workplace along with the rise of a global marketplace make 'economic literacy' a high priority in today's school" (NJDOE, 1999, p. 241). Here economic literacy is described as the "students' comprehension of such basic economic ideas as the role of money, wants and needs, supply and demand, the market and its role, and the workings of a [capitalist] economic system" (NJDOE, 1999, p. 241).

This economic literacy also includes the capitalistic notions of wants, needs, and scarcity. Wants can be described as frivolous desires that are not necessary, but within the *Curriculum Framework* wants are described as "things we would like to have to make our lives or that of our country better" (NJDOE, 1999, p. 247). This implies that wants are not frivolous, but necessary to improving our world and our lives. However, this idea is immediately countered with the idea that not all wants can be met as the concept of scarcity is legitimated in the following section that states, "Scarcity is a basic concept. . . . There is simply not enough resources to satisfy everyone's wants" (NJDOE, 1999, p. 247). While scarcity is certainly present within our world, the implications are that some people will not be able to have the things that "make our lives or that of our country better" (NJDOE, 1999, p. 247).

By teaching the concepts associated with economic literacy throughout school, capitalist ideology is sustained and perpetuated as students develop understandings of their role within a capitalist economy. This curricular treatment of capitalism disallows the kind of critique students need to refute issues of power and domination within a capitalist system. Students are unable to see the extensive boundaries of domination perpetuated through the economic system. Legitimation takes place again through a process of telling students that capitalism and their role within this system is important as early as kindergarten (NJDOE, 1999, pp. 245, 249). Students are presented with an extant system and are only asked to examine one economic system, the capitalist system, rather than examining the viability of other economic systems such as a socialist system or even a barter system. They come to believe that "[i]mplementing effective trading strategies is the ultimate measure of success" (NJDOE, 1999, p. 248) and see that as workers they become "important participants in American economic life" (NJDOE, 1999, p. 245). Students also begin to recognize that "[w]e make contributions to the general good through the work that we do in what is called our job. The jobs we have . . . make life better for all of us" (NJDOE, 1999, p. 249). Through all this, students' consent is given to supporting a system they come to believe is right, even though it is the cause for much hardship, unhappiness, and poverty throughout the world.

Reification: Domination as Common Sense

The standards present knowledge, values, and civic practices in a way that lift them out of their historical or contemporary context and place them into an unproblematic and natural position. Reification is the attempt to "reestablish the dimensions of society without history at the heart of historical society" (Thompson, 1987, p. 527). The reification of particular ideas and practices perpetuates the idea that they are *natural* and are void of a particular history and context, and they are presented as outside of time (Thompson, 1987). Students accept this knowledge as naturally occurring and unproblematic. Imposing ideology upon people amounts to domination, and because this ideology is not representative of all people, it represents a method of ideological control that marginalizes some groups; as we accept a knowledge or conception of society as legitimate, any other group's knowledge becomes viewed as *illegitimate*. This "truth claim" imposes the idea that social reality is somehow objective and natural as truth claims are presented as unproblematic and free of relation to oppressive forms of power.

The standards implement reified knowledge of democracy by suggesting that it is only through studying the documents of democracy, such as the Constitution, Bill of Rights, and Declaration of Independence, that students will become better democratic citizens and a more democratic society will exist. This concept is presented as though this simple process is obvious and self-evident. It is believed that in order to practice democracy, citizens must be literate in the historical texts of democracy. Peter McLaren (1989) notes that the concept of cultural literacy can be used against students who are viewed as culturally illiterate because the canonic knowledge in great books "often deflects attention away from the personal experiences of students and the political nature of everyday life" (p. 177) and renders these experiences worthless.

In deferring the sources of knowledge of democracy only to that which is located within the canon of so-called great books, the standards ignore *other* sources of democracy, texts that may reflect not only democracy, but also the struggles of groups to bring about changes in a society that they find to be *undemocratic*. These could include the writings and speeches of Dr. Martin Luther King, Jr., Malcolm X, and Che Guevara, the historical analysis of Howard Zinn (1999) in *A Peoples History of the United States*, or the classics *Black Elk Speaks* (Neihart, 2000), *Bury My Heart at Wounded Knee* (Brown, 2003), and *Custer Died for Your Sins* (Deloria, 2003).

If, for example, the study of Civics focuses only on the reified versions of democracy, and not the multiple experiences of *living* democracy, which are markedly different from reified versions, this insures that the full extent and history of oppression will never be discussed, examined, or explored by American students. The ideas that the standards ignore the historical realities of lived democracy can be seen in the following passage:

> We live in a time and place of increasing ethnic and cultural diversity. We see our country, our state, and our community changing day by day. It is essential to educators to help children understand that the essence of America is diverse cultures and ways of living all combined into an American culture *and that we are all immigrants or children of immigrants*. We should know about and value the contributions of the many cultures and the different ethnic and racial groups in our country. We must also recognize that the immigration experience was not always positive. (NJDOE, 1999, p. 168, emphasis added)

The standards frame the American experience in such a way that most white Americans can relate to as immigrants or children of immigrants, but completely ignores and disregards the experiences of a large group of Americans who were either abducted from their homeland and brought here in chains, or who were the original people of this land against whom a genocide was committed in order to secure their land, or were subjects of a defeated nation that expanded American boundaries. We are not all immigrants here, and to look at it any other way is to perpetuate a lie that furthers and solidifies the oppression and domination of blacks, Native Americans, Asian Americans, Hispanics, and other groups.

Many groups had experiences that are not reflected in the "American experience." This sentiment is noted in this passage:

> The experiences of Latinos, Native Americans, Asians and other US minorities have not embodied the American credo, nor have their experiences reflected the just and equal treatment implied in the words inscribed on the Statue of Liberty: "Give me your tired, your poor, your huddled masses yearning to be free . . ." Manifest Destiny was one of the justifications for herding Native Americans into desolate locations without economic, social or educational equality. It also served as grounds for conquering the West and storming Mexico City in the Mexican-American War to obtain part of Mexico that then became the state of California, a result that later made Latinos a

minority in a land they had once controlled. National security was a claim that presumably justified the incarceration of Americans of Japanese descent into desolate camps without economic, political or educational equality. These actions exemplify neither justice or equality, but rather demonstrate an unpleasant streak of racism and prejudice in the American character, at least in its political and governmental character. (Nelson and Pang, 2001, p. 145)

In short, there has never been a common experience for all Americans; these differences extend from the ways in which we arrived in this land to the limited experiences that some groups have enjoying the benefits associated with the concepts of justice and equality. The notion that "we are all the same" ignores the real historical and social legacies and reifies a false history.

The multiple interpretations of such events are completely disregarded as the idea of a common culture is continually presented in the New Jersey standards. For example, students are required to "understand the views of the people of other times and places regarding the issues they faced" (NJDOE, 1999, p. 153). This appears uncontroversial, but the text then asks students to consider "how individuals and groups survived and prospered in the face of difficult issues like scarcity, overpopulation, conflicts and discrimination?" (NJDOE, 1999, p. 153). Students focus on oppressed groups' ability to overcome adversity and allow their creative spirit to flourish and prosper as they

learn that this human impulse can be suppressed temporarily in situations where people are mistreated by a government, by social groups or by a part of society. But the creative spirit eventually emerges as people learn to cope and to find alternatives. The Harlem Renaissance is an example of how a more-secure environment fostered the creativity of its inhabitants. (NJDOE, 1999, p. 153)

Certainly the Harlem Renaissance was a period of great cultural, musical, and creative production. However, by focusing only on the creative spirit that emerged during that era ignores the severe racism, discrimination, oppression, and the entire historical, social, and cultural context of the African American experience.

This is an attempt to reify the value of hard work in the face of adversity as a core American value that should be held by students—particularly minority students. The message is clearly saturated in meritocracy and implies that the oppressed must simply try harder to overcome the adversity associated with their domination. Encoded within this message is the implicit idea that if they feel oppressed, responsibility lies not with larger cultural practices, but in their own lack of drive and determination to overcome the conditions of their own making. The response of a small segment of America's oppressed minorities to cultural and racial oppression is canonized and put forth as a response that all oppressed minorities have employed—

or should have—throughout their long history of oppression. Reifying a transitory state of history in which oppressive conditions produced great art relieves the oppressors from any guilt or responsibility associated with the mental burden of domination. The reified knowledge practically states, *if the oppressed can prosper in the face of such extreme oppression, then the oppression itself cannot be that bad.*

The process of reifying limited sources of knowledge is in itself problematic, but the impact that this process has on the consensual acceptance of domination must be considered. The message within this knowledge is clear: not only are the experiences of marginalized groups not important, but neither are *they as people.* This negative message will most certainly become internalized by these groups and will impact their conceptions of self and place. Not only are these beliefs uncoded by oppressed youth, they are also internalized and uncoded by the children of higher socioeconomic groups who come to believe that their superiority is a product of their ability and skill as determined by meritocratic practices and is reflective of the natural order of things.

Fragmentation: Consent through Erosion of the People

The acceptance of domination, or the giving of consent, also occurs through the process of fragmentation. The ideology in the standards works to fragment groups and place them in opposition to one another, reducing the effectiveness of oppressed groups to resist and change the dominant hegemony. Because they are fractured, they become focused on the Other as the source of the problem rather than the dominant ideology that controls and influences their lived experiences. Inevitably groups fragment along the lines of those who have best accepted or most closely approximated the culture and knowledge of the dominant group and those who have not. An example of this is the representation of Asian Americans as the model minority or the group that is most like the majority because of their hard work.

Groups that accept and attempt to model the dominant point of view gain the rewards offered by their acquiescence, which nullifies their potential for resistance. Because competition has been forced upon them, they come to see other groups—with whom they actually have a lot in common—as rivals for the benefits that they enjoy, making it even more difficult to recognize the negative implications that the dominant hegemony has on their own lives. Groups who are in opposition to accepted practices and ideology often find themselves further marginalized, powerless, and unable to change the status quo. At this point, their consent to the limitations of their oppression is gained as their inability to challenge an oppressive, seemingly all-encompassing system of thought, action, knowledge, and experience leads them to either spend the remainder of their lives working to break into the box of dominant ideology, or they succumb and begin to see themselves and their experiences as inferior to that of the other groups.

Once again the theme of commonness is used to oppress as groups fragment when measured against notions of common culture, and marginalized groups are instantly thrust outside the culture because they do not reflect the contrived notions of a common culture. This puts groups into opposition, as marginalized groups become the Other and forces groups in the borderlands to compete against one another, thus fragmenting the groups that have the most in common and the most to gain from their solidarity. Marginalized groups are presented in an odd or negative manner and their historical legacy is glossed over and the historical significance is reduced. This accomplished both aspects of fragmentation as more dominant groups confirm their negative views and marginalized groups look at the negative portrayal of other marginalized groups and develop the same negative views as the dominant group.

The portrayal of the status quo can be seen in the following example. "Students are expected to study Western civilization as a foundational element of social studies" (NJDOE, 1999, p. 9) so that they can understand "our cultural and intellectual heritage [which] includes . . . the Hellenic-Judeo-Christian tradition" (NJDOE, 1999, p. 5). The intent and message is clear: the dominant and most important historical and religious traditions of this country is seeped in the rich, elite, and culturally refined traditions of Western Europe; all other cultures are secondary in importance to these experiences. Marginalized children are forced into a position where they must accept these ideas and are forced to confront an unresolvable paradox of empowerment, where they lose themselves by accepting the dominant knowledge or lose themselves to the borders by rejecting it.

The New Jersey standards also possess examples of cultural oppression that downplay the historical legacy of African Americans. It is as though by casting their legacy in a more positive light other marginalized groups will view them with hostility and contempt and think to themselves, "why are they complaining *they* did not have it so bad," and thus the first fissure in the fragmentation occurs. Standard 6.4, which focuses on social history, discusses American slavery by comparing it to Russian serfdom. The standards ask students the reified question, "How did global economic trends contribute to the growth of forced labor systems in Russia and the New World?" (NJDOE, 1999, p. 188).

An answer is provided that takes away the burden of oppressor from white landowners and forgives their misdeeds as a reaction to changing economic markets. The standard states: "The opening of new trade markets around the globe generated demand for agricultural products, prompting landowners to seek cheaper forms of labor" (NJDOE, 1999, p. 188). This excuse creates fragmentation by whitewashing history to minimize and underscore the oppression that generations of African Americans have endured and immediately debunks any legitimacy in their claims of oppression because their legacy contributed to America's financial success.

Minimizing marginalized groups' claims to oppression is not limited to African Americans; the oppression that Native Americans faced at the hands of their white oppressors is given little attention within the standards. The standards focus instead on cultural aspects of Native American lifestyles that are cast as odd or foreign. In one section the standards make a comparison between a human and an alien encounter to that of the encounter of whites with Native Americans. Students are asked "if they felt that a parallel could be drawn between an alien visit to Earth and European–Native American encounters" (NJDOE, 1999, p. 212).

In the same section the destructive impact of white oppression on Native Americans is addressed in a way that is consistent with the treatment of slavery. While the standards do acknowledge the historical accuracy of the whites' hostile approach to Native Americans, the entire concept of oppression that led to the genocide of the native peoples of this land is shrugged off as an aggravated conflict over cultural differences, not as a systematic genocide and cultural oppression. The standards put a very positive, but historically feeble, spin on this entire oppressive history with the statement: "Cultural conflicts frequently occur when there are differences between the beliefs and customs of the two interacting cultures. Such conflict is, of course, aggravated when one group is encroaching on another's homeland" (NJDOE, 1999, p. 211). There is no mention of the underlying racism, prejudice, and destructive greed that informed the European's belief in cultural, economic, religious, and racial superiority.

The curricular treatment of the experiences of both African Americans and Native Americans minimalizes their claims to an oppressive history and fractures any solidarity that could be developed between these groups. At the same time all of humanity becomes fragmented as people are unable to understand the oppression and struggle faced by some groups and to aid them in securing justice and equality. This is meant to project an image that the dominant group, while admitting to a few mistakes here and there, has on the whole been a group that has positively impacted the creation of American democracy and culture.

Dissimulation: Accepting Ideology that Obscures Domination

Another mode of operation for ideology that produces consent for domination is dissimulation. Dissimulation is the process through which the relations of domination are obscured. When domination is difficult to recognize and legitimated, the obscured ideology is accepted precisely because it is not evident. People accept a form of thinking that hides or diverts their attention from oppression and dominant ideology. Their consent is given to domination as they accept the visible ideology and hidden ideology. Ironically people are often not even aware of their own oppression because they have been so blinded by the ideology that is passed off as common sense.

The *New Jersey Curriculum Framework* obscures relations of domination by focusing on issues of domination within *other* countries. One standard indicator asks students to "identify events when people have engaged in cruel and inhumane behavior" (NJDOE, 1999, p. 172). The suggested activity that accompanies this standard discusses the friendship between a gentile girl and Jewish girl, on the eve of the Nazi invasion of France that ends in a fight. The next day the Jewish girl is forced into the labor camps and the two former friends never have the opportunity to resolve their conflict. While children come to recognize the power of words and the capacity they have to hurt others, they are not given a more accurate or real understanding of inhumane behavior that surrounded the Holocaust. Furthermore, by focusing solely on the Holocaust, our own struggle against inhumanity is obscured, and the many historical instances such as slavery, the genocide of Native Americans, as well as the inhumane conditions that still exist in the United States are ignored.

Another section asks students to examine apartheid in South Africa and define the hardships faced by native Africans under the oppressive conditions of apartheid. The standard offers the insight that "the struggle to achieve those rights everywhere is a struggle that we as Americans should always support" (NJDOE, 1999, p. 141). Certainly an examination of apartheid will shed light on oppressive conditions within South Africa, but this language implies that America is free of oppression or of conflicts related to human rights. The notion that we should support others' efforts to end oppression implies that either we have no related problems or that our problems are not worthy of focus or attention. Either way the message is clear: a study of the violation of human rights and the oppression of people is one that should be carried out when examining other countries or other historical eras, but not our own.

This attempt to shift focus away from our own historical and contemporary practices of oppression works to obscure domination and oppression within the United States. If students accept this, they will be unable to recognize the oppression that exists within our own country. It should be stressed that *all* people are oppressed by logic that distorts the relations of power and domination within our own country because it does not allow those who are oppressed to understand the nature of their own oppression or for others to recognize the full implications of their own oppressive acts.

Disempowered: Transmitting the Skills for Consent

I have seen firsthand the impact of oppressive practices on the lived experiences of students, where they internalize the dominant messages to such a degree that they are seldom able to recognize their own oppression and to distinguish the ways in which they have accepted a negative conception of self. One of my former students, a boy from a working-class family, decided to join the military because he felt that this would improve the way that society viewed him. He told me, "Davies, people see me as a scumbag and that's all they'll ever see me as. But the military will give me honor and pride and people will see me as a Man." While he was unaware of why he was oppressed or the factors that contributed to his oppression, he was acutely aware that his knowledge and experiences were not deemed as valuable or worthy as others' experiences.

Acceptance of "common knowledge" or "common experiences" as illustrated in the standards stratifies learning and experiences, like those of this boy, into low-status experiences and others into high-status experiences. Students who possess the knowledge that is deemed low status are degraded and undervalued and are prepared for failure in a system that does not reflect them or their experiences. The standards not only fail to empower students with the skills and vision necessary to challenge the very notion of high status versus low status, hierarchical systems, or recognize the ways in which they willingly accept their own oppression, but they actually prepare students for failure by blaming their inability to succeed on them. As McLaren (1989) notes, a student's "failure" in school "cannot be interpreted as resulting simply from individual deficiencies; it must be understood as part of a play of differences between radically disparate *cultural fields*" (p. 214). But these radically disparate cultural fields are never taken into account, as it is far easier to blame the victim than condemn the entire system.

The standards need to provide students with the skills necessary to become empowered citizens who can develop a vision of a more democratic society and change the practices that prohibit the realization of such a vision. One such skill is that of critical praxis, or the ability to examine forms of oppression, unequal relations of power, and unjust and inhumane practices and then to *act* on the knowledge gained from this critical examination. But the notion of critical praxis is not present within any of the standards. The language of the standards suggests, through posing questions, an inquiry will be undertaken by teacher and students in order to explore the nature of democracy and citizenship and to create answers. However, this inquiry is controlled by the authors of the standards and is answered by them, and does not allow for personal exploration or critical inquiry into the daily experiences of lived democracy and the interpretation of these experiences by students.

CURRICULUM FOR [DIS]EMPOWERMENT | DAVIES | 65

Exploring difference and the creation of multiple identities and lived experience is crucial to the creation of empowered students. As Giroux (1992) notes, "Difference can be incorporated into a critical pedagogy as part of an attempt to understand how student identities and subjectivities are constructed in multiple and contradictory ways" (p. 75). Examining differences in this form of knowledge allows a student to situate their own experiences in a historical, political, and social context that has been informed by competing notions of knowledge and power and allows them to recognize and identify the forms of power that have dominated and controlled their experience.

While the process of examining difference is empowering to students, it does not guarantee the creation of empowered students; creating dialogue between the Other about difference, culture, and class is a powerful mediator to students in a micro sense, yet it fails to fully remove or alleviate the impact of hegemony on the formation of the concept of self. Wendt (2001) is critical of those within the critical pedagogy tradition because they seem to favor a critical body of knowledge over all others. He states, "They do not take seriously the idea of alternative, creative knowledge, nor do they attempt to expand the theory of power beyond what critical modernism has decided it to be" (Wendt, 2001, p. 148). He also feels:

> Post modern pedagogy must recognize the productive, micropolitical, and less-than-rational dimensions of power relations at the same time it follows the post modern imperative to problematize rational thought and master narratives. (Wendt, 2001, p. 148)

The type of critical pedagogy presented by Giroux seems to represent a master narrative of the dual opposites of oppressed and oppressors.

If students are to be empowered and given the skills to analyze dominant relations of power and to change these, they must first come to recognize the negative impact that power and oppression has had on their own life, they must undo the multiple layers of internalized hegemony that even in an empowered environment will continue to dominate their soul. Kohli (1993) recognizes the transformative possibilities in this practice because the "aim is 'to *begin* the healing of wounds sustained in an oppressive society,' [it] focuses on the affective moments in ideology and hegemony but always within the context of specific historical, structural realities" (p. 130).

Hope and Possibilities: Disrupting the Cycle

The standards attempt to impose a particular ideology upon students, but even if the standards are not applied consistently, or even if they are not applied at all, the best we can expect is a continuation of the conditions that have deteriorated the existence of marginalized people, because, after all, the status quo will continue to allow these conditions to fester and advance. Nothing short of a radical reexamination of the ideological concepts that are accepted as a fundamental part of this society will allow us to transform this society into the type of democratic society that would place justice and equality ahead of competition and capital, people ahead of profit, and democracy ahead of capitalism.

Despite the oppressive ideology within the standards (and for that matter any dominant oppressive practices), room exists for counterhegemony or the creation and implementation of alternative ideologies that run counter to the dominant practice; counterhegemonic pedagogical practices present an alternative to a hegemony-filled education, an alternative with transformative potential to undermine domination and oppression.

In doing this, educators must begin to explore the cracks within the dominant and oppressive system and work to exploit these existing cracks. The standards represent the type of document that, while it is a document of the state, has cracks that allow for counterhegemony, which can potentially address hegemonic practices and allow students the opportunity to examine their own internalized hegemony. Much of the language within the learning activities and the curriculum that accompany the *New Jersey Social Studies Curriculum Framework* reflect domination, but the standards themselves, or the statements made about what students should know, provide opportunities for empowering students with the skills necessary to critically examine and ultimately change oppressive forms of power. Consider Standard 6.3, Indicator 8. It states students should "understand issues, standards, and conflicts related to universal human rights" (NJDOE, 1999, p. 141) or Standard 6.4, Indicator 11, which asks students to "analyze historical and contemporary circumstances in which institutions function either to maintain continuity or to promote change" (NJDOE, 1999, p. 187). Both standards allow for the opportunity to critically examine the sources of domination that have allowed for the violation of human rights and the institutions that exist in large part to perpetuate this domination. Most importantly, this examination does not have to travel beyond our own borders in order to find many examples upon which to base the study. This provides teachers and students the opportunity to examine contemporary problems that limit the ability to imagine, create, and realize more just, humane, and democratic practices and values.

Still other standards provide the opportunity to examine the ways in which dominant knowledge and power is transmitted and maintained. Standard 6.5, Indicator 16, allows for students (and teachers) to "analyze how beliefs and principles are transmitted in a culture" (NJDOE, 1999, p. 233). The curricular activity, which is presented as a method to teach the standards, focuses on the education of young patriots and the process that socializes young citizens to the values of patriotic democracy; it is not required that teachers teach the learning activities, but that they teach to the standards themselves. If teachers teach to the standards by taking the opportunity to explore the particular standards that allow for the examination of domination and our historical legacy and policies of oppression, students will be empowered to identify, critically examine, and change dominant forms of power and recognize the manifestations of power in its many oppressive forms.

However, while the opportunities for counterhegemonic action exist within the standards, there are several roadblocks that limit the potential to exploit these holes and cracks. These limitations include (1) teachers who do not choose to exploit the holes; (2) students who resist efforts to expose how they are oppressed or even how they contribute to the oppression of others; and (3) teacher resistance to change administrative directives that often undermine teachers. These limitations within the schools seem to hinge upon teachers' willingness to confront oppressive forms of power and engage in an education that allows students to explore and question issues, expose domination, examine power, and ultimately develop skills that at the very least provide students with the knowledge and ability to attempt to change and challenge the hegemonic forms of their own oppression. In this way the knowledge that is transmitted to students is empowering and not oppressive; what a student decides to do with this knowledge is up to her or him.

It is imperative that educators with a real commitment to creating the best educational practices for all children dedicate themselves to pedagogical practices that seek to emancipate students from oppressive practices, and empower students with skills to recognize and work to change social injustices, assess the impact of domination and power within their lives, create open dialogue about the lived experiences under an oppressive system of domination, and work to reveal, uncover, and undo the multiple layers of negative self-concept and the consent that allows oppression to continue. In short, if an educational strategy is to be empowering it must liberate students from both the outer and inner forms of oppression and domination, the marginalized self needs to be reclaimed from within the dominated lives of students, and the notion of commonness that comes at the expense of a marginalized other must be reconstituted and exposed as an ideological practice that oppresses all people and results in their domination.

References

Brown, D. (2003) *Bury my heart at wounded knee: An Indian history of the American West*. New York, NY: Henry Holt and Company, Inc.

Deloria, V., Jr. (2003). *Custer died for your sins*. Norman, OK: University of Oklahoma Press.

Giroux, H. (1992). *Border crossings: Cultural workers and the politics of education*. London and New York: Routledge.

Kohli, W. (1993). Raymond Williams, affective ideology, and counter-hegemonic practices. In D. Dworkin and L. Roman (Eds.), *Views beyond the border*, 115–132. New York, NY: Routledge.

McLaren, P. (1989). *Life in schools*. New York: Longham.

Neihart, J. G. (2000). *Black Elk speaks*. Lincoln, NE: University of Nebraska Press.

Nelson, J., and Pang, V. O. (2001) Racism, prejudice in the social studies curriculum. In E. W. Ross (Ed.), *The social studies curriculum*, 143–162. Albany, NY: SUNY Press.

New Jersey Department of Education (NJDOE). (1996). *New Jersey core curriculum content standards* [Electronic version]. Trenton, NJ: New Jersey Department of Education. Retrieved January 24, 2003, from www.state.nj.us/njded/cccs/1996.htm

New Jersey Department of Education (NJDOE). (1999). *New Jersey social studies curriculum framework*. Trenton, NJ: New Jersey Department of Education.

Thompson, J. B. (1987). Language and ideology. *The Sociological Review*, 35(3), 516–536

Wendt, R. F. (2001). *The paradox of empowerment*. Westport, CT: Praeger Publishers.

Zinn, H. (1999). *A people's history of the United States*. New York, NY: Harper Collins Publishers.

4

Hidden in Plain Sight

The Problem of Ageism in Public Schools

GLORIA GRAVES HOLMES

When those who have the power to name and to socially construct reality choose not to see you or hear you, whether you are dark-skinned, old, disabled, female or speak in a different accent or dialect than theirs, when someone with the authority of a teacher, say, describes the world and you are not in it, there is a moment of psychic disequilibrium, as if you looked into a mirror and saw nothing.

ADRIENNE RICH

Introduction

It comes as no surprise to anyone who is even casually observant that America is an ageist society that loves the Young and hates the Old. This ageism is confounding in an American culture that has, as an essential element of its character, a reverence for the future. In America, future conjures up images of youthfulness, vitality, productivity; future is not synonymous with "old age." Although aging, by definition, is a future-oriented process, "old" people, those who are successfully moving through the process, are not valued. This is partly because they are seen as part of the past, not part of the future. And yet, demographics show us that "old" people are part of the present, and are increasingly linked to the future. As a society, whether we like it or not, or are prepared for it or not, the young, and the "old" must coexist. They must see each other as part of the wholeness of human experience rather than from oppositional positions at the extremes of the age spectrum. A challenge to ageism means revising the images, and the underlying attitudes that allow us to equate "old age" with impotence and obsolescence, and difference from the idealized and socially acceptable "norm."

Ageism is partially an outgrowth of what Audre Lorde calls a mythical norm. She argues, "In America, this norm is usually defined as white, thin, male, young, heterosexual, Christian and financially secure. It is with this mythical norm that the trappings of power [and privilege] reside within society" (Lorde, cited in Tatum, 1997, p. 22). Being able-bodied is also part of the mythical norm, and of course, any deviation from the "norm," mythical or otherwise, sows the seeds of discrimination and bias. In the case of older adults, the outcome is ageism (Woolf, n.d. c).

It can be argued that ageism itself may be part of the normative order of American society, and "[a]s such it is passed from generation to generation through the process of socialization much like other cultural phenomena—love of country and church, motherhood, the success ethic, and so forth" (Levin and Levin, 1980, p. 85). Therefore, it is not surprising that the young and the old see each other's experiences through lenses clouded by pernicious ageist attitudes and related stereotypes, embedded in literary themes and characters, textbooks, media images, public policy, and cultural mores (Barrow, 1996; Couper and Pratt, 1999; Kettering, n.d.; Markson and Pratt, 1996; Robinson, 1994; Tupper, 1995). Yet, aside from recognizing the term, ageism, defined by Robert Butler (1969) as "any attitude, action or institutional structure which subordinates a person or group because of age, or any assignment of roles in society purely on the basis of age" (p. 243), educators have done little to address or redress this form of bias that damages both the victim and the perpetrator in tangible and mutually reinforcing ways (Couper and Pratt, 1999; Moseman, n.d.). Although ageism can be interpreted as bias against any age group, for the purposes of this chapter, I am defining it as a form of discrimination against older adults that has unique implications especially for young perpetrators. I want to dispel the idea that the subjects of aging and ageism are relevant only to old people, and demonstrate that aging and ageism have implications for individuals of all ages and for society at large.

In the twenty-first century, although we have the potential to live longer healthier lives, ageism in children and young people can erode that potential. Children and young people must be taught that (1) they have the power to influence their own longevity; (2) how and how well they take care of their bodies as children and throughout their life span is directly related to their future health and longevity; (3) ageism can lead to self-destructive and/or asocial behaviors; and (4) developing positive attitudes about aging and the aging process are essential first steps in challenging ageism.

Yes, we have the potential to live longer, healthier lives, but teachers have the responsibility to teach these life-changing lessons to their students. Whether or not children learn these lessons has far-reaching implications because the young are central to our perception of aging. They define the issues, "determine the status and position of the old person in the social order" (Rosow, 1962, cited in Levin and Levin, 1980, p. 63), and have the power to shape society's response to aging. Their social conditioning and their assumptions about old people will determine how the young define the issue of aging. When assumptions are based on misinformation and prejudice, teachers have a responsibility to interrupt ageist thinking, and correct any misguided notions.

Despite the nation's increasing sensitivity to, and acceptance of human diversity, and despite the recognition by most schools that they must produce citizens who respect difference and oppose oppression, when difference means advanced years, there is often a benign acceptance of prejudice against older adults that may take the form of benevolent ageism. Traditionally, there has been a socially accepted marginalization of older adults and issues that focus on the aging process. But future demographics demand our attention because ours is an aging society. Since life expectancy continues to increase, resulting in what some are calling a "longevity revolution" (Couper and Pratt, 1999) in the coming years, those sixty-five and over will comprise over 20 percent of the U.S. population. Although policymakers on both the national and local levels have begun to address these realities, teachers and schools have not reckoned with the sociocultural, political, or educational implications of these projected changes. Yet there is a great deal that schools and teachers can and should do. This is especially true in an age where schools are expected to do more than talk about social justice. More and more, schools are expected to dissolve the walls that separate them from their surrounding communities and the social problems of community members, and engage students in real-life situations. The issues surrounding aging and ageism are not only relevant and important to schoolchildren in their formative years but these issues will also impact their lives and the choices they make as adults.

Teachers can address these issues by adopting a *life span* approach to teaching and learning, which integrates a discussion of aging issues into all subject matter, demystifies aging, gives students a balanced view of older adults and aging, and contextualizes the aging process as part of the natural life cycle. In addition to providing a sociocultural and historical context for ageism, this chapter presents a rationale for bringing the discussion of ageism, the aging process, and a life span approach to teaching and learning into classrooms at all grade levels, and presents creative ideas and practical activities for teachers to use.

Schools and the Problem of Ageism

One of the difficulties of persuading teachers to confront ageism is its complexity. Ageism has been internalized, neutralized, and trivialized through jokes ("You're forty? Some people have been known to live for weeks after that"), through language ("You can't teach an old dog new tricks"), and through music ("Where's that young Romeo?"); it has been tightly woven into the social fabric of American culture (Tupper, 1995). Society, and implicitly, educators themselves, have grown comfortable with these types of references and may consider them harmless or funny. We all laugh at the jokes, sing the songs, and close our eyes to the underlying problems ageist thinking conceals. But ageism is no joke, especially when research shows that it increases the damaging effects of other forms of discrimination and creates a double jeopardy for the victims (Pampel, 1998, p. 79). For example, it is not funny that ageism, sexism, and racism can intersect, giving older black women the highest poverty rate in the United States. Or that older women in general are twice as likely as men to live at or below the poverty level (Calasanti and Slevin, 2001, p. 23).

According to psychologist Beverly Daniel Tatum (1997), since we all have multiple identities because of various group memberships, we are all vulnerable to multiple forms of bias. Yet "when one is targeted by multiple isms—racism, sexism, classism, heterosexism, ableism, anti-Semitism, ageism—in whatever combination, the effect is intensified" (p. 3). Although Tatum suggests that the intensification of bias can come from a random combination of isms, I argue that ageism is more subversive, and can reinforce all other forms of bias because it is a common denominator. Whatever your race, ethnicity, religion, sexual orientation, or gender, you will age. "Old age does confer a loss of power, even for those advantaged by other social positions . . . age relations carry with them a unique form of oppression" (Calasanti and Slevin, 2001, p. 191). Importantly, age relations provide unique opportunities for teachers to help students see the inequities implicit in the privilege conferred by youth, the disadvantage associated with old age, and develop the skills and dispositions needed to be productive citizens in an aging society.

Since aging is a process that we all experience from the moment we are born, at some stage in our lives, we could be either a victim or perpetrator of age discrimination. Schools and teachers should be prepared to deal with the implications of this, but research suggests that they are not (Couper and Pratt, 1999). This is partly because ageism is so pervasive, and so embedded in our culture that it is a bias that is hidden in plain sight. Also, we

> tend to not see the importance of age relations when we are "not old"—even if we are disadvantaged in other ways. Often, it is when we begin to lose privilege, the importance of age relations—slowly or suddenly—becomes apparent. (Calasanti and Slevin, 2001, p. 191)

Therefore, in order to tackle it, teachers must first be encouraged to see ageism to understand how it can reinforce and solidify other forms of bias, and how they themselves can unknowingly perpetuate it.

In America, ageism is ubiquitous, but unlike racism or sexism, there are few social or political sanctions against it because other more politically correct social issues tend to subsume age discrimination. It, therefore, comes as no surprise that schools not only ignore, but also perpetuate this hidden bias in both formal and informal ways. For example, most teachers would be reluctant to make openly racist, sexist, or homophobic statements to their students, yet teachers are often purveyors of ageism. Many unknowingly or unwittingly transmit their own socially constructed biases to their students through random comments or behaviors that make aging an excuse for failure, ineffectiveness, or poor performance (i.e., "I didn't remember that. I must have Alzheimer's" or "I'm too old to learn/do that"). Such comments subtly reinforce negative ageist stereotypes that associate aging with diminished intellectual capacity, and older adults with disease, decline, and death. Implicitly, this makes thinking about aging and aging issues distasteful, and can instill gerontophobic attitudes in children by indirectly teaching them to fear aging and perhaps fear old people. One sad outcome might be that a child who has already internalized racist or homophobic attitudes may be less willing to appreciate the humanity of an old black woman or an old gay man.

Deeply held ageist assumptions can also influence curricular design, the selection of texts used in the classroom, and how information is presented (Markson and Pratt, 1996; Moseman, n.d.; Tupper, 1995). In America, curricular materials have been influenced by a "Peter Pan" syndrome—a refusal to think about growing old, and standard curricular materials avoid looking at human experience in terms of a normal life span that includes old age. In general, society has

> constructed growing old as a medical problem—a sickness that can be treated and cured. This "biomedicalization" of old age (Estes and Binney, 1991) leads to a focus on diseases associated with old age. Thus old age, equated with illness, is frequently seen as "pathological or abnormal," so that this condition, as well as those "afflicted" with it, are to be avoided. (Calasanti and Slevin, 2001, p. 16)

Therefore, when curricular materials do discuss aging, they tend to omit references to the healthy aspects of aging, and the cause-and-effect relationship between lifestyle choices and healthy aging.

Several studies of children's literature show that older adults are either absent from books entirely, or when they do appear, they are marginalized or restricted to stereotypic roles (Kettering, n.d.; Kupertz, n.d.; Reese, 1998; Robinson, 1994). Older women are often depicted as "little old ladies," harmless eccentric old maids, or as the ugly and disagreeable hag/crone/witch. Older men are often characterized by odd or asocial behavior. The "dirty old man" or sexual pervert is also a common media stereotype. Too often, older men and women are shown in a state of decline, living physically apart from others, like cast-offs, on the periphery of society in some form of isolation. Edward Ansello's (1977) groundbreaking study of 600 children's books showed, among other things, that younger characters were fully developed, multidimensional, and active, while older adult characters were flat, one-dimensional, and passive (Ansello, 1977, cited in Couper and Pratt, 1999, p. 9; Robinson, 1994). The ageist implications of these characterizations are clear. If a teacher chooses a story about an innocuous, seventy-year-old, wheelchair-bound grandfather, it encourages the biomedicalization of older adults, and sends a very different message from a book about a successful, vigorous, seventy-year-old astronaut who chooses to return to space travel. Both images are realistic, but studies show that students are not getting a balanced view of older adults and aging in their classrooms (Couper and Pratt, 1999; Woolf, n.d. a; Woolf, n.d. b). This influences their relationships with the people in their lives outside of the classroom. Moreover, it is a forecast of how they may see themselves in the future, as useless, dependent, isolated, and impotent.

Ageism in textbooks points out how effectively this bias has been institutionalized, and presents some special problems for teachers and students. Unlike children's storybooks, textbooks usually play a more critical role in curriculum development because of their high cost and long shelf life. This means that teachers may not have the option to replace these books, and may be forced to rely on biased materials for long periods of time. Markson and Pratt (1996) published a comprehensive study of how high school textbooks dealt with aging issues. They found that most textbooks either ignored aging issues altogether, or presented misleading or biased information. Many biology textbooks failed to even mention the aging process. For example, Couper and Pratt (1999) point out:

> Although aging is a universal experience of all living things and the aging process involves fundamental biological changes, such basic realities have escaped the attention of most authors, editors, and publishers of biology textbooks. . . . The only term with any relationship to aging found in a majority of textbooks was menopause, and even then, it was relegated to a short one-paragraph definition. (Couper and Pratt, 1999, p. 10)

There were parallel findings in history and sociology textbooks that virtually ignored the social and political implications of the "graying" of America, and institutional ageism.

One of the most troubling findings from the study is the absence of aging issues from health textbooks. It represents missed opportunities to teach students about the relationship between healthy lifestyle choices and longevity. The Centers for Disease Control conducted research to determine what factors had the greatest impact on longevity. They looked at environment, heredity, lifestyle, and medical care, and found that lifestyle is the greatest predictor of life expectancy. This means that students must be taught that "good health habits or lifestyle choices developed during youth and maintained through adulthood influence longevity and health status more than any single factor" (AARP and NATLA, 1997, p. 6)

The persistence of ageism is ironic in an age when schools, increasingly influenced by the civil rights initiatives of the 1960s, have begun to move beyond a rhetorical embrace of diversity to the actual creation of social justice pedagogies that explicitly challenge most forms of bias. Yet schools barely acknowledge the existence and significance of ageism or the part that they play in institutionalizing it (Robinson, 1994). If teachers fail to equate ageism with other forms of discrimination, it becomes part of a hidden curriculum that has implications for society as a whole as well as for its individual members. Un-addressed ageism can foster prejudicial behavior toward older adults because of group membership rather than actual behavior. It predisposes children "to discriminate . . . to avoid contact, victimize or otherwise do injury to old people based on their age status alone" (Levin, 1975, cited in Levin and Levin, 1980, p. 73). Further, it can teach children to marginalize, rather than revere, the older adults in their families and in their communities. This has important societal implications because recent trends show an increase in multigenerational families, or families in which grandparents are primary caregivers. These family structures create new roles for both children and older adults and increasingly bring young children into contact with older adults with whom they must coexist. Yet, since American children grow up in an ageist society, and are not systematically taught to respect, revere, and care for older adults, they are more likely to undervalue older adults, marginalize them, or treat them with contempt. However, bias damages both the victim and the perpetrator, and research shows that the most damaging aspect of ageist thinking may be what it does to those who have internalized it as children (Couper and Pratt, 1999; Couper et al., 1995; Newman et al., 1997).

Although it is not surprising that the average teacher ignores ageism, it is surprising that multiculturalists—those educators whose raison d'etre is to celebrate diversity, expose bias, and help redress discrimination—are themselves replicating the same social patterns that perpetuate ageism. These educators either marginalize or ignore ageism both in their texts and research, and contribute to the silence surrounding these issues in public schools.

Aging and U.S. Demographics

Gerontologists describe the present and future trends toward longer life expectancy as a "longevity revolution" (Couper and Pratt, 1999). They hypothesize that whether we are ready for it or not, increased longevity will have a tremendous impact on how we think about aging, and how we live in an aging society. This longevity revolution should also influence how and what teachers teach (Hodgkinson, 2002–2003). Globally, people are living longer, healthier lives; and the socioeconomic, political, educational, and cultural ramifications of this are significant (Allen and Wircenski, n.d.; Barrow, 1996; Couper and Pratt, 1999; Robinson, 1994). If current demographic trends continue, within three decades, approximately 20 percent of the U.S. population will consist of youth under eighteen, and 20 percent will consist of people over sixty-five. This means that the young and the old will comprise about 40 percent of the American population. These demographic shifts have already begun to create the conditions for socioeconomic and cultural conflict between the generations. In "Shades of Gray", Keller (2000) points out that those under eighteen and those over sixty-five may be competing for public resources in the future. This tension has already surfaced in discussions about funding for public schools. For example, Keller examines questions such as the following: Should property taxes continue to be the mainstay of schools especially when older adults have no children in them? Should tax money be spent on K-12 education, or on retraining older workers (Keller, 2000)? In his book *Gray Dawn*, Peter G. Peterson refers to population aging in metaphoric terms, and sees "icebergs" ahead. He says, "Lurking beneath the waves . . . are the wrenching social and economic costs that will accompany this demographic transformation—costs that threaten to bankrupt even the greatest powers, the United States included" (Peterson, 1999, cited in Keller, 2000, p. 30).

Aside from the monetary issues, ageism is a predictor of other sociopolitical "icebergs" ahead. As previously indicated, the young are central to our perception of aging because they define the issues, "determine the status and position of the old person in the social order" (Rosow, 1962, cited in Levin and Levin, 1980), and have the power to shape society's response to aging. In America, growing old has been defined as a problem. This biomedicalization of old age has led to a mischaracterization of aging that affects perceptions of older adults and policy decisions that can have a significant impact on their quality of life. Biomedicalization of old age "diverts attention from social arrangements that produce inequalities in old age, including differences in health and health care delivery. By making old age a medical problem, what should best be understood as a social issue is construed as a medical or personal problem that should be treated by medical intervention. Power relations based on class, race, ethnicity, gender and sexual orientation are left untouched (Hendriks, 1995)" (Calasanti and Slevin, 2001, p. 17). This suggests that the seeds of intergenerational conflict are deeply planted in the American experience.

Images of Older Adults

In *Ageism*, Palmore (1990) points out that ageism, like any other form of discrimination, may cause the objects of discrimination to internalize the negative images directed at them, and adopt the negative behaviors associated with those images. For example, a person may become disinterested in life, or disengage from active participation in social events and "act old" according to a predetermined social expectation even though these behaviors may contradict the individual's natural instincts (Palmore, 1990, cited in Robinson, 1994, p. 2). This shows that the victims of discrimination are often complicit in perpetuating it, and underscores the complexity involved in changing ageist attitudes. Adding to the complexity is the fact that the social manifestations of ageism vary widely. Ageist stereotypes can be positive or negative; they can be subtle or overt. Edith Stein (1994) illustrates some examples of negative ageism:

> Older persons forget someone's name and are charged with senility and patronized . . .
> Older persons are called "dirty" because they show sexual feelings . . .
> Older persons are called "cranky" when they are expressing a legitimate distaste with life as so many young do . . .
>
> (Stein, n.d., cited in Robinson, 1994, p. 3)

Positive stereotypes may be more difficult to change because people are less likely to challenge them. In recent years, a new positive stereotype of old age has developed. It posits a cluster of positive character traits and portrays old age as healthy, wealthy, and wise. Couper and Pratt (1999) describe variations of these superhuman models of longevity that

> run parallel to images of old age as sick, senile and poor. "Positive" images of the sweet old lady, wise old man, and golden-ager are as stereotypical as "negative" images of impoverished, senile, elderly invalids. Euphemistic glorification of old age as the golden years, and inflammatory portrayals of greedy geezers, add feelings of envy and contempt to other feelings of sympathy and pity . . . both stereotypical images overlook the diversity among older adults. (p. 7)

Couper and Pratt (1999) also point out that despite the increased focus on diversity and the development of culturally competent pedagogy in the last few decades, teachers continue to ignore aging as a diversity issue that has relevance for classroom instruction. This trend ignores the fact that "diversity is a fundamental characteristic of aging. . . . The older we become, the more different we are, as we create our own unique combinations of backgrounds, interests and abilities" (Couper and Pratt, 1999, pp. 77–78). Yet, older adults continue to be lumped together as one homogeneous group, and curricular changes tend to focus on racial, religious, and ethnic diversity, rather than the diversity that comes with aging.

The work of Couper and Pratt has focused on developing a rationale for teaching about aging by examining a variety of lessons and activities for classroom use. In their research study, Children's Images of Aging, Couper et al. (1995) studied hundreds of children aged six through eleven to determine their attitudes toward older adults. The children were simply asked to draw a picture of an "old" person and a "young" person.

They found that even young children displayed the same ageist biases commonly expressed by adults. They equated "old" with shrunken, poor, dependent, deformed, disabled, and approaching death. The study concluded that the way children view old age could affect the way they view older adults and themselves as they age (Couper et al., 1995). Their research supports the development of an approach to K-12 Aging Education that is centered on a Life Span Approach to Teaching and Learning.

A Life Span Approach to Teaching and Learning and Multicultural Education

A life span approach to teaching and learning is another dimension of multicultural education. Its goals and objectives are consistent with the overall goals of multicultural education as well as with the major educational objectives common to virtually all curricula. For example, an effective life span approach to teaching and learning would aim to reduce bias; develop critical thinking skills; affirm difference/different points of view; create social equity; and focus on academic success.

Like most forms of multicultural education, a life span approach to teaching and learning addresses omissions, stereotypes, and misleading information that can lead to biased thinking and behavior. This means encouraging students to critically evaluate the media's role in perpetuating gerontophobic attitudes. A life span approach to teaching and learning is designed to counter ageism by helping students develop realistic and balanced attitudes about aging, and create healthy attitudes about themselves and the older adults in their families and communities.

A life span approach to teaching and learning teaches children that aging is not a problem, but a natural part of the life process that should not be feared. Developmentally, young people are anchored in the present, and do not connect present lifestyle choices with future outcomes. Teachers can change this misconception by helping students to connect their youthful decisions to later life, and gain the knowledge and skills they need to live and work successfully in an aging society (AARP and NATLA, 1997; Couper and Pratt, 1999; Pratt, n.d.).

The current institutionally sanctioned silence in schools about ageism and aging is similar to that which had surrounded other sensitive issues such as race/racism and sexual orientation/homophobia. However, unlike other diversity issues, aging cannot be placed at arm's length because it cannot be rationalized away. It does not simply apply to other people. It applies to all of us. That alone makes it a relevant subject for the classroom. However, there are a number of other important reasons to bring education about aging into the classroom. Aging education, or a life span approach to teaching and learning, is designed to:

Encourage *healthy lifestyle choices* in children from an early age,
Give students a *balanced view of aging,*
Prepare students for *future demographics,*
Develop *positive attitudes* in children about older adults and themselves,
Improve relationships in *multigenerational families,*
Improve *understanding of cultural diversity,*
Give children knowledge and skills needed to live/work in an aging society
(AARP and NATLA, 1997; Couper and Pratt, 1999).

A life span approach to teaching and learning not only recognizes that ageism in children can turn inward and become a catalyst for self-loathing in adulthood but it also attempts to pre-empt these damaging attitudes through both discipline-specific and interdisciplinary activities and lessons. This approach to teaching and learning is not meant to be an add-on, nor is it meant to be peripheral to core curricula. Yet it does not require radical curricula change. Teachers across disciplines not only can, but should, integrate a life span approach to teaching and learning into present curricula because according to NATLA (1997):

Instructional materials that ignore aging topics or associate aging only with decline and death should be unacceptable in today's classroom. They are as unacceptable as the basal readers that portrayed girls and boys only in stereotypical ways and excluded diverse cultural images and content. Real life does not end at age 21, nor should it in our schools' curricula and instructional materials. (p. 13)

Although a life span approach to education does not require additional topics, it does require a reframing of topics in a way that stimulates critical thinking and allows them to be discussed as they relate to situations throughout their lives. Curricula change may involve substituting rather than adding texts. For example, age-stereotypic literature can be substituted for non-ageist literature; math problems or science projects can be centered on age-demographics; English teachers can introduce intergenerational books into the classroom, or discuss the presence or absence of older adults in texts that they presently use. They can also include aging and related topics as writing themes. Social studies teachers can introduce themes like those found in the Connecticut State Department of Education publication *Schools in an Aging Society* (1992c). As with all effective education, the fundamental goal is to promote skill development in reading, writing, listening, speaking, analyzing, problem solving, math, and computer literacy, while connecting students to the social, physical, and economic implications of aging.

Teaching about Aging: Steps to Take

As with any type of multicultural education, a life span approach to teaching and learning must begin with self-evaluation and reflection by teachers. Teachers must search for ageist biases within themselves before they can effectively integrate aging education into their subject matter. They must first understand, accept, and become comfortable with their own aging. The following process should be accompanied by appropriate staff development:

> Self-reflection,
> Integrate lifespan approach into existing curricula,
> Provide materials that offer balanced insights about aging,
> Focus on healthy living, healthy aging and the relationship between them,
> Develop lessons that encourage critical thinking about the media's role in promoting ageism and poor lifestyle choices,
> Incorporate ageism into multicultural/antibias initiatives
> Develop partnerships with colleges/universities; share resources.
>
> (Couper and Pratt, 1999)

Sample Activities

These activities are excerpted from *Teaching About Aging: Enriching Lives Across the Lifespan*:

Elementary Level

Language Arts and Social Studies

> Have students list activities they can or cannot do now; examine the list for activities they can or cannot do when they grow older. Discuss growing older as a process of growth, development and change.

Math

> Develop a timeline showing the ages of students and their siblings, parents or guardians, grandparents, and great-grandparents.

Secondary Level

The Arts

> Provide students with lists of long-lived artists, poets, and musicians, photographers, architects, dancers, or actors. Have students note the age at which important accomplishments were made. Include historical figures along with contemporary celebrities.

Language Arts

> Compare older characters in popular fairy tales and nursery rhymes with contemporary cartoons and television programs.

Mathematics, Economics

> Use age-related data, such as age demographics, changing life span, Social Security finances, to devise problems by which students simultaneously practice math skills and learn about aging.

Social Studies

> Introduce and explore the topics of ageism (age prejudice) and gerontophobia (fear of aging) by gathering and analyzing advertisements, cartoons, comic strips, birthday cards, book illustrations, and common sayings.

Conclusion

> *We should all be concerned about the future because we have to spend the rest of our lives there.*
> CHARLES KETTERING (N.D.)

Children "learn" whether schools teach them or not. We tend to think of schools only as places that "teach" students. Yet, very often schools are in the business of "unteaching" students, of helping them "unlearn" values and reshaping their thinking; replacing misinformation or misguided notions with balanced perceptions and fact-based conclusions. Children are learning, every waking moment of every day, whether the "lessons" are formal or informal, acknowledged or unacknowledged. And the "teachers" are not just those who are paid to do the job in structured classroom settings. The negative lessons about what it means to be "old" are coming from TV, books, music, parents, and even teachers. Perhaps the worst kind of education we could provide students, according to Couper and Pratt (1999),

> would be to teach them that their own future can be seen in the conditions of older people today . . . for better or worse, those who are now growing up and growing older will largely determine what it means to grow old in the years to come. (p. 103)

If schools do not systematically provide aging education that gives balanced views of the process, children will have little or no support to counter the misinformation that is swirling around them. Further, children will not acquire the attitudes and develop the skills that will enable them to live in a future that will be dominated by age/aging-related issues. If we do not teach students about aging, we are "teaching" students about aging. Although the lessons are subliminal, they may be the most affective.

References

Allen, J. M., and Wircenski, M. D. (n.d.). Training older learners: Issues for the new millennium. Retrieved February 9, 2002, from National Academy for Teaching and Learning About Aging University of North Texas Website: http://www.unt.edu/natla/age share.training older learners.htm

AARP American Association of Retired Persons and National Academy for Teaching and Learning About Aging and NATLA National Academy for Teahing and Learning About Aging. (1997). *Teaching about aging: Enriching lives across the life span*. Denton, TX: National Academy for Teaching and Learning About Aging.

Barrow, G. (1996). *Aging, the individual & society*. Saint Paul, MN: West Publishing Company.

Butler, R. N. (1969). Ageism: Another form of bigotry. *Gerontologist*, 9, 243–246.

Calasanti, T. M., and Slevin, K. F. (2001). *Gender, social inequalities, and aging*. New York: Altamira Press.

Couper, D., Donofrio, L., and Goyer. A. (1995) Children's images of aging. Programs Division of American Association of Retired Persons. Soutington, CT: National Academy for Teaching About Aging.

Couper, D., and Pratt, F. (1999). *Learning for longer life, a guide for developers of K-12 curriculum and instructional materials*. Denton, TX: National Academy for Teaching and Learning About Aging.

Couper, D. & Pratt, F. (1997). Teaching about Aging: Enriching Lives across the Life Span. Denton, TX: National Retired Teachers and National Academy for Teaching and Learning about Aging.

Hodgkinson, H. (2002–2003). Educational demographics: what teachers should know. *Multicultural Education*, 02/03, 2–5.

Keller, B. (2000, November 29). Shades of gray. *Education Week*, 29–35.

Kettering, C. F. (n.d.). Problems of ageism in literature. Retrieved December 16, 2002, from

National Academy for Teaching and Learning About Aging, University of North Texas Website: www.cps.unt.edu/natla/web/problems.htm

Kupertz, B. (n.d.). Overcoming ageism through children's literature. In *Texas Child Care*, published by the Texas Workforce Commission.

Levin, J., and Levin, W. (1980). *Ageism: Prejudice and discrimination against the elderly*. Belmont, CA: Wadsworth Publishing Company.

Markson, E. W., and Pratt, F. (1996). Sins of commission and omission: Aging-related content in high school textbooks. The status of aging content in high school textbooks. *Gerontology & Geriatrics Education,* 17 (1), 3–32.

Moseman, L. (n.d.). Aging education in the classroom. Retrieved February 9, 2002, from National Academy for Teaching and Learning About Aging, University of North Texas Website: unt.edu/natla/aged/.htm

National Institute on Aging (n.d). What's your aging IQ? Bethesda, MD: National Institute on Aging.

Newman, S., Faux, R., Larimer, B. (1997, June). Children's views on aging: Their attitudes and values. *The Gerontologist*, 412–417.

Pampel, F. C. (1998). *Aging, social inequality, and public policy.* Thousand Oaks, CA: Pine Forge Press.

Pratt, F. (n.d.). Why teach about aging. Retrieved February 9, 2002, from National Academy for Teaching and Learning About Aging, University of North Texas Website: http://www.unt.edu/natla/why.htm

Reese, D. (1998, June). Children's attitudes about older adults. Parent News Archives. Retrieved December 16, 2002, from http://npin.org/pnews/1998/pnew698f.html

Rich, Adrienne. Cited in Maher, F. A. and Tetreault, M. K. T. (2001). *The Feminist Classroom, Dynamics of Gender, Race, and Privilege.* Oxford, England: Rowman and Littfield, Publishers, Inc., p. 201.

Robinson, B. (1994) Ageism. Retrieved March 5, 2001, from University of California at Berkeley, School of Social Welfare website: http://socrates.berkeley.edu/~aging/ModuleAgeism.html

State of Connecticut Department of Education and Department of Aging. (1992a). *Schools in an aging society: Health/Home economics classroom activities for secondary schools.* Hartford, CT: Author.

State of Connecticut Department of Education and Department of Aging. (1992b). *Schools in an aging society: Language arts classroom activities for secondary schools.* Hartford, CT: Author.

State of Connecticut Department of Education and Department of Aging. (1992c). *Schools in an aging society: Social Studies classroom activities for secondary schools.* Hartford, CT: Author.

Tatum, B. D. (1997). *Why are all the black kids sitting together in the cafeteria?* New York: Basic Books.

Tupper, M. (1995). The representation of elderly persons in primetime television advertising, Master's thesis. School of Communications. University of Southern Florida. Retrieved December 16, 2002, from http://www.geocities.com/Athens/8237/

Woolf, L. M. (n.d. a). Effects of age and gender on perceptions of younger and older adults. Retrieved March 5, 2001, from Webster University Website: http://www.websteruniv.edu/~woolflm/ageismtheory.html

Woolf, L. M. (n.d. b). Empirical evidence. Retrieved March 5, 2001, from Webster University Website: http://www.websteruniv.edu/~woolflm/ageismempiricalevidence.html

Woolf, L. M. (n.d. c). The theoretical basis of ageism. Retrieved March 5, 2001, from Webster University Website: http://www.websteruniv.edu/~woolflm/ageismtheory.html

Teaching Story

Using Mediated Teaching and Learning to Support Algebra Students with Learning Disabilities

JUDI HIRSCH

Along with the rise in expectation of greater student achievement has come a search for effective interventions for those students whom we have failed to prepare for success. Typically, the majority of high school students in the United States fail to learn Algebra—only 6 percent of seventeen-year-olds can solve multistep problems involving simple Algebra (Dossey et al., 1988). The situation is worse for low-income students of color, immigrants, and those identified as having Learning Disabilities, many of whom do not even graduate from high school.

For the past few years, we have been using Mediated Teaching and Learning, a constructivist approach, to support students with special needs to succeed in learning Algebra. Mediated Teaching and Learning frees the teacher to walk around the room, to observe, and encourage the students as they work collaboratively to solve problems. As the students begin to believe that they can learn, they start to take responsibility for their education; attendance improves, and there is more engagement and less disruption.

This essay focuses on what two teachers accomplished during the course of one year while working with low-income, special needs high school students of color. We describe the pedagogy and the philosophy that is the basis of our approach. We share our struggles and our successes and what questions or challenges still remain. The math is consistent with the National Council of Teachers of Mathematics (NCTM) standards. Our approach dovetails with Bob Moses' (2001) program as described in his recent book, *Radical Equations: Math Literacy and Civil Rights*, in which he connects learning Algebra to becoming empowered as a citizen, in ways that are reminiscent of the content and process of the Civil Right Movement of the 1960s. Our pedagogy relies on the work of Lev Vygotsky (1986), Reuven Feuerstein (1979), and Paulo Freire (1978), for whom the heart of Mediated Teaching and Learning is the teacher's thoughtful and respectful interactions with young people. We focus on learning rather than teaching, and believe that if we can support students when and where they need help, they will succeed.

The theory of Mediated Teaching and Learning arose from the work of Lev Vygotsky, an early twentieth-century Russian psychologist and contemporary of Jean Piaget. Vygotsky recognized that children learn best in a social context when assisted by a caring adult, or mediator, who engages with them in their zone of proximal development (ZPD). This ZPD is the "distance between the actual developmental level as determined by independent problem solving, and the level of potential development as determined through problem solving under adult guidance or in collaboration with more capable peers" (Vygotsky, 1986, p. 86).

A constructivist approach to teaching and learning implies that the learner constructs knowledge rather than receives it via direct instruction (Noddings, 1973). This has important implications for pedagogy. Instead of lecturing in front of the classroom, teachers provide appropriate challenges for student engagement and offer support and resources necessary to encourage mathematical exploration. As with Mediated Teaching and Learning, the focus of constructivism is always on the student, and in order for us to ascertain what our students know, we need to focus on their learning process.

A big concern for special education teachers has always been how to teach our underprepared students so that they can really learn. Teachers have to balance our belief in the need for students to know more mathematics with the need to be thoughtful about respecting students' thinking and sense of self-worth. Our challenge is to learn how to teach young people both the content—of Algebra and other subjects—and, more importantly, the fact that they can learn Algebra and other subjects. It is not easy to do this with students who, because they have "failed" for so many years, truly believe they cannot learn. They are so afraid of humiliation that they had often rather be considered troublemakers than take the risks necessary to learn that might result in someone calling them "stupid."

High school students labeled as learning disabled frequently lack not only the basic competencies in mathematics expected of entering college students (Intersegmental Committee), but also the problem-solving skills that are used in daily living. Moreover, they also lack persistence; they often cannot find patterns or make conjectures; and they are unable and/or unwilling to verify that that their solutions to problems are reasonable. We needed to figure out both how to teach underprepared students to take risks and trust their own thinking and also how to organize lessons so that the students are supported while learning to take increasing responsibility for their own education.

What we noticed was that nearly all of our students believed themselves to be unable to learn most high school academic subjects. Feuerstein et al. (1979) have shown how the limited performance of low-functioning individuals results directly from their perception of themselves as passive recipients of information rather than from some immutable genetic or cultural characteristic. Thus, it became imperative that we, their teachers, act on a different assumption, one that sees them as bright and capable. Fortunately, there is evidence that teaching African American and Mexican American students, identified as learning disabled, high-level cognitive skills, rather than giving them drill-and-kill worksheets, can lead to an improvement in academic achievement and adjustment as well as an increase in measures of achievement such as standardized test scores (Hirsch, 1987). This can be accomplished by providing opportunities for cooperation and dialogue rather than competition and isolation.

The Bird
If I had cut its wings
it would be mine;
it wouldn't have escaped.
But then, it wouldn't be
a bird anymore;
and what I wanted
was a bird.

This Basque poem expresses our dilemma: How can we help our students learn without destroying them in the process? How can we set up sustainable communities of learning? How can we as teachers learn to ask more than we tell, and listen more than we talk? One source of inspiration comes from Paolo Freire's (1978) little known book *Pedagogy in Process: The Letters to Guinea-Bissau*. Based on his remarkable success in helping to overcome illiteracy in many parts of Central and South America, Freire was invited to come to a newly liberated African country and collaborate on literacy education for adults. He responds by saying that "If there is anything that we learned in Brazil that we were able to repeat in Chile it was not to separate the act of teaching from the act of learning" (p. 9). And that it is "only through such praxis—in which those who help and those who are being helped help each other simultaneously" (p. 8).

We were aware of the political nature of schools and classrooms, and the tremendous power teachers wield over their students; but we figured out how to use this to our advantage. By consistently and continually verbalizing and demonstrating our belief in the innate intelligence of our students and the knowledge that they could learn Algebra, we slowly began to erode years of self-doubt. We knew that learning the mechanics of mathematics was really a lesson in empowerment that had ramifications far beyond the classroom walls. If one could learn Algebra, then one could learn almost anything.

I am a veteran teacher, having spent more than thirty years working with children in special education who are rarely taught much of anything, least of all that they are brilliant and capable of passing Algebra. After spending fifteen successful years as the Resource Specialist at a small, alternative K-12 public school, I was asked to teach two classes of Algebra at our district's most poverty-ridden, lowest-performing high school to a mixed-age group of high school special education students who could not be mainstreamed due to very low academic skills. Despite truancy and dropout/push-out rates of well over 50 percent, the hope was that by continuing to act on the assumption that all students are brilliant, I would somehow be able to instill in them the same kind of confidence that I had helped to create among my former special education students. The woman who job-shared with me the previous year continued in that role. I worked four days, she worked one.

One way to improve the learning environment is to carefully choose the textbook, and not use a prepackaged curriculum that assumes that "one size fits all" (Ohanian, 1999). When underprepared students are faced with a typical high school Algebra textbook, with pages upon pages of indecipherable and often meaningless formulas and equations, instead of stimulating the learner's curiosity, it reinforces a passive, receptive attitude, which contradicts the creative act of knowing (Freire, 1978, p. 11). Students give up, misbehave, and drop out.

We decided that our students would learn not only Algebraic concepts but also how to collaborate, how to organize a binder, how to write a summary of a problem, and how to keep orderly notes. We were using Algebra to teach more generalizable skills—that they could store and later retrieve information—an important competency that is often not taught in our schools today (Hirsch, 2001).

We knew these attitudes would be essential to their success because we planned to use *College Preparatory Math* (CPM), a program designed to foster mathematical competence and understanding by developing individual problem-solving skills via a group process, while encouraging students to take increasing responsibility for their achievement in mastering the material. CPM was written to ensure success, and it requires a change in teaching methods. Units are organized thematically around problems, and concepts are introduced using easy numbers and revisited in a spiraling fashion, so the students have ongoing opportunities to use what they know and add to their knowledge base at the same time, all the while becoming more confident.

The first thing we did was to replace individual desks with tables and chairs. One of our sneaky aims was to get the children to like each other. Then I went to a recycling center. Every student was given a sturdy three-ring binder with five dividers and told what to write on each: textbook, class notes, and tool kit (CPM's idea of where to keep their tools of the trade—things like rules, formulas, and definitions—that could be carried to a test like a plumber or carpenter would carry theirs); class work and homework; tests and quizzes; and graph and lined paper.

When students arrived, they were asked to write a letter of introduction, telling us what they liked about school, what was hard, how they learned best, and something about their math history. When they were called up to get their Algebra books, I made them sign a paper that said, "I understand that I am getting a brand new CPM Algebra book. I promise to take good care of it and return it at the end of the year (or pay for it) in order to get a grade." Everyone signed it and at the end of the year only one book was lost. CPM books cover one semester each, are soft-covered, and are designed to be kept in a binder.

The students "graded" themselves each week and calculated their averages. We had simple, four-function calculators available for their use. We made up a rubric, which had the words "College Preparatory Algebra" in very big bold letters at the top of the page. The students loved it; we told them this did not mean that they *had* to go to college, but that it would prepare them if they chose to. The rubric gave 4 points for trying everything, 3 for trying most things, 2 for trying some things, 1 for trying a few things, and 0 for trying nothing; these numbers corresponded to the traditional A-F grades, but we did not focus on that. The "things one can try" included attendance, perseverance, cooperation, respect, class work, homework, preparedness, among others.

At the end of six weeks, grades were due, and because of our conviction that good organizational skills were a necessity for success in this class (Hirsch, 2001), we gave each student a folder and asked them to put their notebook pages in chronological order, make up a table of contents, and write a summary of what they learned so far, including what they struggled with. Then, on at least four pages of their work, we asked that they write: "This was easy because" or "This was hard because." Though they moaned and groaned, they did a beautiful job. Spelling was hard for them, of course, and we always helped with that. They kept asking, "Do we *have* to?" and we kept saying, "Yes, you do."

We worked with low-income students of color who were not used to seeing themselves as academically successful. Our students could not do the homework often because they had no homes, but also because they had other things to do. Many were caring for elderly relatives, living with extended family, or sleeping in shelters. Some had jobs. There was just no way we or they could follow the suggested pace of the CPM program. Unlike middle-class CPM learners our students had problems with attendance and attitude—coming to class prepared to work with at least a pencil and a willingness to struggle. Additionally, there were students who could not read. Finally, there were many students who did not have the prerequisite math knowledge required for success in this program. What could one do?

We started off very slowly. I insisted that they put their name, date, and problem number at the top of each page of class work and then file it in the correct section of their binder when they were through. We worked *very* slowly with them, reinforcing each and every positive thing they did, naming and praising their struggles. Frederick Douglass looked down on us from a poster above the blackboard, saying, "Without struggle, there is no progress." As the students worked, we walked around the room helping them to get started and encouraging them to keep struggling. When they got stuck, we listened to their doubts and reminded them they are brilliant and capable by pointing to some work they had already done, some challenge they had overcome.

We made it a rule to support POSITIVE behavior and NEVER to call home and complain, because that always backfires. Telling a parent that their child is not behaving is the same as saying that the parent is not doing their job—not a good way to have a relationship. Also, with constant praise and a pre-inked stamp I could usually avoid reinforcing disruptive behavior and instead reinforce positive actions. We walked around with a clipboard and a list of students' names, and a few categories that we checked off every day, such as "came prepared with a notebook," "has textbook and pencil," "works cooperatively," "completes the assignment." They knew what we were doing and would call out "Look, I have a pencil," or "Check my homework," or "Dante and I are working together," or "We just finished a problem, come and stamp it." Interestingly, these high school students made fun of the stamps when we first introduced them, but quickly started asking for stamps when they saw that others were OK with it.

A *big* challenge for all of them was setting up *Guess and Check* tables, CPM's way of introducing a format for translating word problems into tables, which eventually leads students to write and solve equations using the familiar "x." The beauty of this approach is that the students are using a process that will not let them focus on finding the answer until it emerges from their guesses. It strengthens the students' number sense, which is critical for life outside of school, and makes memorization of meaningless rules—such as a negative times a negative is a positive (or is it a negative *and* a negative)—unnecessary. Even the most reluctant/terrified student was able to perform the final "guess" on his or her own after getting help with setting up the table and making the first few "guesses." It was so easy to reinforce their struggles because they really wanted to be able to solve problems that allowed them the luxury of using their minds to figure things out. We also asked students to write a lot about what they were learning regarding themselves as learners, and about working in a group. While their writing needs much improvement, they are becoming better at expressing themselves.

By the end of the semester, most of the students were coming to class regularly and were engaged with each other and with their assignments for the entire period. Unfortunately, due to a high truancy rate, moving forward with the whole class was hard, as was encouraging group work, since the groups differed each day. The most important thing that was happening is that *these students are learning that they can learn.* They are developing good *habits of mind.* Some do homework and have learned to work cooperatively. Some have let us call their homes to brag to parents, grandparents, and guardians about what great students they are. In all, we believe they are moving in a positive direction, and we think that many will actually get good grades in this class.

Much of what is happening is because of the strong belief that my teaching partner and I share regarding our mission: *we teach children that they can learn math and then we let them do it.* We also have had the help of a wonderful Instructional Assistant who quickly adapted to our way of doing things and was very supportive of the efforts made by our students. We all believe it is our job to get the students to engage in the struggle to learn that they are capable of mastering the material, and that any behavior to the contrary is just leftover stuff from many years of failure, criticism, and lack of confidence. We just persist and never give up on any of them, and it turned out to be a very good year for all of us. We all enjoyed coming to class and were rarely absent—a testimony to what is possible.

We are learning as much or more than the students are, and still have lots of questions:

1. What are the *big* ideas in Algebra? Can these ideas be taught at all levels of school and in a variety of classes or only in a high school "Algebra" class? Can these ideas be learned by students who are far behind their peers?
2. What math do students *really* need to know for *life?* Here we are thinking about REAL math, like problem solving and noticing patterns, rather than the kind of computation that can be done by a calculator.
3. How can we best ensure that our students learn the most important lesson—*that they can learn?*
4. Does it make sense to require Algebra for all students? If so, when should it be introduced? Who should teach it? What is a good student/teacher ratio? Is there an optimum teaching/learning situation? Developmental level? Knowledge base? Attitude? Organizational competence? What kind of support is needed to ensure success? How do we provide it?
5. What should be taught in an Algebra class? How long should that take? Should publishers, politicians, or teachers, who have a sense of their students' readiness to move ahead, make this decision?

6. How can we ensure that our students are learning a unified field of study, a coherent system, rather than the piecemeal approach, which seems to be so widespread? How can we improve the articulation of mathematical instruction so that it makes sense to students?

7. What is our overall goal? What is our priority? Do we want students to pass tests? To learn the beauty and excitement of struggle and engagement? To succeed in life? Should we ever make curricular needs a higher priority than the needs of our students?

8. How do we find the balance between the students' need to know and our need to teach? Who decides?

9. What's happening to our students now? Were they able to maintain a strong belief in themselves as being capable of learning? Was this belief strong enough to withstand the reality of racism, poverty, and hopelessness?

10. Can this kind of success be replicated?

References

College Preparatory Math Educational Program. 1233 Noonan Drive, Sacramento, CA 95822.

Dossey. J. A., Mullis, I. V. S., Lindquist, M. M., and Chambers, D. L. (1988). *The mathematics report card: Are we measuring up?* (National Assessment of Educational Progress Report). Princeton: Educational Testing Service.

Feuerstein, R., Rand, Y., Hoffman, M., and Miller, R. (1979). *The dynamic assessment of the retarded performer: The learning potential assessment device, theory, instruments and techniques.* Baltimore, MD: University Park Press.

Freire, P. (1978). *Pedagogy in process: The letters to Guinea-Bissau.* New York, NY: Seabury Press.

Hirsch, J. (1987). *A study of a program based on Feuerstein's theories intended to teach high-level cognitive skills to African-American and Mexican-American junior high school students identified as learning disabled.* (Available from UMI, 300 N. Zeeb Rd., Ann Arbor, MI 48106).

Hirsch, J. (2001). Mediated learning: dynamic assessment and mediated learning: Teach them all to fish. In J. L. Kincheloe and D. Weil (Eds.), *Standards and schooling in the United States. An encyclopedia,* 667–694. Santa Barbara, CA: ABC Clio.

Intersegmental Committee of the Academic Senates of the California Community Colleges, the California State University and the University of California. (1997, October). *Statement on competencies in mathematics expected of entering college students.* Long Beach, CA: Academic Senate SCU.

Moses, R. P., and Cobb, C. E., Jr. (2001). *Radical equations: Math literacy and civil rights.* Boston, MA: Beacon Press.

National Council for the Teaching of Mathematics. (2000) *Principles and standards for school mathematics.* Reston, VA: The Council.

Noddings, N. (1973). *Constructivism as a base for a theory of teaching.* Unpublished doctoral dissertation, Stanford University.

Ohanian, S. (1999). *One size fits few: The folly of educational standards*. Portsmouth, NH: Heinemann.

Vygotsky, L. S. (1986). *Thought and language*. In A. Kouzoulin (Ed.). Cambridge, MA: MIT Press.

Conversation

Unearthing Hidden Curriculums

MARK R. DAVIES, JUDI HIRSCH, & GLORIA GRAVES HOLMES

On Silences, Aging, and Social Justice

Gloria: In America, when we think about social justice, and the dynamic of the *oppressed* and the *oppressor*, many forms of individual bias or institutionally embedded social inequities come to mind. Foremost among these are racism, sexism, homophobia, and religious intolerance. Ageism is rarely equated with the most deleterious forms of discrimination; silence muffles the response to ageism, so it is usually left out of the debates about social justice even though aging, the process that provides the catalyst for ageism, is a noncontroversial, biological reality that links all human beings. Some of the same impulses that cause us to dismiss and discard older adults also cause us to ignore ageism as a social justice issue. We fear aging. We associate it with a profound sense of loss, because in our society, aging means disease, decline, and impending death. Society has developed a number of defense mechanisms for responding to these fears. For example, some attempt to neutralize their fears through humor, hence the endless, often tasteless, jokes about older adults. Others handle fear of aging by avoidance and denial while some mask their fear by showing contempt for older adults. All of this provides fertile ground for ageist thinking and ageist behavior in all levels and sectors of society—even schools.

Ageism poses some special challenges for social justice educators because of its difference from other "isms." First, because everyone grows older with time, one's age classification is not static. Throughout the life span, individuals experience different perspectives on aging and different responses to ageism depending on where they are in their individual life span. In other words, age is constantly changing where-as the manifestations of race/racism and gender/sexism, for example, remain constant throughout one's life span. Second, aging is a universal experience; therefore, everyone has the potential to experience ageism regardless of his or her race, gender, sexual orientation, or religious affiliation. Finally, when ageism is coupled with other biases, the damaging effect is intensified.

According to Sonia Nieto and others, our goal as educators is to design *education that is multicultural.* Ageism is a form of bias that should be part of the multicultural education initiatives to ensure social equity and support teaching for social justice. Students must be taught *how* they are connected to the communities that surround them, and *why* injustice to any segment of their community degrades everyone in the community. If we were doing this, social justice would be embedded in our teaching, and effective pedagogies that acknowledge diversity and challenge oppression would be pervasive rather than exceptions. Taking a stand against ageism is as much a responsibility of schools as taking a stand against any other form of bigotry, and is consistent with social justice pedagogies that promote social activism, democratic principles, and proactive citizenship. Moreover, unlike racism or sexism or homophobia, ageism is not limited by color or gender or sexual orientation or religious affiliation; it can be directed at any of us because we are all aging every day.

Mark: Silence is indeed oppressive. Silence is perpetuated by the hidden curriculum and through the inclusion of particular groups and the exclusion of others. Gloria's critique of the treatment of ageism illustrates how silence through exclusion works to distance, alienate, and oppress. Social justice educators must recognize that silence oppresses all people. If we fail to include the diverse voices that resonate within society, then we are effectively neutralizing those voices that have been distanced by the status quo. We tend to think about those who are distanced by race and class, but often fail to consider those who are distanced by age, gender, sexual preference, religion, ability, and other qualities. It is imperative that we unmask oppression within the curriculum, but it is equally important that we give voice to those who have long been silenced by the hidden curriculum. The challenge to all these ideas is working to move anti-oppressive ideas into the very real world of classroom practice, so that our ideas are working with students in meaningful ways.

Judi: Concerned teachers are looking for ways to ally themselves with their students, but they are being silenced, too. Rather than allow teachers to continue to use their professional judgment in deciding how to approach and support emerging readers and "at risk" youth, teachers are instead being forced to use scripted series such as "Open Court," which mandates pacing, testing, and where posters are to be placed in a classroom; it is also forbidden to have any trade or library books in the room other than those that are part of that series. Teachers are watched and written up if they fail to adhere to the rules. All teachers at the same grade level have to be at the same lesson at the same time every day. There is no room for flexibility or accommodation within the classroom of standardized accountability. But who needs caring, concerned teachers when all they are being asked to do is test preparation?

We are reminded of the words of James Baldwin in his 1970 letter to his sister Angela Davis: "If they take you in the morning they will be coming for us that night." The message is the same, only the players have changed; it's now students and teachers who fill the roles that Baldwin then attributed to blacks and whites. If they take the students today, then there won't be any need for teachers. In fact, distance learning via computers is fast replacing human beings in classrooms.

Privilege and Oppression within Policy

Mark: The "No Child Left Behind Act" is the latest educational policy in a long line of educational reform policies that focus on reforming students and teachers in order to reform the schools and, ultimately, society. By focusing on reforming students and teachers, it can be inferred that their "deficiencies" are the cause for much of the economic and social problems today. The deficiencies reform approach has a long history and dates back to the twenty-year-old document "A Nation at Risk," which asserted that America was at risk of completely losing its eroding economic power base unless the deficiencies of the students and the schools were addressed. This policy spawned the educational platforms of the last four presidential administrations, including the present Bush administration, and has left an indelible scar on the educational landscape.

Because the philosophy that undergirds present educational policies focuses solely on the deficiencies of individual students, teachers, and schools, and assumes that these deficiencies created many current societal problems, it ignores other more obvious culprits who have long perpetuated a system of injustice cloaked in the language of freedom, equality, and choice. In order to unearth how such policies and the subsequent curricular reform efforts are oppressive, a simple look at what deficiencies are addressed reveals a more poignant revelation as to who is believed to be deficient. The examples from the New Jersey Curriculum Framework, as cited in the earlier chapter, reveal the belief that students lack a collective, binding identity and the curricular models work to supplant individual identities and experiences with what is expressed as a common or normal American identity and experience.

Simply put, because students from ethnically and racially diverse backgrounds or from poverty lack the skills, experience, and knowledge associated with what is thought to be "the normal class," they themselves are seen as deficient. In essence the real deficiencies are in an oppressive system that blames its victims and that sees these victims as an anchor holding back progress. If democracy is to be realized, educational policies must begin to address the very real roadblocks associated with oppression. We cannot afford to silence a great number of voices any longer.

Gloria: The "deficiency" model that blames children and communities instead of schools and institutional racism is anchored to the tenacity of "white privilege," which remains deeply embedded in the American psyche. Until we address white privilege in schools and school systems, significant curricular change will be compromised. Addressing white privilege requires a paradigm shift; it means power sharing and a respect for multiple perspectives.

I agree that certain hegemonic practices need to be challenged because they are both *oppressive* and *antidemocratic*. Not only are they harmful to students, they corrupt the "democratic" system. And yet I can't help but feel that we continue to struggle with these issues because, to a large extent, there is a huge void between the *dream* of democracy and the *reality* of democracy. Those who have traditionally been silenced know this. Their voices have always been missing from the *chorus*, and yet the patriotic music of democracy plays on. Even now we continue to define what democracy means (i.e., Are we a melting pot or a salad bowl?).

Judi: When teaching low-income students of color, immigrants, and those identified as having learning disabilities, there are many challenges. The traditional demoralizing affects associated with institutional racism and class oppression have taken a backseat to new and more insidious threats related to the *No Child Left Behind* (*NCLB*) policy of our federal government that has been in place since January 2002. Teachers no longer have the academic freedom to decide on how to teach English, math, science, and history. In fact, many schools have cut out those subjects entirely in which students aren't being tested. In Oakland, California, for example, many students who failed to meet certain standards in reading are being forced to take three periods of remedial English a day and they are losing out on the opportunity to discuss issues that would make them more aware and concerned citizens, more connected to their peers, better prepared to find a job, and more likely to want to stay in school.

Here in California, which once led the nation in the field of public education from kindergarten through graduate school, we are now near the bottom of the fifty states in what we spend per pupil, and for school and public libraries. And the cuts go on. We must figure out how to save our system and it won't come if we're quiet. As a bumper sticker says, "Your silence won't save you." The answer, of course, is to organize around this crisis facing those of us who work and attend our public schools. We can do this by joining coalitions within local neighborhood and with other unions; informing people about the insidiousness of NCLB; and meeting with other educators across the historical divide between K-12 and the university. We can win this fight. There are more of us than there are of them, and once we get to know each other, there's every reason to believe that we'll be working together across lines that have divided us in the past. In the end we can be stronger than we were if we work together.

Mark: As Judi points out one way that we can resist these policies of oppression is to join together and organize all people who are concerned with creating real democracy. We have not fully realized the consequences of silenced voices on the chorus of democracy. We must do so before it is too late. But at the same time we need to educate students from privileged groups about the very real oppressive practices that are ongoing in our society, because many are blind to the negative societal impact of cultural reward and privilege gained through their dominant race, class, gender, and sexual identity. If these educational practices continue then we will never be capable of realizing, creating, and perpetuating a democratic society, because as long as any human life is degraded and devalued, the result will always be a hierarchical and fragmented society. The dominant curriculum of injustice can only be challenged when educators, students, and community members are willing to unearth and challenge oppressive practices within schools and society.

Making the Necessary Movement from Theory to Practice

Judi: I have been greatly influenced by the theoretical positions of Reuven Feuerstein and Paulo Friere. From Feuerstein, with whom I worked in Israel from 1970 to 1979, I learned about Vygotsky's notion of the ZPD, and of Mediated Learning. I also learned about Feuerstein's belief that we can never know how much a child could achieve if offered enough support and encouragement, so it's always best to act on the assumption that each student is brilliant. From Friere I learned that we can only start where the student is, not where we'd like them to be; I also learned humility, and the necessity of both practicing praxis (thinking about what I do and then revising my thinking based on my interactions with the students), and reciprocity (that teachers are learners and students are teachers).

Most of the struggles I faced "converting" theory into practice were with peers and administrators, people who thought they knew best about where students ought to be, and some internal oppression from the students themselves, who had come to believe that they weren't very smart. The biggest opposition to practices supported by these theories comes from the institutional belief that we must make the student fit the curriculum; because of this it has often been the teachers who were the most resistant to our ideas about curriculum. I think this comes from their need to find someone to blame, and since it's hard to fight the powers that be, such as textbook companies, administrators, or laws such as the *NCLB*, teachers often blame the students. It's the students' fault if they don't know the required material, and they can't go on until they do, so that means weeks, months, and sometimes years of making students remember things such as multiplication tables by heart, rather than spending the time trying to help them figure out how to solve problems. At the end, if we are able to do some introspection, we find that we've done them a great disservice, and ourselves, too, because we've gone over to the enemy and stopped being teachers. We've become test preparers, pimps for the *NCLB*.

The dilemma of figuring out how to help our students learn without destroying them in the process is unfortunately ongoing and unanswerable. I believe that my job and moral imperative is to be there for my students as a support and reminder that they are brilliant when they forget, but it is so hard to remember that they are more important than the content that we are trying to teach them. I think that as we mature in our profession, we tend to get a sense of each child's breaking point, and can learn that nothing that we want to teach them is more important than maintaining their sense of integrity and connection to their family and culture. If we don't set up an adversarial situation with parents, where children are forced to make an impossible choice between "us and them," parents can be our strongest allies in the process.

I was lucky in that I shared my job with a colleague who shared my pedagogical beliefs. We were always discussing both what we were doing and how the students were progressing. This allowed us to monitor our practice so that we didn't unconsciously slip into a dominating, oppressive pedagogy while using our liberatory techniques. I am sad to say that without ongoing support—which luckily I am allowed to provide to some teachers—many of my colleagues aren't able to sustain their nascent belief in the theories of Freire and Feuerstein, and often give up on the students, and on themselves as their teachers, because they lack the belief that the students are really capable.

Mark: It is hard moving theory to practice. It is also hard to assure that the practice is free of hidden oppression. Judi's point about the difficulties in teaching students without destroying them was quite real to me when I was a public school teacher. I was concerned about teaching my students all the ideas that the state demanded they know, yet at the same time I was cautious of the unintended messages within the knowledge. I too found practical wisdom in Freire's idea to teach students not only how to read the word, but how to read the world. With this in mind I began to use techniques that opened up the curriculum (and the world) to questions, critiques, and to create discussion that examined problems. However, this demanded that I provide opportunities for my students to develop their "decoding skills," so that they could decode or unearth oppressive ideas.

    I found that students were quite skilled at decoding and recognizing oppressive messages about gender within print ads and commercials. This became the starting point for discussions and questions as we began to examine glossy, glamorous ads as reflective of a problematic but culturally accepted exploitation of women. From here we were able to move into decoding other ads for racial and class messages. After sharpening their decoding skills, many students commented that they could not view advertising or television shows the same way again. We were able to then make the move from decoding visual images to decoding text as students began to use their decoding skills within the class (district-mandated) textbook. Students became quite adept at analyzing and questioning the text and were able to uncover much of the problems with the standards that I pointed out in the previous chapter. While these forms of decoding were easy I struggled with getting all students to decode societal practices and how these practices impacted their lived experiences; some were able to get it and others resisted. I fear that the reality of the oppression as well as the difficult work needed to challenge and change these practices were too much for some students. From my experiences as a teacher educator, I know that these very same fears are encountered by preservice teachers. But all educators and students must work to move beyond fear and engage in the difficult challenge of anti-oppressive education, so that we might realize the transformative possibilities of such an education.

Gloria: I agree with Judi that the greatest challenges come from educators who, because of entrenched belief systems, are resistant to change. Any efforts to combat hidden curricula that support oppressive practices must be aimed at bringing about fundamental changes in the belief systems of educators. This must begin with a thoughtful examination of their own beliefs, and classroom practices, if they are to be efficacious practitioners who challenge oppressive practices, and promote the goals of equal educational access for all of their students. However, Judi also points out that internal oppression can come from the students themselves, which is a manifestation of problems with student belief systems as well. In addition to belief systems, research shows that the deep structure of schools can also inhibit change in schools. But the concept of deep structure embraces more than schools; it refers to the larger society's widely accepted beliefs regarding what schools are for, how they should function, and what constitutes success. The pervasiveness and complexity of oppressive practices in schools suggests that school systems must be both willing and able to reinvent themselves. This means a commitment to training for faculty and administration. This training would allow school systems to begin conversations about oppressive practices in its many forms, and open the door to much needed systemic change.

Part III

Learning to Read Critically

From High School to College to Teacher Education

5

Color Me Purple

How Gender Troubles Reading

CAROL RICKER-WILSON

No Rose-Colored Lenses: Outlining "the Trouble"

In this chapter I examine how students at an urban Toronto secondary school read in ways that alternately secured and vexed their understanding of mainstream, heterosexist discourses about gender, sexuality, and sexual orientation. From a critical, feminist perspective, I attempt to make visible how gender, as a social category, made students vulnerable in a host of ways that directly affected their academic achievement.

The focus on gender and academic achievement has shifted in the last decade from the girl shortchanged by androcentric curriculum and instruction to the at-risk male reader and underachiever (Broude, 1999). Currently a wide spectrum of popular and academic texts give educators access to diverse, but often contradictory, advice about how they might modify instruction and curriculum to address the "boy" problem. Essentially, however, these texts rely on one of three theoretical approaches through which to describe the complex connections between gender and academic achievement, particularly as these relate to adolescent literacy problems.

Proponents of "brain-based" research maintain that purportedly "innate" neurobiological differences largely account for the different learning styles and needs of male and female learners, which should lead to modifications in instruction (Gurian et al., 2001). Tending to perceive "maleness" as a homogeneous category, they show minimal regard for what might account for academic differences *among* boys or girls. Limiting their analysis to "anatomy is destiny"—for which one at least might compensate—they cannot account for why working-class and visible minority students continue to be disproportionately identified as weak or reluctant readers, and tracked, to their detriment, into lower-level classrooms (Curtis et al., 1992; Darling-Hammond, 1995).

Advocates of a second approach emphasize providing more male-oriented content and/or instructional strategies to offset what they perceive to be the largely cultural differences that account for girls' and boys' disparate engagement with texts. This approach has considerable currency among adolescent educators because of its seeming immediacy in addressing the problem. Certainly, all students need to see themselves included in texts and require engaging text selections. However, simply acknowledging and serving gender or cultural differences can be a means of perpetuating rather than examining how difference is defined, defended, and regulated, and with what consequences. Moreover, an unproblematic call for more male-oriented textual content is curious given that, even in the most "progressive" mainstream textbooks, the roles of women—and people of color—in history, government, culture, science, and invention continue to be underrepresented. A singular call for more male-friendly fiction is no less perplexing. There is currently no dearth of readily accessible children's and young adult fiction featuring resonant male protagonists and subjects of interest to boys. And, at the secondary level, English course outlines continue to be distressingly narrow in their "feature" offerings that include, and are almost limited to, Shakespeare and a dozen twentieth-century white male authors predominantly featuring white male protagonists (Applebee, 1993). As to "boy-friendly" instructional strategies, a popular one is to accommodate males' purportedly "more active" learning style. While all children would benefit from less sedentary and Socratic instruction, and from more interactive learning strategies, as is, this suggested accommodation neatly reproduces the sexist notion that boys as a category are more "active" than girls. Indeed, it neatly reproduces the status quo by not inquiring into how we understand "active," and how teachers encourage or discourage specific types of classroom behavior and activity. Fundamentally, while certain male students might indeed be receptive to new or underutilized learning strategies, a *singular* or *predominant* reliance on them by teachers and school boards is unlikely to alleviate other issues of academic equity, such as women's (Tolusso, 2003) and visible minorities' continued underrepresentation in university-level science, technology, and computer science programs, and in high prestige positions and careers (AAUW, 2000).

The two aforementioned approaches rely on gender differences ("natural" or cultural) to *account for* academic performances with an emphasis on accommodating these differences. A third approach is concerned with making visible how social differences become constituted and with what effects. Its advocates (Alloway and Gilbert, 1997; Moss, 1998) perceive adolescent literacy *itself* as a gendered (as well as raced and classed), highly nuanced, and perpetually shifting performance. They suggest that social and, particularly, peer group interactions are significant in *constructing* "problem" students and that merely providing more "male-oriented" text selections or instructional strategies will do little to help either male or female students understand how gender operates as a form of social control to circumscribe academic and other behaviors and opportunities. By the terms of the third approach, one cannot understand how literacy is a problem without simultaneously considering how "masculinity" and "femininity" are problematic constructions. That is, as I will reveal, the very acts of reading and responding (particularly to fiction) in a school venue are highly fraught because of what they might suggest to one's peers about identity. Later I describe how certain students performed both gendered—and heterosexist—readings, and performed gendered literacy roles in manners that obfuscated learning. I then describe how using questioning strategies form current literary theory offers a means of focusing on these troubling phenomena.

Color Me Red: Passionate Readings

Gender is a significant regulator of classroom social interactions (Gallas, 1998; Sadker and Sadker, 1994; Thorne, 1993). Children actively take up what they learn from parents, the popular media, religion, and other sites about gender roles and use this—often contradictory—information to influence each other's behaviors. They dictate what is more or less "acceptable" and "unacceptable" through a host of practices including name-calling and peer group ostracization. In multiple ways children are actively involved in constructing their own and each other's gender roles. But rarely does schooling call into question gendered practices and the power of these constructions. Several excellent accounts (e.g., Davies, 1989; Gallas, 1998; Stedman, 1982) describe the complexity of the engendered interactions among primary school children with their peers and with texts. In this account I highlight several intersections between gender and literacy in the senior grades.

I taught at what I will call "Simcoe Collegiate," an inner-city school with a highly diverse population. In my classrooms, issues of representation and identity were of ongoing concern to students. Toronto is one of North America's most culturally diverse cities. It is a place where, if you play any thoughtful role in the educational process whatsoever, you cannot pretend that visible difference does not matter, or adhere to the myth, in your classroom, that "everyone is the same." Elsewhere I have described how race was a factor in reading responses (Ricker-Wilson, 1998); in this chapter I limit my focus to gender.

At the beginning of one term, I assigned a Grade 11 advanced English class *Input* (Bulger, 1990), a short story about a job interview. A two-day, barely contained conversation about sexual harassment ensued in which multiple and conflicting discourses about women's bodies and economic opportunities circulated, were analyzed, engaged with, and disputed. This conversation also suggested to me that these students needed time and space in which to "unpack" the rhetorical extremes around which the conversation transpired ("She was asking for it" "No means no") and to consider where sexual transactions themselves became ambivalent; where danger and desire intersected; and where women were alternately compelled by the culture toward complicity in their sexual objectification and forbidden to express their own sexual desires (Fine, 1993).

In this class, female students outnumbered males by three to one, and I observed that no matter how passionate the discussion became, the males remained silent—or rather, they occasionally whispered among themselves. Several young women picked up on this and demanded their opinion but one young man said that, with all the girls in the class, he would not dare give one. Outraged protests ensued. One girl called that a "chicken shit" response. No one stepped in to "save" the boys who, by their body language, and expressions, looked ready to disappear into the floor. Would it have been "gender transgression" for one of them to *agree* that there was something wrong with sexual harassment? Was it really such a risk? Part of me was delighted to see the boys so uncomfortable, to have them experience a *gendered discomfort*, and to experience the ramifications of their own silence in this overtly gendered discourse. But I also knew that adolescent males lived by rigid gender codes of their own and that being able to speak against the peer group required modeling, guts, and practice. In addition, given their silence, I had no way to assess their own understanding of this text.

Color Me Purple: Reading "Straight," Missing Meaning

A major way in which certain male students manifested their gender anxiety was by exercising their homophobia. At least once a month a male student in one of my classes would ask aloud why "those people" would do "such things" and express his disgust for homosexuals. This became the period's curriculum. A familiar pattern would emerge: several students would invoke a primary Western source of homophobia—the Old Testament—dragging out such terms as "sinful" and "unnatural." If they were really sophisticated, "abomination." We would then spend some time deconstructing their biblical exegeses. Most had only a passing familiarity with Jonah, Noah, Lot and his daughters, or the Ten Commandments; but they all knew that homosexuality was a sin. Many males did not think fornication was sinful, however (if they even knew the term), and conceded that such "unnatural" acts as oral sex were okay if they were on the receiving end and a female was doing it. Interestingly very few female students ever sided with the male homophobes. To some degree, given the instability of "maleness" as an identity category, I suspect the young men mainly wanted female confirmation that it was okay to be sensitive or nonathletic or anything else that signaled a departure from macho behavioral conventions.

I believe these conversations that disrupted the "official" curriculum were not initiated simply as a break from business as usual. On the contrary, the students, in the throes of coming to terms with their own sexual identities, were insisting on the time, space, and need to know—need to demystify—whatever they had previously learned. From numerous sources, I knew how frequently any conversation about sexual orientation was silenced in education. I have attended conferences at which gay and lesbian students testified that homophobic comments directed at them and overheard by their teachers were recurrently ignored in classes. Teaching candidates in an English education course that I taught related frequent occasions in their intermediate/senior classrooms where conversations about sexual orientation were suppressed. In one instance a senior student had inquired as to whether it was true that some of Shakespeare's sonnets had been addressed to a man. The "master" teacher replied, "We don't have time to waste on such trivia."

Jonathon Silin (1995) maintains that "the curriculum has too often become an injunction to desist rather than an invitation to explore [children's] life worlds. . . ." He perceives teachers' efforts to silence exploration of the forbidden and controversial as actions that make the curriculum socially irrelevant. By sticking with the program, or dismissing questions about difference, he argues, "We judge differences as inadequacies or weaknesses rather than alternative but equally valuable ways of knowing. We also protect ourselves from looking at existing power arrangements across the generations" (1995, p. 49). In my own case, student need suggested it was essentially to make a space for the most unpopular expressions of racism, heterosexism, or homophobia because only by creating a forum in which these concerns could be voiced, contested *by other students*, and to some extent deconstructed and demystified could authorized "ignorance" be exposed for what it was. These conversations were often painful for the participants, and rarely concluded with any sense of a shift in positions. But students insisted on returning to them.

On the other hand, despite my agenda to include difference, sometimes students insisted on mystification. When six or seven students gave presentations on *The Color Purple* (Walker, 1983) in that same class, neither male or female could mention the term "lesbian" with reference to the relationship between Shug and Celie. While I have no idea how sexually experienced or naive these sixteen- and seventeen-year-olds were, I believe that had they read the novel (or had simply seen the film), here was a case where understanding had to be truly suppressed, to the point where the text lost its meaning. Indeed, I suspect it took considerable cognitive *effort* to misunderstand or elide the nature of Shug and Celie's relationship.

Silin (1995) claims that people "are purposefully ignorant and that ignorance is not the opposite of knowledge but rather an integral part of the same dynamic system" (pp. 170–171). He believes that people's "preferred ignorance, like their knowledge, is allied to a specific regime of truth, one that privileges conformity over distinction, the Caucasian over the person of color, the heterosexual over the homosexual. Regimes of truth establish fields of force, exert controls over thought and behavior, our knowing and not knowing" (pp. 170–171). This is another way of explaining how thoroughly dominant discourses about what is the norm for appearance, desire, or behavior construct and circumscribe subjects and do them social and psychological violence.

This incident allowed me to understand how simply staging student encounters with "difference" creates a problem for both learners and teachers within the compulsory venue. The students' reading quandary forced me to address the limitations of reason, of reader response theory itself (How can you respond to what is significant when you do not "believe" it is?), and of conventional assessment practices. How could I accurately—let alone justly—assess students' understanding of *The Color Purple* when understanding depended on the willingness to engage with issues and ideas that generated such cognitive and emotional dissonance? On the other hand, how *was* one to respond to students who, quite bluntly, were exercising a very powerful and stubborn (albeit irrational) resistance to the "counterhegemonic"—that which challenged the regime of truth, the dominant and conventional ways of thinking about a subject? For clearly, this was a case where "not knowing" forbade homosexuality from exerting its very presence. This was confirmed for me when I finally asked why no one would say the word "lesbian." One young woman replied, "If you know what [Celie and Shug] were doing someone might wonder *why* you know it." This astute student recognized that counterhegemonic knowledge, like counterhegemonic behavior, could complicate your life. As Britzman et al. (1993) observed, "[student] 'ignorance' of how identities work is, in actuality, an effect of the 'knowledge' these students already hold, namely that race, class, gender and sex are the explanations of 'trouble' and 'discomfort' and thus are best left alone" (p. 196).

To proclaim your knowledge was to become suspect, contaminated, and allied with the socially unpopular. No wonder you suppressed it. No wonder you *performed* ignorance. Thus, I learned in what a complicated manner and to what degree homophobia exerted major social control over both sexes, and began to recognize that simply encouraging dialogue about it—putting it into *rational* discourse—had its limitations. While I had been led, throughout my English education, to believe that reading and discussion presented routes out of the taken for granted, I continually discovered that both presented a cognitive and affective minefield.

Color Me Blue: Lower-Track Readings

Another distressing manifestation of how gender regulated learning was evident mainly in my lower-track, or general-level, classrooms in which working-class male students were disproportionately represented, gendered behaviors were more extreme, and most students practiced, in their seating and group work arrangements, self-regulated sex segregation. The fact that my advanced-level students generally showed considerably more willingness to interact with the opposite sex suggests that somehow the fears and expectations of general-level students might play a part in their gendered classroom behavior. While the occasional, relatively self-assured girl would interact with some of the quieter, more mature-acting boys, it was my impression many girls seemed clearly intimidated by the loud brashness of male clusters who intermittently practiced an overt if generally good-natured "resistance" to most manifestations of compulsory education. Perhaps they did not recognize that the boys, far from displaying unequivocally macho personas, frequently displayed a touching vulnerability, manifested in comments easily heard by anyone in the room, such as, "I can't write a poem. It'll sound dumb" and "Will you read this, Miss? How bad does it suck?" I wondered to what degree the boys' own vulnerability accounted for the segregation.

In her exploration of how gender is lived in elementary schools, Raphaela Best identified an early connection between reading skill and male social status in which "The boys who were rejected from peer group membership lost macho points because they were reading 'baby' books—first-and second-grade readers" (1983, p. 22). Best maintained that such humiliation affected them to the extent that they lost all desire to become better readers. She also observed that the process of masculine socialization is such that by second grade, it is common for boys to begin to bond with their male peers and situate themselves in opposition to girls and female authority figures through rebellious, aggressive, and offensive behaviors. Not surprisingly, in such a context, "[t]he concern of the rejected boys themselves was far less with their academic progress or lack of it than with their inability to achieve acceptance in their peer world" (p. 51). As a consequence, Best notes, these male students frequently engaged in antisocial behavior and/or showed signs of depression. She maintains that this dynamic was only evident in boys in school. While more research is needed to confirm this, Best's work suggests one possible way in which reading and literacy acquisition in our culture becomes gendered, and the nascent construction of the student most commonly found in elementary remedial and secondary lower-track classrooms: the "at-risk" male with "behavioral problems," which, I believe, could be defined as the practice of "hypermasculine" behaviors to gain status and negotiate power.

Connell (1995) identifies those practices of masculinity, so resonantly and vigorously perpetuated by popular culture and mass media, that are understood to grant men high status and ability to wield authority as "hegemonic" masculinity. At present, Western hegemonic masculinity is associated with

> physical rigor, adventurousness, emotional neutrality, certainty, control, assertiveness, self-reliance, individuality, competitiveness, instrumental skills, public knowledge, discipline, reason, objectivity and rationality. It distances itself from physical weakness, expressive skills, private knowledge, creativity, emotion, dependency, subjectivity, irrationality, co-operation, and empathetic, compassionate, nurturant and certain affiliative behaviors. (1995, pp. 20–21)

It is, not surprisingly, hard to sustain, and men who are otherwise marginalized by the dominant culture often exaggerate these behaviors in order to ensure that they are recognized by the dominant culture as "real" men. Such an identity excludes what it perceives as subordinate masculinities, which are often rigorously, if only partially, defined as being tainted by the "feminine."

While hegemonic maleness can be positively reinforced in our culture—through athletic dexterity in competitive situations and spatial–mechanical expertise—schooling and the job market primarily award those with high grades. When other identity categories are factored in, literacy habits may become even more complicated. Genre theorists argue that lower-income students tend not to acquire the socially powerful language register and vocabulary at home, and are denied access to it in the lower-track courses in which they are frequently placed in school (Martin and Rotherty, 1980). Moreover, the English classroom has been deemed a "feminized" sphere of knowing (Morgan, 1990; Pirie, 2002).

The ongoing emphasis on narrative reading, on responding personally to literary texts, and on acquiring the codes to read aesthetically (affectively) rather than efferently (for information) (Rosenblatt, 1978) has little currency with many working-class North American male students who likely sense and resent the vestigial or overt impetus to "civilize" them by—effete—middle-class standards. Given that it is predominantly working-class and lower-income males who are deemed to have reading problems, to a certain degree working-class male il-literacy might be constituted first by a lack of access to the socially powerful dominant discourse; and then by a rejection not just of its language register but of its literacy habits. People resist and reject knowledge in gendered, raced, and classed manners (Mac an Ghaill, 1994; Ogbu, 1988; Willis, 1977). To some degree, those who are confrontational, those who fail, skip, and drop out might be signaling both their disaffection with and resistance to an educational system that they feel marginalizes them and challenges their identity.

By the time they enter high school, their low-level reading ability puts these male students at even greater risk. To be illiterate might confirm maleness but at the same time, particularly in the English classroom, it reduces one's stature since it makes you look "dumb" and ultimately delimits your opportunity for higher education.

Furthermore, you are no longer at the age when sitting next to a girl (whom your peers read as properly "feminine") contaminates you. On the contrary, it enhances your standing with other males—but only in very specific situations— where a girl could not possibly show you up, where it is assumed you will have the upper hand or be able to "score." The English classroom is not necessarily such a place. On the contrary, it can expose your lack when called on to read or write. Here is a place where you are in a double bind: to be too literate is to be "fey"; to be illiterate diminishes your prestige and economic future. Either way you are in danger of emasculation. As Bronwyn Davies notes, "[M]aleness in our society is defined in large part in terms of one's capacity not to behave like a girl " (1989, p. 87) and is thus construed by some boys as something that has to be continuously achieved. In a sense, there may be safety in lower-tracked classrooms for reluctant male readers, where they have, and can continue to cultivate, a classroom culture of resistant maleness: edgy, brash, bellicose, hyperphysical, and hormonally charged. On numerous occasions I counseled male students to switch to advanced-level courses and was told "those courses are too hard." When I suggested that they are quite capable of such work and that it might broaden their future options, several male students responded: "I feel safer here." Interestingly, however, the female students I counseled seemed merely to need that encouragement to make the switch.

I discovered that one's relationship with literacy seemed gendered in ways I had never before considered. One did not simply read "as a woman" or prefer certain genres. Rather, it seemed, one *practiced* literacy (in)expertise in a gendered way—in a way which, perhaps, secured both gender and sexual orientation. If high school literacy was not complicated enough, it seemed its practice might suggest something about one's wo/manhood. Following de Laureates (1987) I began to understand how gender, an artificial and unstable category, exerted real and significant effects on literacy practices. My struggles with how to theorize about such incidents and what strategies I might employ to address the nuanced and multiple suppressions of all unofficial discourses about gender and sexuality led me to examine how English education itself suppresses textual understanding.

Reading in Technicolor

Reading in technicolor happens to a significant degree, cultural theorists (Batsleer et al., 1985; Faust, 2000) charge, because of the kind of questioning protocols teachers habitually apply to texts. These continue to be almost exclusively informed by two types of literary theory (Applebee, 1993). The most prevalent, New Criticism, emphasizes the structural features and conventions of texts: character, plot, theme, imagery, and unity. It provides no opportunities to address how narrative might simultaneously represent, perpetuate, and challenge, through the heterogeneous voices of its characters, the best and worst practices of its culture. Nor does it provide lenses through which to make gender or any other social categories "visible" to readers. The second, Reader Response theory, recognizes that reading is idiosyncratic, and that textual interpretation depends on personal experience and social location. However, rarely do curriculum documents or textbooks encourage teachers to use such theory to encourage students to challenge authoritative interpretations of literary works, or to provide students with strategies to critically examine textual relations between power, identity, and representation.

Throughout my teaching career, I naively struggled to guide student reading with more resonant questions. This practice, however, was not particularly visible to me as employing a particular type of literary theory. Having received all-too-minimal professional development with each new era of curricular "reform," I did not understand what informed the questioning protocols presented in curriculum documents and textbooks. Fortunately, my encounters with contemporary literary theorists—particularly feminist and Marxist—provided me with new lenses through which to read and analyze texts. Since Millett (1971) initially made gender dynamics visible in her 1970 focus on how women are represented in men's texts, subsequent feminist critics, diverse in interests (black women's writing, Shakespeare, science fiction) and approach, have examined (cf. Showalter, 1981) how women write about their own experiences and representations (Gilbert and Gubar, 1979; Showalter, 1977); how they read about themselves (Fetterley, 1978; Schweickart, 1986); and how to read through feminist lenses (Davies, 1993; Fetterley, 1986). While I lack the space in which to name and describe their diverse approaches and debates in which they engage, I discovered that feminist literary theory prompted a variety of questions through which to examine issues of gender and representation in texts such as the following:

> How are women/men depicted (physically, emotionally, etc.)? How fair/accurate/stereotyped/contradictory are their depictions?
> How does gender, within the social and cultural context of the text, operate to enable or inhibit the characters' actions and options?
> How significant are gender issues in this text?
> How do narratives featuring women differ from those featuring men?

Feminist literary theory, far from homogeneous, is informed by linguistics, psychoanalysis, political, and social theory, among others. Some of its interests overlap, for instance, with those of Marxist critics who make visible how narrative texts, far from presenting "fictitious" worlds, are cultural artifacts with ideological value that might perpetuate (even as they critique) prevailing beliefs and social norms (Bonnycastle, 1996). Significant questions raised by Marxist-informed critics include the following:

> How does power in all of its manifestations (social, sexual, economic) operate in text and with what effects? Who has power and of what sorts? How do they negotiate it and with whom? How does this change as a text progresses?
>
> How are class issues evident, and how do they create conflict in a text? How are working-class/middle-class, low-income/high-income people depicted? How fair or accurate are these depictions? In what texts are working-class people depicted in favorable or complex manners?
>
> What political and ideological biases are evident in the text? How does this text/author challenge my own beliefs or values? (Graff, 1987)
>
> How does the text's narrative conventions manipulate my emotions? What strategies or devices does the author use to get readers to sympathize with the protagonist? To distance themselves from the antagonist(s)? (Brecht, 1964)

New Criticism focuses on the structural elements of texts (e.g., plot, imagery) and their purportedly "inherent" meaning. Much current criticism, including the two I have mentioned, along with postcolonial and queer theories shifts outside the structural conventions of texts themselves in order to consider how meaning gets produced, focusing "on how language works, in whose and what interests, on what cultural sites, and why. "A post structural literacy," advises Davies, "offers one effective means of addressing the coercive character of texts to shape desire, to constitute 'real selves' that are positioned in 'real worlds'" (1993, p. 148). Suspect of traditional reverence for literary works, poststructural literary theorists invite readers to consider the following:

> What is literature?
>
> Why are we reading this text? Why are we not reading something else?
>
> Should this text be taught in schools? Why or why not?
>
> Who decides what is worth reading?
>
> Why is one book considered art and another trash?

From whose position does the author wish me to read this text? Why and how does that affect my understanding of other characters' positions? What in my past experience might cause me to read from a particular position? To identify with certain characters or ideas?

I recognized that I had never explicitly taught students how to read texts through different lenses, and that some of these lenses magnified what had previously been invisible. As I read current critics, I began to introduce more questions on representation, power, and reading position. Once the students began to acquire a vocabulary to talk about gender and power in its varied manifestations, I found that my general-level students spoke and wrote lengthily about father/son and male/female power dynamics in David French's *Leaving Home* (1972) in ways that suggested their personal and academic struggles with these dynamics and efforts to articulate them. Further, their articulations confirmed their emotional engagement as well as their analytic and interpretive capabilities. When we focused on French's representation of working-class Newfoundlanders, many were willing to return to the text to find supporting evidence for their opinions, to thoughtfully dramatize their understanding of power relationships, and to discuss working-class representations. When Shakespeare's focus on gender became visible to them in *Macbeth*, the majority of my Grade 11 advanced class (male and female) chose to write their exam on how the notion of "manliness" itself created problems for the protagonist. Such questioning strategies provided and legitimized opportunities to consider both the multiple and conflicting seventeenth-century discourses about women's spiritual, social, economic, and sexual rights and representations; and those to which we are currently subject in texts and in life.

In addition, I found that such questioning strategies enabled us to study popular texts critically. When five female students in one general-level class requested to read Danielle Steel (1989) novels for their independent study, I drafted a romance questionnaire, informed by current literary theory, which I hoped would enable them to focus specifically on the "sexual politics" inherent in these texts—that is, the ways in which engendered power operated in interpersonal and social relationships. For example, I asked them to:

Compare the heroine and her lover in terms of age, occupation, social, and economic status.
Examine who has power and of what sort in the novel? Over whom? How does this power balance change as the novel progresses?
How is sexuality (male and female) described?
How believable is the ending?

All five students submitted extensive and thoughtful responses to the assignment. In one ensuing discussion, I determined that they were able to get outside the text and begin to consider production values themselves. Recognizing its significance, I transcribed it immediately after the class, attempting to retain its gist and their style. I have used pseudonyms to protect their privacy:

> "Why," asked Rosa, about *Star's* (1989) male lead, who would not officially leave his loveless marriage, "did he have to worry so much about his image? He could've gotten a divorce and another job anywhere. It says he was a hotshot lawyer. So staying with Elizabeth don't make sense."
>
> "He uses her as an excuse," replied Maria. "I don't think he really wants to marry Crystal all that much."
>
> Rosa asked, "So why can't Crystal figure that out. Why'd she marry him in the end?"
>
> "I don't think [the writer] wants you to think about that," said Maria. "That would make him not look good and then it wouldn't be a happy ending."
>
> "But you did think it," I said. "You got right outside the logic of the novel. So what do you think that means?"
>
> "That she's not a very good writer?" ventured Rosa.
>
> "Maybe she couldn't figure it out herself. Maybe she doesn't know or want to know what it means," suggested Maria.
>
> "But if we figured that out maybe other people could too," said Tamara.
>
> Maria added, "Maybe people'll stop reading her novels. Maybe they'll think they're stupid if she doesn't give them what they want."
>
> "She makes women look smart and dumb at the same time. She kind of tricks you into liking them dumb," declared Tamara. "I liked the book but I don't like being tricked."

The students, supposedly not very careful readers, were busily unraveling some of the text's loose ends, and were in the nascent stages of discovering the constraints on women's writing and desire. Barely aware of how to identify them, I recognized the significance of Maria's comments. She had begun, in a fundamental manner, to examine the power of discourse itself to masquerade its construction and control behavior, and to employ what I now recognize as deconstructionist questioning techniques. These students were beginning to escape the confines of traditional literary theory on its own, in a general-level classroom. Using different questioning protocols from the two to which they are most commonly given access in English courses, they had begun a complicated unraveling of author from reader from text.

In What Colors Are You Reading?

I have argued that literacy practices are bound up with identity and are subject to peer interactions and expectations. To some degree, the practices help construct problem readers. I believe particular reading practices, along with teacher expectations for and about literature also bear a role in constructing problem readers. Lower-level readers, in particular, need a reason for reading beyond finding directly stated information (What color was the door?), and beyond the fact that some teacher thinks it is beneficial to absorb the author's message about "the inherent evil of man." The notion that a particular text is "good" for someone—or everyone— does an injustice to the text and to potential readers. Why take any risks if the English teacher already guarantees the outcome? Why read in monochrome?

To my delight I discovered that reading became less of a problem once students acquired strategies to examine how "masculinity" and "femininity," among other signifiers, are problematic constructions. Both the quality of reading and of peer group interactions changed. Current literary theory offers one of the richest imaginable repositories for initiating exploration of conflicting discourses about gender and sexuality, something desperately needed by secondary school students, who hear virtually nothing suggesting a discourse on female desire (Fine, 1993); who cannot even speak the word "lesbian" when discussing *The Color Purple*; and who beg not to be put with someone of the opposite gender during group work. Surely discussion of female and male representation in texts might engage students in an examination of how their own behavior has been so rigidly regulated and circumscribed. Critical questioning protocols gave me "permission" to legitimize such study. Several excellent works are currently available to help secondary school teachers and students learn how to explore texts through the lenses of diverse literary theories that are explained and made visible as such (e.g., Applebee, 1993, Soter, 1999; Thompson, 1993).

I do not mean to suggest that with critical questioning all reading problems were suddenly "cured," or that everyone in my classrooms was categorically more receptive to reading. But I believe such questioning protocols have the potential to disrupt notions of school texts as canonical artifacts decodable primarily by those who have power to call the shots. Far from troubling their reading, I determined that many of my students were more willing to take the trouble to read carefully. Such questions make reading more permissible because they make *resistant* and *iconoclastic* readings and responses permissible. They permit—or rather demand—a youth-friendly "bad attitude" toward all texts—"high" and "low" print and visual. They create a space for students of diverse identities, abilities, and social locations to challenge texts, and to identify and articulate how gender and other social categories operate. They allow all students to examine and critique our troubled cultural narratives, and to examine and respond with some immediacy to the forces of subjection and domination in which we are all embroiled.

References

Alloway, N., and Gilbert, P. (1997, March). Boys and literacy: Lessons from Australia. *Gender and Education*, 9(1), 49–60.

American Association of University Women (AAUW) Educational Foundation, Commission on Technology, Gender, and Teacher Education. (2000). *Tech-savvy: Educating girls in the new computer age*. Washington, DC: Author.

Applebee, A. (1993). *Literature in the secondary school: Studies of curriculum and instruction in the United States*. NCTE Research Report No. 25. Urbana, IL: National Council of Teachers of English.

Appleman, D. (2000). *Critical encounters in high school English: Teaching literary theory to adolescents*. NY: Teachers College Press.

Batsleer, J., Davis, T., O'Rourke, R., and Weedon, C. (1985). *Rewriting English: Cultural politics of gender and class*. London: Methuen.

Best, R. (1983). *We've all got scars: What boys and girls learn in elementary school*. Bloomington, IN: Indiana University Press.

Bonnycastle, S. (1996). *In search of authority: An introductory guide to literary theory* (2nd ed.). Peterborough, Ontario: Broadview Press.

Brecht, B. (1964). *Brecht on theatre: the development of an aesthetic*. Translation and notes by J. Willett. London: Methuen.

Britzman, D. P., Santiago-Valles, K., Jimenez-Munoz, G., and Lamash, L. M. (1993). Slips that show and tell: Fashioning multiculture as a problem of representation. In C. McCarthy and W. Crichlow (Eds.), *Race, identity and education*, 188–200. New York: Routledge.

Broude, G. H. (1999, July 15). Boys will be boys. *The Public Interest*. v. 136.

Bulger, L. (1990). Input. In J. Borovilos (Compiler), *Breaking through: A Canadian literary mosaic*, 127–130. Scarborough, ON: Prentice-Hall.

Connell, R. W. (1995). *Masculinities: Knowledge, power and social change*. Berkeley and Los Angeles: University of California Press.

Curtis, B., Livingstone, D., and Smaller, H. (1992). *Stacking the deck: The streaming of working class kids in Ontario schools*. Toronto: Our Schools/Our Selves Education Foundation.

Darling-Hammond, L. (1995). Inequality and access to knowledge. In J. A. Banks and C. A. M. Banks (Eds.), *Handbook of research on multicultural education* (pp. 365–483). New York: Macmillan.

Davies, B. (1989). *Frogs and snails and feminist tales*. Sydney: George, Allen and Unwin.

Davies, B. (1993). *Shards of glass: Children reading and writing beyond gendered identities*. Cresol, NJ: Hampton Press.

de Lauretis, T. (1987). *Technologies of gender: Essays on theory, film, and fiction*. Bloomington, IN: Indiana University Press.

Faust, M. (2000, August). Reconstructing familiar metaphors: John Dewey and Louise Rosenblatt on literary art as experience. *Research on the Teaching of English*, 35, 8–34.

Fetterley, J. (1978). *The resisting reader: A feminist approach to American fiction*. Bloomington: Indiana University Press.

Fetterley, J. (1986). Reading about reading: "A Jury of her Peers," "Murders in the Rue Morgue" and "The Yellow Wallpaper." In E. Flynn and P. Schweickart (Eds.), *Gender and reading: Essays on readers, texts and contexts,* 147–165. Baltimore: The Johns Hopkins Press.

Fine, M. (1993). Sexuality, schooling and adolescent females: The missing discourse of desire. In L. Weis and M. Fine (Eds.), *Beyond silenced voices: Class, race and gender in U.S. schools,* 75–100. New York: State University of New York Press.

French, D. (1972). *Leaving home.* Toronto: New Press.

Gallas, K. (1998). *Sometimes I can be anything: Power, gender, and identity in a primary classroom.* New York: Teachers College Press.

Gilbert, S. M., and Gubar, S. (1979). *The madwoman in the attic: The woman writer and the nineteenth-century literary imagination.* New Haven: Yale University Press.

Graff, G. (1987). *Professing literature: An institutional history.* Chicago: University of Chicago Press.

Gurian, M., and Henley, P. with Trueman, T. (2001). *Boys and girls learn differently! A guide for teachers and parents.* San Francisco: Jossey-Bass/Wiley.

Mac an Ghaill, M. (1994). *The making of men: Masculinities, sexuality and schooling.* Buckingham: Open University Press.

Martin, J., and Rotherty, J. (1980). *Language, register and genre: A reading in the Deakin University B. Ed. Children Writing Course, Course Reader.* Geelong, Victoria: Deakin University Press.

Millett, K. (1971). *Sexual politics.* New York: Avon.

Morgan, R. (1990). Reading as discursive practice: The politics and history of Reading. In D. Bogdan and S. B. Straw (Eds.), *Beyond comprehension: Reading, comprehension and criticism,* 319–336. Portsmouth, NH: Boynton Cook.

Moss, G. (1998). *The fact and fiction research project. Interim Findings.* Southampton, UK: University of Southampton.

Ogbu, J. (1988). Class stratification, racial stratification, and schooling. *Class, race and gender in American education.* Lois Weis, ed. Albany, NY: State University of New York Press.

Pirie, B. (2002). *Teenage boys and high school English.* Portsmouth, NH: Boynton/Cook Heinemann,

Ricker-Wilson, C. (1998, March). When the mockingbird becomes an albatross: Reading and resistance in the language arts classroom. *English Journal,* 67–72.

Rosenblatt, L. M. (1978). *The reader, the text, the poem.* Carbondale, IL: Southern Illinois University Press.

Sadker, M., and Sadker, D. (1994). *Failing at fairness: How America's schools cheat girls.* New York: Charles Scribner's Sons.

Schweickart, P. (1986). Reading ourselves: Toward a feminist theory of reading. In E. Flynn and P. Schweickart (Eds.), *Gender and reading: Essays on reading, texts and contexts,* 31–62. Baltimore: The Johns Hopkins Press.

Showalter, E. (1977). *A literature of their own: British women novelists from Brontë to Lessing.* Princeton, NJ: Princeton University Press.

Showalter, E. (1981, Winter). Feminist criticism in the wilderness. *Critical Inquiry, 8,* 179–205.

Silin, J. G. (1995). *Sex, death, and the education of children: Our passion for ignorance in the age of AIDS.* New York: Teachers College Press.

Soter, A. (1999). *Young adult literature and the new literary theories: Developing critical readers in middle school.* New York: Teachers College Press.

Stedman, C. (1982). *The tidy house: Little girls writing*. London: Virago.

Steel, D. (1989). *Star*. New York: Dell Publishing.

Thompson, J. (1993). Helping students control texts: Contemporary literary theory in classroom practice. In S. B. Straw and D. Bogdan (Eds.), *Constructive reading: Teaching beyond communication*. Portsmouth, NH: Boynton/Cook Pub.

Thorne, B. (1993). *Gender play: girls and boys in school*. New Brunswick, NJ: Rutgers University Press.

Tolusso, G. (1999). Grappling with the gender gap. Retrieved November 15, 1999 http://magazine.carleton.ca/1999_Fall/6.htm

Walker, A. (1983). *The color purple*. New York: Pocket Books.

Willis, P. (1977). *Learning to labour: How working class kids get working class jobs*. New York: Columbia University Press.

6

Ways of Reading, Ways of Seeing

Social Justice Inquiry in the Literature Classroom

MARY BETH HINES

Over the last ten years I have worked with a variety of English teachers engaged in exploring the challenges, conflicts, and complexities of claiming the classroom as a site for social justice—whether in middle, secondary, or postsecondary institutions, alternative schools, or mainstream schools. In using the term *social justice*, I am referring to the broad range of issues related to linguistic and cultural differences, equity, and social responsibility in a multicultural society (Delpit, 1995; Delpit and Dowdy, 2002; Edelsky, 1999; Goebel and Hall, 1996; Hynds, 1997; Moller, 2002; Oliver, 1994; Pratt, 1996; Slevin and Young, 1996). While some may refer to this set of issues as cultural criticism, critical pedagogy, multiculturalism, teaching for tolerance, or cultural studies, I deliberately use the term *social justice* because it suggests not only an interrogation of signifying practices, but also because it challenges us to move beyond—to change the material conditions and lived experiences that create and sustain inequities. Thus, social justice pedagogy not only includes cultural critique, but also extends such work by emphasizing social action.

Scholarship on social justice explores in various ways the question of what counts as social justice. While an array of taxonomies exist, taken together they make the case that there are competing ways of seeing social justice, and those visions and versions have implications for teachers and learners. While these discourses vary in emphases, there are basically two opposing perspectives. On one hand, some locate the problem and solution for injustice within the individual, fostering explanations that focus upon physical, psychological, or cognitive elements. This orientation is sometimes called liberal, liberal humanist, or psychological, and views social change occurring as individuals pull up their proverbial "bootstraps," as Villanueva (1993) and others (e.g., Belsey, 1980; Boyle-Baise, 2002; Sleeter, 1993) explain. In contrast, others (including myself) argue that competing, contradictory, interlocking, and mutually reinforcing forces and systems (often invisible) create and perpetuate such inequities. This orientation reflects priorities in Althusserian Marxism and its antecedents. The perspective is referred to as structural or systemic (Boyle-Baise, 2002; Roman, 1993; Sleeter, 1993).

This multiplicity of theoretical perspectives on social justice has compelled many discussions of what counts as effective social justice practice in the English classroom and in the culture. Most recently, I have been able to explore such issues with teachers in the Indiana English Teachers Collaborative (ETC), a teacher-research network dedicated to social justice, an organization that I have helped to establish and direct. As I studied the ways in which members have worked as agents of change in their respective classrooms and communities, teacher-researchers have conducted research projects driven by their own questions about teaching and learning. I wanted to understand how and why teachers engaged in such inquiry, and how that work affected students and schools. The unsettling questions that typically preoccupied these teachers arose when the particularities of their respective classrooms did not embody the prevailing wisdom of the profession. In many cases, these conscientious and cutting-edge teachers blamed themselves, rather than the profession, for the lacunae. Implicitly, these omissions indicated that their practices, rather than our theories, are deficient. In this chapter, I trouble that perspective as I point to the limits of prevailing principles for conceptualizing the English classroom as a site for teaching and learning about social justice. After years of working with teachers, I have more questions than answers about what it means to enact and to promote social justice in the English classroom, questions that are at the heart of this essay.

As a way to address some of the vexing pedagogical issues that accompany social justice inquiry in the classroom, I draw from a qualitative case study of one college literature classroom taught by a committed Marxist with strong feminist leanings, Richard (all names are pseudonyms in this essay). I attended, videotaped, transcribed, and analyzed half of the semester's classroom discussions, attempting to identify recurring themes and patterns of discourse in relation to social justice issues. I also collected and analyzed all written work completed in relation to these discussions, and interviewed Richard and several case study students repeatedly throughout the semester. In so doing, I generated hypotheses about what counted as social justice, analyzed more information, and adjusted the hypotheses accordingly.

Richard forged a conceptual framework for literary inquiry with Marxist schol-arship in order to enact and to promote social justice in the classroom. Aside from the critical expertise and pedagogical vision that Richard brings to the classroom, this case is important because the trajectories and traditions of Marxism have had a significant impact upon the history of ideas, past and present, especially in rela-tion to social justice. Today, strands of Marxism crisscross the interdisciplinary discourses of cultural studies, literary studies, media studies, composition, literacy studies, critical pedagogy, critical ethnography, feminisms, and other fields within the humanities and social sciences. Thus, it is not only that Marxist instructors may see themselves in Richard, but it is also true that this case may prove salient to teach-ers developing feminist or cultural studies pedagogies. Focusing on the specific dynamics of Richard's classroom and the generative dilemmas that arose, I hope to promote even as I problematize social justice inquiry in the literature classroom. That is, I will use Richard's class as the springboard for identifying issues that developed in the nexus of literary pedagogy and social justice. In so doing, I hope to laud the work of the teachers with whom I have worked, arguing that at this moment our profession has as much to learn from classroom teachers as it does from theorists and critics.

Background on Richard

Richard was a white, middle-class instructor from England who taught at a large, Midwestern research university enrolling 30,000 students, 98 percent of whom were white, in a state that was 96 percent white. The state was predominately rural, and its citizens boasted students' high marks on standardized tests. He had taught the course I studied four times prior to the semester of my investigation. This course was the only literature course required for non-English majors, a sequel to a required composition course, part of the general education program and an English Department staple. Designed in a discussion format, Richard's course was a survey course focusing primarily upon American writers of the twentieth century. Students were typically required to write several formal essays and a variety of informal responses. Richard's class had 18 students and reflected the demographics of the state.

Richard was a doctoral candidate specializing in nineteenth-century colonial-ism and landscapes of imperialism, themes reflecting his interests in cultural stud-ies and Marxism. He culled most of his literary pedagogical priorities from the work of Louis Althusser (1977, 1969/1990, 1990), considered by many to be the most sig-nificant academic Marxist since Karl Marx. In light of the contributions made by scholars drawing upon Althusser's work (i.e., Bennett, 1990; Hennessy and

Ingraham, 1997; Morton and Zavarzadeh, 1991), Richard also undertook to explore with students the role of language not only in reflecting, but also in constituting society, a view of language with implications for literary studies that are discussed in a subsequent section.

I feature Richard's classroom in this chapter for several reasons. His ways of seeing the world, the classroom, and his role in them issued from his commitments to Marxism and were informed by his passion for social justice. Widely known on campus as a Marxist, he used an array of Marxist analytic tools for social justice inquiry in his classroom. He consciously designed curriculum and instruction to reflect his commitments to social justice. That is, he developed a scaffolding that challenged students to move from simpler to more complex understandings of the issues, and from simpler to more complex texts. In so doing, he created an innovative pedagogy that challenged long-standing educational norms and literary educational practices. Moreover, his consistent enactment of social justice pedagogy complicates and calls into question our profession's "givens," and our ultimate purposes, challenging our assumptions about the roles that teachers should play, not only in the classroom, but also in society.

Ideology, Literary Pedagogy, and Social Justice: Richard's Views

In a series of interviews Richard explained that his beliefs about social justice were intricately interwoven with his goals as a literature instructor and his ethics as a socially responsible human being. He described himself as an oppositional instructor whose ultimate aim was not to "simply" and "freely" discuss and write about literature. Rather, his ambition was "to disturb," to challenge the dominant powers in our society. In this respect Richard agreed with the Marxist view that ideological critique is a first step toward changing the conditions of oppression in the world. According to Richard, students needed to learn to critique the culture because students have been taught to see the world in the way that newspapers, their parents, the schools, and church represent. They have a certain way of seeing that what they are told is a natural, commonsense way of seeing. Underlying that there are certain assumptions. What I want students to do . . . is to question these assumptions.

Richard explained that he typically began the semester by inviting students to help him draw an advertisement for a company that specialized in producing and marketing lawn care chemicals. He would ask students to consider "what messages were being sold" to consumers, and what the professional ad campaign designers might do to enhance the class's ad and to reinforce its messages. In addition, he would ask what information was suppressed to market the product and why.

By raising questions Richard taught students to critique the social "givens," or what Marxists and others call hegemonic practices; because students "have been taught to see things, taught to see themselves in certain ways." He would ask a variety of questions to invite students to construct alternatives to the "givens," or what Marxists and others describe as counterhegemonic stances:

> We sit back and say, "Okay, what are these ways? Does this benefit you? Whom does it benefit? What does it actually do? We should question these because a lot of assumptions are seen as "natural" or "common sense" ways of looking at things. I want to say that nothing is common sense. Nothing is natural, inherent or unique.

In order to expedite this inquiry, Richard said that he would ask students to think about what notions seemed to be constructed as "common sense" in the lawn care ad that the class developed.

Just as Richard encouraged ideological critique by focusing upon the constructed nature of the lawn care ad, he would later emphasize the constructed nature of language, texts, and culture:

> The main thing I want to stress is that we, ourselves, as readers, as people, and the text, are social constructs. . . . If it's a social construction, then who constructed it, what's it doing, and what are the elements going into this construction?

As students responded to these questions, they learned to become critical readers of texts and culture, rather than mere consumers, understanding, for instance, that the lawn care ad the class constructed was designed to sell a product that also sold the "normal" American family and home life.

Richard explained that he relied upon several key strategies when teaching students to critique dominant ideologies. Underlying his approach was a respect for the individual's beliefs, even those that perpetuated the status quo. That would mean valuing, for instance, even those who "buy into" the toxic chemicals as "necessary" for a beautiful yard:

> I think the best way of doing it is to take everyone's comments as legitimate, which they are. And then discuss those comments and try to show where they are coming from. What are their effects? What is their history?

Richard describes a repertoire of questioning strategies designed to promote awareness of ideologies, and how those are socially constructed. At the same time, he emphasizes that all viewpoints and experiences are valid and valuable, even those that support the status quo, because as members of society we all are susceptible to inheriting certain ways of seeing and not seeing: no one is immune.

Richard encouraged multiple perspectives from students as a way to counteract hegemonic belief systems:

> If you go into your classroom and say that we're going to talk about how this piece of literature enriches us all as human beings, how it teaches us all as human beings to respond in the same way to love or to death—big universals—then that is very biased because it allows the political status quo in society—which exploits women, which exploits through the class system—to continue. It doesn't engage with them at all, and it doesn't even try. It says we're all the same, which of course, we're not—you're a different class, a different color, and I would say your relationship to death and love is different.

In other words, hegemonic belief systems produce consent through an appeal to the innate and the universal that, on closer examination, turns out to be insupportable. As Richard went on to point out, "dealing with universals" is "at best complicitious with and at worst, actually supporting, the political status quo. And I suppose I cannot see society in any other way than it is a political system and is exploitative."

In practicing an oppositional pedagogy, Richard taught students to critique ideologies by recognizing two identifiable elements contributing to the making of hegemonic belief systems: universalism and essentialism. Universalism is the myth that all humans across all cultures share a common element or trait, as if it is a "given," when, in fact, it is common to some, rather than to all, human beings. Essentialism is the assumption that a trait is inherent to all members of a certain group, that it is an innate biological, physiological, or psychological quality, that group members are all similarly predisposed. Richard rejected the notions that students are universally or essentially the same, that they all read and experienced life in similar fashion. To help students challenge these ideas, Richard would, in the instance of the lawn care ad, situate the ad within various social, historical, and cultural contexts. He might begin by asking students to consider how responses to the house, family, and picket fence images might vary among urban, suburban, homeless, or incarcerated individuals. He might ask how World War II veterans might respond differently than Generation X-ers, or how Americans pre– and post–9/11 might respond.

For Richard, critique of the lawn care commercial would lay the groundwork for challenging universalism and essentialism in the analysis of literature:

> We have to set the piece of literature in its historical context. It was not written without social forces. I want to stress that because I want to say that we can look at our own lives, or information that we receive, and say this is part of our historical context. Just bringing up the history of Shakespeare's time doesn't help them [students] either. That's very interesting, but it's more like a history lesson.

Richard distinguishes between "just bringing up the history" and the *use* of history to point to and to critique the social and historical variables affecting the writing and reception of texts. His views resonate with recent Marxist critics and many others working in cultural studies (e.g., Angus and Jhally, 1989; Bennett, 1979; During, 1993; Eagleton, 1976; Giroux and Shannon, 1997; Young, 2001).

Interrogating "Student-Centered, Constructivist" Ideologies

It should come as no surprise that Richard interrogated educational norms and values, particularly notions of student-centered and constructivist inquiry. Mainstream and progressive discourses define "student-centered" inquiry as that in which student discourse prevails over teacher discourse, where students are the active producers of knowledge (see, e.g., Hynds, 1997). These are "givens" in educational theory, underwritten, as Richard argues, by the liberal humanist conception of the individual as autonomous, born with the power of understanding that transcends history and societal circumstances:

> I think the liberal humanist way of teaching literature is to just throw out ideas, and students would pick them up or bring in their own . . . like a free market. You can throw things out, ideas will be circulated freely, and students will have a free voicing of their ideas. Then the best ideas, the best products, will win out. I just do not subscribe to that because it ignores that there are dominant ways of seeing.

From this perspective individuals "freely" buy and sell ideas in the marketplace, all oblivious to the power relations, institutional, social, and historical systems in which such "free" markets operate.

In rejecting these definitions, Richard claimed that his classroom was indeed "very student-centered" because he was dedicated to uncovering the ultimate "best interests" of his students even as those interests challenged the status quo. He had to perform as "definitely an authority" when students did not "naturally" see the ways in which the dominant groups shaped values and practices. For this reason, he alternated between "exposing" and "selling" counterhegemonic perspectives:

> I have to sell ideas they are not familiar with. So I don't feel I can just throw out ideas and have a "free" discussion—just kind of "pick up on things"—because they're trained to see things in a certain way that I want to resist.

While literature teachers may encourage a multiplicity of viewpoints, Richard reminds us that any and all interpretations are value-laden, that they carry political implications. In light of the pervasiveness of the dominant ways of seeing, Richard emphasized that students were not at fault for subscribing to them: "I don't say, 'You're wrong,' because they're not wrong. It's just a different way of seeing the text. It's just as valid. In terms of the majority, they are right—but I want to say, What does that buy into?"

Richard's analytic strategies were designed to generate counterpoints to prevailing views and practices. If immersion in dominant ideologies is a "given," then the teacher or other students can point to the pull of the dominant ideologies rather than to the failures of an individual, when talking about commitments to those entrenched and "received" views. It is opportunity, not innate capacity, that leads students to counterhegemonic knowledge and practices.

Additionally, Richard's views on "free voicing" resonate with the radical critiques of "voice" found in feminist and critical pedagogical discourses, as well as in cultural studies (Aronowitz and Giroux, 1991; Giroux, 1983; Orner, 1992). These arguments counter the "commonsense" claim that voice is the expression of one's individualism, a liberty due to all people in a democracy. Such a view, Richard and other critical teachers argue, obscures the power relations operating within and beyond the classroom; and it ignores those systemic and structural forces that reproduce the economic, political, and cultural arrangements that benefit the dominant group.

Enacting Social Justice through the Curriculum

Another way that Richard enacted his social justice priorities was through the formulation of an inventive curriculum that challenged the "commonsense" logic prescribing that a course be organized thematically or chronologically. In contrast, he envisioned inquiry as a series of progressions moving from relatively easy reads to the more challenging, from single elements of oppression to multiple. For instance, he began the semester with media advertising, short essays, and stories, ending the semester with novels. The class began by charting single and obvious issues of injustice to complex, mutually reinforcing, and dynamic forms of oppression (i.e., race, class, and gender issues). While some may assume that a Marxist would only focus upon economic issues, Richard's priorities mirrored those of many post-Althusserian and post-Marxist theorists (e.g., Barrett, 1988; Bennett, 1990; Hartsock, 1990) who analyze the multiple, interlocking systems of oppression constituting the cultural arena.

Within this novel framework, he typically initiated students into this particular community of readers, or "reading formation" (Bennett, 1983, p. 3), via a consideration of gender issues rather than class struggle. Class oppressions were "not as visible" as gender biases to his students, Richard explained, and race issues, while "visible," were all the more elusive a topic of inquiry because of the state's demographics (96 percent white). A predominately white institution in a predominately white state, most students knew few people of color so they "didn't have a personal relationship to issues of race." However, as Richard maintained, many students would "immediately relate" to gender inequities through their lived experiences. Women could invoke their personal experiences and men could critique their experiences as boyfriends, fathers, and brothers. In addition, when we consider that 10 percent of the population is gay, lesbian, bisexual, or transgender (GLBT), and that GLBT young adults experience higher suicide and depression rates than heterosexual young adults, and that they are more often the victims of school violence, gender issues become even more pressing to discuss in the literature classroom (Daniel and McEntire, 1999; Day, 2000).

Ideological Critique in the Classroom: What Counts as Knowing Literature, Culture, and Social Justice?

The segment of discussion featured in this section illuminates several key patterns characteristic of the first half of the semester's discussions: (1) students identified and explored competing ideologies and generated counterhegemonic perspectives, producing knowledge of media, culture, and history as well as texts; and (2) Richard activated a repertoire of strategies to engage students in ideological critique and cultural criticism. These included (a) inviting students to juxtapose "the facts" or empirical data with prevailing myths; (b) inviting students to unpack the interests at stake with "Why" questions; and (c) inviting students to turn to culture, rather than exclusively to the text, as "evidence" to support and illustrate assertions.

To suggest the dynamics of the discussions conducted in the early part of the course, the following excerpt begins with Greg, a white, outspoken, middle-aged student, who turned the class's attention to the following excerpt from *Out of Focus* (Davies et al., 1987, p. 98), offering a critique of the *Oxford English Dictionary*:

> Its definition of the verb "to beat" is truly unbelievable (or is it) in these supposedly enlightened days: "to beat—to strike repeatedly, as in to beat one's wife." Not only does this show the presumed sex of the reader (at least one half of the population does not have a wife), but it also clearly demonstrates that beating "one's" woman is an acceptable way for men to behave. Would it not otherwise have been struck from the "thinking man's bible"?

> Greg: On page 98 talking about wife beating, "not only does that show the presumed sex of the reader, but it clearly demonstrates that beating one's wife is an acceptable way for men to behave." I can't draw that conclusion from what's found in the dictionary.

> Richard: Why would they put that in the dictionary? It makes it very commonplace.

As in beating one's wife. Like it happens all the time, right? And the dictionary is supposed to be the definitive meaning of the word.

John: The author sends subtle unconscious messages which shape our attitudes.

Jack: But a dictionary isn't the place where you make comments.

Greg: I sort of find it degrading women, but some people do beat their wives, and it does explain the word "beat." Striking repeatedly. But as I see it, they're putting the word "beat" in a certain context, and I don't think they should have used it. But at the same time I don't necessarily think it is a statement that it's okay to beat your wife.

Linda: By being in the dictionary it's something that people look at every day; they are stating that it's commonplace. You open a dictionary every day. If you read "beating one's wife," it may seem that that's what happens.

Todd: It's kind of, I guess to add on to this, I was looking in my friend's room the other day and on his bulletin board, Charles Barkley, the MBA Basketball player—I guess he was losing a game and was talking to a reporter and said, "Yeah, this is the kind of game that after you're done with it you go home and beat your wife." Did you notice how in the end she was cheering and he was—the newspaper person was like, do you want me to just quote you on that or do you want it off the record. He said, "No just quote me on that." That's kind of glamorizing. That it's okay. Some little boy might think, Charles Barkley is my hero, my idol, after a game you just go beat your wife. This kid will grow up and think that's okay.

Jay: Going back to the dictionary thing, when I read that I can see how that could be degrading women, all because of the word "wife," but to assume that wives get beaten is just as degrading to the male attitude I think . . . It's just assuming that wives get beaten and that men are doing it. How do males come out on top on that one? I'd say it's almost equal. It makes us look terrible for being beaters and the women for being frail and getting beaten.

Richard: Why does it happen? It's domestic violence. That means beating one's wife. They have shelters all over every city for women who leave their husbands from beating. That's the leading health threat to women. Why does that happen?

Tammy: When you're little you don't hear them say to a little girl, "You're not supposed to hit little boys." But it comes to that; little boys aren't supposed to hit girls, but they play with GI Joes and stuff. So the whole thing is that they get those messages when they're little, from basketball players or cartoon characters, who are mostly male. A kid is too little to say, "Yeah, but that's not the way real life is." That's the point of the cartoon character. It is directed toward little kids, and that's the way life goes on.

Jim: When we look in the dictionary, what you see is what you believe. That's what you're taught. I think that what they're trying to say in this one quote is that something like that in there almost condones it. Like it's okay. Like a message if you're male it's something that is done or is okay to be done. It's tied in with a definition. It's just a message. But it's there.

This dialogue reveals several of the distinguishing features of social justice inquiry in Richard's classroom. First, Richard chose texts that both demonstrate and spark ideological critique. In this case, he focused on an assigned reading that features an ideological critique of a dictionary definition. He provided an explicit model of ideological critique and counterhegemonic perspectives, thereby offering a scaffold so that students could learn to generate hegemonic and counterhegemonic perspectives.

Second, in this and most discussions, participants registered a multiplicity of perspectives on this and every issue. When Greg challenged the argument made in the readings—that language itself is never innocent and is always a site for ideological critique—he took a stand that can be said to reproduce rather than to challenge the status quo (i.e., that dictionary definitions are "given" or "true"). At the same time, Linda and others challenged his interpretation, claiming counterhegemonic stances that offered varying degrees of opposition to Greg's.

Indeed, this discussion suggests that students do consider the polyphony of viewpoints, and in so doing, fostered counterhegemonic perspectives, including social justice perspectives. Greg's comments suggested that he has been affected by the viewpoints of others. Although he did not wholeheartedly support the view that the *OED* is misogynistic, he eventually conceded that the definition is "degrading women."

Third, this conversation excerpt also illustrates the kinds of knowledge about literature, culture, and social justice that students produced in Richard's class. It emphasized students' experiences and personal knowledge of media figures, and pop culture. Students mentioned, for instance, cartoons, ads, and famous athletes. Students not only brought them up as examples to illustrate assertions but they also interrogated them for competing ideologies, unpacking "the messages being sold to us." Thus, pop culture functioned as a text and as a site for ideological critique.

Equally important, this discussion illustrated the role of formalist analysis and close reading in the first half of the course. In the first half of the course little attention is paid to these ways of knowing literature. For instance, a citation from the text served as a springboard for this discussion episode, but the discussion immediately shifted from text to culture. "Support" for assertions was not drawn from textual details but was garnered from pop culture and media. This pattern offers a countervailing example to the text-centered patterns documented in the research on literature classrooms and simultaneously suggests new possibilities for literary education that enacts and promotes social justice.

In terms of the role of the teacher, Richard's strategic interventions worked in important ways: (1) to open a space for counterhegemonic views he posed "why" questions to point to the constructed nature of the dictionary; and (2) to encourage students to consider how and why misogyny became "naturalized," as Marxists and others in cultural studies say. He also relied upon "why" questions when he situated the definition against "the facts," or statistics that suggest "one in four women have been raped." In addition, in his last turn Richard resisted closure and did not attempt to reduce the discussion by offering simple solutions to complex problems. As the next section suggests, these patterns shifted as the semester progressed, raising questions about what counts as knowledge in the literature class, and about what it means to enact and to promote social justice.

What Counts as Knowledge: The Function of Close Reading in Richard's Class

As the research on literary education suggests, close reading is a staple of classroom literary inquiry. Close reading is used frequently by literature teachers, often to generate knowledge about the characters, plot, or theme—all in service of understanding the formal features of the text. Close reading of any kind was rare in the first half of Richard's class, but became more important in the second half when students read more complex texts.

What is significant about close reading in Richard's class is that the kinds of knowledge that close reading produced were not about genres and textual conventions, but about the text's social formation. He asked students to situate particular passages within and against other discourses written about that society. Illustrating how close reading worked in service of social justice inquiry, the following excerpt features Richard and his students discussing characters in *The Great Gatsby* (Fitzgerald, 1925/1992), considered by many to be a "classic" American novel because it so effectively portrayed society in the United States during the 1920s:

Richard: What else in the first three chapters: Other ways that Tom is depicted or how Daisy and Jordan are shown? How does society show them?

Matt: Tom sets himself up as superior.

Richard: Where is this?

Matt: Page seven at the bottom.

Richard: This is a place that should have a number of asterisks. Because these are very important. Fitzgerald chooses to give Tom these lines, right? It shows where Tom is coming from. Where his superiority is rooted. (Reads text:) "Civilization's going to pieces," broke out Tom violently. I've gotten to be a terrible pessimist about things. Have you read *The Rise of the Coloured Empires* by this man Goddard?

"Well, no," I answered, rather surprised by his tone.

"Well, it's a fine book, and everybody ought to read it. The idea is if we don't look out the white race will be—will be utterly submerged. It's all scientific stuff; it's been proved."

"Tom's getting very profound," said Daisy with an expression of unthoughtful sadness. "He reads deep books with long words in them. What was the word we—"

"Well, these books are all scientific," insisted Tom, glancing at her impatiently. "This fellow has worked out the whole thing. It's up to us who are the dominant race to watch out or these other races will have control of things." (p. 17)

After reading the text verbatim, Richard says,

"Racism. That's all it is. That's why these late eighteenth century books, early nineteenthcentury, were written, to legitimize slavery. You can find, if you go back, supposed biologists, doctors writing long books proving the white race had bigger brains, therefore is superior. Now it seems ridiculous, but at the time it was scientific proof . . . What does this tell us? Does it tell us anything about the upper class? What's he really scared of? We talked about what racism is based on. It's not just a kind of fear. Does it tell anything about the ideology that the upper class has? How it functions?"

This transcript illuminates several key patterns of discussion. The episode begins with the close reading of the text. Richard opens the episode by inviting students to analyze the main characters. When one student volunteers a character (Tom) and a trait ("superior"), Richard asks the student to cite evidence from the text to support her analysis. These patterns resonate with those found in the research on literature classrooms, so at first glance Richard's approach seems only too familiar.

However, as important as it is to examine the ways Richard constructed the content of his turns, it is also important to notice what Richard did not do and why. To put this in the context of research on literary education, episodes in the research frequently focus upon the traits of the main characters, as Richard has done here. However, these discussions feature episodes that analyze one key trait and then another, with the goal of understanding each of the main characters and how their interactions illuminate the conflict, plot, motifs, and themes of the art. If we look at Richard's questions that follow, however, it becomes clear that close reading serves other purposes:

> What does this tell us? Does it tell us anything about the upper class? What's he really scared of? We talked about what racism is based on. It's not just a kind of fear. Does it tell anything about the ideology that the upper class has? How it functions?

Rather than performing uptake, that is, generating additional probing questions, asking for other traits and textual support, he linked the character to history and culture. With these questions Richard encouraged students to see Tom's character traits not as individual elements or motifs but as signifiers of ideology—how Tom enacts particular beliefs and interests of the upper class. Richard thus consciously oriented students to the ways in which "the cultural resonates in the particular" (Joan Pong Linton, personal communication, June 10, 2002).

Visible in this discussion excerpt is another key move that Richard made in discussion of the longer works that carried on the work he did with the shorter texts. That is, Richard periodically reminded students that the text is not a transparent window onto reality, but is an artifice carefully fashioned by an author. For instance, in this discussion he said, "This is a place that should have a number of asterisks. Because these are very important. Fitzgerald chooses to give Tom these lines, right?" After this episode, Richard reiterated: "How else does Fitzgerald allow us to see Tom?" These questions prompted students to view texts as constructed and language as constitutive of society. In so doing, Richard reinforced the view that language not only mediated but also shaped our understanding of what counts as "real" and as "truth." With such questions he invited ideological critique and encouraged counterhegemonic perspectives, thereby contributing to social justice inquiry.

Richard's curricular design raises questions about what counts as "knowing" literature and culture, and how such knowing can contribute to larger movements for social change: Does ideological critique of a text's social formation necessarily motivate, inform, or enrich students' commitments to social justice in contemporary society? By extension, does "reading the word" actually "translate" into "reading the world," to use Freire and Macedo's (1987) terms? Do those reading practices channel into social action within and beyond the classroom doors? And by extension, does such work produce socially responsible citizens acting for justice? I think it is as important to question even as we applaud Richard, ourselves, and other teachers working for social justice, and, in doing so, to acknowledge the limits of social justice pedagogies. That is, despite all the wonderful work that Richard and his students have done, the question still remains: Is this pedagogy transforming teachers and learners? The culture?

While there is no easy, direct translation from "word" to "world," it is clear that literature teachers such as Richard give us hope that classrooms can be the site of work for social justice, that teachers can and do make a difference in helping students to develop new ways of seeing texts and cultures. Engaging in cultural criticism of textual and actual worlds, exploring the cultural through the particular, students and teachers can realize the power and possibility of literary education to contribute to the community, to connect with larger movements for social justice. These goals make literary inquiry richer and more relevant to students and teachers living in a multicultural society. Richard invites us to think about what it means to be a teacher, not only in the classroom, but also in the culture—challenging not only the "givens" of literary education, but also the "givens" of society.

References

Althusser, L. (1969/1990). *For Marx* (B. Brewster, Trans.). New York: Verso.

Althusser, L. (1977). Ideology and ideological state apparatuses. In L. Althusser (Ed.), *Lenin and philosophy and other essays* (pp. 127–186) (B. Brewster, Trans.). London: New Left Books.

Althusser, L. (1990). *Philosophy and the spontaneous philosophy of scientists and other essays.* (B. Brewster Trans). New York: Verso.

Angus, I., and Jhally, S. (Eds.). (1989).*Cultural politics in contemporary America*. New York: Routledge.

Aronowitz, S., and Giroux, H. (1991). *Postmodern education: Politics, culture, and social criticism*. Minneapolis: University of Minnesota Press.

Barrett, M. (1988). *Women's oppression today*. London: Verso.

Belsey, C. (1980). *Critical practice*. New York: Methuen.

Bennett, T. (1979). *Formalism and Marxism*. London: Methuen.

Bennett, T. (1983). Texts, readers, reading formations. *MMLA Bulletin, 16*(1), 3–17.

Bennett, T. (1990). *Outside literature*. London: Routledge.

Boyle-Baise, L.(2002). *A journey toward shared control: Community service learning for multicultural education*. New York: Teachers College Press.

Daniel, P., and McEntire, V. (1999). Rights of passage: Preparing gay and lesbian youth for their journey into adulthood. In J. Kaywell (Ed.), *Using literature to help troubled teenagers cope with family issues* (pp. 193–224). Westport, CT: Greenwood.

Davies, K., Dickey, J., and Stratford, T. (Eds.). (1987).*Out of focus: Writings on women and the media*. London: Women's Press.

Day, F. (2000). *Lesbian and gay voices: An annotated bibliography and guide to literature for children and young adults*. Westport, CT: Greenwood.

Delpit, L. (1995). *Other people's children: Cultural conflict in the classroom*. New York: The New Press.

Delpit, L., and Dowdy, J. (2002). *The skin that we speak: Thoughts on language and culture in the classroom.* New York: New Press.

During, S. (Ed.). (1993). *The cultural studies reader*. New York: Routledge.

Eagleton, T. (1976). *Criticism and ideology: A study in Marxist literary theory*. London: Verso.

Edelsky, C. (Ed.). (1999). *Making justice our project: Teachers working toward critical whole language practice*. New York: Teachers College Press.

Fitzgerald, F. (1925/1992). *The great Gatsby*. New York: Collier.

Freire, P., and Macedo, D. (1987). *Literacy: Reading the word and the world*. South Hadley, MA: Bergin and Garvey.

Giroux, H. (1983). *Theory and resistance in education*. South Hadley, MA: Bergin & Garvey.

Giroux, H., and Shannon, P. (Eds.). (1997). *Education and cultural studies: Toward a performative practice*. New York: Routledge.

Goebel, B., and Hall, J. (Eds.). (1996). *Teaching a new canon? Students, teachers and texts in the college literature classroom*. Urbana, IL: National Council of Teachers of English.

Hartsock, N. (1990). Foucault on power: A theory for women? In L. Nicholson (Ed.), *Feminism/postmodernism* (pp. 157–175). New York: Routledge.

Hennessy, R., and Ingraham, C. (Eds.). (1997). *Materialist feminism: A reader in class, difference, and women's lives*. New York: Routledge.

Hynds, S. (1997). *On the brink: Negotiating literature and life with adolescents*. New York: Teachers College Press.

Moller, K. (2002). Providing support for dialogue in literature discussions about social justice. *Language Arts*, *74*(6), 26–36.

Morton, D., and Zavarzadeh, M. (Eds). (1991). *Theory/Pedagogy/Politics: Texts for Change*. Urbana, IL: University of Illinois Press.

Oliver, E. (1994). *Crossing the mainstream: Multicultural perspectives in teaching literature*. Urbana, IL: National Council of Teachers of English.

Orner, M. (1992). Interrupting the calls for student voice in "liberatory" education: A feminist poststructuralist perspective. In C. Luke and J. Gore (Eds.), *Feminisms and critical pedagogy* (pp. 74–89). New York: Routledge.

Pratt, M.L. (1996). Daring to Dream: New Visions of Culture and Citizenship. In J. Slevin and A. Young (Eds.), *Critical theory and the teaching of literature: Politics, curriculum, pedagogy* (pp. 3–20). Urbana, IL: National Council of Teachers of English.

Roman, L. (1993). White is a color! White defensiveness, postmodernism, and anti-racist pedagogy. In C. McCarthy and W. Crackle (Eds.), *Race, identity, and representation in education* (pp. 71–88). New York: Routledge.

Sleeter, C. (1993). How white teachers construct race. In C. McCarthy and W. Crackle (Eds.), *Race, identity, and representation in education* (pp. 157–171). New York: Routledge.

Slevin, J., and Young, A. (1996). *Critical theory and the teaching of literature: Politics, curriculum, pedagogy*. Urbana, IL: National Council of Teachers of English.

Villanueva, V. (1993). *Bootstraps: From an American academic of color*. Urbana, IL: National Council of Teachers of English.

Young, A. (2001). *Postcolonialism: An historical introduction*. Malden, MA: Blackwell.

Teaching Story

Anti-Oppressive Pedagogy and Curriculum in Secondary English Methods

Focusing on Critical Literacy

JOCELYN ANNE GLAZIER

This chapter describes an approach I have taken in a secondary English methods course to support students' learning about anti-oppressive and socially just teaching.

Students in my *Recent Developments in the Teaching of English* course have completed at least a semester's worth of student teaching and, occasionally, are immersed in their first year of teaching. At this point, students have finished nearly all of their program coursework. This is the second of two methods courses these students take at the university, the first having been taken early in their academic careers. It is at this juncture in their program when I ask my students to take an important step back, to see what they have done, where they have been, what they are teaching, why they are teaching it, and how the choices they are making are impacting the various students within their secondary classrooms. Essentially, I ask my students to deconstruct their own teaching as well as their curriculum. I ask them to deconstruct what they have learned primarily about literature and text more generally, leading many students to become "unsatisfied with what is being learned, said, and known" (Kumashiro, 2000, p. 43). I invite my students to assume an inquiry stance within the course, among other things "making problematic the current arrangements of schooling; the ways knowledge is constructed, evaluated, and used; and teachers' individual and collective roles in bringing about change" (Cochran-Smith and Lytle, 2001, p. 50).

The focus of the one-semester course is critical literacy; we immerse ourselves in its exploration. Despite their backgrounds in literature and/or writing, the students often have little knowledge of and practice in critical literacy. They have rarely thought about the notion that "every novel has silences and every novel privileges certain ideologies over others; every novel, in other words, provides only a partial perspective" (Kumashiro, 2000, p. 34). I choose not to give students a specific and rigid definition of critical literacy, rather I ask them to create it themselves from the course readings. However, I do start them in their definition building by providing them with a model of the type of work they will be involved in during the semester. On the syllabus, I explain to my students that they will be asked, among other things, to do the following during the course:

1. Examine your stance/position and identify its influence on student learning through the use of autobiographical reflections and readings;
2. Explore traditional and alternative definitions of literacy through both identifying personal definitions of literacy and illiteracy and interrogating the definitions of others including peers and published authors;
3. Develop an understanding of critical literacy through readings including those by Paulo Friere, Linda Christensen, Barbara Comber, and Henry Giroux;
4. Reflect on your experience in school settings to determine both what is being taught—and how—and what could be taught—and how—in middle and secondary school settings by examining such things as curriculum models in current school settings and pedagogical examples used by critical educators (e.g., Linda Christensen, Bill Bigelow, and Tom Gaughan);
5. Examine the relationship between critical literacy and national and local standards for the English Language Arts by revisiting the NCTE standards and applying them to your own unit;
6. Strengthen skills related to creating integrated units of study that appropriately address the needs of all students and incorporate multiple and critical literacies through collaborative unit planning.

Each of these points is representative to an extent of the ways I am defining critical literacy. My current perspective builds on a definition by Shor (1999): Critical literacy

> Involves questioning received knowledge [from text] and immediate experience with the goal of [disrupting grand narratives], challenging [stereotypes] and inequality and developing an activist citizenry. (p. 8)

However, as I tell my students, my definition continues to evolve as I pursue this work in both my teaching and my research.

Why Critical Literacy?

Given the amount of time my students spend with text—reading it alone and with their students, teaching it, and talking about it—asking them to critically analyze both texts and their approaches to the texts seems to me like an appropriate way to prompt students to think about possibilities of anti-oppressive pedagogy in their secondary English classrooms. Whereas wrapping one's head and mind around anti-oppressive education can feel like a daunting task, particularly when we erroneously assume it comes in one form, requiring an intensive and exhaustive look at the world, exploring critical literacy strikes me as a manageable and necessary means to that end, particularly in an English classroom. Like anti-oppressive education, which explores the political and oppressive nature of schools and institutions more generally, critical literacy focuses on the same with regard to literacy and text. Indeed critical literacy may be perceived as nestled within the larger framework of anti-oppressive education. Critical literacy essentially asks one first to understand how it is that texts perpetuate systems of oppression and suppression (Comber, 1999; Lankshear and Knobel, 1998; Luke, 2000).

Course Design

One of my objectives in the course is to help my students "learn to read texts in multiple and anti-oppressive ways" so that they can do the same with their own students (Kumashiro, 2001, p. 7). To that end, the course is focused on the notion of critical questions (Simpson, 1996). We begin the semester interrogating notions of literacy: *What is it? How does school shape it? What is "in-school" literacy? What is "out of school" literacy? What does not count as literacy in school and why? What forms of literacy are valued and why? What could count as literacy in school? Should we teach/value multiple literacies/multiple discourses in school? Why or why not?* These questions are important ones to allow students to begin to reflect on the narrow vision of literacy we tend to privilege in school, a vision that validates the language of some, invalidates the languages—and with that the experiences and cultures—of others.

Course readings focus in particular on notions of multiple literacies allowing students to begin to envision possibilities other than those traditionally perpetuated in school settings where only one literacy, the Secondary Discourse—a Standard English—(Gee, 1989) is valued (Gallego and Hollingsworth, 1999). I begin this exploration with students by asking them to do an inquiry around literacy, first writing about their own definitions of literacy and illiteracy and then looking to community definitions of the same, conducting informal interviews with members of the local university community.

We then examine what literacies are taught in school by engaging in a brainstorming session. Comparatively, we focus on individual students we have had and imagine their literacies outside of school: *What are they reading? What are they speaking? Do these overlap with in-school literacies? If not, why not? And, finally, if there is no overlap between a student's school and home literacy, how might that affect a student's performance in and outlook on school?* Class discussions often result in my students experiencing a number of "aha" moments as they reflect on students they have had in class whose failure, they now realize, may be linked to this disjuncture between home and school literacy.

Next we move to a focused exploration of critical literacy: What is it? What does it look like? To help my students arrive at a collective definition, we read works by authors and thinkers including Barbara Comber (1999), Alan Luke (2000), Peter McLaren (1998), Linda Christensen (2000), Paulo Freire (Freire, 1970, 1998; Freire and Macedo, 1987), and others. Simultaneously, we engage in active exploration and interrogation of texts, using literature where messages are explicit and those in which the message is more implicit (e.g., the short story "Girl" by Jamaica Kincaid [1987], excerpts from Maya Angelou's *I Know Why the Caged Bird Sings* [1969], and the children's book *Babar* by Jean de Brunhoff [1933]). We interrogate the literature, asking such questions as *Who is the author (or what do we think we know about the author)? Who is the (intended) audience? What are the messages? How are they carried?* These questions prompt students to unpack texts and interrogate the possibility of the intentional construction of texts, that texts are purposefully written and far from neutral. Conversations around texts take multiple forms, from students sharing and exploring a single text to our investigation of a text as a whole class. Simultaneously, students are beginning to choose and read literature that they believe may allow for different voices to be expressed in the classroom context, acknowledging the limitations of single texts and single voices. Later in the semester, we critically explore their choice of texts, identifying the silences still maintained in and through these texts.

As students come to understand notions of critical literacy, I ask them too to explore their own role in oppression and/or empowerment: *How do their choices and actions impact a student's experience in the English classroom? How might their language be positioning students in particular ways? Or how might their own position—as raced, classed, gendered, among others—be impacting what and how they see and teach?* I ask my students to view themselves, in part, as texts, thus critically reading themselves. After all, "Theoretical assumptions [histories] and ideologies shape the decisions that affect how and what we teach in English classrooms and, in turn, how our students come to understand and use literacy in their lives" (Yagelski, 1999, p. 11). They engage in this process by journaling on their own and dialoguing with their teacher colleagues. And they begin to raise these questions with one another as the course evolves, particularly as they engage in developing collaborative unit plans. Indeed this self-exploration is challenging and students leave the semester having only just begun this self-interrogation.

The final aspect of the course involves students in actively creating curriculum and pedagogy that is anti-oppressive. This course component is critical given the "uncertainties of what critical literacy looks like in classrooms" (Lewison et al., 2002, p. 390). I believe it would be irresponsible of me not to allow my students to "act on their knowledge" (Christensen, 1999, p. 212), something I would expect them to do with their own secondary students.

Practical Applications

Once my students have come to understand the partialities of texts as well as the limitations of their own teaching given their histories and identities, how do they move to enacting anti-oppressive pedagogy, particularly in traditional school settings that continue to be "contested sites where power struggles are played out" (Cochran-Smith, 1999, p. 117)? In an effort to help my students move theory to practice and ultimately transform school structures, I ask them to collaboratively construct unit plans, a traditional technique used in this case toward a more progressive end. Of course I remind students that "lesson plans need space for the unpredictable and uncontrollable things that always get in the way of knowing our students and achieving our objectives" (Kumashiro, 2000, p. 10); thus what they construct will have to be modified considerably depending on students and context. Furthermore, I encourage them to think of the unit plan as part of a larger curriculum framework. Otherwise, anti-oppressive pedagogy exists simply and potentially ineffectively as an "add-on" similar to the less critical multicultural approaches employed in many classrooms. Finally, realizing the constant discussion of standards in the school districts surrounding the university and the requirements my students have to meet these standards, I ask my students to envision how this work speaks specifically to the NCTE/IRA English Language Arts Standards.

Analysis of students' unit plans consistently reveals that they have developed an inquiry stance and have essentially made critical literacy their "own," employing language of "critique and hope" (Lewison et al., 2002; Freire and Macedo, 1987) as they reflect both on where they have been and where they want to go with their own students. In a final course text, one student group wrote: "Critical literacy is an approach to the curriculum that fosters (1) Study in which the students view texts as biased by social, political, and cultural contexts and forces; (2) Exploration of texts and underlying ideas that lead to (self)reflection on students' own values and viewpoints and where they originated; and (3) Student involvement and social action based upon students' analysis, synthesis, reflection, and anticipation of needed social change." Moving from "critical thought to critical practice" (McLaren, 1998, p. 52), these preservice teachers applied their definition to their pedagogy and curriculum, beginning by identifying literary texts to be used in a unit that they said "reflected immigrants' experiences in America" and would allow "students into reflection and analysis of the issues surrounding acculturation and 'becoming American.'"

In an attempt to bring their own secondary students into the critical literacy fold, this group began their unit "with reading, questioning and mining the various [unit] texts for interpretations and critique. We will focus on literary structure and literal meaning as well as social contexts and authorial intent." The preservice teachers here are conscious that before "reading the world" (Freire and Macedo, 1987), their students need to be able to read the word. The teachers then described their intentions to involve their students in exploring their own life stories; essentially inviting the students to insert themselves into the curriculum and, ultimately, the larger conversation as the students would then publish their autobiographical reflections on a class website. Critical literacy brings students' voices, and students' lives to the front and center, introducing students to multiple texts, multiple stories, and including their own and those of their peers. The preservice teachers noted the opportunity for their students to do this using multiple and home literacies or discourses (Gee, 1989). At the end of the unit, the secondary students would be involved in a social outreach project, thus allowing the students to "act on their knowledge" (Christensen, 1999, p. 212). Examples included creating a guide for ESOL (English for Speakers of Other Languages or English as a Second or Other Language) students at the school and/or a letter writing campaign to address policymakers about issues of immigration. Another project the group identified was an archive of oral histories from the students' communities, ultimately allowing students opportunities to "recover their own voices so that they [could] retell their own histories" (Giroux, 1988, p. 68).

Another group of preservice teachers in the course discussed in their unit plan the "common tendency among English teachers . . . to simply teach their interpretation of the text. . . . We believe that critical literacy challenges both the teacher and the students to look at not only what is in the text but why it is there." These teachers focused in particular on helping their own students realize the partiality of text: "Literature is simply a VERSION of life that is oftentimes offered as political aims and based on cultural assumptions." These teachers described further,

It is not enough to realize and talk about the political agendas and "power relationships" but critical literacy requires students to DO something about it. . . . Our students must learn that they are not "clean slates" on which vast amounts of knowledge can be "written into" them without their input. No, they are thinking beings who can analyze what is given to them, ask critical questions of it, and come up with their own opinions. Once these opinions are formed, it is not enough to say "I disagree," but "What am I going to do about it?"

These teachers summarized with

We believe that to be "literate" means that you understand the "what" of text, but to be "critically literate" means that you also understand the "why". The text is not something that is just created, but it evolves from the political and social assumptions of the author. It is up to us as readers (and teachers) to ask critical questions of the text to determine why it was written that goes beyond its theme. Once we have students who can truly analyze the texts they are given, use the text as a way to determine where they fit into the larger society, and be inspired to effect change in society, then we have truly created critically literate students.

Conclusion and Limitations

I believe that anti-oppressive teaching in the English Language Arts requires critical literacy as a starting point, leading ultimately to the creation of new texts, new discourses, and new actions. I hope my students leave the methods class realizing how to support their own secondary students' understandings of how literacy can help them "make sense of and negotiate—and change—[the] world" (Yagelski, 1999, p. 3). Therein lies a limitation of my work. I do not have—nay, I do not make—the opportunity to follow my students into their classrooms to support their "walking the walk," in school contexts that too often try to constrain this sort of work. I have no evidence, other than anecdotal, of whether or not my students practiced critical literacy and anti-oppressive pedagogy in their own classrooms, in their own schools. Will my students of teaching participate in and challenge the discourses that surround them? Will they begin new conversations? I must be more vigilant in finding ways to continue to support my students as they enter the teaching field, prepared to change the world. Until I do, my work remains partial and unfinished: there is much yet to be done.

References

Angelou, M. (1969). *I know why the caged bird sings.* New York: Random House.

Christensen, L. (1999). Critical literacy: Teaching, reading, writing, and outrage. In C. Edelsky (Ed.), *Making justice our project.* (pp. 209–225). Urbana, IL: NCTE.

Cochran-Smith, M. (1999). Learning to teach for social justice. In G. Griffen (Ed.), *The education of teachers.* (pp. 114–144). Chicago: University of Chicago Press.

Cochran-Smith, M., and Lytle, S. (2001). Beyond certainty: Taking an inquiry stance on practice. In A. Lieberman & L. Miller, *Teachers caught in the action: Professional development that matters* (pp. 45–58). New York: Teachers College Press.

Comber, B. (1999). *Critical literacies: Negotiating powerful and pleasurable curricula: How do we foster critical literacy through English language arts?* Paper presented at the Annual Conference of the National Council of Teachers of English, Denver, CO.

de Brunhoff, J. (1933). *The story of Babar the little elephant.* New York: Random House.

Freire, P. (1970). *Pedagogy of the oppressed.* New York: Continuum.

Freire, P. (1998). *Teachers as cultural workers: Letters to those who dare to teach.* Boulder, CO: Westview.

Freire, P., and Macedo, D. (1987). *Literacy: Reading the word and the world.* MA: Bergin & Garvey.

Gallego, M., and Hollingsworth, S. (Eds.). (1999). *What counts as literacy: Challenging the school standard.* New York: Teachers College Press.

Gee, J. (1989). What is literacy? *Journal of Education, 171*(1), 18–25.

Giroux, H. (1988). Literacy and the pedagogy of voice and political empowerment. *Educational Theory, 38*(1), 61–75.

Kincaid, J. (1987). Girl. In A. Charters (Ed.), *The story and its writer: An introduction to short fiction* (pp. 1190–1191). New York: St. Martin's Press.

Kumashiro, K. (2000). Toward a theory of anti-oppressive education. *Review of Educational Research, 70*(1), 25–53.

Kumashiro, K. (2001). "Posts" perspectives on anti-oppressive education in social studies, English, mathematics, and science classrooms. *Educational Researcher, 30*(3), 3–12.

Lankshear, C., and Knobel, M. (1998). *Critical literacy and new technologies.* Paper presented at the American Educational Research Association, San Diego, CA.

Lewison, M., Flint, A., and Van Sluys, K. (2002). Taking on critical literacy: The journey of newcomers and novices. *Language Arts, 79*(5), 382–392.

Luke, A. (2000). Critical literacy in Australia: A matter of context and standpoint. *Journal of Adolescent & Adult Literacy, 43*(5), 448–461.

McLaren, P. (1998). *Life in schools: An introduction to critical pedagogy in the foundations of education.* New York: Longman.

Shor, I. (1999). What is critical literacy? In I. Shor and C. Pari (Eds.) *Critical Literacy in Action,* 1–30. Portsmouth, NH: Heinemann Press.

Simpson, A. (1996). Critical questions: Whose questions? *The Reading Teacher, 50*(2), 118–127.

Yagelski, R. (1999). *Literacy matters: Writing and reading the social self.* New York: Teachers College Press.

Conversation

Learning to Read Critically

From High School to College to Teacher Education

JOCELYN ANNE GLAZIER, MARY BETH HINES, & CAROL RICKER-WILSON

Jocelyn: In reading the three chapters together, I was struck by the seeming subversive nature of the work we do and report. Although we wrote our pieces without conferring with one another, the three chapters share a set of images and metaphors that serve to name characteristics of that subversive work. For instance, "silence" is a term that appears regularly in your chapter, Carol, is evident in mine and is alluded to in yours Mary Beth. And it's that silence that we seem to want to give sight to—to break open. Even the images we use in our texts—the lenses you refer to Carol, and Mary Beth—your "ways of seeing"—and my attempt to have my students "focus"—suggest the importance we place on supporting the development of a different type of seeing: a seeing beneath that prompts an interrogation of text and of, as you describe Mary Beth, "signifying practices" that continue to privilege some over others.

I feel as though the work we do and report is similar to the work of archaeology: In essence, our efforts as teachers and teacher educators in support of socially just and anti-oppressive pedagogy is focused on supporting our students' and colleagues' "uncovering" that which remains too often hidden.

Carol: Your observations confirm for me that we're struggling with what critical theorists identify as the "hidden curriculum," Jocelyn. Giroux (1988, p. 5) defines the hidden curriculum as the unspoken messages and values students receive throughout the course of their schooling. Messages that come from the kinds of classroom interactions in which they're encouraged—or required—to engage, and from the inclusion—as well as exclusion—of particular types and forms of knowledge. Also from the infrastructural taken-for-granteds such as the way desks are arranged—all of schooling's habitual practices.

I'm also intrigued by your archaeology simile. A major concern in English education and for pedagogy in general is that between the academy's and a ministry or department of education's conceptualization and teachers' execution of curricular policies lie only several days' worth of professional development. Within a condensed schedule of implementation, curricular theory and the ideologies that inform it have a way of getting watered down or skimmed over to the point that its context is unapparent to those required to learn new methodology and/or a new set of content criteria for their subject. When a particular round of curriculum reform is introduced, teachers are rarely informed and supported in understanding how, say, critical practices collide with or contradict positivist practices. Thus a lot of what one can end up doing is contradictory. One set of practices and round of curriculum reform indeed settles like dust over earlier ones. This takes tremendous effort to uncover.

Mary Beth: Jocelyn and Carol, I like your thinking, and it inspires and challenges me to extend my own thinking. How can these ideas inform my work as a teacher educator committed to social justice? How can I help my preservice teachers to "focus," as Jocelyn says, using the "lenses" as Carol says, of anti-oppressive pedagogy so that they can teach their own middle and high school English/language arts students to "uncover" the hidden curricula?

Jocelyn: Right—these are key questions, questions to which we seem to have some similar responses. The efforts we describe at arriving at that uncovering are similar. All three examples center on using critical questions as a way to interrogate practices and texts. Richard raises questions, Carol—you raise questions, I raise questions and although all questions are not similar, they ask students to move beneath a surface understanding of text and, more broadly, society.

Mary Beth: I think, taken together, our chapters point to the importance of "reading" silence in discourses, especially in discussions of social issues and in classrooms invoking critical pedagogies. Across our chapters, we have concentrated on defining critical literacy in practice and in process. However, I wonder if we have simultaneously confined our definitions and constrained our understandings by focusing upon that which is spoken.

Jocelyn: Yeah—I agree. In many ways the texts we have written here explore the spoken, not the unspoken.

Mary Beth: Like both of you, I am motivated to explore the silences in Richard's classroom, seeking to understand how such silences work, and for whom, under what conditions. In my study I lacked a grid of intelligibility, a cartography of the competing, conflicting discourses of the "unsaid" (Macherey, 1978).

Jocelyn: Depending on who engages in the silence, it can be either power or powerlessness. Both concern me. For my primarily white, middle-class students, however, I think silence is what allows them to continue living a myth of meritocracy (McIntosh, 1988) and an oppressive reality ultimately.

Mary Beth: How might we begin to name other uses and types of silences marking classroom discourse?

Carol: I'm aware of secondary schools attended by predominantly white middle-class students whose parents complain when there's a departure from the focus on the canon in English courses. That's a very powerful form of silencing, making it quite difficult for the teachers who wish to introduce literature that contests dominant discourses to argue for change.

Jocelyn: Which is problematic given the powerful potential of literature to open voices.

Mary Beth: I take as a point of departure the work of Stephanie Carter (2001), who studied the ways in which two African American high school girls in a predominantly white British Literature class used silence to communicate with each other; to reaffirm their respective identities as young, African American women, surrounded as they were by white men and women, reading texts written by white males. While some researchers view silence as an absence, Carter sees silence as a repository of resources for critical meaning-making, and she has analyzed the rich, complex, and complicated meanings of the girls' silences. In so doing, she, in effect, gives voice to the silent focal students and makes visible their critical literacies. If we define critical literacy as the display of knowledge that involves analyzing power relations, invoking cultural criticism, or interrogating taken-for-granted patterns in society, then we must be able to recognize the ways in which silence works in and around such conversations, how it mediates and complicates "the meanings" of such demonstrations, how it embodies and advances "the meanings" that students attribute to their lived experiences. As a result, we, as teachers and researchers, can't afford to "perform ignorance," to invoke your chapter, Carol. This leads me to ask how we might decipher the varied codes impacted in classroom silences and how we might come to understand how those silences function. How do we learn to "read" those silences that ostensibly signal student engagement but that also might be designed to disrupt, to defer, and to denounce "the official" classroom discourses?

Carol: Karen Gallas (1998) has also thoughtfully examined how silence operates in her elementary school classrooms, particularly with reference to gender relations, in which women's silence is traditionally understood to signify passivity. I've learned a lot from Gallas about how one might read the nuances and complexities of silence as a significant form of manifesting power—or powerlessness—in difficult circumstances. Gallas argued that one young girl effectively "controlled the flow of spoken ideas by recognizing the mediating role of talk in the classroom, but not participating in it" (p. 52). Her silence alternately focussed attention on her and enabled her to become, at times, almost invisible in the fraught atmosphere of the classroom. Gallas also read the girl's silences as having a tone to them as well, manifested by her body language and gestures. Clearly, as you've noted, Mary Beth, reading silence depends so much on context and considering the multiple ways in which it might be used resistantly. It also calls for us to consider how we can encourage students to exercise their public voice, and under what circumstances this might be beneficial or—as significantly—detrimental to them.

On a different note, if I may, in my role as an English consultant to secondary teachers, it's significant to learn from you both the manner in which English teaching candidates are receiving opportunities to explore the complexities of critical literacy. And it is complex! I see English Education, as practiced in secondary schools throughout North America, as a patient—subject to multiple and conflicting discourses about what has value and what should be prioritized: skills or content—as though these are a la carte items rather than components of a package.

Thus, Mary Beth, I value your clear, accessible description of how, for Richard, Marxist theory becomes praxis, in which modeling reading strategies and providing support for reading serve an anti-oppressive agenda. Richard's work shows how teachers might marry strategies for reading better and more carefully with access to a resonant discourse for reading critically. This is very important for me, because I often hear teachers say that they have "no time" to think about how to change content if they're to teach "skills" and how they can't "cover" all the required curricular content. Your description of his work is helpful because it actually adds to my repertoire of critical reading strategies.

Jocelyn: And yet how does context impact what Richard is able to do? Does he feel the same constraints my students do as they set out to teach in secondary classrooms? Likely not.

Mary Beth: Definitely not—by a long shot.

Carol: He has more institutional freedom than they would in their venues. Your answer, Mary Beth, suggests that the actual venue in which Richard teaches would make it difficult for him to practice critical theory or invoke Marxism in the classroom. Of course your narrative is partial and subject to space considerations.

I understand you, Jocelyn, to also be concerned that I or other readers not assume that they can read Mary Beth's description of Richard's practice like a recipe that they can follow to succeed with their own students. Clearly the specific relational interactions in which Richard and each of his students are engaged are crucial to determining the "extraordinarily complicated conversation" (Pinar et al., 1995, p. 48) he can have with each of them—and the outcome. Your concern about context raises for me the problem of how to represent or describe critical practice. How to tell a critical tale? How might what we write be read and used? How does it offer potential for helping others engage in different sorts of practices? How might it be misused? In what way do we make critical theory and practice accessible to teachers and student teachers? And in what ways can we, without misrepresenting its frustrations, make critical practice attractive?

Jocelyn: That reminds me of something one of my students said this summer. I was teaching a course on literacy and we were exploring critical literacy in particular on this day. The student essentially said that the readings on critical literacy made him feel illiterate! And this from a graduate student who had been highly successful in the teacher education program.

Mary Beth: Your questions, Carol, are at the heart of another study I am doing with a group of excellent and wonderful English teachers, members of the Indiana English Teachers Collaborative, an organization of teacher-researchers conducting inquiry projects on issues of social justice. One of the findings of our study is that the teacher-researchers in our group define leadership as an ability to work within and against the system, what we refer to as "systems savvy." In other words, they know how to effectively navigate the educational systems and powers-that-be that shape their immediate circumstances, but they also know how to effectively disrupt those systems. But these teachers are all well-established in-service teachers. How do we teach preservice teachers to navigate in like manner?

Jocelyn: Right—the navigation within traditional and oftentimes oppressive systems, even if students leave us well grounded in critical literacy and/or social justice, is difficult at best.

Carol: Taking another slant on context, if we think of it as most generally, the evaluative educational milieu, in which both Richard and beginning school teachers possess symbolic and institutional capital, and this suggests that both must come to terms with the meaning of their own authority in their (ever transitory) classrooms. Thus I valued your observations, Mary Beth, of how Richard "had to perform as 'definitely an authority' when students did not 'naturally' see the ways in which the dominant groups shaped values and practices." Drawing on Brenda K. Marshall's (1992) understanding of a poststructuralist reader reception theory, Orner et al. (1995) perceive the relationship between teacher and students as one in which

the teacher takes control and manipulates the students into the position of taking responsibility for the meanings and knowledge they construct. . . . This paradox is not another version of: The teacher empowers students by giving up her authority. And it certainly is not: The teacher empowers the student by practicing reciprocal, dialogic relations that equalize power relations among teachers and students. This paradox exceeds these formulations; it cannot be contained by any of these resolutions. Yet it can be enacted. It can be performed in the classroom. (pp. 77–78)

If I understand this correctly, the writers have captured the fundamentally inequitable, highly improvisational, intrinsically fleeting nature of all pedagogical transactions. It does no one justice in compulsory education to pretend that authority is openly negotiable or can be unproblematically benign. Likewise it does no one justice to pretend that all opinions are of equal "value" in a democratic venue. The way in which one enacts pedagogical authority—and it is always an enactment, and innately unstable—the ways in which one might perform "control" is dependent on the actors and situation, requiring sensitivity to one's own and students' ever-changing desires and epistemic resistances. To manipulate students into taking responsibility for making meaning might in one circumstance require gentle nurturing. Subsequently it might require one to temporarily relinquish all "control" of classroom conversation. At another moment it might depend on refusal to "rescue" students from the cognitive cul de sacs in which they become entrapped. It might even mean demanding that certain students read a text against their will. But ultimately it depends, in diverse ways, on inviting students to examine the origins and implications of their own opinions. There is nothing innately empowering about this. On the contrary, it can lead to confusion, resistance, anger, and other responses indicative of epistemic and ontological crisis. At the end of the term, it is not likely that the teacher will have led the students out of their darkness into her or his light. This certainly makes a critical project challenging—faced with considerable constraints.

Jocelyn: And yet I wonder if that's what Richard tries to do in a sense—lead students into his light. Is that the goal? Should it be? I was struck by the control Richard seemed to assume in the classroom, control that in some ways is reflected in the words you just used Carol, to describe approaches educators may take. Words like manipulative, demanding, and inviting. Indeed, this is an imbalance of power. I agree, Carol, that teachers always remain in positions of authority—but how do we use those positions? I could not be Richard in my teacher education classroom—that wouldn't fly. And yet his explicitness of his position is something I think I could and should borrow, particularly if I want my own students to do the same for their students.

Carol: How do we use these positions—our teaching positions—most ethically? How do we do the least harm when new and counterhegemonic knowledge might be painful?

Mary Beth: Your point, Jocelyn, makes me wonder how we might extend our chapters so that they intersect with and are enlarged by recent research frequently referred to as the New Literacy Studies (Cowan, 2004; Hull and Schultz, 2002). These ethnographies emphasize power relationships and out-of-school literacies, especially as they stand in contrast to school-sanctioned literacies. While critical literacy and pedagogy focus upon the classroom, the New Literacy Studies focus upon practices in the community. These studies document the specific "funds of knowledge" that linguistically and culturally diverse groups gain in their respective homes and communities, and these studies frequently juxtapose these skills with the kinds of literacies expected in schools.

Carol: Yes! Reading about the New Literacy Studies has helped me recognize how I might invite students to bring their own literacy practices as well as reading interests and needs into class—especially their engagement with pop cultural texts. It's also made me aware of how little I know about multicultural literacy practices.

Mary Beth: Situating our chapters within and against the larger backdrop of the New Literacy Studies and larger movements for social change, I am left with more questions than answers. They include: (1) What does it mean to know and to practice knowledge of anti-oppressive education? (2) Can we, by studying classroom practices, know whether or not teaching with a critical literacy orientation has ultimately contributed to the formation of socially responsible citizens? (3) Can we ever know if and when our teaching has ultimately been transformed into students' social action for social justice? (4) Have we, in fact, changed the world by changing our teaching practices?

Carol: I found significant Jocelyn's comment that "she has no evidence, other than anecdotal, of whether or not [her] students practiced critical literacy and anti-oppressive pedagogy in their own classrooms." Thus I'd like to add three interrelated questions: (1) To what degree is it feasible or how might we gather data—and of what sort—on the efficacy of our work as critical practitioners? What does "efficacy" look like? For Ellsworth, the critical leads to more questions and uncertainties, to narratives of partiality, uncertainty. (2) Mary Beth's documentation on Richard's student teachers regarding the word "beat" shows that some are developing a counterhegemonic perspective, but not all. How might one assess—fairly—the quality of ideological critique—especially in a compulsory educational venue? How does one assess resistance to the counterhegemonic? (3) What kind of resistance was there to Richard's project and approach? What kind of resistances did you encounter, Jocelyn, from your students as your methodology called into question power arrangements?

Jocelyn: Indeed all of these questions are ones we need to continue to explore as we engage in this work. As I reflect on our reporting of the shattering of silences around issues such as gender and class, I can't help but wonder about the silences we enact as authors of these chapters. What is it we aren't including here and why? Mary Beth, how is your story similar to or different from Richard's? What role did you play in his classroom conversations? Carol, where is your voice in the conversation about Danielle Steel's book? And, for myself, how did my own discourse and actions disallow certain conversations from happening in my classroom? Seems we have lots to continue to think about collectively and individually.

References

Carter, S. (2001). *The possibilities of silence: Adolescent African-American female cultural identity and secondary English classrooms.* Unpublished dissertation, Vanderbilt University, Nashville, TN.

Cowan, P. (2004). Devils or angels: Literacy and discourse in lowrider culture. In J. Mahiri (Ed.), *What they don't learn in school* (pp. 47–74). New York: Peter Lang.

Gallas, K. (1998). *Sometimes I can be anything: Power, gender, and identity in a primary classroom.* New York: Teachers College Press.

Giroux, H. (1988). *Teachers as intellectuals: Toward a critical pedagogy of learning.* Granby, MA: Bergin and Garvey Publishers.

Hull, G., and Schultz, K. (2002). Schools out: Bridging out of school literacies with classroom practice. New York: Teachers College Press.

Macherey, P. (1978). *A theory of literacy production* (G. Wall, Trans.). New York: Routledge.

Marshall, B. K. (1992). *Teaching the postmodern: Fiction and theory.* New York: Routledge.

McIntosh, P. (1988). White privilege and male privilege: A personal account of coming to see correspondences through work in women's studies. Working Paper 189. Wellesley College Center for Research on Women, Wellesley, MA.

Orner, M., Miller, J. L., and Ellsworth, E. (1995, Fall). Excessive moments and educational discourses that try to contain them. *Educational Theory, 45*(4), 71–91.

Pinar, W., Reynolds, W., Slattery, P., and Taubman, P. (1995). *Understanding curriculum.* New York: Peter Lang.

Part IV

Addressing Resistance

Uncertainties in Learning to Teach

7

After the Soup

A Feminist Approach to Service Learning

RITA M. KISSEN

Introduction: Service Learning in Teacher Education

A 1998 survey of over 1,100 teacher education programs revealed that over 200 were currently integrating service learning into their curricula and another 175 were interested in learning more about doing so (Wade and O'Reilly, 1998). Rationales promoting community service as part of teacher education praise the opportunities it fosters for student reflection, for challenging assumptions, for applying knowledge to problem solving, and for increasing preservice teachers' sensitivities to their students' home communities (Anderson, 1998; Bok, 1982; Education Commission of the States, 2000; Erickson and Anderson, 1997; Swick et al., 1998; Wade and O'Reilly, 1998).

At its simplest, service learning can mean little more than serving dinner once a week at a soup kitchen or participating in a neighborhood cleanup on a Saturday morning. Students in these programs experience little contact with the recipients of their service and virtually no interaction with the communities they serve. Such community service suggests a "'missionary ideology' . . . a series of decisions intended to 'do good things' for others," and is oblivious to "what those others . . . might have to offer" (Weah et al., 2000, p. 675).

Recognizing that such experiences offer preservice teachers little to foster reflection or genuine connection with the lives of their students, some service learning advocates have looked beyond "volunteerism" to the ethic of care developed by Nel Noddings (1984, 1992), Sara Ruddick (1989), Carol Gilligan (1982), and others. Robert Rhoads (1997), for example, calls for service learning initiatives that help "restore the 'lost connection' which is at the heart of the demise of community" (p. 8). Others argue that service learning can reinforce the importance of caring in teaching (Swick, 1999), and "give students the sense that they live in the world, in a community" (Meyer, 1985, p. 20). Still others argue for "transformative" service learning (Kahne and Westheimer, 1996, p. 595), with a pedagogy connecting class, race, gender, and other oppressions (O'Grady, 2000). For example, Adams et al. (1997) propose a "multiple issues curriculum" that provides a more sustained and integrated learning experience than the "single issue" workshop or module (p. 261), while Swadener and Lubeck (1995) urge us to challenge the "otherness" of poor people (p. 265).

Service Learning and the TEAMS program: A Work in Progress

TEAMS (Teachers for Elementary and Middle Schools) is a four-and-a-half-year undergraduate program at the University of Southern Maine in which five cohorts of about twenty students each move through a series of academic and internship experiences based at the university and a group of partner schools. From the beginning, the program was designed as a cohort experience where students would work in the schools while pursuing an academic major and education courses, culminating in a full-fledged internship during the senior year. The first two years are built around a unifying theme: family and literacy during the first year, culture and community (C & C) during the second.

During their sophomore year, students take a thematic course, Culture and Community in American Life (C & C), which I team-teach with a Women's Studies colleague from the History Department. They also volunteer at several Portland agencies serving mostly poor and working-class white families with a sprinkling of refugees from Asia, Africa, and Europe.

Starting the Program: "Why Don't They Smile?"

During the 1999–2000 school year, the first year that the C & C cluster was offered, students spent 12 hours in elementary school classrooms and 12 hours at agencies that included a community center offering food, clothing, and other support services to poor and homeless people; the local branch of the Portland Public Library; and several after school programs and Head Start sites. Weekly seminars helped students process their feelings, but their journals revealed that we had not prepared them adequately for their experience. Some were overwhelmed by the sheer discovery that some people in Portland did not have enough to eat; others were embarrassed to wait in line at the soup kitchen or dismayed when their clients did not seem grateful. Acknowledging their own economic privilege often made students feel guilty, troubled, and confused all at the same time. As one student expressed:

> I smile at them all morning long and no one returns it. It's so disturbing. I know they appreciate what we are doing for them, but I almost feel resentment because I'm on one side of the food line, and they're on the other.

The following year, we revised the C & C course to focus more directly on the social, political, and historical contexts of community. As Women's Studies colleagues, my teaching partner and I bring feminism to all of our classes. Since women were the majority of our students, the majority of their school and community hosts, and the majority of the clients served by their host agencies, we wanted to make women's issues more visible in our course. Though our feminisms vary according to our disciplines (history and teacher education) and our temperaments (she leans more toward traditional labor politics, I am interested in the spiritual and the emotional as well as the material), we both view gender as a social construct, and agree that understanding what happens in schools and societies requires an understanding of the unequal power relationships between women and men.

To provide this social and historical context for our students, we began the second year of the course with four weeks of American history and a strong emphasis on women's roles in the United States and Maine. As a prelude, we showed *Hopi: Songs of the Fourth World*, a film portraying a community where art, ceremony, and work are intimately connected, and where the symbolic planting and growing cycle of corn represents a philosophy in balance with nature. Students shared our admiration for the Hopi, but we pointed out how a close-knit traditional community can limit women's choices. For while the Hopi women's creativity and wisdom were respected, they were expected to fulfill narrowly defined roles as wives and mothers.

Our basic history text was Howard Zinn's *A People's History of the United States* (1995), which presents American history through the eyes of the less powerful in American society and, in Zinn's words, highlights the "fierce conflicts of interest . . . between conquerors and conquered, masters and slaves, capitalists and workers, dominators and dominated in race and sex" (pp. 9–10). Although Zinn focuses more on class than on race or gender, his discussion of women's history fit with our feminist emphasis on power and powerlessness. We supplemented his discussion with such handouts as the Seneca Falls Declaration and an article my colleague had written on Irish women immigrants in Portland.

Students found Zinn difficult. For one thing, the book's sheer volume of information, most of it new to them, required more sustained time and effort than many of them were used to. In addition, Zinn's emphasis on what had been omitted from conventional history books shocked and troubled many. Some were angry because they did not like what they were learning. Others, remembering their elementary and high school teachers' upbeat, optimistic version of American history, wanted to know why they had not been told the truth.

Despite our students' discomfort with Zinn, we felt it was important for them to come to terms with the issues he raised, and we continued to raise them ourselves as the course progressed. We also continued our emphasis on women. Discussing *Grapes of Wrath*, we pointed out how Steinbeck's mythic portrayal essentialized women even as it celebrated the dignity and courage of Dust Bowl refugees. We paired *Grapes of Wrath* with *Salt of the Earth*, a classic 1953 portrayal of a strike in a New Mexico zinc mine. The film describes how, after an injunction barring the miners from picketing, their wives walk the picket line and help win the strike. The film also connects the personal and the political, as the newly empowered miners' wives begin to challenge the patriarchal structures of their marriages and family lives. *Salt of the Earth* was a universal favorite with our students, and it has remained so over the years. Despite the distance between these white working- and middle-class undergraduates and the oppressed Mexican American miners, students responded to the clear-cut depiction of heroes and villains, and to the narrator/heroine, Esperanza, luminously portrayed by the Mexican actress Rosaura Reveultas.

During the second year we also gave the students excerpts from Studs Terkel's *Working* (another big success, largely for its accessibility and anecdotal style) and *Wednesday's Child*, a memoir by local author Rhea Cote Robbins, who visited us and talked about her experiences of gender and class as a Franco-American woman in Maine.

The major writing assignment was an article about an actual community, which had to include at least one interview. We required the TEAMS students to interview a director or provider at their agency, focusing on relations with the larger community it served. Though they wrote sensitively about culture and community, they generally failed to take into account the nature of gender and power within social service agencies, despite our emphasis on women and women's history.

Listening to the Students: The Interviews

At the end of the semester, I interviewed 10 of the 15 students in the cohort, hoping to discover whether our emphasis on women had influenced their service learning experiences. The interviews took place informally, after a holiday party at my home. I began by asking about their initial assumptions, and whether these had changed.

I was not surprised to hear that this cohort of young, traditional-age students had entered the program with many stereotypes about poor people, but I was pleased and touched at their willingness to acknowledge these assumptions and to talk about how they had changed:

> The first day we were there we walked down to the playground and I noticed all the kids were not playing yet, and I was like, what's going on, and we had to check the playground for glass and needles and things that could harm the children. . . . I grew up with a huge yard, and . . . all they have is the playground, and then people are abusing it that way. And that really hit me hard.

> When I first arrived I was pretty shocked by the actual outside of the building [an afterschool center]. There were bars on the windows and really very few windows at that, and it was just this light green hexagonal building that just sat there in the middle of like a rusted park, and I was just like, oh, gee—I didn't know what to expect once I entered the door.

> I've come from a pretty rich part of a neighborhood where we don't have any children like this, no programs like this, and I expected parents that just didn't love their children, that didn't have enough money, to just kinda put them in a day care or on welfare. . . . But once I got there, you know, it's not that parents don't love their children, it's just that they were never taught parental skills that they need.

Students were forced to rethink their definitions of wealth and poverty, as one young woman, who worked at a family resource center, explained:

> Before I went there I figured these kids as being unprivileged [*sic*] children and once I went there I realized that just because they didn't have a lot of wealth it didn't mean that they were unprivileged at all. . . . Like every Monday night they have like a little free food party, and the guy, he's a baker, and he cooks pizza and he'll just bring free food over. And the firefighters are always having their house open so the kids can explore it, and Casco Bay Lines [the local ferry service] gives them free tickets so they can explore the islands, and they have really rich culture and really connected community.

They clearly connected their discoveries with their developing identities as teachers:

> I never realized how important it was to create community within your own classroom, and to create a safe haven where kids feel respected and loved, because I never realized that kids would not get that at home.

Students' comments also showed that they were beginning to relate the issues we had talked about in the Culture and Community course to their service learning experiences. One of our films, *Anchor of the Soul*, describes the life of Maine's small but vibrant African American community, and helped students understand the African American children they were meeting. As one student remarked:

> There were three African American students that were at [the family center], and all
> of them had practically the same pickup list and they all had about thirty people on it,
> because if their parents couldn't come, their neighbor could come, if their neighbor
> couldn't come, the guy down the street could, and they were all exactly the same. This
> shows how much trust that community has, and when we'd walk the children down to
> the playground, the kids would know everybody, they'd, "Oh, hi, so-and-so, hi, so-and-
> so," pet the dog, talk to the person across the street, everybody. . . . I don't know every-
> body even on my street. But they know everyone.

> It's almost like taking a vacation to somewhere you've never been before in a different
> country. It's just a different experience for you that you now know stuff about and you can
> use it, and you just feel like so much bigger after, like you've done something like that, I think.

Most significant from a feminist perspective, students began to develop an ethic
of care that some writers have placed at the heart of feminist pedagogy. Such an
ethic, writes Nel Noddings, "is rooted in receptivity, relatedness, and responsiveness"
(1984, p. 2), in which the carer must always "try to apprehend the reality of the
other" (p. 14). Noddings's later work explores the dimensions of caring in schools
and other social institutions (see, e.g., 1992, 2002), using the model of "the good
home" where basic human needs are met in an atmosphere of dignity and respect.
Noddings's emphasis on human relationships draws on the work of Carol Gilligan,
whose groundbreaking *In a Different Voice* (1982) contrasts women's relational
approach to morality with men's focus on judgment and rights.

Although neither Gilligan nor Noddings asserts that women are inherently
more caring than men (in fact, Noddings specifically refutes this view), the specter
of maternalism lurks behind the discussion of caring, for it is sometimes difficult
to separate the celebration of qualities that have been culturally bred in women from
a celebration of "women's nature." As Noddings says of Gilligan:

> [Her] approach was identified in the voices of women, but Gilligan did not claim that
> the approach is exclusively female, nor did she claim that all women use it. Still, the
> avalanche of response from women who recognized themselves in Gilligan's descrip-
> tion is an impressive phenomenon. (1982, p. 21)

Caring is an explicit value in the TEAMS program. Mentors support students'
social and emotional development along with their academic preservice preparation,
and encourage them to become a community of learners helping one another succeed. The students I interviewed brought this ethic to their interactions with the
children, though they were saddened by the unmet needs they saw all around
them:

> I wish I could do more, cause I didn't feel like I did enough. But I think by showing
> up there, I think it showed the children more than the parents that there are people that

care, and I know when the parents see the volunteer log they see that there are other people in the world that care for their children and are trying to support them and help them.

I wanted to give them so much more than what they had, but yet the only thing I knew that I could give them was my support and my love for these children, and that was what I was there for. . . . I mean their parents took care of them but it was just a different type of care than my parents had given to me, and so I kind of took the role of providing care and nurturing for these children.

One kid, when I first got there, he was very kind of wild and didn't really want any[thing] to do with any of the teachers. . . . I just started playing with him on the playground one day, and like the last time I was there he was sitting in my lap and he wanted me to rub his back when he went to sleep. And so that was good but . . . then I left, so I felt guilty leaving, just like another person in their life that came into their life and left.

A Theory about Theory

Despite their evidence of relationship and care, my students' responses told me that the feminist framework I had hoped to provide did not ultimately inform their experience. While they did learn a considerable amount about culture and community, their learning tended to be experiential and anecdotal. They rethought their assumptions about poor people, they became more aware of the meaning of community, and they came to care deeply for the children they met. However, they did not consider their experiences theoretically. In an effort to help them think systemically, I asked whether they could envision a world where their agency might no longer be necessary. None of them could:

You'd have to get rid of greed. Like, a lot of people are very greedy and very selfish.

If we didn't have to worry about getting pregnant and having the father take off, or drug addiction, or any of that stuff that plays a role in that society, then the world would be a better place.

There's a lot of good people out there but there's a lot of evil people out there.

Though they had begun to see the families and children they served as real people rather than stereotypes, students still held negative assumptions about those whom George Bernard Shaw's antihero Alfred P. Doolittle called "the undeserving poor" (1913/1953):

There are some people that have horrible situations, how they were brought up, or what they've witnessed, and that tends to really affect them in their actions. Other people who've gone through the exact same or worse experiences and they're better because of it. I mean, everyone has a conscience that says, this is right or this is wrong, and I think it's just, how people deal with the hand that they're dealt depends on how they turn out and how they are, whether good or evil.

Like I mean there are some people who are on welfare because they're lazy, there's other people that are on welfare because they work as hard as they possibly can and they just—when they were younger, maybe they didn't have the financial circumstances to go to college, and so since they didn't go to college maybe they can't get a good job. . . . But in the end I really think that how you deal with it reflects on who you are as a person.

When it came to gender, students were nearly oblivious, despite the fact that we had discussed it repeatedly in the Culture and Community class. When I asked them to think about how gender affected their community service experience, they reported that the little boys had tended to gravitate toward the one male member of the cohort and toward a male volunteer at one of the after school programs:

I think it's because maybe they don't have the father figure at home, maybe they just want another boy to connect to, because there were more girls in the program than boys.

Beyond this conventional discussion of male role models and father figures, the students seemed genuinely surprised to realize that, as I pointed out previously, most of the clients in the families they served were women; most of the staff members at their agencies were women; and most of the elementary teachers at their host school were women and most of them were women. Furthermore, it was difficult for them to see that the dismal conditions they deplored were directly connected to the devaluation of caring and women's work, which in our society means more resources for corporate welfare and military budgets than for schools and childcare.

Initially, the students' unwillingness or inability to place their experience within a theoretical framework made me decide that we had failed to give them an understanding of feminism and of theory in general. But as I thought about my own undergraduate development and talked with colleagues and friends, I began to wonder whether there was not also a developmental path to theory, a level of experience and maturity needed to understand the big picture. My theory of "theoretical development" was confirmed when the faculty leader of the TEAMS cohort described student reaction to the required Seminar readings he had assigned. They found Jonathan Kozol's *Amazing Grace* and Mike Rose's *Possible Lives* (both long on powerful stories and anecdotes) accessible and thought provoking; they had a great deal of trouble with John Dewey's more abstract *Experience in Education*, even though it dealt with the very issues they were encountering (L. Goldsberry, personal communication, April 3, 2001). I have found similar resistance among my traditional-age Women's Studies students, especially when compared to the nontraditional students, many of whom have personally experienced oppressive marriages, single motherhood, and a disempowering welfare system.

Gender and Feminism in Service Learning: A More Troubling Question

The total invisibility of gender in my students' interviews, and in oral and written comments by subsequent cohorts raises a more troubling question. Searching the literature on service learning in teacher education, I discovered that gender is almost as invisible as it was in my students' interviews. A survey of the major national reports on service learning reveals almost no mention of women, feminism, or gender (Belbas and Shumer, 1993; Education Commission of the States, 2000; Gray et al., 1999; Shumer et al., 1999, 2000). While writers on service learning celebrate caring (e.g., Swick, 1999), few teacher educators have connected that ethic to an explicitly feminist model (Rhoads, 1997; Warren and Rheingold, 1993). Fewer still have studied service learning in education through a lens that "takes as problematic the structured dependence of women on men" and aims at "interrupting relations of dominance" (Gelenian, 2000; Lather, 1987/1994; Manicom, 1984).

Both teaching and unpaid social service have traditionally been "women's work," seen as the natural extension of women's maternal role (Barnard, 1981; Hobson, 1994; McCarthy, 1990; Rubin, 1982; Walsh, 1995). And since the majority of poor people in the United States are women and children, women make up the majority of clients in most social service environments. It would seem that such gender imbalances would invite a feminist analysis of service learning. However, few teacher educators have looked across campus at the insights gleaned from the internships that have been part of Women's Studies programs for decades (Harvey, 2000; Novek, 1999; Rubin, 1982; Trigg and Balliet, 1997; Warren and Rheingold, 1993; Weiler, 1992).

Further, as I have pointed out, the ethic of care carries its own contradictions for feminist educators and may actually reinforce inequities of power between women and men. Eugene (1989) reminds us that some kinds of caring may encourage women and minorities to accept unjust and inhumane conditions, rather than trying to change them. Even if we "de-genderize" the care ethic (Lister, 1997, p. 101) by rejecting the essentialist assumption that women are inherently more caring than men, we are left with an ethos that seeks to counter the impersonality of modern life by humanizing the Other, but ignores the social and political conditions that give rise to "otherness" in the first place. In the context of service learning, maternalism leaves unchallenged the neediness of the "needy." As one student wrote, "I will, of course, care for my students, but I know that this is not enough. I also care deeply for my houseplants and they perish under my care" (Van Galen, 1996, p. 147).

Feminism in Teacher Education: Another Explanation?

Still seeking to understand my students' responses (or lack) to gender, I have turned to feminist educators who describe the almost total absence of gender in teacher education. Mader and King, in their 1995 survey of 30 Michigan teacher education programs, found only "moderate" or "minimal" instruction on gender with most of the emphasis on "equity" rather than power or oppression. Another study by Coffey and Acker (1991) found similar biases in teacher preparation programs in the United Kingdom. Susan Laird (1988) analyzed two key educational documents, the Carnegie Forum's 1984 report, "A Nation Prepared: Teachers for the 21st Century" and the Holmes Group's 1986 document, "Tomorrow's Teachers." Both have strongly influenced teacher-education programs during the past 15 years, yet neither acknowledges the emergence of feminist pedagogy. Similarly, the National Network for Educational Renewal, of which my own teacher-education program is a member, speaks in its Twenty Postulates of the teacher's moral obligation "to ensure equitable access to and engagement of the best possible K-12 education for all children and youth," but says nothing directly about gender (National Network for Educational Renewal, 2000). None of these highly influential public documents acknowledges the truth put forward by Sara Lawrence Lightfoot:

> Both [mothers and teachers] are required to raise children in the service of a dominant group whose values they do not determine . . . to socialize children to conform to a society that belongs to men. (cited in Lather, 1987/1994, p. 245)

It is here, in the intersection between the politics of the family and the gender politics of the teaching profession, that I find the most provocative explanation for my students' resistance to feminist theory during their service learning experiences. If, as Ann Manicom (1984) asserts, "a feminist framework is a world view that takes as problematic the structural dependence of women on men" (p. 77), then a feminist analysis of the family is essential for understanding the oppression of women and children. My students sympathized with the parents of the children at their agencies, but clung to the traditional concept of "maternal deprivation" rather than "[what] should be thought of as *mothers'* deprivation" (Manicom, 1984, p. 83). Their resistance to feminism echoes that of the Canadian primary school teachers interviewed by Manicom, and of the students in Jordan Titus' Multicultural Education course, who asked, "How is this stuff going to make us better teachers?" (Titus, 2000, p. 23).

The Problems that Remain

During the past two years, we have continued to modify the C & C course and the service learning experience. My teaching partner and I continue to point out how the power inequities between women and men shape and are shaped by culture and community. New texts, such as Robert Putnam's *Bowling Alone*, give students more concrete and explicit definitions of community. Student group presentations now focus directly on real-world communities, including several comparing women's and men's communities. In light of our early experiences, we have moved the elementary school placement to another part of the program and expanded the community service requirement from the original 12 hours to 24. The current service learning instructor and I now regularly discuss students' progress and work to strengthen the connection between the course and the field experience. We have also tried to establish closer ties with our host agencies, though students still occasionally find themselves preoccupied with "busy work," and some placements are still based on student schedules rather than aptitudes and interests. We will continue to address these problems within the confines of site-based teacher education, where the benefits of extensive clinical work often mean less time for reflection and discussion.

Because C & C is a team-taught course, our enrollment cap is 60, twice the cap for the usual USM course. The large class size is a constant challenge. Students in the TEAMS cohort, which has remained at about 15 each year, tend to band together; and other class members sometimes complain about their cliquishness. In addition, the numbers make it difficult for us to get to know students well, and even more difficult to get a sense of where they are emotionally and pedagogically. Small group discussions have helped, but group work brings its own challenges, allowing students who have not done the assigned reading or reflecting to hide behind their more conscientious peers.

What Next? Conclusions and Challenges

Two years after my interviews with the second cohort, I am increasingly convinced that asking nineteen-year-old students to engage in feminist analysis—or any analysis—while they are still overwhelmed by needles in the playground and unfriendly clients on the soup line contradicts pedagogic wisdom. I have been helped to this conclusion by anthropological and psychological research on culture shock, a term first used by Kalvero Oberg (1958) to describe the experiences of those living and/or working abroad. Oberg wrote of a "honeymoon phase," a hostile or aggressive phase, a period of adjustment, and finally, acceptance and adaptation to the cultural differences of the host country (Oberg, 1958). Other accounts of culture shock in Outward Bound participants (Kraft, 1992; Richards, 1977); returned Peace Corps volunteers (Dubrowsky, 1964); and students who have studied abroad (AFS, 1984) echo the disorientation, dismay, and resistance I hear as my students discover the culture of poverty at their service learning sites.

My reading and reflection have led me from that conversation in my living room to an awareness of the difficulties inherent in helping students barely out of adolescence to think theoretically, and to a consideration of the possible links between feminism and the entire teacher education enterprise. But in the end, I return to my students. How can I challenge them to understand the political as well as the personal? What tools can I give them to see the children in their service learning placements as part of a system that disempowers women and children? And most important, how can I encourage them to bring an awareness of power and gender into their own classrooms?

First I know that I must remember, as Sandra Hollingsworth (1995) advises, that mere exposure to feminist literature does not necessarily lead to action, just as knowledge and understanding about cultural differences does not necessarily enable students to function comfortably within culturally different settings (Steward et al., 1998). Like Hollingsworth, I must give my students more opportunity to examine their own history as women and more direct guidance in connecting feminist insights to their service learning placements. I will certainly continue encouraging them to care for the children they serve, yet at the same time, I will seek a feminist pedagogy that, as Kathleen Weiler (1992) puts it, celebrates the nurturing work of women teachers—but "not unproblematically" (p. 335).

As a feminist, I want my students to ask why the children waiting for their evening meal at the soup kitchen are hungry in a land and in a city of plenty and to think about what needs to happen in order to change that reality. But as a caring teacher educator mindful of developmental learning theory, I know I must honor their journey from encounter to theory. In this regard I can think of no better advice than Atticus Finch's to young Scout in Harper Lee's *To Kill a Mockingbird*: "You never really understand a person until you consider things from his point of view . . . until you climb into his skin and walk around in it" (1960/1980, p. 34). Walking around in the skins of the people at the soup kitchen may be only the beginning of my students' journey, but I know now that I must allow them to make it one step at a time.

References

Adams, M., Bell, L. A., & Griffin, P. (1997). *Teaching for diversity and social justice: A sourcebook*. NY: Routledge.

AFS Orientation Handbook, Vol. 4. (1984). Available from Research Department, American Field Service International, New York.

Anderson, J. (1998). Service learning and teacher education. *ERIC Digest* (Report No. EDO-SP-91–1). Washington, DC: ERIC Clearinghouse on Teaching and Teacher Education.

Barnard, J. (1981). *The female world*. NY: Free Press.

Belbas, B., and Shumer, R.D. (1993). Frequently cited sources in service learning. Available from the National Service Learning Clearinghouse, University of Minnesota, St. Paul, MN.

Bok, D. (1982). *Beyond the ivory tower: Social responsibilities of the modern university*. Cambridge: Harvard University Press.

Coffey, A. J., and Acker, A. (1991). "Girlies on the warpath": Addressing Gender in initial teacher education. *Gender and Education, 3*(3), 249–261.

Dubrowsky, K. (1964). *Positive disintegration*. Boston: Little Brown & Co.

Education Commission of the States. (2000). *Learning in deed*. Issue paper. Denver, CO: Educational Commission of the States.

Erickson, J., and Anderson, J. (1997). *Learning with the community: Concepts and models for service learning in teacher education*. Washington, DC: American Association for Higher Education.

Eugene, T. (1989). Sometimes I feel like a motherless child: The call and response for a liberational ethic of care by black feminists. In M. Brabeck (Ed.), *Who cares? Theory, research, and educational implications of the ethic of care* (pp. 45–62). New York: Praeger.

Gelenian, K. (2000). Multicultural Education. Course syllabus. Retrieved from www.campuscompact.org/syllabi.

Gilligan, C. (1982). *In a different voice*. Cambridge, MA: Harvard University Press.

Gray, M., Ondaatje, E., and Zakaras, L. (1999). *Combining service and learning in higher education*. Summary Report. Santa Monica, CA: Rand Corporation.

Harvey, I. (2000). Feminism, postmodernism, and service-learning. In C. D. Lisman and I. Harvey (Eds.), *Beyond the tower: Concepts and models for service learning in philosophy*, 35–52. Washington, DC: American Association for Higher Education.

Hobson, D. (1994). Across the generations: Conversations with retired teachers. In P. Joseph and G. Burnaford (Eds.), *Images of schoolteachers in twentieth-century America: Paragons, polarities, complexities* (pp. 78–95). NY: St. Martin's.

Hollingsworth, S. (1995). The "problem" of gender in teacher education. *Mid-Western Educational Researcher, 8*(2), 3–11.

Kahne, J., and Westheimer, J. (1996, May). In the service of what?: The politics of service learning. *Phi Delta Kappan, 7*(9), 593–599.

Kraft, R. J. (1992). Closed classrooms, high mountains and strange lands: An inquiry into culture and caring. *Journal of Experiential Education, 15*(3), 8–15.

Laird, S. (1988). Reforming "women's true profession": A case for "feminist pedagogy" in teacher education? *Harvard Educational Review, 58*(4), 449–463.

Lather, P. (1994). The absent presence: Patriarchy, capitalism, and the nature of teacher work. In L. Stone (Ed.), *Education feminism* reader, 242–251. New York: Routledge.

Lee, H. (1960/1980). *To kill a mockingbird*. New York: Warner Books.

Lister, R. (1997). *Citizenship: Feminist perspectives*. New York: NYU Press.

Mader, C., and King, C. (1995). *Awareness of gender within teacher education programs*. Paper presented at the meeting of the American Educational Research Association, San Francisco, CA.

Manicom, A. (1984). Feminist frameworks and teacher education. *Journal of Education, 166*(1), 77–88.

McCarthy, K. (Ed.). (1990). *Lady bountiful revisited: Women, philanthropy and power*. New Brunswick, NJ: Rutgers University Press.

Meyer, T. (1985, February 27). More students finding time to give the needy a hand. *Chronicle of Higher Education*, 20.

National Network for Educational Renewal. (2000). *Twenty postulates*. Retrieved from http://depts.washington.edu/cedren/publications.htm.

Noddings, N. (1984). *Caring: A feminine approach to ethics and moral education*. Berkeley, CA: University of California Press.

Noddings, N. (1992). *The challenge to care in schools*. New York: Teachers College Press.

Noddings, N. (2002). *Starting at home: Caring and social policy*. Berkeley, CA: University of California Press.

Novek, E. (1999). Service learning is a feminist issue: Transforming communication pedagogy. *Women's studies in communication, 22*(12), 230.

Oberg, K. (1958). Culture shock and the problem of adjustment to new cultural environments. Address to the Health, Welfare and Housing Division, US AID/ Brazil. Eric Document #-068424.

O'Grady, C. (Ed.). (2000). *Integrating service learning and multicultural education in colleges and universities*. Mahwah, NJ: Lawrence Erlbaum.

Rhoads, R. (1997). *Explorations of the caring self: Rethinking student development and liberal learning*. Paper presented at the meeting of the American Educational Research Association, Chicago, IL.

Richards, G. (1977). Some educational implications and contribution of Outward Bound. Eric Document #194266.

Rubin, S. (1982, December). The dialogue between voluntarism and feminism: Implications for higher education. *New directions for experiential learning (New partnerships: higher education and the nonprofit sector)*, n. 18, 35–46.

Ruddick, S. (1989). *Maternal thinking: towards a politics of peace*. Boston: Beacon Press.

Shaw, G. B. (1913/1953). *Pygmalion*. New York: Modern Library.

Shumer, R., with Dutweiler, P., Furco, A., Hengel, M., and Willems, G. (2000). *Shumer's self-assessment for service learning*. St. Paul, MN: University of Minnesota Center for Experiential and Service-Learning, Department of Work, Community and Family Education, and the College of Education and Human Development.

Shumer, R., Treacy, A., Hengel, M., and O'Donnell, L. (1999). *Recent dissertations on service and service-learning topics*. St. Paul, MN: Learn and Serve America National Service Learning Clearinghouse. Retrieved from www.umn.edu/~serve.

Steward, R. J., H. Jo, and A. Roberts. (1998). *Empathy and cross-cultural sensitivity*. Paper presented at the Great Lakes Regional Conference, Division 17 of the American Psychological Association, Bloomington, IN.

Swadener, B., and Lubeck, S. (Eds.). (1995). *Children and families "at promise": Deconstructing the discourse of risk*. Albany, NY: SUNY Press.

Swick, K. (1999). Learning helps future teachers strengthen caring perspectives. *Clearing House, 73*(1), 29–32.

Swick, K., Winecoff, H.L., Kemper, R., Rowls, M., Freeman, N., Somerindyke, J., Mason, J., Williams, T. (1998). *Service learning and teacher education: Linking learning with life*. Clemson, SC: National Dropout Prevention Center, Clemson University.

Titus, J. (2000). Engaging student resistance to feminism: "How is this stuff going to make us better teachers"? *Gender and Education, 12*(1), 21–37.

Trigg, M., and Balliet, B. (1997). Finding community across boundaries: Service learning in women's studies. In Guarasci, R., and Cornwell, G. (Eds.), 51–71. *Democratic education in an age of difference: redefining citizenship in higher education*. San Francisco, CA: Jossey-Bass.

Van Galen, J. (1996). Caring in community: the limits of compassion in facilitating diversity. In D. Eaker-Rich and J. Van Galen (Eds.), *Caring in an unjust world: Negotiating borders and barriers in schools*, 147–170. Albany: SUNY Press.

Wade, R., and O'Reilly, K. (1998, Winter). Service learning in preservice teacher education: Understanding cooperating teachers' experiences. *National Society for Experiential Education Quarterly*, 7–11.

Walsh, E. (1995). *Schoolmarms: women in America's schools*. San Francisco, CA: Caddo Gap Press.

Warren, K., and Rheingold, A. (1993). Feminist pedagogy and experiential education: A critical look. *Journal of Experiential Education, 16*(3), 25–31.

Weah, W., Simmons, V. C., & Hall, M. (2000, May). Service-learning and multicultural/multi-ethnic perspectives: from diversity to Equity. *Phi Delta Kappan, 81*(9), 673–675.

Weiler, K. (1992). Teaching, feminism, and social change. In C. Mark Hurlbert (Ed.), *Social issues in the English classroom*, 322–337. Urbana, IL: NCTE.

Zinn, H. (1995). *A people's history of the United States 1942–present* (Rev. and Updated Ed.). New York: Harper Collins.

8

Putting Anti-Oppressive Language Teacher Education in Practice

MARY CURRAN

As a teacher educator who teaches for social justice, I believe it is of utmost importance that the in-service and preservice teachers who pass through our programs are exposed to the concept and practices of anti-oppressive pedagogy in order to raise their awareness of educational (and other) inequities and foster a sense of responsibility for engaging in anti-oppressive educational practices in their classrooms. I work in a language education program at a large state university in an urban setting. Our program is responsible for training pre- and in-service English as a Second Language (ESL), English as a Foreign Language (EFL), bilingual education, and world-language (Spanish, French, German, Italian) teachers. While knowledge about anti-oppressive pedagogy is a necessity for teachers of all disciplines, I believe it is especially important for language educators due to the way issues regarding language, education, and inequities are often linked. In this chapter, I briefly explain the unique role language educators play in anti-oppressive education, and I describe the way I have designed one of my courses, Language and Culture, to prepare language educators to assume these roles. I focus, in particular, on the pedagogical tool of the book club that I used with my pre- and in-service language teachers to demonstrate the way this activity may serve to foster both learning and unlearning about self and Others as we work toward becoming anti-oppressive educators.

Language, Education, and Discrimination

In the words of Reagan and Osborn (2002), "[L]anguage is at the heart of virtually every aspect of education, and indeed of social life" (p. 34). As we know, most learning in educational settings takes place through the medium of language, and one of the principal goals of education is the acquisition of socially and academically appropriate oral and written language forms (Clearly and Linn, 1993; Reagan and Osborne, 2002). At the same time, many learners experience discrimination in educational (and other) settings because of language.

Skutnabb-Kangas (1988) coined the term "linguicism" to refer to discrimination on account of language. Linguicism refers to the ideologies that "legitimate, effectuate and reproduce an unequal division of power and resources (both material and non-material) between groups which are defined on the basis of language" (p. 13). Lippi-Green (1997) writes how ideologies about language serve to create the norms, standards, and preferences that tell us who is worth listening to. Linguistic discrimination has been well documented (Lippi-Green, 1997; Macedo, 1994; Macedo and Bartholomé, 1999; Nieto, 2001; Roberts et al., 1992). As Lippi-Green (1997) explains,

> It targets not all variation, not all language varieties, but only those which are emblematic of differences in race, ethnicity, homeland, or other social allegiances which have been found to be less than good enough. (p. 240)

She explains how these discriminatory ideological stances with regard to language are

> introduced by the schools, vigorously promoted by the media and further institutionalized by the corporate sector. It is underscored by the entertainment industry and underwritten in subtle and not so subtle ways by the judicial system. (p. 72)

In other words, linguistic discrimination is everywhere, and attitudes toward language play a big role in determining who succeeds at school and in the workplace.

At the same time, "some of the most comprehensive approaches to multicultural education, while including race, class and gender concerns, have failed to include language issues in their conceptual framework" (Nieto, 1996, p. 187). This omission is not possible within the framework of anti-oppressive education because anti-oppressive education does not reduce identities to an essentialized or exoticized limited set of characteristics. Instead, anti-oppressive education considers the multifaceted nature of identities and their shifting positions within the many forms of oppression, which are "multiple, interconnected and situated" (Kumashiro, 2000, p. 41). An anti-oppressive stance requires that issues regarding language and the complex and multiple ways language plays out in educational (and other) systems in practice and policy need to be examined by our future teachers, especially our future language teachers.

Language teachers working in ESL, EFL, bilingual, and world-language education are seen as experts with regard to language issues. This puts language teachers in positions of authority in which they may influence educational practice and policies with regard to language and beyond. If a language teacher works from an anti-oppressive educational perspective, he or she is in the unique position to serve as an advocate for language rights, working toward "1) the rights of freedom from discrimination on the basis of language and 2) the right to use . . . [one's] languages in the activities of communal life" (Macias, 1979, p. 41). Moreover, these anti-oppressive language teachers can become advocates for a multilingual society, in which we are all encouraged to learn languages other than English. This effort can work to combat the monolingual and monocultural ideologies so predominant in U.S. society (Reagan and Osborn, 2002).

Pennycook (1994), Macedo and Bartholomé (1999), and others have written how language politics (e.g., in the English Only movement or recent cuts to the funding of bilingual education programs) may possess hidden agendas and have become acceptable substitutes for racial politics. Critically aware language educators can work to reveal the many ways linguicism impacts our educational system and, as a result, our students. For example, they can work to show how nonnative English-speaking students are often seen from a deficit perspective (i.e., as the "problem students") and may receive fewer resources than their native-speaking counterparts (Nieto, 2001). They can unmask the irony that while monolingual English-speaking students are encouraged to learn a second language, students who arrive at schools speaking a second language are usually not provided with bilingual education that would support the maintenance of their home language and the acquisition of English (Reagan and Osborn, 2002). They can show how the language of some students is questioned for its legitimacy, as we see in the case of students who speak African American vernacular English (Delpit and Dowdy, 2002) or in the decision about which Spanish to teach in classrooms that are assigned Spanish as a world language. They can educate others on how language teaching, especially the teaching of English as an international language, has been linked to colonialism and global capitalism (Pennycook, 1994; Phillipson, 1992). In each of these examples, language educators can work to reveal how belonging or not belonging to particular language communities can have a big impact on educational opportunities and achievement. Anti-oppressive language educators can work to show how beliefs, attitudes, and assumptions about language have material effects.

To do this work, language teachers need an awareness of the pivotal role they can play within the cultural politics of education. Pedagogical tools to raise this awareness must be interwoven into teacher education program design and curricula. In addition to knowledge of their respective content areas and teaching methodology, language educators need to gain an in-depth knowledge of the complicated relationship between language and discrimination. To understand this, I suggest that they need an awareness of the dynamic identities of their students and the many communities in which students live and how language plays a role in the social construction of these identities and communities. At the same time, and perhaps more importantly, they also need to work to understand their own identities and their unique and shifting locations within the playing fields of linguistic (and other) discrimination (e.g., they can examine their positions as a nonnative or native-speaking teacher; as a speaker of a dominant or nondominant variety of a language; as a teacher in a second-language or foreign-language context, etc.).

Gaining this understanding about self and Others requires both learning and unlearning. By *unlearning*, I mean the process of disrupting our commonsense notions about our self and Others (those groups who are traditionally marginalized by society). Unlearning asks that we go beyond exoticizing or essentializing how we look at Others, while raising to conscious awareness the unsaid about ourselves and Others. Unlearning asks us to suspend our search for the "truth" about self and Other and requires that we question the processes for the normalization and marginalization of certain identities. It asks us to use this knowledge not as an end in itself (as we do when we claim to have the "right" answer), but rather as information to be used to challenge previous and future assumptions. In this way, lessons learned are not facts, or whole, true stories. Instead they become "both catalysts and resources for students to *use* as they learn more" (Kumashiro, 2000, p. 34). Disruptive knowledge, then, becomes a tool for *looking beyond* toward learning that leads to "unpredictable, uncontrollable, and unforeseen goal[s]" (Kumashiro, 2000, p. 39). Clearly, this inability to predict or control inhibits our ability to talk about teacher education strategies that work for all teachers, with all students, in all situations. However, we can talk about strategies that encourage a particular type of labor in which we work against the harmful repetition of the normalizing and marginalizing practices. It is in the work to change these practices where we may enact change—hopefully, moving us to a better place (Kumashiro, 2000).

From this perspective, language education becomes more than simply teaching (and learning) an additional language. It requires that a language educator teach his or her students about the intricate relationships between language and discrimination (in both the target and the first-language cultures). It also requires that we engage our students in the process of learning and unlearning about ourselves and Others and reflecting upon our locations in linguistic hierarchies. It also asks that we design and participate in activities with our students that aim to transform existing social injustices based on language. This knowledge and these activities take us beyond the traditional responsibilities and outcomes of language education.

Reagan and Osborn (2002) write about the extended power of language education:

> The study of languages other than one's own cannot only serve to help us understand what we as human beings have in common, but can also assist us in understanding the diversity that underlies not only our languages, but also our ways of constructing and organizing knowledge, and the many different realities in which we all live and interact. Such understanding has profound implications not only epistemologically, but also with respect to developing a critical awareness of language and social relationships. In studying languages other than our own, we are seeking to understand (and, indeed, in at least a weak sense, to become) the Other—we are, in short, attempting to enter into realities that have, to some degree, been constructed by others and in which many of the fundamental assumptions about the nature of knowledge and society may be different from our own. We are, in fact, creating new selves in an important sense. Such creation and recreation forces each of us to reflect more deeply on many of the core questions related to being an educated person, as well as requiring that we become not merely tolerant of differences, but truly understanding of differences (linguistic and otherwise) and their implications. (p. 13)

When language educators strive to raise "critical awareness of language and social relationships," we open the possibilities of creating new selves (for both ourselves and our students), which may lead to the creation of new social realities. In this way, we engage in a pedagogical process that has the potential for transformation—changing teachers, students, and society (Kumashiro, 2000). In terms of education, the hope is that this transformation will lead to higher achievement for all students and a social order based on equity.

Anti-Oppressive Language Teacher Education in Practice

Where does one begin in this endeavor? What does anti-oppressive language teacher education look like in practice? There are many ways that we can teach and model this type of educational practice for our students. In fact, I tell my students that an orientation toward anti-oppressive education needs to be infused in all we do. The objective is to design opportunities in which students will learn and unlearn about themselves and Others, which will encourage them to question normalization and marginalization processes and which will lead to a greater understanding of the broader social, cultural, historical, and political contexts in which they live and work. These opportunities will help foster "analytical and critical skills for judging the truth and merit of propositions, and the interrogation and selective appropriation of potentially transformative moments in the dominant culture" (Ellsworth, 1992, p. 96). Further, "[t]his critical knowledge and thinking is what impels students toward action and change, toward resisting and challenging oppression" (Kumashiro, 2000, p. 37). As an example of anti-oppressive language teacher education, in the following section, I discuss my experience with a course I have designed, Language and Culture, and the ways my students and I engaged in the learning and unlearning process.

The Course: Language and Culture

Language and Culture is a required course for students in our ESL, EFL, world language, and bilingual education Master's in Education and certification programs. The three overarching goals for this course are to cover how we learn culture (both our own and Others'), how we can teach culture (both our own and others'), and how we can work as anti-oppressive educators in language education. As I introduce the course to my students, I explain how I see these three as interrelated and inseparable goals.

The course is based upon a critical, experiential, and narrative approach to learning—critical in its emphasis on anti-oppressive education; experiential in its aim to link course content to personal experience; and narrative for the importance I give to the analysis of our stories for the multiple and disruptive meanings they shed on how we make sense of language and culture. Over the course of the semester, we engage in many activities. We read (e.g., Peggy McIntosh's [1988] *White Privilege and Male Privilege* in which she examines and lists the unearned benefits white people experience in U.S. society); we watch videos (e.g., *Color of Fear* produced by Lee Mun Wah [1994] in which nine men discuss racism); we write (the students write a Cultural Identity article in which they describe their identities and the possible implications of their identities for their teaching); and we venture into the local community (we visit ESL high school classes and attend a culture fair at an adult ESL learner program). These are just a few of the activities we engage in over the semester. In this chapter, I want to focus on one particular pedagogical tool I used in Language and Culture—the book club—and discuss how it may work as an anti-oppressive education practice to offer the students the opportunity to learn and unlearn about self and Others. I will also use the example of the book club to discuss some of the inherent difficulties in practicing anti-oppressive education.

The Book Club

The book club idea was modeled after the recent popularity of book clubs, as we see on a large scale with Oprah Winfrey and through small social groups at libraries, bookstores, or with friends. My students, together with local high school ESL students, local adult ESL learners, and a group of EFL pre- and in-service teachers in Mexico read Richard Rodriquez' (1982) *Hunger of Memory: The Education of Richard Rodriquez.*

Rodriquez' memoir was chosen for several reasons. First, it holds almost canonical stature as an oft-cited book in the language education literature. Rodriquez has become notorious for his anti-bilingual education and anti-affirmative action stance. Due to the controversial nature of this book, it provides rich fodder for discussion as students grapple to articulate their reactions to Rodriquez' description of his experience growing up as a Mexican American in California and the implications for language teaching. Second, although ten years old, the book deals with very timely topics as seen in the recent Supreme Court decision regarding the University of Michigan's affirmative action policies and the Bush administration's reduction of support for bilingual education in the implementation of *No Child Left Behind.* Third, our university is located within a community with a large Latino population. As such, Rodriquez' experience may strike personal chords with many who participated in our group club. Moreover, with the growth of the Latino population in the U.S., all teachers in our public schools will be working with these students and will need more knowledge about their communities. Rodriquez' book offers one perspective, and our conversations about the book offers many others.

I worked on the book club project in collaboration with two local ESL teachers (one who teaches high school, and the other who teaches adults) and an EFL teacher trainer in Mexico. It was very important that we design our interactions to be mutually beneficial for all participants. Our students read selections from *Hunger of Memory* and met either in person or via the Internet to discuss the readings. Our goal was to break beyond the insularity of our classrooms and engage in authentic conversations in an effort to learn and unlearn about our own and Others' language communities. In exposing the students to multiple perspectives on language issues, we hoped to lead them to an enriched understanding of their broader social, cultural, historical, and political context and ramifications. In addition, for both high school and adult ESL learners and the EFL pre- and in-service teachers, this activity provided authentic opportunities to practice their English, and my students had the opportunity to use their world-language skills with local community members.

The English as a second language and world-language standards both emphasize the importance of the community (*ESL standards for P-K-12 Students*, 1997; National Standards in Foreign Language Project, 1996). Without the community, language is meaningless. As Magnet (1990, cited in Crawford, 2000) argues, "[T]he right to utilize a language is absolutely empty of content unless it implies a linguistic community which understands the speaker and with whom that speaker can communicate . . ." (p. 293). Moreover, "[l]anguage rights are collective rights"

(Crawford, 2000). As such, linguicism (discrimination on account of language) always impacts a linguistic community. Language issues cannot be understood outside of their community context. Language learners, in order to gain critical language awareness, need a sense of their own identities as members of linguistic communities. They need to learn about the target linguistic communities and form connections with these community members. They also need an understanding of the way the target language community is located within broader contexts. Unfortunately, this does not always occur in language teacher education or in ESL, EFL, bilingual education, or world-language classrooms. Language educators often spend the majority of their time teaching language as isolated skills that are practiced within the confines of the classroom. As anti-oppressive language teacher educators, we need to model ways to link students to the community and raise awareness of the different ways linguistic communities experience discrimination or privilege. It is through interactions such as these that students will have the opportunities to learn and unlearn more about themselves and Others.

Interactions between My Students and the Adult ESL Learners

In this section, I am only going to discuss the ways in which the book club interactions between my pre- and in-service teachers and the adult ESL learners were organized and the way this activity afforded anti-oppressive learning opportunities for learning and unlearning about self and Others. To begin our project, the collaborating teacher and I introduced our students to the idea of the book club. We asked them to read selections from *Hunger of Memory*. My students were asked to read the entire book, but to focus on specific sections, and her students, because of their developing English proficiency, were only asked to read specific shorter selections. For the first meetings, the ESL adult learners joined us at the university during our class time, and we asked the students to begin with a general discussion about culture and schooling. We gave the students some suggested questions to ask each other (both groups had these questions in advance of the meeting so that they could prepare their responses).

I had two groups of students in Language and Culture—one class of 14 students, and another of 30. Thirty-three ESL adult learners participated. The ESL adult learners visited our university upon two occasions so that they could meet with each group of my students. When we met, each participant briefly introduced himself or herself to the large group and then we broke into smaller groups to focus on the topic of culture and schooling and to begin discussing *Hunger of Memory*. At the end of each large group meeting, the students who were going to partner with the adult learners (my students had the option of meeting with either an adult or high school ESL learner) were introduced to their book club partners. My students were required to schedule at least two meetings with their partners to continue their discussions of *Hunger of Memory*. They also had to write a brief response article about this experience.

For the analysis of this project, I saved the texts and evaluations produced by the students, so that we could critically reflect upon the activities as the collaborating teachers and I engage in future planning. I also kept notes in my teaching/research journal about the class. In what follows, I rely on these notes and data from the student-produced texts. It is also important to note here that the three teachers and I have committed ourselves to working on a collaborative self-study in which we are conducting "an intentional and systematic inquiry into one's [our] own practice" (Dinkelman, 2003, p. 8). This type of self-study is important for anti-oppressive educators, so that we can take careful look at the pedagogical tools and the student learning and unlearning (or lack thereof) happening in our classrooms. In addition to this chapter in which I offer *my* perceptions on what occurred as a result of the book club activity, I am in the process of writing another essay with the collaborating adult ESL teacher and two of our students. As such, this chapter offers only one way to make sense of the book club activity.

The First Visit

I remember the first time the adult learners came to visit our class. My students and I had discussed the questions about culture and schooling, and we took a break while we waited for our guests. I remember thinking that my students did not seem to be very enthusiastic about the visit. For example, each student in this class had signed up to work with high school students instead of the adults for their paired meetings. When I commented upon that, one of my students made a comment along the lines of, "working with adults can be too strange." At 7:00 when the adults arrived, our room was quickly filled by 33 adult ESL learners representing more than 20 countries (in contrast to my 14 students, all of whom—except one—had been born in the United States). I watched as my students straightened in their chairs, and one came up to me, smiling and said, "We're outnumbered." After the introductions, we broke the students into small groups—two or three adult learners to one of my students. We told them to work through the questions for about an hour. We had arranged for a large space for this activity, and the room quickly filled with conversation. After an hour, we met as a large group to discuss their conversations. They shared their observations on U.S. schooling practices and practices in other countries—discussing both similarities and differences. For example, they talked about how in many other countries children are required to wear uniforms in school. A Russian adult learner gave his opinion that this takes away some of the stress students and their families experience from the inequities experienced because of differences in social class. Others commented on how school days are longer in some countries, like Korea, for example. Others spoke about the formality of schooling in other countries, citing how students must rise to speak in class. They discussed the important value all cultures give to schooling.

At one point, Miguel,[1] an adult learner from Ecuador, spoke to the large group, directing his words to my students. He said:

> Tonight you spoke with three of us, and you learned something about us and our countries. You will be teaching our children. You need to continue to learn more about all of us. Tonight was just a beginning for you. I hope you continue to have interactions with people like us. And, when you are teaching, don't think that parents like us, who are new to this country, don't care. If we don't come to speak to you, if we don't go to your PTO meetings, it isn't because we don't care. It's because we don't have good enough English to speak to you, or because we are working two jobs, or it's because we don't think that *you* really care to hear what we have to say. So, please keep learning and keep trying to speak to us.

Of course, I was thrilled to hear his comment, because I had often said similar things to my students, but I knew that it would be much more believable and powerful coming from him. When we met the second time with my other group of students, I asked Miguel whether he would not mind expressing this idea again. After these two meetings, the students were on their own to arrange their individual meetings to discuss *Hunger of Memory*.

In the articles my students wrote, responding to their interactions with their adult ESL learner partners, there was evidence of many kinds of learning. Both groups of students delved deeply into the content of our course and learned multiple perspectives on the issues. First, they wrote about their discussions of Rodriquez, commenting on how they agreed or disagreed with his views on bilingual education and affirmative action. They discussed how their personal experiences were either similar or different than his. For example, one student wrote that a Korean ESL adult learner said that her children's teacher in the United States had requested the same thing as the nuns who taught Rodriquez—that the family speak only English at home. Second, they learned about cultural similarities and differences in schooling, in terms of the products (i.e., uniforms), practices (i.e., standing to speak, or the use of traditional educational methodology for teaching languages), and perspectives (i.e., the value of education). This information should help prepare teachers to understand some of the difficulties their new immigrant students might encounter, and it should inform the new immigrant about the culture of U.S. schools. Third, the interactions served to allow my students to learn more in depth about the immigrant experience, an experience common to many of their future students' families. For example, Julie wrote:

> Meeting with Rodrigo and Alonso has affected me pretty profoundly. I work with, and plan to continue working with, adult English learners, but never before have I had the opportunity to speak so in-depth with my students about the whys and wherefores of leaving their countries or the struggles they endure to stay here.

My students wrote about the complexity of their partners' lives—writing about their professions (as they revealed themselves to be chemical engineers, dental technicians, preachers, marketing researchers, etc.) and their desires for future education (to study theology, art, or mechanical engineering). Fourth, the students served as mutual resources for each other. One of my students helped her partner get information on graduate school admissions at our university and tutoring for her son. Another student helped her partner with her ESL homework. The ESL learners also provided language practice for some of my students who are nonnative speakers of the world languages they plan to teach. Fifth, many of these relationships grew beyond the two-visit minimum course requirement. I learned that one of my students and her Chinese partner meet regularly and practice English and Chinese. The student who had said that adults "can be so strange" wrote, "I'm so glad that I chose to meet with an adult ESL learner instead of a high school student. I have a new friend now, and someone I can go to for help [with my Spanish]."

My hope is that the relationships begun in the book club will flourish into genuine connections with the community, and at a minimum, will help overcome stereotypes and conquer fears that teachers may have in reaching out to students and families. As a group, we discussed how language teachers can work to make similar connections for their future K-12 students by planning activities (e.g., a book club, pen pals, or other activity) in which their students reach beyond the classroom to engage in authentic, meaningful language practice focusing on issues related to linguistic discrimination with members of the target linguistic community.

I would like to think I can claim that the book club activity has worked to help my students learn and unlearn about themselves and others, and reflect upon the way linguistic identities and communities fit into broader social, cultural, historical, and political contexts and become advocates and agents for transformation. In an informal course evaluation, many students wrote about the value of working with the adult learners, asking for more interactions. For example, I received comments such as the following: "Most of all I liked interacting out of the classroom with the non-native speakers of English," and "I loved working with the ESL learners and learned a great deal about myself." The following are some examples of comments written by the students:

1. Learning about self:
"I was able to learn a lot about myself as well as others. I took my first steps to becoming interculturally competent."

" . . . it was wonderful to be able to take the time to look at myself and get to know who I really am in terms of culture. It was definitely a really great learning experience that put everyday life in cultural perspective."

"I learned a lot about myself and how to teach culture."

"I never considered myself privileged before, as far as being white. I like how in 'Color of Fear' [a video we watched in class] a man said, 'you don't know what it means to be white because you never had to think about it.'" And that's true. I never did. I take all of my privileges for granted. But I don't think they should be called privileges. I think that they should be everyone's divine right, and that everyone should enjoy these 'privileges.'"

2. Learning about Others:
"This class has urged me to become more aware of the people around me and what makes people who they are. Until this class I felt that dissecting culture and its implications [for teaching] was important, but now it's necessary."

"This class has really changed me . . . more than any class I have ever had at Rutgers. It made me see the world and others in a different light. I am thankful for that. I now realize so many things I never even considered."

3. Advocate behavior:
"I enjoyed this course a lot. I think that it made me more culturally aware, and more of an advocate. Now, whenever I hear a comment (racist, bigoted, ignorant) I don't ignore it; I say something."

"I feel like a more very well rounded individual after this class. I have been able to speak to others about issues of race, prejudice with more confidence and with a lot more knowledge to back up my ideas and thoughts on it."

When I read these comments, I am pleased. But I know that I can never really know what has been learned/unlearned or what real transformations in attitudes, beliefs, assumptions, or behavior have taken place. I know that these comments do not prove that we have made a difference (Ellsworth, 1997), nor do they show that all students were affected in the same way or at all. All students enter the educational process at different stages and will take away different lessons. This is inherent in anti-oppressive education, which acknowledges that

> [t]here is always a space between the teaching and the learning, and rather than try to close that space (and control where and how the student is changed), the teacher

should work within that space, embrace that paradox, and explore the possibilities of disruptions and change that reside within the unknowable. (Lather, 1998 cited in Kumashiro, 2000, p. 46)

I offer the following as an example of this uncomfortable space between the teaching and learning.

Between Teaching and Learning

The week when we began the book club and the adult learners came to visit my class, I was feeling very good about my week's classes. I remember telling some colleagues, "I *know* these interactions must have made some impact; they [the students] *must* have learned something." I had been struck by how, after the first visit, the student who had told me "adults can be too strange" asked whether she could change to work with adults instead of the high school students. And in our large group discussion after the visits, several of my students commented on how they had been surprised by the adult ESL learners. One honestly admitted to the class that, although she knows better, she finds herself thinking of all these new immigrants as poor and uneducated. She explained that as her conversation partners revealed that they were medical doctors in their countries, she found herself confronting these stereotypes. I was also very pleased by the opportunity the students had as they listened to Miguel, when he asked them to learn more about the new local immigrant communities. After the visits, I felt that my students had had the opportunity to learn something about themselves and Others. It seemed that some students had the opportunity to question and perhaps unlearn what they had previously learned as normal.

At the same time, I quickly relearned how I cannot assume that my students are learning what I expect. The following week, after class, one of my students followed me to my office so that I could remind her of the name of her conversation partner. I told her that it would be Miguel, the student who had spoken so passionately about the necessity that my students learn more about these adult ESL learners' communities. She surprised me when she said she was not sure whether she remembered who he was, saying that she had not remembered his comments. I was crushed, because I had assumed that all of my students present had been as powerfully impacted by his comments as I. The lesson learned was mine: We cannot make assumptions about what our students are learning, and we must remember that they are all located at different points in the journey to become anti-oppressive educators. For each student, learning is happening in different ways at different times. I consoled myself with the knowledge that this student would be spending more time with Miguel, hoping that perhaps similar learning/unlearning opportunities would present themselves in their future interactions.

What *I* have learned (or unlearned) is that I cannot assume that I have changed my students. I leave myself with the hope that perhaps I have *moved* them, as Lather (1998) argues, or I have created the conditions within which they *will be moved.* The hope is to nudge them off center so that they will begin to think on their own. In this sense, education is like a caress. After a while, unless there is movement, we stop feeling someone's touch. We feel a caress because of movement, because of change. It is the same thing with education: the important thing is that we move in our thinking, that we unlearn the norms, making them salient to ourselves so that they are noticed. Then we can decide whether and what actions are necessary and proceed to make a difference (Ellsworth, 1992). The difficult thing is ensuring that this will happen. There is no guarantee.

Since there is no guarantee, it is important that anti-oppressive educators engage in collaborative self-study. Even though we may not arrive at a definitive "truth," collaborative self-study (Dinkelman, 2003) is a vehicle for reflection and knowledge production, so that lessons learned (or unlearned) may be infused into future teaching and programmatic development or disseminated in scholarly literature. The teachers with whom I collaborate meet regularly to plan our practice and to reflect upon and analyze our experiences. We want our students to be aware of the value we place on collaborative self-study. They need to observe their teacher educators modeling collaboration, making connections with the community, and engaging in reflection. We invited the students who participated in our book club to join us as coresearchers in our analysis of the projects we engaged in. We need to learn/unlearn from their perspectives, and at the same time, foster the development of their identities as anti-oppression language education scholars as well.

In the same way, the conversations that ensue as a result of this volume will also provide rich fodder for reflection. Reflection upon and engaging in anti-oppressive language education is a must if we hope to change the often discriminatory ways we think about and treat Others because of their language. As I point out in this chapter, language educators can play an important role in revealing the way that language (and other) discrimination works in society. This chapter begins this conversation by sharing one experience of working toward preparing language educators within an anti-oppressive educational framework.

Note

1.   All names are pseudonyms, except for Donna, the collaborating teacher.

References

Clearly, L., and Linn, M. (Eds.). (1993). *Linguistics for teachers.* New York: McGraw-Hill.

Crawford, J. (2000). *At war with diversity: U.S. language policy in an age of anxiety.* Clevedon, UK: Multilingual Matters.

Delpit, L., and Dowdy, J. K. (2002). *The skin that we speak: Thoughts on language and culture in the classroom.* New York: New Press.

Dinkelman, T. (2003). Self-study in teacher education: A means and ends tool for promoting reflective teaching. *Journal of Teacher Education, 54*(1), 6–18.

Ellsworth, E. (1992). Why doesn't this feel empowering?: Working through the repressive myths of critical pedagogy. In C. Luke and J. Gore (Eds.), *Feminisms and critical pedagogies* (pp. 90–119). New York: Routledge.

Ellsworth, E. (1997). *Teaching positions: Difference, pedagogy, and the power of address.* New York: Teachers College Press.

ESL standards for P-K-12 Students. (1997). Alexandria, VA: TESOL Publications.

Kumashiro, K. (2000). Toward a theory of anti-oppressive education. *Review of Educational Research, 70*(1), 25–53.

Lather, P. (1998). Critical pedagogy and its complicities: A praxis of stuck places. *Educational Theory, 48*(4), 487–497.

Lippi-Green, R. (1997). *English with an accent: Language, ideology, and discrimination in the United States.* New York: Routledge.

Macedo, D. (1994). *Literacies of power: What Americans are not allowed to know.* Boulder, CO: Westview Press.

Macedo, D., and Bartholomé, L. I. (1999). *Dancing with bigotry: Beyond the politics of tolerance.* New York: St. Martin's Press.

Macias, R. F. (1979). Choice of language as a human right: Public policy implications in the United States. In R. V. Padilla (Ed.), *Bilingual education and public policy* (pp. 39–57). Ypsilanti: Department of Foreign Languages and Bilingual Studies, Eastern Michigan University.

Magnet, J. (1990). Language rights as collective rights. In K. L. Adams and D. T. Brink (Eds.), *Perspectives on official English: The campaign for English as official language of the USA* (pp. 293–299). Berlin: Mouton de Gruyter.

McIntosh, P. (1988). *White privilege and male privilege: a personal account of coming to see correspondences through work in women's studies.* Wellesley, MA: Wellesley College, Center for Research on Women.

Mun Wah, L. (Producer) (1994). *The color of fear* [video recording]. Available from Stir-Fry Productions, Oakland, CA.

National Standards in Foreign Language Project. (1996). *Standards for foreign language learning: Preparing for the 21st century.* Lawrence, KS: Allen Press.

Nieto, S. (1996). *Affirming diversity: The sociopolitical context of multicultural education* (2nd ed.). New York: Longman.

Nieto, S. (2001). *Affirming diversity: The sociopolitical context of multicultural education* (3rd ed.). New York: Longman.

Pennycook, A. (1994). *The cultural politics of English as an international language.* New York: Longman.

Phillipson, R. (1992). *Linguistic imperialism.* Oxford: Oxford University Press.

Reagan, T. G., and Osborn, T. A. (2002). *The foreign language educator in society: Toward a critical pedagogy.* Mahwah, NJ: Lawrence Erlbaum Associates.

Roberts, C., Davies, E., and Jupp, T. (1992). *Language and discrimination: a study of communication in multi-ethnic workplaces.* London: Longman.

Rodriquez, R. (1982). *Hunger of memory: The education of Richard Rodriquez, an autobiography.* Boston, MA: D. R. Godine.

Skutnabb-Kangas, T. (1988). Multilingualism and the education of minority children. In T. Skutnabb-Kangas and J. Cummins (Eds.), *Minority education: From shame to struggle.* Clevedon: Multilingual Matters.

Teaching Story

Reflections upon Racism and Schooling from Kindergarten to College

ANN BERLAK & SEKANI MOYENDA

Ann: A Classroom Encounter

One July day toward the end of the millennium I asked the students in my Cultural and Linguistic Diversity course—preservice and experienced teachers—to finish writing responses to a video we had just seen and then to take a break. When we reconvened, Sekani Moyenda, an African American woman who teaches in an elementary school that serves predominantly poor Chinese immigrant and African American families, would make a presentation to the class.

Sekani had been a student in the course the previous semester. I invited her to speak because, after completing the course, she had told me that, in her opinion, graduates of our teacher education program were not being adequately prepared for the realities they would face as teachers of African American, Latino, Asian, or poor white children. I responded by inviting her to take three hours of class time to address the class in any way she chose. She decided to engage the class in a simulation she called "Boot Camp for Teachers." I had no idea what she had in store for us. One thing I knew for sure was that we would not be bored. By the time the presentation was over and the students had left the classroom, I was reeling from the trauma that this encounter with Sekani had provoked. During the session two white women shed tears, one fled the room before the presentation was over, and a heated argument erupted between Sekani and Jim, a white man who had volunteered to play the role of teacher.

That evening, Jennifer, a white student, wrote: "It was one of the most valuable classes I have ever had." Another white student, Denise, wrote: "I am upset and enraged by the message I heard from today's guest speaker." Isaiah, the only African American, wrote: "Sekani touched a nerve in our classmates. . . . She gave them more in two hours than they will get from any course at the university." Wong Wan Shan, an immigrant from Hong Kong, responded, "Teachers . . . must never at any time while inside a classroom be carried away by our emotions. Yesterday, the guest speaker let her emotions take over. . . . We are all eye witnesses to the result. . . . The original good intentions of the guest speaker got totally washed down."

A few weeks later I had decided to write about the encounter, primarily because I thought doing so would help me begin to understand what had happened. But I did not want to reflect upon it solely from my privileged perspective as a white middle-class professor, so I asked Sekani whether she would write about it with me. The story of the encounter and our reflections upon it were published in a book called *Taking It Personally: Racism in Classrooms from Kindergarten to College* (Berlak and Moyenda, 2001) from which this chapter is partially drawn.

Five years have passed since our initial efforts to mine the encounter for lessons about racism and schooling. In this chapter Sekani and I reflect upon what writing the book taught us about personal and institutional racism and anti-oppressive teaching and schooling. In the section "Sekani: The Boot Camp Presentation," Sekani briefly tells the story of the encounter. In the section "Making Sense of the Encounter: Conversations Across Time and Space," I consider how the events affected my understanding and my teaching over time. In the section "A Love Letter to the Staff at Rosa Parks" Sekani narrates a series of events that was set in motion when she presented *Taking It Personally* to her colleagues at the school where she has been teaching for the past nine years.

Sekani: The Boot Camp Presentation

My goal for the presentation was simply to give Ann's students some teaching tips that they had not learned in the credential program. I hoped to address the students' greatest fear: managing behavior in predominately black, and especially poor black, classrooms. I wanted to bring some reality to students unfamiliar with the true scope of the responsibilities and difficulties they were likely to confront as they begin to teach.

I had no idea we would end up dealing with racism. Though I felt certain the students would not have overcome their racist conditioning entirely, I assumed it would at least remain covert, as it almost always had in the classes I had taken in the credential program. I introduced myself by telling the class I had come of age in the Civil Rights generation and, strongly influenced by my mother who had been a Black Panther, was a great proponent of "I'm black, I'm proud." I told them I thought one of my primary functions as a teacher of black children was to prepare the children to become militant adults. I then told several stories to convey the forms of racism I had observed and experienced throughout my life, including at Rosa Parks where I was teaching. One example I gave was about a white fourth-grade teacher who refused to intervene when I was being racially harassed by a white girl. I told the students I finally took matters into my own hands and beat the little girl up.

My presentation depended upon using the role-play to re-create the level of chaos I walked into after being assigned to what I have come to call a crisis class-room: a classroom that had been taught by a succession of uncredentialed mostly white substitute teachers. I provided a shortage of supplies, little information about the children, a list of school rules that the teacher would be unable to enforce, and no backup outside the classroom. In addition, I was going to give the teacher only 20 minutes to teach a skill. At the conclusion of the role-play we would see what we could learn from discussing it.

Seven Minutes of Chaos

A young white man named Jim volunteered to be the teacher. I was pretty sure he would not get through the lesson, though I doubted we would be able to re-create the chaos of a real classroom in crisis. The credential students seemed so—well—tame. I did not realize they would inhabit their roles—how shall I say it—so robustly. I reminded Jim he was set up to fail. He asked me whether he could try to succeed. I responded, "Of course, you can *try.*"

I set the timer for 20 minutes and the play began. There was immediate chaos as the students, as directed by their "scripts," became possessed by their disruptive roles. Jim, in the teacher role, immediately called a "class meeting" to reiterate the class rules I had taped upon the wall. None of the "children" paid him any heed. Jim became visibly agitated. "*Sit down,*" he yelled. "*We're having a class meeting.*" After seven minutes of chaos, the classroom a virtual madhouse, I called the role-play off.

From Simulation to College Classroom Confrontation

With all players in position, Jim and I begin the "heated argument" all the students referred to that evening in their journals. It included the following interchanges:

Jim: This situation is totally unrealistic. I've been teaching for a year and I've never seen it happen.

Sekani: Well, I've seen it happen many times in the school where I teach. Especially in the classrooms of white teachers. It's based on my experience. I don't know where you've been teaching.

**

Sekani: What could you have done to diffuse the situation? Why didn't you use the "para" to send the children who were out of control to the counselor?

Jim: I would never throw a child out of my classroom, no matter what. They'd never trust me if I did that.

Sekani: Perhaps knowing you will teach them what the limits are might be just what they need in order to learn to trust you.

At one point during the dialogue between Jim and me, Jim went over to the list of classroom rules I had posted and below rule number 8 wrote number 9, "HAVE FUN," in bold letters. He told the class:

I love being with kids. I'm just a kid, myself.

Sekani: These children don't need an adult kid. They need adult role models, not buddies; they can have fun *after* school. Your job is to teach. If you can't control the classroom, you can't teach. You better not sacrifice the learning of my children to what you think might be the needs of an out-of-control child. If you want to play, become a camp counselor.

Then, addressing the entire class, I said that many white teachers do not understand children who have been abused and have experienced violence. At this, one white woman broke into tears and, speaking through her sobs, told me I did not know much about it if I thought that there is no alcoholism and violence in white middle-class homes. I responded:

With all due respect, I am a total stranger; I don't know you. If what I say doesn't apply to you, it doesn't apply. But I'll say this: If I can make you cry by making an off-the-cuff comment, you're in even bigger trouble when you get into a classroom and school filled with people like me.

Making Sense of the Encounter: Conversations across Time and Space

In *Taking It Personally* I conceptualized the encounter and its aftermath as a moment in time in which multiple conversations, composed of innumerable responses to and anticipations of the responses of others, converged and reverberated across time and space. At the moment of the encounter, I was aware that my invitation to Sekani was a response to my conversation with her about the relevance of the diversity course. Later, I understood that I also invited her because I wanted the students to engage with her militancy. I wanted, among other things, for the students to join a conversation I first participated in with Inuka Mwanguzi, who had been my student more than three decades before.

On the day following the encounter I initiated a discussion of Sekani's visit so the students could hear their classmates' responses to what she had said. My intention, only partly conscious then, was to spur ongoing conversations within themselves, with one another, with friends and family, and with me through the journals.

In response to Sekani's presentation, Wong Wan Shan had written: "Some of us let our emotions take over. That is bad." I wrote in response: "One lesson I take from what you say is that there are significant differences between you and Sekani in cultural style." My words were intended to encourage Wong Wan Shan to listen to Sekani and, more generally, not to discount what people say just because their voices are filled with passion. My intentions had been shaped in part by a paper about Chinese immigrants Sekani had written while she was my student. In that paper she had told of two Chinese immigrant women who became her aunts through marriage to her uncle and the difficulties these women faced dealing with the complexities of a culture for which they had no frame of reference. That paper shaped my grasp of the difficulties and importance of understanding between Chinese immigrants and African Americans.

Lifetimes of conversations that Seknai and I had engaged in before we ever met were also present during the hours we spent together trying to make sense of the encounter. When we finally sent the book to press, though our conversations had powerfully affected each other's understanding, there were many ways in which we still did not see eye to eye. Nevertheless, all our conversations are present in every interchange I have with every student in every class I teach.

Anger in the Classroom

Though nearly all the students took for granted that we would be speaking one of the liberal or mainstream "languages" that are commonly spoken in classrooms, in the years prior to the encounter I wanted the students to learn to think and speak in an antiracist or critical multicultural "language"—that is, a language structured around concepts that draw attention to systematic group differences in personal and institutional power. Early reflections upon the encounter revealed that though the languages the students were most familiar with and the critical antiracist talk I wanted students to become conversant in differed in important ways; they were in common in that they took for granted that classroom talk should be "civil," "polite," and "respectful." This meant in practice that we should speak to one another without expressing feelings, particularly feelings of anger.

Anger (Moral and Defensive)

Until Sekani's visit, the students had discussed racism in tones that might as easily have been used to talk about the weather. However, on the day of the encounter, Sekani broke the rules of "polite" conversation by telling stories of racism she had observed and experienced in a voice inflected by anger as well as humor. She also responded to some of the students' comments in angry tones.

That day for the first time a number of the students also expressed anger, either in their journals or in the open forum of the class. Apparently, Sekani's breaking of the cultural and classroom norms against expressing feeling gave permission to some students to break that norm as well. With the exception of Jennifer and Isaiah, however, the anger they expressed was not moral anger—anger at socially induced suffering—directed at the injustices Sekani had spoken of. It was, instead, defensive anger. Defensive anger is a response to being held, or feeling one is being held, responsible for injustices (Boler, 1999).

For example, Kathy expressed defensive anger when she wrote, "I am enraged by the messages I heard from today's speaker. I found her hostile, condemning and close-minded." Denise, another white woman, wrote, "She started spouting off . . . I felt it was an insult to you." Some students expressed anger at Sekani less directly. Christina (a Latina) wrote, "I felt (the presentation) revealed that she (Sekani) still has some personal issues to deal with" (i.e., the problem was in Sekani rather than in a racist society).

As I reflected upon the encounter I came to understand for the first time the significance of the fact that the tacit classroom rule not to express feelings applied to everyone equally, to those who experience injustice and those who may benefit from it. For example, the person who is the target of a racial slur and the one who speaks it are both subject to the same prohibition against expressing anger. I came to realize that silencing passionate expressions of anger supports the powerful, weakens dissent, and drains the energy from challenges to the status quo. As I came to understand the ways in which views about expressing anger were produced by social, historical, and cultural experience, I began to grasp how pervasive and deeply normalized the prohibition is.

Some Reflections upon Reflection

The morning following the encounter I began with a debriefing exercise designed to encourage students to reflect upon and share how they felt about Sekani's visit. Though the students' responses revealed that at least half the class initially felt some degree of defensive anger, and no moral anger at the racist experiences Sekani had recounted, apparently hearing how others felt provoked some of the students to reevaluate their views and feelings. The previous night Sally had written that she "associated militant with words like military and war" and expressed resentment toward Sekani for feeling hostile to white people. However, during the debriefing, after hearing her classmates' responses, she wrote, in response to my question about what Sekani meant by "militant," "that children would have pride in themselves and be prepared to defend themselves in the real world."

Jim wrote, "Today's class [the debriefing session] helped me internalize the messages that were hard for me to grasp yesterday. While the role play exercise was in progress . . . it was very hard to look beyond the feelings I was having. . . . I was angered and defensive." Kathy wrote:

> I feel much better after today's class. I had such a violent reaction on Tuesday that I was unable to focus on any positive aspect of Sekani's presentation. After hearing others' perspectives I realized I had learned and gained more than I thought. It was good for me to hear her anger and to examine the deep feelings it brought up for me.

Isaiah wrote:

> I'm really glad you did the [debriefing] exercise so the many emotions of our classmates could be heard . . . I know you would like me to speak more when we have open discussions, but I don't believe our classmates can even hear ME. . . . This is how I FEEL right now. ANGRY. Thanks Professor Berlak. I needed to see how people really see me. . . . This class has been an awakening for me.

Journal entries written after the processing activity suggest that students' views continued to change during the remainder of the course. In his final journal entry Jim wrote: "I'm really starting to GET IT." On the evening of the day we had debriefed the encounter Wong Wan Shan wrote: "As teachers we must never . . . while inside a classroom be carried away by our emotions." However, in his final journal entry he said: "The tension grew, the anger exploded, the self image challenged . . . yet the feelings so true. Through pain we learn more about pain. . . . Through argument we see truth and through struggle we see hope."

Another white woman, Margie, wrote in her final entry:

> I'm still thinking of Sekani's visit. Of course I am. I feel like my insides have been ripped out, and I think it will take some time to heal! So far, my range of emotions has been: Intimidation, fear, defensive attitude, hopelessness, realization, guilt, confusion, hope, understanding, admiration and respect. And I would say that's just the tip of the iceberg.

I now see that offering students this opportunity to broaden their awareness of various possibilities for "reading" the classroom crisis by listening to their classmates' views increased the likelihood that they would supplement and alter rather than merely maintain their initial responses to the encounter. I think the processing session prompted students (e.g., Isaiah and Jim) to reconsider how they were implicated in the dynamics of oppression, and to bring this knowledge to bear on their senses of self, as indicated by Jim's and Kathy's journal entries.

Anger in the Classroom since the Encounter

In *Taking It Personally* I wrote that confrontation with an other or others who speak passionately may be traumatic for those who have been taught that expression of intense feeling is inappropriate and is, therefore, not to be taken lightly. I argued that those who have been socialized to express feelings publicly may have to learn ways of speaking that do not so strongly jar the sensibilities of those who have not.

I concluded, however, that a transformation of understanding of racism by members of both dominant and nondominant groups may *require* that teachers and students expand their views of the array of acceptable classroom speech genres. I had come to believe that there are some people who may be unable to grasp the degree of damage that racism wreaks upon people of color (and upon white people) unless they engage *face-to-face* with expressions of anger and pain, and then have an opportunity to reflect upon or "process" their responses.

I thought that people who have participated in cultural communities that are reticent about emotional expression needed to adapt to a more expressive public culture, as Wong Wan Shan had seemed to be doing right before our eyes (Guitierez and Rogoff, 2003). My concern that Wong Wan Shan would acculturate to a more publicly expressive pattern of communication flowed from my awareness that he was likely to interact with African American children and adults as a teacher and perhaps as an administrator. His ability to listen with respect to passionate voices might, I thought, in the future stand him in good stead.

I have taught the Cultural and Linguistic Diversity class more than a dozen times since I came to believe that expressing feelings is an essential component of successful antiracist teaching. One might think that in subsequent classes I would, therefore, use opportunities that presented themselves, or create opportunities, to promote and encourage passionate expression. The truth is that sometimes I have done so, but many times I have not. My classes are almost always characterized by decorum. And I believe without a doubt that it is precisely because of this that at the end of the semester I feel my courses have fallen short. Some students who have read *Taking It Personally* share this feeling, saying they wish something "real" like the encounter had happened in the class.

There are, of course, many reasons why the expression of feeling is regularly muted. These include social norms and asymmetries of power. However, I realize that I (as well as they) feel comforted by decorum. I think students are less likely to express angry feelings because they have correctly read my ambivalence; my understanding of the crucial role that expressing and processing anger is likely to play in unsettling oppressive worldviews does not trump my fear of the discomfort that is generated when students express anger, moral or defensive, in the classroom. Even after I had written of the value of expressing anger, it took several years to recognize that my enforcement of the "agreements" or rules for conducting classroom discourse, which are widely presumed to insure "classroom safety," indicated that I remained in the grip of the oppressive fiction that classroom "decorum" is the bedrock of a trusting community and anti-oppressive pedagogy.

I have rarely been aware while in the teaching moment that I am choosing decorum over crisis. However, upon reflection I can see that not being personally subjected to racism makes it easier for me to make that choice, even though I am less likely than colleagues of color to be censured by students or administrators for exploring the depths of feeling that racism can evoke. A former student who grew up in Iran responded to my reflections upon the gap between my intentions and my actions:

> Of course they are shocked when they hear Sekani. They cry, they deny and they tremble in anger. Sekani is the toughest pill to swallow but they must and as educators it is our duty to administer it to them. You will do an unforgivable disservice if you hold back your beliefs, awakening and awareness. It would be unconscionable if you see, hear, feel, sense, smell racism and racist comments and do not speak up against it.

The Unconscious: Ubiquitous and Uninvited Guest

Sekani's and my initial conversations yielded a second insight: the role the unconscious played in the encounter. At the time I had unwittingly assumed that if teachers rationally expose injustice, students will both recognize and resist it.

Though I, like at least some of the students, "believed in," and had explored the unconscious in therapy, I had become accustomed to leaving this lens outside the classroom door.

As we wrote *Taking It Personally* I began to understand that my "forgetting" about unconscious processes was motivated in part by my own unconscious fears and desires. I considered the possibility that rather than wanting to know more about what was going on, I had a passion not to know. Perhaps, I thought, I was afraid to face the implications of Sekani's view that the lesson of the blond-haired girl story was that violence is one way to challenge racism. Or perhaps I did not want to know how powerfully implanted were Jim's unconscious fears of and disrespect for black people, in part because such an awareness would remind me how deeply I had been implanted with the same. Perhaps I was resisting knowing that my carefully constructed curriculum had left these fears and attitudes untouched because I wanted to believe that I could change, in 30 hours, the way my students thought.

I realized that I was not the only one whose unconscious had been active during the encounter. The students' journals provided clues to feelings that apparently remained unconscious and unexamined. The most prominent of these was fear. Denise's comments "our community was stormed by the militia" and "the discussion became invasive, violent . . . militant" suggest that she feared Sekani.

What was there to fear? Perhaps, I wrote, these students' fear of Sekani was an instance of a largely unconscious but deeply ingrained fear of encirclement by dark-skinned others. Perhaps some saw Sekani as the embodiment of the loud black female who denaturalizes the norm of white male power (Lei, 2003). Perhaps they were associating Sekani with the terror they felt at the prospect of teaching a class populated by what they—with the assistance of mass media, schooling, and the criminal justice system—had come to see as violence-prone and dehumanized Black children. Perhaps at least some of the students, though they were unaware of it, were deeply invested in keeping at bay Sekani's view that she and other people of color were unjustly disempowered because that challenged their understanding of how rewards and punishments are meted out in a society that they learned to think of as just.

Maybe, I wrote, Jim and others resisted acknowledging racism because they were trying to maintain the floodgates that protected them against a dawning awareness that their positions in the racial hierarchy, which provided important sources of self-esteem, were unearned and undeserved. Maybe Julia's view that Sekani had a chip on her shoulder flowed from an unconscious attempt to differentiate herself (a relatively light-skinned Filipina) from people darker than she. Their need to protect themselves from these largely unconscious fears and desires may have mobilized their defensive anger at Sekani's claims to be an expert who is capable of judging their qualifications to teach Black children.

As we were writing *Taking It Personally* I came to see the encounter as a trauma that activated or reactivated anger, fears, and desires at various levels of consciousness without suggesting any way to adequately respond to them. I wrote that had I been as attuned then to unconscious processes as I had now become, I would have considered students' questions. For example, "What makes her [Sekani] an authority?" These were clues to unconscious fears and desires, and important to recognize in future classes. I felt that once I had become aware of the presence of the unconscious I would surely ask a student like Denise who characterized Sekani as "infested with negativity," to bring to consciousness the fears and desires implicit in this choice of words, and the genesis of these fears and desires. I planned to change the rules of the classroom game—by inviting the unconscious into future classrooms.

I have come to think of the encounter and its aftermath as a set of responses to trauma, anxiety, resistance, and mourning (Salverson, 2000). I saw Sekani's naming of racism as traumatic because it activated fear and socially prohibited anger as well as sorrow that flowed from a new awareness of the immense distrust and disconnection deeply buried in those on all sides of the racial divides. These feelings aroused anxiety—a generalized feeling of dread. The most common initial response to the anxiety was denial and resistance in the guises of defensive anger and numbness.

However, I had come to understand that anxiety can also set the stage for a moment of creative change in those who have the spirit to acknowledge their resistance and denial and go beyond them. In fact, I began to see trauma, anxiety, and resistance as *essential precursors* to the complex dynamic involved in mourning. Mourning is a process of naming and confronting our own or others' suffering. It is set in motion when one resists experiencing trauma but subsequently witnesses oneself denying the feelings the trauma has provoked. A number of students engaged in this form of self-reflection when they later acknowledged the defensiveness they felt during and immediately following the encounter. Reflecting upon the encounter suggested to me that mourning can enable those who experience it to participate energetically in unraveling the institutional structures that keep racism in place.

My understanding of the importance of bringing the unconscious to consciousness has not changed my teaching as much as I would have thought or hoped. Now that I am aware that students who have read *Taking It Personally* anticipate Sekani's presentation with dread as well as fascination, I encourage them to bring to consciousness and explore their fears before she visits our class. I now more comfortably respond to students' anxieties, guilt, and the defensive anger that is often directed at me with understanding that these reactions are essential if students are to experience the pleasures of participating in the construction of a more just and joyful world.

However, I do not always write in response to journal entries or pose in classroom conversations "thought-provoking" questions designed to probe what I interpret as clues to students' unconscious and dehumanizing fears and desires. I think one reason is that I still struggle against my own fears of crisis that, though brought to consciousness during periods of focused and systematic reflection, usually return underground when I teach. Thus, I have often failed to seize the opportunity to challenge the decorum of the classroom by asking students to consider what their unconscious fears and desires might be.

Before Sekani's visit I had felt intuitively that it was important to provoke the unconscious fears and defensive anger that I now think must be mobilized if students are to achieve the state of mind Jim and Isaiah called "getting it." However, I had not found a way to activate students' fantasies and feelings as powerfully as the face-to-face encounter with Sekani. Since the encounter, no coincidence of forces has provided the conditions necessary for students to take the classroom experience quite so personally.

In the Long Run

In the conclusion to the book, I described our conversations that summer in that classroom as threads in the complex weave that is the future. What Jim and Isaiah "got" when they wrote, "NOW I GET IT" or "I think I'm beginning to get it," would be transmitted, contested, and transformed by future generations, including, perhaps, generations of their students, children, and colleagues. I considered that Denise, who had never heard the words "can't afford" from her parents, might, at some future time, speak of militancy in terms of action for social justice, thinking about her experiences and the experiences of others through frameworks other than the same ready-made ones that channeled her thinking throughout most of the course. I thought it within the realm of possibility that Kathy would, as a result of the encounter, sometime in the future see and speak out against racial discrimination in the allocation of school resources or the disciplining of students.

I thought of Sekani's presence as having reactivated particular and partially dormant historically powerful revolutionary languages. I saw these new readings of the racial world sparked by the encounter and the continuing conversations that directly or remotely descend from them as culture in the making. I was, in a word, optimistic about the potential of people to unlearn racism. I did not in any way imagine what would happen when Sekani shared *Taking It Personally* with her colleagues at Rosa Parks.

A Love Letter to the Staff at Rosa Parks

Dear Staff,

Let's Reminisce! Remember when you were kind enough to give me a ride home when I couldn't walk? How about the times we went to dinner or the movies, and bowling together? Or when I came to your home to fix your computer? Or when one of the students overwhelmed you to the point of exhaustion and I took him off your hands? Those were the years in which I regularly received "Highly Satisfactory" evaluations. Though I received my clear credential in 1998, I really learned how to be a teacher at our school—not in a college classroom. We took a building that looked like a slum and turned it into a school—together. We created a safe learning and working environment because we all gave more than one hundred percent.

A friend of mine teaches at another school in the district. One of the staff members there is also a published author. They had a special assembly to honor her. At most school sites they would display a book written by a teacher and use it to promote their school. But what did you do when I displayed *Taking It Personally* in the office and you discovered I was a published author?

A few white staff members got together, copied a few pages out of the book, anonymously wrote in bold letters down the side of the copies "*Not appropriate for display*," and put the pages in everybody's mail boxes. You waited until I was in the hospital to pull this little stunt. Soon after, the principal pulled the book from display. Of course an Uncle Tom took great pleasure in calling me while I was in the hospital to tell me *ALL* about it.

After that is when I began to feel the tension in the school. Sure, you were all "courteous," pretending it was "*all good.*" But the absence of any mention of the book was evident. On the last day of the school year, when I had just come back from surgery and we had our little gathering for awards and appreciations, I picked up the first signs of your hostility. You told staff people, who many of you had complained all year were too incompetent for words, how wonderful it was to work for them. People who were pregnant or getting married were given gifts, but nothing— absolutely nothing—was said about my book. I didn't even receive a get well card which everyone at the school always got—even when you didn't like them. At the time I still didn't see what all that meant. I still thought it was just a few of the white staff who was disturbed by the book. And I thought the silence about the book was because the principal was simply trying to avoid conflict on her last days before retirement.

When we got back to school in the fall our ethical and competent principal had been replaced. I told the new principal about your resentments and my willingness, in fact, my desire, to have a meeting to discuss the situation with the help of a mediator. Her response appeared supportive, even compassionate, polite, and professional as I, following district procedures, was attempting to arrange mediation. I now know she was actually working with some of you to start a campaign of harassment by building false evidence of my misconduct, fraud, and sabotage.

First the principal interrogated me about the number of workers' compensation claims I had submitted the year before she came to Rosa Parks. Two weeks later she told me she had to confiscate my key to the building. She claimed the district told her to do it. Sure, it was in the back of my mind that she didn't trust Black people. It didn't occur to me that her behavior might also be a response to the claims about racism at our school that I had made in *Taking It Personally*.

Not long after that, and without warning, the locksmith arrived when I would usually be in class at the University. It seemed strange that the principal asked that the new keys be given to her first and then she would give them to me. Though I agreed to this, I felt my chest constrict. Still, I told myself I was "just trippin.'" The locksmith had known me for years. I, the school technology teacher, was the dragon at the gate who kept our equipment safe from theft and he never questioned me when I insisted that the locks be changed and that only I and the principal and the secretary were to be given copies.

Once the locksmith's work was complete the principal asked if the locks to the storeroom in my office had been changed as well. We said of course—the storeroom always had the same lock as my office because the store room was located there. A large closet/room inside my office/classroom, it was the safest room in the school. It was where the network server, expensive equipment, my personal stuff, and dangerous supplies were located, and no one else was allowed there without me being present.

The principal started to stutter and fumble her words as she told the locksmith the storeroom had to have a different lock than the classroom. The locksmith and I asked why. She said this was an order from "The District." The way she averted her eyes confirmed my suspicions but I needed her to say it. She finally admitted that I was not to have a key to my own closet. I told her that was unacceptable and that the locksmith would have to go to lunch until we worked this out. I got madder and madder. She wouldn't admit that she was accusing me both of no longer being trustworthy enough to have keys to the building and to my storeroom, and of being crazy/paranoid as well.

I had invested literally thousands of hours trying to get the infrastructure necessary to support our school's technology needs operational; but my phone calls, e-mails, letters, and memos had been ignored for years. Now that Information Technology had new leadership and explanations were in order for why hundreds of thousands of dollars had been spent but the computer labs in poor, predominantly Black, schools like ours were still not operational, I was being used as a scapegoat by the district. And some of you were going around telling people I had "not done any work" all those years even though you knew the difficulty I was having, to say nothing of having failed to help or lend support. You preferred to sit back on your butts and pass judgment. Someone at the district level had his or her hands in the till, and the money that should have gone to the schools had gone into some-one else's pocket. And now I was being treated as untrustworthy, as a potential if not an actual thief. HELL NO!

I connected what was happening to district corruption, and its need to find a scapegoat for the rampant incompetence. I thought the principal's now obvious prej-udice against black people in positions of authority and trust simply fed into it. All the frustration of five years of trying with no success to get an operational comput-er lab for our school filled up inside of me. I knew I was being accused of a crime and if I didn't stop the accusations they would be held over my head and I would be beat with them as long as I worked there. *That* I wasn't going to tolerate. So, I FLASHED!!!!!!

Yes, folks, with no regard for my profession, my position, or my status as a role model, I turned into the angry Black woman you all fear. I blew off the pretense of "decorum." I opened my mouth and shouted loud enough to be heard in the next city: *"You have been accusing me of deceit since you met me. First the workers comp. forms, then the key to the building . . . I'll be damned if after all the work I put into that lab I am going to be accused of a fucking crime and let the district or your racist ass get away with it. you will give me those fuckin' keys by the end of the goddamn day or fucking arrest and fire me! get me my goddamn union rep noooowwwwww!"*

Yes, I showed my ass that day. But I was resolved. It was make or break and I was completely clear that the district and principal would do right by me or would have to openly lie and put me under arrest. How far were they willing to go in order to bring me down? It was time to find out. It was the assistant superintendent who finally spilled the beans. A manager in Info-Tech who hadn't visited the school in over three years had accused me of sabotaging the computer lab. What proof was there? None, of course. She claimed that since a set of keys had come up missing she was only looking out for my best interest—to remove any doubt—and it was "*normal* procedure." I said, "Bullshit"! I had previously told the manager and the principal that the missing keys had been found and, more importantly, asked why they didn't tell me their plan was to lock me out of my own storeroom before they changed the locks? More to the point, did they plan to change the locks to the stor-age spaces that other teachers had? Did they lock the computer labs of all the com-puter teachers in the district? Well, I got the keys back and a shit load of vague apologies for this "simple misunderstanding." It had all been hyped bullshit. It had simply been their way of trying to put me in my place. But it didn't work. However, it wasn't over because you people couldn't keep my name out of your mouth and your nose out of my business.

Later the following week, your principal (she's yours cuz you picked her, not me—I was in the hospital remember) helped you get all the staff into the library by calling a mandatory "emergency" staff meeting with no agenda. She simply took five minutes to announce the date on which the technicians will finally arrive to set up the lab. Something she could have put in a memo. She and I then left the room. I thought the meeting was over. I went to the bathroom and she to her office. Then I got a knock on the bathroom door for an "emergency" union meeting. I was the building representative, so how could the staff call an emergency union meeting without consulting me first?

The purpose of the meeting was to inform me that due to my "misconduct" you had decided I was no longer welcome at Rosa Parks Elementary School and that you wanted me to resign. Where did you get the notion that you were entitled to openly discuss my personal matters since the issue of staff discipline is between me, my immediate supervisor, and Human Resources? I was devastated. My pain was compounded because the attack was led by a person I had seen as a respected Black Elder, but who turned out to be nothing but a bully and "massuh's overseer." The image of this black woman, surrounded by whites and Asians, pointing her cane in judgment of me, as if being the "fist of whitey" was the same as the right hand of her Christian God, is forever burned into my psyche. She was now willing to give me a verbal lynching thanks to the authority the principal had given her. This woman I had called friend, whom I had phoned in the hopes of discussing the matter, had never returned my calls. She was now standing before Klan and Toms alike, drunk on this little bit of power. It was the greatest betrayal I have ever experienced.

I was symbolically lynched by people I had worked with for years. Not one of you had talked to me about any of your concerns before that day or has done so since. I would have preferred a real beating—those wounds would have healed by now and it would be over. You people truly realized your potential for emotional and institutional violence. This is what you do to the black kids in the class when no one's looking, isn't it?

My righteous expression of indignation was all the excuse some of you needed to justify the punishment you wanted so badly to inflict on me for writing a book that told more truth about your racism than even I had been aware of at the time I wrote it. The book was primarily about prospective teachers in a college classroom who couldn't suppress their racism. It turns out that you were even worse than they when provided with institutional support. Some of you argued that I gave you the ammunition by yelling. You are missing the point. That is your rationalization. The truth is the institution, as represented by the principal, allowed you to avoid having to openly acknowledge to anyone your true feelings about me writing a book that dealt (though only tangentially) with the subject of racism as it was practiced at our school site. Where did this contempt for me come from? Why am I so special that for nine years it was impossible to get the entire staff into one room—but the opportunity to spill my blood built you into a unified force? I find it hard to believe you felt this way about me before the book or when we had an ethical and professional principal. I can't be that thick or naïve.

The hardest part was not that you didn't like me, or even that you didn't want to be fair and hear my side of the story, or offer any support, but that you destroyed the respect and loyalty and, yes, even affection I had for you. You killed my faith that you could grow and learn. You have proven to me that your racism or internalized racism was much deeper than just a character defect, as I naïvely saw it then. I now see it as a well thought-out conscious choice that having a corrupt principal who supported such conduct allowed you to let loose without fear of consequences. Some of you so-called good people with nice manners sat around and methodically planned your attacks with the premeditated coldness of serial killers, while the rest sat around like the German citizens and pretended not to smell my flesh burning. You exercised your white privilege even when you weren't white.

It may not have been "proper" for me to holler in the hallway, but it was the right thing to do to defend myself. I had been cornered: I had tried to talk to the principal and to some of you in order to negotiate and communicate my fears and concerns before that day. I had sent several letters to the principal that took a civilized and professional approach. That didn't work. Expressing my anger in the way I did was apparently the only way to keep my job and the keys as well.

A month doesn't go by when another stunt isn't cooked up that I have to defend myself against. All that is left is my contempt for you because you have devoted so much energy to being vindictive in the name of "professionalism." So let me put this in terms you can understand as we begin another academic year. Thanks to you, I have asthma and suffer from depression, on top of my diabetes. So you are good at causing harm—a dubious achievement unless you're an overseer, tom, or other type of oppressor. But guess what, mother fuckers! I've also got my civil rights, and I still have a fucking job. I have all this because authentic good people with courage, people with highly developed understanding of the true importance of "justice for all"—not "just us"—suffered and died to protect people like me from people like you. I will have justice one day or die trying. Either way—I'm already free.

So bring it on bitches—bring it ON!

Love,

Sekani Moyenda

References

Berlak, A., and Moyenda, S. (2001). *Taking it personally: Racism in classrooms from kindergarten to college.* Philadelphia, PA: Temple University Press.

Boler, M. (1999). *Feeling power: Emotions and education.* New York: Routledge.

Lei, J. (2003). (Un)Necessary toughness? Those "loud black girls" and those "quiet Asian boys." *Anthopology & Education Quarterly, 34*(2): 158–181.

Gutiérrez, K. D. & Rogoff, B. (2003). Cultural ways of learning: Individual traits or repertoires of practice. *Educational Researcher,* 32 (5),19-25.

Salverson, J. (2000). Anxiety and contact in attending to a play about Landmines. In R. Simon, S. Rosenberg, and C. Eppert (Eds.), *Between hope and despair: Pedagogy and the representation of historical trauma,* 59–74. Totowa, NJ: Rutgers University Press.

Conversation

Addressing Resistance: Uncertainties in Learning to Teach

ANN BERLAK, MARY CURRAN, RITA M. KISSEN, & SEKANI MOYENDA

Sekani   (to Mary): Whenever I read articles like this I always think about what it means to have "street smarts." I'm grateful that I have them. Street smarts have taught me to know when I can speak my mind without fear of the kinds of retaliation that most White Americans fear. When I read your article I wondered to what extent your responses to your students are motivated by fear, fear of causing pain or of experiencing it. For example, the student who didn't recognize Miguel or remember him was proof to me that, as I have always argued, racism makes you "stooped." Why didn't you challenge this student with the questions: "Why don't you remember someone who said something so important? Was it because you're afraid of causing students discomfort, let alone pain?" It's my opinion that if you're going to be effective in helping your students to "unlearn" their racism, you're going to have to challenge their self-concept and self-esteem and that will result in having your credibility as an educator threatened.

     As a teacher educator, is it enough to "move your students forward" as opposed to challenging them on a deep personal and professional level? I don't think it is: the standard of "movement" is noble, but is insufficient when you try to reach the "thick headed." So my question is, how far are you willing to go to reach your students? Is it worth the risk to your professional career to challenge their racism when it rears its ugly head? There may go your nice course evaluations; you become the teacher bitch from hell. But if your department head will support your effort to help students "unlearn" racism, he or she should understand that there are times when your students may not like you—as is normal. In your chapter, it seemed that every time you had a teaching opportunity you backed away and fell into a safe academic research and theory place which enabled you to support your unwillingness to challenge your students' racism effectively.

Mary: Sekani, your response challenges me to question my pedagogy. I ask myself, why didn't I respond with anger? Why didn't I link this student's failure to hear Miguel to her grade? Although this type of critique can be difficult to hear, I know it's important for me to be vigilant about my practice, and I welcome this opportunity to see my practice through your perspective. You're right that I need to find a way to confront my students about the racism inherent in their choice to not hear certain information. You're right that my interactional style with my students is an ingrained part of my white, academic discourse and that by keeping within this safe academic research and theory place I may not be taking the necessary risks to fight against oppression.

I appreciate your speaking so directly to me—not many people will do that. In fact, so few people in my usual milieu do speak as frankly and directly as you, Sekani, that I find myself having to actively search them out. My most valued friends are people I've called my sandpaper people—people who, through our encounters, challenge me in my thinking. I feel that by rubbing against them, I (and hopefully they too) have the opportunity to see or feel something differently, and as a result, grow.

Many people, especially mainstream, white Americans, are quite uncomfortable with displays of confrontation and anger. It's such a perfect double-bind: getting emotional, being passionate and challenging the status quo are natural and normal reactions to injustices. However, by labeling challenging behavior as anger and, therefore, an unacceptable discourse style for polite conversation or academic forums, we deny the possibility for communication and find powerful ways to discount claims of injustice.

It would have been easy for me to have reacted with a litany of the reasons why I responded to my student as I did and to have not heard your message, Sekani, because I was wading through a mixture of denial, anger, and pride. Instead, I'm thinking about how the institutional constraints you bring up (concerns about teaching evaluations and tenure promotion) impinge upon my actions, even though my first gut reaction was to deny that I'm concerned about that. I'm really trying to listen and see where my own fears keep me from doing what I consider my most important work and to consider ways I may need to change.

At the same time, I'm questioning what it is that keeps me listening and engaging in this discussion and why my student (and many white students) tune out. I know we need to awaken our students and that discomforting challenges to their self-concept and self-esteem are necessary. However, if the approach taken with the students causes them to engage in total resistance or rejection of the message, is that of any benefit? Might that not, in effect, push them away and eliminate the possibility for change even more? Don't we lose all in that case? Your comments make me think that I could have MADE her learn. It seems that you believe that MAKING her learn is possible. I wonder if it is. Or, would it only have pushed her to a more defensive, and perhaps racist, position as she would have had more fodder to see me as a hypocritical, radical teacher who only wanted to receive the answer that she wanted to hear.

Sekani: I want white teacher educators like yourself to challenge your white students 'cuz we as educators of color are sick of always having to do extra duty at the job site. Not being heard and not having credibility is probably my greatest peeve when it comes to racism. You have to understand that when you are trying to get through to someone who isn't listening to you—you are getting only a small taste of my daily life.

You are at the other end of the spectrum. You believe that if you say or do something a certain way, these people will hear you. My problem is I have tried hundreds of ways for thousands of times in the course of my life to get people to hear me and I am still invisible—until I snap!

I don't think the question is whether or not being angry will shut them off. For me, it has been my experience that they don't hear me unless I express my true feelings. I don't think you understand that the reason your student didn't hear Miguel is the same reason I have to shout to be heard. The racist or oppressive mind is not wired the same way as a just and reasonable mind. The oppressive mindset does not respond to kindness and respect—it responds to instant gratification and threat. The racist mind is a fearful mind with myopic vision and severely dulled senses.

Don't forget—Miguel had said what needed to be said in a sane, kind, respectful, and reasonable manner. We all take that approach first. As a matter of fact, I see white males throw tantrums and make demands much more frequently than people of color. Being rude and threatening seems to work for them and doesn't seem to change people's perception that they are intelligent and capable.

And yes, I do think it is possible to *make* someone learn. It happens all the time. But because I'm open about it people are afraid of me. Which I find strange since people are forced to do all kinds of things they wouldn't do if they had a choice. In the example we are discussing with the student who can't hear Miguel, I was suggesting you provide incentive to pay attention. In reality, I don't know your student and, as you described, perhaps what I suggested wouldn't have been appropriate at that time. What I was implying was that you needed to institutionalize your standards of anti-oppressive learning. While you provide a safe environment for exploring an issue X, you don't provide a just one. A just environment must deal with the abuse of that safe environment. Your classroom should not be a safe haven for the racist *mentality*. If a racist gives you a bad review, runs to your boss pissed off claiming you're incompetent and drops out of your class because you're a bleeding-heart, tree-hugging, justice junkie with delusions of goddesshood, you've done your job. Take the reprimand and frame it.

How else is learning forced? When white men do it, they are leaders and CEOs; when the district does it, they call it professional development; when the college does it they are called exams, and we pay for it too. The difference is that all these forces tell us it is a choice. For five years I had the Success For All cops on my ass to teach their curriculum which I had to learn. Now I have the Houghton Mifflin Nazis with another scripted program that has nothing to do with teaching stalking me to learn *their* program. But I'm never *forced* to learn it. They aren't *making* me do it. They are providing me with support, encouragement, and pay for the professional development days. When I am under surveillance, I mean when they come to observe, they aren't assessing whether or not I keep my job, get tenure, receive more money, have money taken away. Noooo, none of that is force, we just don't leave any child behind.

The purpose direct confrontation should serve is to get adults who are considering teaching in a community different from their own to make well-informed decisions, not to lead to any specific action. I want all white wanna-bees to know what they are getting into, what their responsibility is to that community, to know what it will cost them if they put their loyalty with people of color instead of the dominant culture where they enjoy white privilege. If they choose to maintain their loyalty with the dominant culture and if they come into a community like mine to basically enforce assimilation, they are my enemy and they will spend their entire career battling the kids, their parents, the community leaders, and the allies who share our social justice ideologies.

As educators, like in any other profession, there are losses that must be grieved, examined, learned from, and remembered, but for God's sake don't give them a teaching credential. Sure, I would get pissed if someone came up to me like the student you write about in your chapter came up to you, but don't confuse my style with the issue. The issue here is: should a racist pass a cultural diversity course? Or better yet, let me ask it this way. How the hell does a racist pass a cultural diversity course? That would be like a baby-killer getting a license to run a foster home, or a person who tortures animals for fun becoming a veterinarian. How can a racist, no matter how passive in their expression of it, get to the MSAT when there are teacher educators who consider themselves anti-oppressive teacher educators giving these students passing grades?

You can't be kind all the time. Sometimes you have to be strong and you have to have the faith they need to know that by becoming social justice educators they make the world a better place in all they do as long as they do it ethically, intelligently, and faithfully. Those are the academic standards that we must apply. They aren't easy and they sure aren't easily mapped out into a nice little recipe that anyone can apply. If so, then *anyone* could be a teacher and there would be no need for *social justice educators* to exist. But we do exist, and we have a purpose to serve. Whether we can agree on the strategies is not nearly as important as standing as leaders and rising to the occasion to do whatever is necessary, including giving our students a quick kick in the butt when they need it.

Ann: Mary, I am glad to engage with you about the issue of confrontation and anger in anti-oppressive classrooms. It's an issue Sekani and I have been pondering for several years now. Basically, what we have come to believe (and argued in *Taking It Personally*) is that for some students experiencing a trauma or crisis that results initially in "total resistance or rejection of the message" may be a necessary (though not sufficient) step in the journey to perspective transformation. We agree with

Shoshana Felman and Dori Laub (1992) that "teaching in itself takes place precisely through crisis" (p. 55). However, what we have learned from our collaboration is that it is absolutely essential that teachers and students process or reflect together upon the trauma, carefully and non-judgmentally examining their conscious and unconscious responses to it and the origins of their responses. These responses often involve shame, fear, and grief. We need to observe ourselves being unable to hear claims of racism when they are made in voices inflected with anger. We need to reflect upon the significance of becoming angry at the messenger, but not at the message of racism.

Mary: You're right—we need to learn how to do this, and we have to learn how to do it well. We have to learn to demand the learning—like I would of reading or writing, and take more risks. These days there is such a proliferation of educators who talk about doing social justice work. We all know that many of us (who claim to be doing this kind of work) do not get it. That is truly scary. To get it, I really think that one has to be willing to change one's life—to change in deep ways that cause conflict, discomfort, and pain. For example, at a minimum, as you say, we need to be aware that getting a "bad review" is an expected, even necessary, part of the game if we are really committed to not harboring a racist mentality. And, clearly it's got to be much, much more than that.

The truth is, as I think about this, I know I'd be losing friends right and left if I "called" the racist mentality when I saw it. You write about how hard it is to be able to predict when racism (or other "isms") will appear—we all know we see it even in our closest friends and in ourselves at times. Yet this is exactly why it's perpetuated—and so invisibly and silently. And, this is exactly why teachers, all of us, need some awakening, preparation, and time to reflect upon just what to do in these situations—so that we can become change agents.

Our chapters point to the need for a more careful analysis of our pedagogical tools. As Rita writes, we need to make the link to show how the students will become better teachers. One way to begin answering these questions is by engaging in the type of conversations we're attempting to enter into right now. We need to give more space in our personal and professional lives for this kind of collaborative work that challenges and causes us to question; however, this is not easy. For example, to bring the four of us together via email to engage in this discussion was like pulling teeth, due to time constraints because of work and family pressures, and perhaps also due to a lack of models for how to begin. As I write this response, I feel very constrained by the tool of writing as well. Limiting myself to a few brief words (which then might be taken out of context or at least understood within the limited context of this edited conversation) does not seem like an adequate vehicle to express the complicated responses I had to the three chapters and to Sekani's response to mine. And, I'm very disappointed to find that I am still locked within academic language. As much as I try to write from my gut and emotion, I keep censoring it.

Ann (to Rita): Perhaps your students need to be taught a gut-level grasp of the concepts of capitalism and exploitation before they can "rethink their assumptions about poor people." Without these lenses I think they will continue to be unable to "apprehend the reality of the other," blaming poor children's academic performance on unloving parents who have poor parenting skills, and seeing solutions in individualistic, charitable terms ("I wanted to give them so much more"). They will continue to be "saddened by the unmet needs they saw all around them," while attributing the problems to "evil people," rather than feeling angry at a system that insures the needs will be unmet. They need to be helped to put the glass and needle-strewn playgrounds into the broader context of a political-economic system that is cutting social programs simultaneously with the taxes of the rich.

I wonder whether your students might be better able to "make a genuine connection with the lives of their students" if you offered them lenses that honored race and class as these intersect with gender, and built your pedagogy around their own experiences as Freire and Vygotsky have taught us to do. Only after you have done so will you be in a position to decide if the problem is that they are simply "developmentally unready" (lack the maturity) to become anti-oppressive teachers.

Sekani (to Rita): I found myself wondering if you ever experienced the debate between Black Womanists and White Feminists. While I was a student at San Francisco State University, this debate raged between the Women's Studies Department and the Black Studies Department. When I read your chapter, it reminded me of why I got sick of the Women's Studies Department and finally left.

The perspective you were teaching seems to assume that all women are assigned the same (middle-class white) roles in their cultures and that all men's roles within each culture are the same as those of white males in yours. Does sexism exist in the black community and contribute something to the issues your students will have to face? Yes!

218 PART IV ADDRESSING RESISTANCE

Will teaching your students to use the lens of white feminism help your preservice teachers make a genuine connection with the lives of their students? I don't think so!

If you want the students to learn about the "ethics of care," why weren't your sources of feminist theory the specific communities' leaders and scholars such as bell hooks or Audry Lourde? What perspective on the role of women in that black community was represented in the film "Anchor of the Soul?" Did the film you showed interpret the Hopi culture as sexist ("limited choices for women," "narrowly defined roles") or was this your interpretation? Is this how the Hopi women who live it viewed their culture? How could you integrate into your courses the perspectives and expertise of the children your students will teach and their parents, and of their community leaders and scholars?

What evidence do you have that your teaching strategies were an asset to these communities and not another form of racist missionary indoctrination that undermined and trivialized their culture?

Rita: Reading the chapters by Ann and Sekani and Mary, along with their responses to my chapter and to each other, has been both chastening and validating. Like many white academics, I have been taught, and have taught my students, to be Nice—to respond to others in ways that will not hurt their feelings. Ann's and Sekani's questions demand more of me—they lead me to the same kind of discomfort that Ann's students experienced during Sekani's visit, and that Mary describes on first reading Sekani's response to her article.

On the other hand, I found myself nodding along with much of what Ann and Sekani suggest, since their concerns echo many of the changes my teaching partner and I have made since I wrote the chapter. We now spend more time explicitly explaining concepts related to class, and we discuss race and racism more directly as we continue to use "The Hopi: Songs of the Fourth World," "Anchor of the Soul," and "Salt of the Earth." Each of these films presents a complex view of a non-European culture, relies on the voices of members of that culture, and defies the stereotypes that our students bring to the classroom. Despite the fact that Portland is a Refugee Resettlement Center, Maine remains the "whitest" state in the country (tied with Vermont), with just over 3 percent of the population identifying as nonwhite. Most of our students grow up without any contact with people who are not White, and most will teach and live in overwhelmingly White environments. Talking about race with them poses its own set of challenges.

As my three co-conversationalists point out, anti-oppressive education has consequences. One example from the 2002 to 2003 semester suggests just how threatening a serious discussion of race can be to white students. In an especially powerful segment of the film "Anchor of the Soul," an African American woman raised in Portland describes what happened back in the 1950s when the seniors at her high school decided to hold their prom at the local Elks club. After the school's few black seniors learned that the Elks Club had a policy barring blacks from membership, they asked their classmates to move the prom to a downtown hotel.

The class refused. Unlike other local venues in town, the Elks Club boasted air conditioning. The woman goes on to describe how she and her black classmates contacted the local NAACP, and how a group of black citizens and white allies picketed the prom. She adds proudly that some of the white students in her class were among the picketers, choosing to make a statement against racism rather than to attend their high school prom at a segregated venue.

When we showed the film in the fall of 2002 we asked the class what they would have done if they had been in the black woman's senior class. To our astonishment, a group of preservice teachers responded indignantly that the black students had no right to try to move the prom. Proms were always held in June, they argued, and air conditioning would be really important to such an event. I played my usual role (let everyone be heard, don't alienate students). My teaching partner, a white working-class labor historian, was far more confrontational and dared to use the word "racism." The discussion turned nasty, as a few students came to the defense of the black seniors in the film and the rest remained silent. In their course evaluations that semester, several students accused us of calling them racists. Some wrote that if they wanted a course in black history, they would have taken a black history course. These were the worst evaluations we had ever received.

In her response to Mary, Sekani predicts that challenging students' racism "will result in having your credibility as an educator threatened. . . . There may go your nice course evaluations; you become the teacher bitch from hell." Sekani's predictions describe precisely what has happened to me in the Culture and Community course. Evaluations for this course have consistently been well below evaluations for my other courses and below the university and college course averages. This fall, these low course evaluations have been a major stumbling block in my application for promotion, despite the fact that I have received good or excellent ratings in my other courses and have a strong record of teaching, service, and scholarship. Contesting this decision feels empowering but reminds me that antiracist teaching challenges not only one's students, but colleagues and administrators as well. I am grateful for the voices of Ann, Sekani, and Mary, as well as the others in this volume, who remind me that making change is hard work but infinitely worth doing.

Sekani: I'm so excited by your responses. It is rare that I get beyond that point of polite conversation to authentic dialogue. You've raised legitimate questions that have to be answered by all educators. Whether or not we agree is not my concern as much as wondering how anyone can argue they even have pedagogy when they refuse to investigate, assess, and apply strategies that address issues like anger, power, and anti-oppression education standards?

Ann: I think it's important for us to put this conversation in social and political context. Now in this country the pressures to teach for social reproduction rather than social transformation are tremendous and flourishing. When I came to California 15 years ago, the state required all preservice teachers to take a cultural diversity course. As inadequate as that may have been, it was a far cry from what we have now: state and federal mandates to train teachers to teach their students to score well on standardized tests. Political pressure to teach for social justice has nearly vanished. Conversations like the ones in this book are one way to keep hope alive in these dark times.

Epilogue

Mary has invited Miguel and the student-who-didn't-hear-Miguel to engage in a collaborative case-study research project to analyze the teacher education students' partnership activities with the adult ESOL learners. Sekani and Mary will collaborate on a long-distance (California–New Jersey) project connecting Sekani's first-grade students and Mary's teacher education students.

Reference

Felman, S., and Laub, D. (1992). *Testimony: Crises of witnessing in literature and psychoanalysis.* New York: Routledge.

Part V

Complicating Race

Engaging Anti-Racist Educational Theory and Practice

9

Moving Beyond the "Simple Logic" of Labeling?[1]

CONNIE NORTH

If it is not in the language, it is not in the mind.
And if it is not in the mind, it cannot be in the social structure.
—PARAPHRASING SISTER JOAN CHITTISTER[2]

It is the second week of my students' fourth semester in the elementary teacher education program. When these students arrive in the classroom for the third class session of the mandatory social studies methods course that I teach, they remain unsure about who I am and what I might be scheming to do. I contend that most of them—20 of 23, in fact—see a white female graduate student who, in physical appearance at least, seems like them (in my class, there are 3 students of color and 3 males, one of the males is Latino).

How do the intersection of gender, race, and sexuality shape student perceptions of, and, therefore, responses to, the teacher? As Gloria Ladson-Billings (1996) points out, the status and power attributed to a white male educator can differ dramatically from those assigned to a black female educator. And these attachments differ from those ascribed to a white woman, a Korean American man, a gay black man, etc. When you add the additional status differential between a professor and a teaching assistant, the power dynamics become even more complex.

I have little doubt that my status as a graduate student and female diminished my "authority" in the classroom. However, in a formal university context, I think my race and the cultural capital that I have accumulated via my upper middle-class upbringing and

elite undergraduate and graduate education create a certain faith among most of my stu-
dents in my ability to teach the course. Nevertheless, given the limited number of compet-
ing perspectives introduced into classroom discussions by virtue of the largely homogeneous
racial, gender, sexual, religious, and geographical backgrounds of the students, my repeat-
ed interruption of dominant discourses (e.g., equality means sameness) perpetually threat-
ened to become seen as the actions of a pathological individual (e.g., "Connie is just
crazy"). As Britzman (2003) points out, when instructors do not have the buy-in of their
students, who perhaps do not want to be bothered, feel threatened by alternative points of
view, and/or do not have experience acting as social critics, their efforts risk "being reduced
to the idiosyncrasy of the lone individual" (p. 207).

The first day of the course, however, I attempted to subvert their assumptions.
First, I emphasized that the nearly three years of living in Senegal as a Peace Corps
Volunteer shook up my worldview and my ideas about what constitutes effective
teaching for all children. I also presented them with a quote from Gloria Ladson-
Billing's (1994) *The Dreamkeepers* that emphasized the scarcity of elementary preservice teachers who express, along with their fondness for children, a love of
intellectual rigor or the possibility of using knowledge for empowerment. "I am
assuming that the students of whom Professor Ladson-Billings spoke are not you,"
I told them. A couple of my students—those who resented being treated like the
children whom they planned to teach in other courses—responded with a vocal
"Thank you!" I am somewhat sure that I scared, or at least threw off, a number of
others who remained silent.

What they and I could not know on that first day together was that my 29 years of
living as a heterosexual woman were about to come to an end. A few months after the
semester ended, I began dating a woman for the first time and, thus, living the queer the-
ory that I had been reading for several years. Consequently, I was forced to rethink my self-
ascribed identity and what it might mean for me to claim the labels "queer" and "lesbian"
for myself in public and private spaces. How could I take ownership of the heterosexual
privileges I had enjoyed my entire life and simultaneously recognize that the label "straight"
no longer held? How could I advocate for the queer youth facing violence and perpetual
taunting in their classrooms, playgrounds, hallways, and homes without reducing their suf-
fering or their complex daily lives to a one-dimensional label? Related to Sister Chittister's
message, where was the language to deal with these complex relationships and contradic-
tions? How could I—how can I—fight the silencing that works against such language
making it into and thus transforming our minds, hearts, and social structure?

During the second class, I warned the students that they would be reading a
philosophical article by Ian Hacking (1986) called "Making Up People." To prepare
them for this piece, we discussed the concept of "nominalism"—the philosophical
notion that objects labeled by the same term (horses, for example, or stars) have
nothing *intrinsically* in common but the name that human beings assign to them.

I imagine as they shuffle into class today that they are worried about (or annoyed at) having to confront, once again, some abstract educational theory that they see as having little practical bearing on their future teaching careers. My primary goals for the day are (1) to demonstrate that the naming of phenomena, people, and practices in the world can have real material consequences for both the namers and the named; (2) the superficial use of names (i.e., adopting a label without interrogating how it is used in the world) can be just as problematic as the employment of labels to which we attach significant meaning.

One final bit of background information—after the first class session, the students had to write a short autobiographical piece answering the question, "Why teach social studies?" I asked them to consider how their backgrounds, including their class, race, ethnicity, gender, religion, geographical locale, family constellation, personal attributes, and experiences, had influenced their attitudes toward social studies. They do not know it yet, but I will be linking these personal narratives to that dreadfully theoretical idea of nominalism before the class is through.

Ironically, "sexuality" was not on this laundry list of background factors for the autobiographical essay. Did I assume "gender" adequately covered the sexuality territory? I certainly did not consciously omit this particular identity category. In fact, during the semester I arranged for the local school district's gay, lesbian, bisexual, transgender, and queer (GLBTQ) resource teacher to come in and speak to my students about their legal duty to ensure the safety of all children and to provide curriculum suggestions related to sexuality. During that class, I covered the chalkboard with startling statistics—a nationwide survey's finding that 84 percent of GLBTQ students experienced verbal harassment at school; a recent survey's finding that 33 percent of GLB high school students reported attempting suicide in the previous year in comparison to 8 percent of their heterosexual peers; service providers' estimation that 25–40 percent of homeless youth are GLBTQ (Advocates for Youth, 2006). Perhaps my concern that these future teachers create safe spaces for their GLBTQ students precluded my exploration of how heterosexism was functioning in our classroom.

Incidentally, I recently came out to one of my former students. She wished I had claimed queerness while teaching the class, as she deemed many of her classmates "homophobes" and thought I might have been able to challenge their assumptions with my personal story. As she pointed out, statistics and a lesbian guest speaker and expert on GLBTQ issues did not push her peers to a different place with regard to sexuality—a place in which they were willing and able to perform "new readings, new meanings, and associations with different emotions" (Kumashiro, 2002, p. 63).

Getting Started

Today's session begins with the viewing of a 25-minute clip of the third videocassette in California Newsreel's (2003) series *Race: The Power of an Illusion.* I have three particular learning outcomes in mind when pushing "Play": students will contemplate the social rather than biological roots of race in the United States as well as the complicity of supposedly neutral and just social institutions, like the Supreme Court, in producing and reproducing a racial hierarchy; students will reevaluate the assumption that the subordination and exclusion of people based on their skin color were and are solely Black and white issues; and the students will (re)consider the social studies content area in sociohistorical and sociopolitical terms.

I have chosen the segment that describes U.S. race relations during the early twentieth century. The documentary emphasizes the "mosaic of values, assumptions, and historical meanings" attached to racial characteristics in the United States by showing how the numerous European immigrants who came to the United States from 1880 to 1920 fit into the already established racial hierarchy. The video also emphasizes the laws and practices that advantaged white people during this period and throughout the twentieth century. More specifically, it describes the rise of scientific race theory and the eugenics movement, the 1915 lynching of Jewish Leo Frank, the erratic definitions of racial identity used by particular states so as to prevent miscegenation and to enforce Jim Crow laws, and the Supreme Court's denial of citizenship, first to Japanese Americans via the *Ozawa* decision in 1922 and, three months later, to South Asian Americans via the *Thind* ruling.

The classroom mood is somber when I stop the videocassette and turn on the lights.

Beginning to Make Linkages

After viewing the videocassette, we sit in a circle and each person shares something about the film or Hacking's article that they learned and/or found surprising, problematic, or thought provoking. Intending to create a forum where everyone has an opportunity to express his or her reactions, I ask the students not to interrupt or respond to each other's viewpoints just yet. Soon enough, we will have an opportunity to engage in dialogue.

Several of the students communicate shock at the hypocrisy of the purportedly impartial Supreme Court. Others discuss the ways in which classification has been used as a tool of legitimation for those in power. More specifically, Ashley points out that the association of the "common man" with whiteness establishes white people as normal and others as deviant. Dana asserts that assimilation into the culture of the white majority has demanded that people of color accept an inferior status. Mia wants to know whether there was a time when we did not categorize people according to perceived differences. Stacey conveys her concern that a focus on the ways in which race is socially constructed undermines the real effects of racism on people's lives. She relates an anecdote from a previous anthropology course wherein a second-generation Chinese American student resisted the idea of race as a human creation rather than a biological fact because he felt like it called into question the concrete examples of discrimination that he had faced throughout his life.

Having begun the process of examining the consequences of classifying people according to historical, social, political, and cultural interpretations of (ab)normality, we are ready to face Hacking's argument directly.

Diving into Hacking: The Realm of "Dynamic Nominalism"

> But some of the things that we ourselves do are intimately connected to our descriptions . . . What is curious about human action is that by and large what I am deliberately doing depends on the possibilities of description . . . if new modes of description come into being, new possibilities for action come into being in consequence.
>
> —IAN HACKING

Before asking students whether they have specific questions about Hacking's argument, I address some issues raised by the students in the circle. First and foremost, I want to emphasize that we are exploring how categories like race are socially determined not to suggest that labels like "black" are figments of our imagination but, rather, to emphasize that the socially constructed nature of such brandings means they can be reconstructed in ways that promote a democratic society based on social equality and the inclusion of a plurality of people and viewpoints. In other words, seeing categories and institutions as human creations opens the door to the possibility of a different world, a different reality. Second, I propose that the problem is not classification itself, which seems to be a universal practice, but the values underlying such cataloging of people. Stated differently, it is the work that labels do—the normalizing of some and marginalizing, silencing, and exploiting of Others—that poses a problem, for such labeling, whether intentional or not, results in the inequitable sorting and sifting of resources, individual and group rights, and (dis)respect.

We then move into a discussion of the distinction that Hacking makes between "static" and "dynamic" nominalism, as William admits confusion over Hacking's use of these concepts. I decide to use LeighAnn's resistance to Hacking's argument that "the homosexual" does not exist in the "natural" world as a way to get at this distinction. During the sharing session, LeighAnn insisted that homosexuality has been around since at least the Old Testament where it was repeatedly documented. "Why," she insisted, "is Hacking claiming that human beings, rather than nature or God, have created homosexuals?"

I use the text to point out that Hacking does not claim the nonexistence of homosexuality. He believes, unlike "static nominalists," that "many categories come from nature, not from the human mind" (p. 228). In other words, and as Hacking points out, a horse remains a horse and a planet remains a planet regardless of what we call them. Gloves, on the other hand, take us into the realm of dynamic nominalism, as people, not nature or God, manufacture gloves. While it is not clear whether the thought or the mitten came first, Hacking underscores that the category and the object "emerged hand in hand" (p. 229). That is, the idea of a glove did not exist in the world before human beings undertook the task of producing one.

Hacking, therefore, does not deny that homosexuality, in terms of an attraction between and/or sexual actions involving people with the same sexual anatomy, is real or ancient. Rather, he wants to emphasize that *the* homosexual, as a "kind of person" to whom people and institutions respond in particular, historically contingent ways and, in turn, who performs her identity in particular, historically contingent ways, "came into being at the same time as the kind itself was being invented" (p. 228). Michel Foucault (1978/1990) has identified the nineteenth century as the moment when psychological, psychiatric, and medical discourses in "the West" characterized and, thus, constituted the homosexual. As he wrote, "Homosexuality appeared as one of the forms of sexuality when it was transposed from the practice of sodomy onto a kind of interior androgyny, a hermaphrodism of the soul. The sodomite had been a temporary aberration; the homosexual was now a species" (p. 43).

What, then, are the social implications of this lofty-sounding theory of "dynamic nominalism"? When applied to the notion of "the homosexual," Hacking suggests that the distinction we make between "heterosexual" and "homosexual" influences the lived reality of the people who identify or do not identify with these labels. Relating this notion to social justice, he asserts that by associating certain labels with rigid descriptions—all homosexuals are abnormal, perverted, and/or sick, for example—we diminish "the space of possibilities for personhood." In sum, our labels for and descriptions of people matter because in particular social contexts, such as the classroom, they shape (and often limit) individual actions, beliefs, and understandings of themselves and Others.

Would I have come out to my students if I were teaching the course now? I like to think so. After all, I told my father about my queerness after less than two months of transgressing heterosexual boundaries. And I could not imagine anything more terrifying than this admission, as the effects of disappointing him felt so much scarier than the negative judg-

ments of or sanctions imposed by my students, colleagues, advisors, boss, and/or the University. Then again, when I recently tutored a multiracial group of seventh-grade boys (one was Hmong, another Latino, and the third African American) for the first time, I said nothing when the Latino student called the African American student "gay." I managed to say, "I don't sound like that," when the same boy told the Hmong student he was reading like a "girl," but I felt overwhelmed by the sheer number of labels floating effortlessly off these students' tongues in the space of five minutes.

My silence, in part, stems from the recognition that they, as students of color, face subtle, terrorizing, daily oppressions that I cannot even begin to imagine and do not want to deny. And, yet, they are also contributing to the domination of Others via their gendered and sexualized epithets. Joy Lei (2003) writes that it is within the

> complicated relationship between identities at the interpersonal level and discourses of knowledge at a structural level . . . that the symbolic realm (in which histories, experiences, and people are represented) and material realities collide, interact, and coexist. It is also within this relationship that identities are created, imposed, appropriated, resisted, and embraced. (p. 158)

During the upcoming year, as these students and I struggle to forge relationships across power inequities and identity barriers—barriers that are so often imposed rather than intentionally erected—I trust that we will find ways to challenge and expand our descriptions of each other.

Integrating Hacking into the "Real" World

Aware that Hacking's theory is new territory for many of the students, I want to give them an opportunity to apply his ideas to the concrete world of teaching and learning. I, therefore, ask them to break into small groups and discuss the relevance of Hacking's arguments to social studies education. To scaffold this conversation, I first present them with the following set of questions that relate directly to the material effects of creating "kinds of people":

> The next discussion questions are difficult and require a large degree of honesty with yourself and others. Reflect on and name "some of the things that we ourselves do [that] are intimately connected to our descriptions" (Hacking, 1986, pp. 230–231). How do you think these potentially limit and/or create possibilities for teaching and learning in your future classroom? Some suggestions: Think about what assumptions you have upon hearing the labels "at-risk," "special ed," "urban school," "queer." How might these "modes of description" influence your actions?

To introduce a second line of questioning emerging from Hacking's article, I then reveal a list of concept labels that I have written on the chalkboard, which come directly from the social studies autobiographies they wrote after the first day of class. These labels include the following instructional goals: "teaching for diversity," "understanding cultural differences," and "promoting democratic citizenship." I emphasize that these concept labels appeared throughout the students' autobiographies but have not necessarily been critically examined. Suggesting that Hacking's explanation of "static nominalism" might be useful in an analysis of *why* something like "teaching for diversity" matters, I give them the following questions:

> What do the concept labels up on the board mean in concrete, day-to-day practices? That is, apart from labeling them as significant aspects of the teaching and learning of social studies, what behaviors/social interactions/actions, beliefs, ideas, attitudes, and pedagogical strategies accompany them? In Hacking's terms, what "possibilities for action come into being" as a consequence of describing things like "active citizenship," "understanding cultural differences," and "critical thinking"?

My main objective in asking the second set of questions is to challenge the dominant notion that the learning of educational ideas and/or the facile use of them in class discussions and assignments translate easily into compatible, effective instructional practices. Too often, educators' claims of teaching for diversity and equity are more rhetorical than substantive. Indeed, James Gee (1996) asserts that the primary lesson learned via schooling is how to talk about practices rather than enact them. Accordingly, educators frequently convert "multicultural education" into the superficial teaching of diversity—what Elsie Begler (1998) calls the "Five Fs" (food, fashion, fiestas, folklore, and famous people)—despite the repeated efforts of teacher education programs to instantiate a version of multicultural education that includes attention to institutionalized oppression and the unequal distribution of resources in U.S. society.

Today's class activities and conversations serve as gateways into themes that we will be exploring throughout the rest of the course—namely, the concrete meaning of teaching for social justice and our own complicity in perpetuating labels that diminish rather than expand spheres of human agency. Accordingly, I assure students that Hacking will continue to rear what several of them view as his very ugly head. To push them to practice implementing his ideas, I end the class by asking the students to reread their social studies autobiographies and examine how the discussions in today's class session influence their interpretation of these narratives. They are then to revise their autobiographies in whatever way they see fit. I encourage them to read their narratives through a "Hackingian" lens but do not foreclose the possibility of resistance to his argument. A revised autobiography, therefore, may consist of an addendum to the initial text (rather than an interruption or reinterpretation of it) that explains why Hacking's argument and/or my teaching of it is/are all wet.

Second Round: My Own Need for Revision

Did I tell you that this is my second time using these materials to push students to reflect on the social construction of race, class, gender, (dis)ability, religion, and sexuality as well as the ways in which language may or may not produce significant material effects in the classroom and beyond?

The first time I taught the class, the discussion was explosive. I intended to have the students break into small groups, but the barrage of direct challenges to the ideas I put forth just kept coming. In hindsight, I could have dispelled this adversarial climate, as well as the notion that only I had a competing perspective to offer, by dividing the students up or asking other students to respond to their peers' defiant questions. Instead, I played the role of teacher as expert—or at least "teacher who has thought about these things long and hard"—and several of the students read me as a political propagandist. By diminishing the legitimate spaces in the class from which they could respond, I succeeded in disempowering them (Ellsworth, 1987/1994, 1997).

In effect, I attempted to transfer my own theories and practices onto the students, the underlying assumption being that I could "know and control the processes of teaching and learning" (Ellsworth, 1997; Kumashiro, 2002, pp. 62–68). By not leaving space for the "unknowability" (Ellsworth, 1997) that constitutes human relations within and beyond the classroom, I ultimately mimicked the very "banking education" (Freire, 1970). I had explicitly challenged on the first day of class. I thus failed to push students to make their own meanings of Hacking's argument—to take response-ability for the way they contributed to the creation and fortification of "kinds of people." Returning to Hacking's argument, I limited the students' very "possibilities of description" by reducing them to "Christian," "white," "straight," "suburban" "women." And, unfortunately, I think I forever lost a few of the students that day, as I expressed, through their lenses, a political dogmatism that proscribed an understanding of their positions and knowledges.

I cannot know how the students would have responded to an acknowledgment that I was one of "those"—a homosexual. But my own assumptions about my parents' response to my queerness revealed to me that I still have much work to do when it comes to opening, rather than foreclosing, spaces for anti-oppressive dialogue.

I feared my father's response to my revised sexual status so much that I outed myself to him via a carefully crafted e-mail message. Through this mode of communication, I did not have to face his immediate reaction. However, his response, which took place within a day of sending the missive, was one of love and support. And through his answer, he taught me an important lesson about unknowability: by addressing people as if they have a "fixed and coherent position" about identity categories such as race, sexuality, and gender, and, thus, creating an ideal of how people "should" respond (Ellsworth, 1997, p. 31;

Kumashiro, 2002), we perpetuate vocabularies of deficit and hierarchy and, in turn, human relations that detail "the inadequacies of those who do not compare favourably" (Ludema et al., 2001, p. 197).

Better, I think, is to speak and act from a place of compassion, defined by Thich Nhat Hanh (1992) as a person's ability to suffer with another. While we need to remain critical and reflexive about our own and others' claims related to issues of oppression, what social change might become possible if we considered liberatory words and actions to be those that demonstrate a deep recognition—a "witnessing"—of "the physical, material, and psychological suffering of others" (Hanh, 1992, pp. 81–83)? How might such a view strengthen and deepen my relationships with my students and father, all of whom have their own complicated histories of struggle and suffering?

The second time I taught the class, then, I attempted, whenever possible, to make my pedagogy available for critical examination in both class discussions and assignments. In so doing, I sought to resist the idea that students should "ask questions about content or pedagogy in their teacher education courses" but not " of those teacher education courses" (Segall, 2002, p. 9). However, I am aware that my power to evaluate the students (via their final grade) made such public questioning of my practices an uncomfortable, seemingly risky enterprise (Segall, 2002, p. 160). Nonetheless, to promote a "reflective practitioner" (Zeichner and Liston, 1991) agenda without attempting to practice it is both unethical and dishonest. As Avner Segall (2002) writes, "[R]ecognizing the degree of courage it might take to overcome the difficulties in having those involved in preservice education read their learning environment critically, is not a reason to abandon the project" (p. 160).

And the second time I taught this lesson, I did not face the same sort of resistance. Although different group dynamics and distinctive individual characteristics explain a significant amount of the variation in outcomes, they do not tell the whole story. After taking into account student responses to the lesson last semester, I thought through how to present Hacking's argument more clearly—how I could scaffold deeper understandings of dynamic and static nominalism and the implications of these concepts for social studies instruction. Accordingly, I revised the questions I asked, the examples I used, and the way I presented both of them.

Nonetheless, I still contend that when few competing perspectives are voiced (even when they exist) in educational settings, not only because of a homogenous racial and ethnic student makeup but also because of institutional norms that stress compliance, conformity, and consensus (Segall, 2002, p. 9), the students are more likely to write off a persistently "critical" teacher educator as eccentric or biased. Additionally, like many teacher educator programs, this one uses cohorts. Because the students enter my classroom having already spent three semesters together, they feel like they already know everyone's point of view—as if perspectives were static, impervious entities—and, therefore, have little to gain by delving into controversial issues with one another. To upset this myth of absolute knowing, the students often need their unexamined assumptions laid bare through role plays, case studies, or other forms of experiential education.

To that end, I followed up the second Hacking lesson with a labeling activity that I observed while studying student responses to a high school leadership camp (see North, 2007). Only after throwing the students into emotional "crisis" (Kumashiro, 2002) via this exercise did the students acknowledge that racialization and racism were functioning in our very own classroom. Since this experiential exercise both intentionally Othered every student and invoked their complicity in the act of Othering (thereby attempting to effect what Deborah Britzman [1998] calls "learning from" rather than "learning about"), many of the students expressed emotional distress and pain. And, subsequently, I had to devote a significant amount of time and energy to helping students work through that trauma (Berlak and Moyenda, 2001). In the end, I think the effort was worth it. However, I elected not to teach (and was lucky enough to have this "choice") the course the following year because I felt physically and psychologically spent after a single year of attempting to teach for social justice at the college level.

According to Britzman (1998), the "capacity to love, to work, and to learn without invoking more harm and suffering" demands "both a patience with the incommensurability of understanding and an interest in tolerating the ways meaning becomes, for the learner, fractured, broken, and lost, exceeding the affirmations of rationality, consciousness, and consolation" (pp. 118 and 129). During the past few months, I have tried to cultivate more self-compassion as I work through the internal conflicts and confusion that have emerged through the process of significantly transforming my sexual identity, of letting go of some of my deep-seated attachments to an unambiguous, stable version of Connie. I like to think this sometimes joyous, sometimes traumatic journey will improve my pedagogy and engagement with students who are both visibly and invisibly different from me. I also like to think that my more open-ended view of the world will contribute to the realization of a social reality where finding people, regardless of gender, whom you love and who love you is honored rather than condemned.

But I want to end this revision on a positive note. The Hacking discussion during the first semester was not a total catastrophe. It influenced at least some of the students' thinking about labeling, as demonstrated by their revised social studies autobiographies. Linda, for example, used this assignment to analyze an experience she had during one of her practicums in a local elementary school. I read aloud the following excerpt of her narrative to both the first- and second-semester groups of students to illustrate an articulate application of Hacking's theory to the classroom:

I had thought about how people assign labels to others and embrace them for themselves, but the Hacking article put a different spin on the issue for me. I was interested in the point that labels themselves actually create what they are describing. That is, it is not just that something previously existed without a name, but that it did not exist until there was a name to give it. Once I got that into my head a little, an example from one of my practicums came to me. When I first arrived to work in the classroom, my supervising teacher did not hesitate to tell me what she thought of each student in the class. One of the students had been branded "the troublemaker." I prefer not to make judgments on students, and I would certainly not make decisions about their personalities and roles in the class before even really meeting them, so I listened to what my teacher had to say, but decided to keep my mind open.

****

The first thing that struck me about "the troublemaker" was that he was the one African American student in the class, and actually the only non-white student. He was also a very active child, who did not enjoy sitting still, but was engaged when given something that he enjoyed doing. He had a very mature way of relating to my practicum partner and me, talking to us almost as peers (in an appropriate way). I noticed when I first worked with him that he gave up very easily; when he hit a challenge, he shut down and expected to be handed the answer. I observed my teacher with him, and when he got frustrated in class, she rolled her eyes and gave the answer herself or asked another student to answer. I also noticed that when she addressed him, she always used a sharper tone than with the other students, even when he was not misbehaving. At times when the whole class was inattentive, she almost always singled him out for demerit points. He could say the exact same thing as other students, and she would read a tone in his words that she deemed punishable. I did not make any assumptions at first; after all, I was the new one in the classroom, and I did not know the history. But this way of interacting with this one student continued the whole time I was in the classroom. I saw in that situation that the student in question could read how the teacher categorized him, and he acted accordingly. He was the troublemaker because he was labeled so.

I have held onto Linda's revised social studies autobiography to remind myself that this sort of work can make a difference, even if it is small.

Postscript/Manifesto?

As a teacher educator of predominantly white students, my central objective often entails imagining creative ways to expose their and my multiple privileges so that we can begin a discussion on how to challenge and transform systemic inequalities. I would like to devote more time to mulling over and planning strategic, collective social action to confront these complicated, intersecting oppressions—and should—but also think such work would be putting the cart before the horse when there is little to no recognition of the ways in which the social injustices we study *over there* are functioning right here, in the institutional settings where we spend our days and in the social interactions that take place in those spaces.

Moreover, if we do not attend to the tensions resulting from the simultaneous need to use social group labels for political purposes (since social groups structure our hierarchical social order [MacKinnon, 2002; Young, 1990]) and desire not to reduce individual people to those labels, we threaten to create new forms of silencing, marginalization, and Othering. As Matthew Jacobson (1998) argues, race-based politics (and I would include other social group politics, such as gender-based activism, as well), while a practical necessity, also sustain the concept of race, which can render harmful consequences. In his words, "So deeply embedded is racialism in our national political structures that movements to alleviate racial tension on one front are likely to influence the racial chemistry on another, perhaps in unexpected ways" (p. 272). Still, the dangers of unforeseen costs do not justify paralysis. We all need to respond.

After returning from a major education conference recently, where I heard a lot of talking heads (many white and male) throwing around words such as equity, diversity, and social justice, I despaired over how many conversations take equal access to educational institutions of all "kinds of people" (Hacking, 1986) for granted when such access has not been achieved at the postsecondary level, the administrative/leadership level, and certainly not at the teacher level. Why are we not more outraged that nearly 90 percent of K-12 teachers are white when at least 35 percent of their students (and many more in major U.S. cities) are not (Banks, 2002; Tye, 2000)? How would teacher education (and teacher educators) transform if the K-12 teaching force actually came from and lived with the communities where they teach? How might the learning and daily lives of the three students of color in my class be improved? In more direct terms, how many of us claiming to work for social justice are acknowledging and confronting our own complicity in perpetuating an unjust educational system (Thompson, 2003)?

Francisco Valdes (2002) writes about the need to challenge "Euroheteropatriarchy": "The interlocking operation of dominant forms of racism, ethnocentrism, androcentrism, and heterocentrism—all of which operate in tandem in the United States and beyond it to produce identity hierarchies that subordinate people of color, women, and sexual minorities in different yet similar and familiar ways" (p. 404). What is required of us—each and every one of us—to employ this concept label in ways that destabilize these interconnected forms of unjust privilege? In Hacking's terms, how can we keep the struggle against "Euroheteropatriarchy" dynamic?

Notes

The names of the students in this chapter were changed. Deep gratitude is extended to Diana Hess, Jamie Kowalczyk, Thomas Popkewitz, Simone Schweber, Gloria Ladson-Billings, Bic Ngo, Kevin Kumashiro, and my peers and students in the school of education for introducing me to the readings/resources I used and for pushing me to explore the linkages among them.

1. I am borrowing the notion of "simple logic" from Sharon Razack (2002). As I argue in the chapter, a "simple logic" about labeling works to obscure institutionalized oppression in this society, including its internalization, thereby enabling an imagined, coherent national narrative of meritocracy to prevail.

2. Sister Chittister was on Wisconsin Public Radio's "Here on Earth," hosted by Jean Ferraca, on April 30, 2005.

References

Advocates for Youth. (2005). The Facts: GLBTQ Youth. Retrieved October 2006, from http://www.advocatesforyouth.org/publications/factsheet/fsglbt.htm

Banks, J. A. (2002). Series foreword. In L. Darling-Hammond, J. French, and S. P. Garcia-Lopez (Eds.), *Learning to teach for social justice* (pp. ix–xii). New York: Teachers College Press.

Begler, E. (1998). Global cultures: The first steps toward understanding. *Social Education, 62,* 272–275.

Berlak, A., and Moyenda, S. (2001). *Taking it personally: Racism in the classroom from kindergarten to college.* Philadelphia: Temple University Press.

Britzman, D. P. (1998). *Lost subjects, contested objects: Toward a psychoanalytic inquiry of learning.* Albany, NY: State University of New York Press.

Britzman, D. P. (2003). *Practice makes practice: A critical study of learning to teach, revised edition.* Albany, NY: State University of New York Press.

California Newsreel. (2003). The house we live in. Part three of *Race: The power of an illusion.* San Francisco.

Ellsworth, E. (1987/1994). Why doesn't this feel empowering?: Working through the repressive myths of critical pedagogy. In L. Stone (Ed.), *The educational feminism reader* (pp. 300–327). New York: Routledge.

Ellsworth, E. (1997). *Teaching positions: Difference, pedagogy, and the power of address.* New York: Teachers College Press.

Foucault, M. (1978/1990). *History of sexuality: volume 1: An introduction.* New York: Vintage Books.

Freire, P. (1970). *Pedagogy of the oppressed.* New York: Continuum.

Gee, J. P. (1996). *Social linguistics and literacies: Ideology in discourses* (2nd ed.). New York: RoutledgeFalmer.

Hacking, I. (1986). Making up people. In T. C. Heller, M. Sosna, and D. E. Wellbery (Eds.), *Reconstructing individualism: Autonomy, individuality, and the self in Western thought* (pp. 222–236). Stanford, CA: Stanford University Press.

Hanh, T. N. (1992). *Peace is every step: The path of mindfulness in everyday life.* New York: Bantam Books.

Jacobson, M. F. (1998). *Whiteness of a different color: European immigrants and the alchemy of race.* Cambridge, MA: Harvard University Press.

Kumashiro, K. K. (2002). *Troubling education: Queer activism and antioppressive pedagogy.* New York: RoutledgeFalmer.

Ladson-Billings, G. (1994). *The dreamkeepers: Successful teachers of African American children.* San Francisco: Jossey-Bass.

Ladson-Billings, G. (1996). Silences as weapons: Challenges of a Black professor teaching White students up people. *Theory Into Practice, 35,* 79–85.

Lei, J. L. (2003). (Un)Necessary toughness?: Those "loud Black girls" and those "quiet Asian boys." *Anthropology and Education Quarterly, 34*(2), 158–181.

Ludema, J. D., Cooperrider, D. L., & Barrett, F. J. (2001). Appreciative inquiry: The power of the unconditional positive question. In P. Reason & H. Bradbury (Eds.), *Handbook of action research: Participative inquiry and practice* (pp. 189–199). Thousand Oaks, CA: SAGE Publications.

MacKinnon, C. (2002). Keeping it real: On anti-"essentialism." In F. Valdes, J. M. Culp, and A. P. Harris (Eds.), *Crossroads, directions, and a new critical race theory* (pp. 71–83). Philadelphia: Temple University Press.

North, C. (2007). What do you mean by "anti-oppressive education"? Student interpretations of a high school leadership program. *Qualitative Studies in Education. 20*(1) , 73–97.

Razack, S. (2002). "Simple logic": Race, the identity documents rule, and the story of a nation besieged and betrayed. In F. Valdes, J. M. Culp, and A. P. Harris (Eds.), *Crossroads, directions, and a new critical race theory* (pp. 199–220). Philadelphia: Temple University Press.

Segall, A. (2002). *Disturbing practice: Reading teacher education as text.* New York: Peter Lang.

Thompson, A. (2003). Tiffany, friend of people of color: White investments in antiracism. *Qualitative Studies in Education 16*(1), 7–29.

Tye, B. B. (2000). *Hard truths: Uncovering the deep structure of schooling.* New York: Teachers College Press.

Valdes, F. (2002). Outsider scholars, critical race theory, and "outcrit" perspectivity: Postsubordination vision as jurisprudential method. In F. Valdes, J. M. Culp, and A. P. Harris (Eds.), *Crossroads, directions, and a new critical race theory* (pp. 399–409). Philadelphia: Temple University Press.

Young, I. M. (1990). *Justice and the politics of difference.* Princeton, NJ: Princeton University Press.

Zeichner, M., and Liston, P. (1991). Reflective teaching. An introduction. Saddle River, NJ: Lawrence Erlbaum Associates.

10

Rethinking Ignore-Ance in the Examination of Racism

THOMAS M. PHILIP

Teaching about difference, privilege, and oppression evokes emotions of "desire, fear, horror, pleasure, power, anxiety, fantasy and the unthinkable" (Ellsworth, 1997, p. 46). This space in which one teaches and learns about issues such as racism is occupied by ignore-ance.

Ignore-ance is "an active dynamic of negation, an active refusal of information." The hatred or fear of one's own implication in what's being taught can make forgetting or ignoring or not hearing an active, yet unconscious refusal. And the "inner resistances" that call an ignore-ance into being are stubbornly capable of maintaining it, even against the conscious intentions or desires of one who otherwise wants to learn (Ellsworth, 1997, p. 57).

This chapter situates ignore-ance in the context of hegemony, acknowledging its historical, social, political, and economic development, while developing an analysis of ignore-ance at the level of cognition. Extending diSessa's (1993) theory of knowledge in pieces and Stuart Hall's (1982) understanding of ideology, ignore-ance is understood as a "social space, formed and informed by historical conjunctures of power and social and cultural difference" (Ellsworth, 1997, p. 38). By examining ignore-ance through the lens of ideology, the "unconscious," and complex-knowledge systems, the relationship among societal structures, cognition, and emotions is explicated in people's conceptualizations of race. With this understanding of ignore-ance, the chapter concludes with analysis of common sense embedded in ideology as a pedagogical position to interrupt ignore-ance.

Theoretical Framework

This chapter supports diSessa's (1993) position that people make sense of the world largely through cognitive elements of common sense, which he calls phenomenological primitives or *p-prims*. Examples of such might be "the harder you try, the more likely you are to succeed" or "you're going to be influenced by people around you." *P-prims*, according to diSessa, are self-evident and difficult to further justify, originate in nearly superficial interpretations of experienced reality, and constitute a rich vocabulary through which people remember and interpret their experience. They are cued specific to the context, applied locally and do not require global consistency. In addition to the experiential basis for common sense, there are a reservoir of themes and premises that are "drawn from the long-standing and historically elaborated discourses which has accreted over the years, into which the whole history of the social formation has sedimented" (Hall, 1982, p. 73). I refer to this broader category of cognitive primitives as *naturalized primitives*. I use the term *naturalized* to indicate that these primitives gain the warrant of common sense within particular historical, cultural, and social contexts.

The *naturalized primitives* one employs in making sense of the world around him or her are large in number, loosely organized, and not systematic in application. Therefore, what appears salient in one situation may not be so in another. As diSessa (2002) finds in *p-prims*, "a good candidate model for [*naturalized primitives'*] activation and use is 'recognition.' One simply sees them in some situations and not in others" (p. 39). The very definition of the problem at hand, what is important to pay attention to, is related to the salience these *naturalized primitives* take in a context. *Naturalized primitives* acquire salience "by repetition and by the weight and credibility of those who propose or subscribe to it" (Hall, 1982, p. 81). Particular communities, or even societies at particular historical times, will, therefore, have dominant *naturalized primitives*. While the *naturalized primitives* that a member employs will not be uniform across a community, some will have a preferred salience because of such repetition and associated credibility. *Naturalized primitives*, concepts, and principles do not exist in isolation. Ideology, which is "those images, concepts and premises which provide frameworks through which we represent, interpret, understand and 'make sense' of some aspect of social existence," exists in the interrelatedness of concepts, principles, and *naturalized primitives* into a "distinctive set or chain of meanings" (Hall, 1982, p. 81).

To elucidate *naturalized primitives*, consider how one might reason about parental nonparticipation in schools. Consider two chains of reasoning. These chains of reasoning might be how two different individuals reason about the situation, or how one individual reasons about it in varied contexts. In the first hypothetical case, the *naturalized primitive* "poor parents don't value education" might become salient. Possibly embedded in an ideology of meritocracy, success is viewed through the lens of hard work and the condition of poor communities is explained through their own choices and value systems. In a second case, the *naturalized primitive* "one will not engage with something hurtful" might be invoked. In this instance, school might be seen as a historically alienating and colonizing institution for certain communities, and parental nonparticipation reflects this relationship and apprehension.

Hall (1982) argues that ideological change is exceedingly difficult precisely because the terms of an argument, and what becomes salient, have acquired the warrant of common sense through repetition and associated credibility. Ideology establishes "certain systems of equivalence between what could be assumed to be true about the world and what could be said to be true" (p. 75). Hall argues that "new, problematic or troubling events, which breached the taken for granted expectancies about how the world should be, [are] 'explained' by extending to them the forms of explanation which had served for 'all practical purposes,' in other cases" (p. 75). Drawing from Althusser, ideology tends to "[move] constantly within a closed circle, producing not knowledge, but a recognition of the things we already know. It [does] so because it [takes] as already established fact exactly the premises which ought to have been put in question" (p. 75). Thus, even when one takes an oppositional stance, he or she may likely reproduce the terms of the argument. Paralleling Hall's example of immigration, to challenge the argument that poor children do not do well because of lack of parental attention by the counterclaim that poor parents actually do care, essentially leaves intact the whole set of propositions explaining why students do not do well and, therefore, does not change the terms of the argument. It continues the focus on individual characteristics and obscures any historical, social, economic, political, or institutional analysis.

Ideological change, akin to diSessa's perspective on conceptual change, occurs through a reorganization of *naturalized primitives*. Extending diSessa's (2002) notion of *p-prims*, *naturalized primitives* are not extinguished or replaced by learning new concepts or principles. Instead, *naturalized primitives* might become "an effective special case" (p. 39) of a principle. So while someone with a historical and structural analysis would not use the *naturalized primitive* "children learn behaviors from their parents," to explain educational disparity for a community, there will be specific instances where it is still applicable. It is important to note, however, that when one uses a principle in a "more expert-like" manner, the *naturalized primitives* will no longer function as explanatory primitives. In other contexts, a *naturalized primitive's* salience might decrease in the context at hand but remain useful in other situations. For example, a shift in understanding high school dropout from an individual analysis to a structural analysis might include the decrease of the salience of the *naturalized primitive* "people are influenced by their peers," and an increase in the *naturalized primitive* "one will not engage with something hurtful." Acquiring a deeper ideological position and the salience of related *naturalized primitives* scaffold each other, often making the process of ideological change slow and intermittent.

Methodology

Data

The data presented in this chapter is based on a cognitive clinical interview with a teacher who will be referred to as Stephanie. The interview was modeled after diSessa's (1993) clinical interview. At the beginning of the interview, Stephanie was told that she would be asked to reason through scenarios that she might find herself in as an administrator. The purpose of the interview was explained as seeking to understand how people reason about race and equity in education. The scenarios were described as complex and without necessarily having simple answers. As they would reflect real-world problems, there would be advantages and disadvantages to any proposed solution. It was reiterated that there were, therefore, no right or wrong answers.

Excerpts examined in this chapter are taken from the first scenario in which Stephanie was asked to reason through a scenario in which an African American teacher cites educator and actor Bill Cosby's statement at a 2004 National Association for the Advancement of Colored People (NAACP) event. In this statement, Cosby says, "We cannot blame the white people any longer" and argues that the educational disparity that exists is a problem that originates from choices made by African Americans themselves. This controversial example was specifically chosen so that participants would be placed outside of relatively rehearsed conversations around white privilege and multiculturalism. It is well documented by scholars such as Bonilla-Silva (2003) that educated, middle-class individuals are proficient in speaking about issues such as race without seeming overtly biased, but reason about specific contexts in ways that draw from dominant notions of difference that perpetuate oppressive practices. Individuals tend to stay within acceptable discourses in relatively familiar settings such as short conversations regarding difference, surveys, or prescribed interviews. The cognitive clinical interview, in which participants reason about complex situations and the interviewer draws upon their statements to pose counterarguments or potential contradictions, places the participant out of such relatively rehearsed conversations and, therefore, better reflects how participants actually reason about race in the rich contexts of everyday interactions.

The Interviewee

Stephanie was in a fourteen-month Master's and Administrative Credential program. She was very fluent using reform-oriented language within the context of coursework. The interview took place before Stephanie formally began the program, but after an initial orientation meeting. During the interview, she repeatedly indicated the importance of teachers reaching all students, holding high expectations for students, not labeling students, recognizing that African American students are often misinterpreted because of differences in norms around acceptable behavior, bringing in aspects of a student's culture into the classroom, validating students, differentiating instruction and recognizing the economic hardship of parents who, in some cases, might be working three jobs. She mentioned that she thought about issues of race in her previous Master's program and specifically mentioned Beverly Daniel Tatum, whose work has been extremely influential in addressing race in teacher education, as someone who "gave [her] a framework to work with." She represents, in these respects, a teacher who is comfortable using reform-oriented or progressive language promoted by many teacher education programs.

Relating the Unconscious to the Closed Circle of Ideology

Teaching and learning about difference such as race means simultaneously addressing unpredictability and expectedness, idiosyncrasies and patterns, the individual and the social. If we focus on the unpredictability, the idiosyncrasies, and the individual, we quickly lose sight of the expectedness, the patterns, and the social. While Ellsworth addresses the social space between teaching and learning that is "formed and informed by historical conjunctures of power and social and cultural difference," her focus on the capriciousness of the unconscious obscures the relationship that the "unconscious" has to ideology. Here, I attempt to show that Ellsworth's ignore-ance is related to Althusser's description of the operation of ideology as "[moving] constantly within a closed circle, producing not knowledge, but a recognition of things we already know" (Hall, 1982, p. 75). How is it that when people encounter "new, problematic or troubling events, which breach the taken for granted expectancies about how the world should be," events that one would expect to induce deep questioning of positions, they are able to ignore these inconsistencies, which "are [then] 'explained' by extending to them the forms of explanation which serve for 'all practical purposes', in other cases" (Hall, p. 75)? For instance, in a society where wealth inequality is extreme, the "unconscious" must operate to rationalize this inequity. To implicate the system or the institution would be to implicate ourselves in ways.

Locating the cause of class difference within the marginalized themselves enables an "ignore-ance" of the workings of class oppressions.

This chapter brings the expectedness, the patterns, and the social aspects of the workings of the "unconscious" back into light and thus allows us to extend Ellsworth's contribution.

Bonilla-Silva (2003) argues that because "post-Civil Rights racial norms disallow the open expression of racial views, [people] have developed a concealed way of voicing them" (p. 57). In the interview passages that follow, the absence of racialized discourse is remarkable. While the framing of the scenario highlights race, and the students discussed are "racial minorities," Stephanie almost exclusively refers to "the home," "the family," and "culture" without mentioning race. These, in effect, become post-Civil Rights euphemisms for racial categories. Bonilla-Silva (2003) documents semantic moves whereby "color-blind racism's race talk avoids terminology and preserves its mythological nonracialism" (p. 70). The following excerpts evidence how Stephanie's avoidance or ignore-ance of racial categories operate at the level of individual cognition but is embedded in, and has outcomes related to, the ideology of post-Civil Rights liberalism. By examining four commonly expressed arguments, the power of ignore-ance to avoid potentially troubling new information is explored within the context of this post-Civil Rights discourse.

"Poor Families Have Detrimental Expectations for Their Children"

Consider the following exchange in which Stephanie responds to a question regarding the importance of teacher expectations. The closed circle of ideology operates such that the *naturalized primitive* "Poor families have detrimental expectations for their children" is invoked. This obscures any analysis of institutional causes. Invariably, with middle-class suburban youth, teachers consider a host of reasons that preserve the individuality of students to explain their achievement. With poor urban children on the other hand, the explanations invoke deficiencies in the family (Swadener, 1995; Valencia and Solorzano, 1997). This is not happenchance. A society in which wealth and income are so unequally distributed needs to naturalize the belief that inequality is unavoidable and rooted within the choices of its victims.

Related to Bonilla-Silva's (2003) observations regarding post-Civil Rights' color-blind language, van Dijk (1992) finds that people tend to lighten the implications of potentially discriminatory language. By arguing that most families hold their children to high expectations, but invoking the contrary as an explanation in any particular case one reasons about, enables one to maintain the notion that he or she is fair and open, and that each particular case of poverty is an exception to an otherwise equitable system.

Interview Segment	Comments
Stephanie: [. . .] It's not only things that are happening in school, but things that are happening in your home and culture of what society tells you what you can or cannot be as a child. So it's hard, with everyone saying that to you, it's really hard for a child to understand that that's not the, that doesn't have to be the reality.	Shift from a possible institutional analysis to an individual analysis. One lives up to the expectations of those around him or her. Poor communities limit one's sense of reality.
Interviewer: So can you give me some examples of when a family or community might be telling a kid of what they might be capable of doing.	
Stephanie: So I think society glamorizes a lot of things that are not realistic for most people. That's what I think society does. Families, in terms of, my own family, you know, I was expected to go to college and hold some professional job. That was my responsibility, you know as a product of my family. Or you know, I know of families that I have worked with that don't expect much out of their kids. They just figure that oh, that they will be working some hourly nine to five job and they just don't expect a lot. And then again, I've worked with families, most families, expect their children to go above and beyond what they've achieved. I think that's the case in most cases.	Successful families hold high expectations for their children. Going to college and holding a professional job are the right things to do. Working-class families do not expect their children to "go beyond" their circumstances. See van Dijk reference later.

Stephanie's use of *naturalized primitives* is apparent in the aforementioned interview. These include the following:

> One lives up to the expectations of those around him or her.
> Poor communities limit one's sense of reality.
> Successful families hold high expectations for their children.
> Going to college and holding a professional job are the right things to do.
> Working-class families do not expect their children to "go beyond" their circumstances.

These commonsense notions are an integral part of Stephanie's reasoning. They are given meaning in a particular historical and cultural context and have acquired their validity and salience through repetition and the associated credibility of those who convey them. Ideologically, these *naturalized primitives* focus on individual characteristics or poor urban youth and their families, and thereby cloaks a historical, social, economic, political, or institutional analysis.

"You Can't Reach Every Student"

There is a personal accountability and responsibility one must address in the face of overwhelming inequality. For a teacher, this includes coping with the reality that a number of his or her students may be alienated or academically underachieving. When *naturalized primitives* such as "a teacher can't reach all her or his students" become salient, it obscures the reality that segments of students might not be reached or might even be emotionally hurt through schooling. This process of obscuring is evident in the interaction with Stephanie that follows. As with other segments of Stephanie's interview, she initiates a sequence of the ideal, returns to the practical and then focuses on the deviance of the marginalized. It demonstrates how "ignore-ance" is embedded in an ideology that preserves the status quo and allows hegemony[1] to function through common sense.

"The Problem Family"

Earlier in the interview, Stephanie specifically spoke about the detrimental aspects of labeling students. In the segment that follows, she unproblematically invokes and later supports the use of a "problem" label for a child and his family. In this exchange, Stephanie again positions herself as one who is attempting to undo the negative influences of the home.

Interview Segment	Comments
Interviewer: So how much do you think the teacher can actually do?	
Stephanie: I think they can actually do a lot. I mean as far as reaching out to the whole class, that takes a really good teacher to do that. But even if you can reach one or two, but you have to at least, you know, you can't think that you're not affecting their lives, so I think that the teacher has an important role in trying to, you know, raise the student's esteem and the way they think about themselves and what they can become. And what they can learn.	Begins with the ideal that a good teacher can reach all students. On a practical level, it is sufficient if a teacher affects one or two students. Positively affecting a student is related to raising their self-esteem and their sense of potential. This immediately follows her statement that families play an important role in determining a student's potential. This chain of reasoning again focuses on an individual's characteristic and obscures any institutional analysis of how a teacher or school shapes a student's self-esteem, particularly in relationship to students whose communities have been historically oppressed.

The racialized nature of Stephanie's color-blind speech is evidenced by the similarity that the structure of her speech has with van Dijk's (1992) analysis. van Dijk (1992) proposes that when people engage in speech that might be interpreted as prejudiced, they first attribute it to others but then provide a supporting instance. This suggests that they are at least partly aware of the implications of their speech. Stephanie's use of the "problem" label, in which she first attributes it to other teachers, but then uses it without qualification, fits this discourse pattern.

Interview Segment	Comments
Interviewer: Earlier on you said that some families just don't expect much from their students. Is this from your personal experience, or?	
Stephanie: Well, yeah, that and they teach their children things that they've done. And I just don't think that's expecting much.	

Interview Segment	Comments
Like I had one student who in the family there are three kids, there are a boy, a girl and a boy. And in the first year I had the oldest son and we had this conversation about stealing, how it is bad and the factors of why you shouldn't be doing it and then he is a kid that teachers have labeled a problem child. The whole family is. And he looked confused when we were having this conversation and looked at me and said, "Well, is it wrong because my mom teaches my little sister how to steal and she was four at the time?" Yeah, so, I don't think that's expecting much out of your child if you're wanting them to become a thief at age four.	Teachers like herself attempt to make up for the moral shortcomings of poor and minority children. First attributes the label to other teachers. Uses label without ascribing. Returns to the position that poor and minority parents teach their children deviant behaviors.

In an attempt to shift Stephanie toward an institutional analysis, the problems associated with labeling that she mentioned earlier in the interview were introduced. Almost seamlessly, Stephanie's chain of reasoning shifts from the problem of labeling to a justification for the label based on the nontraditional nature of the family. Here again, Stephanie is "[moving] constantly within a closed circle, producing not knowledge, but a recognition of the things [she] already knows" (Hall, 1982, p. 75). Instead of questioning the validity or usefulness of such a label, Stephanie's "ignore-ance" functions to justify the label because of the family's deviation from the two-parent heterosexual norm.

"Schools Undo the Family's Wrongs"

Continuing the conversation, another attempt is made to have Stephanie consider the implications of the administration and the teachers "writing off" this family. Stephanie transitions in her meaning of "problem," very likely not even noticeable to herself. She transforms the original question regarding the school "writing off" students to a restatement of the important task before teachers to "work on" these families.

Interview Segment	Comments
Interviewer: So if you think a staff, or a set of teachers had already labeled this child as someone who may be a problem child, do you think that can influence how other teachers sort of interact with this child.	Attempt to introduce an institutional analysis.
Stephanie: I think so, definitely. Because over the years I have seen that people say that, "Oh, I can't deal with them." There is nothing I can do. Because the parents don't care, they never show up. You know, as a matter of fact, even the administration takes that stance with that family that there is just nothing they can do. Yeah, actually, I've	Begins with a focus on the institution of schooling as it relates to teachers and administrators.
seen it. They've put a label on this family *because* they are, they're a different family, they're not, you know, a two-parent family. They are a three-parent family with, you know, the father, the biological father, the mother and the mother's girlfriend, living, all living in	Transition from the label that the school has put on the family to a justification for the label. The "because" in this segment not only signifies the reasoning ascribed to the administration, but more importantly is a transition from Stephanie's reporting of the administration's position to her own position about the family.
the same household. So, already, by the family situation they are labeled as different.	The family's label is naturalized by virtue of their difference.
They have issues besides that, they have their issues of violence where the girlfriend has been known to start fights with	Violence is contextualized within the discussion of the nontraditional family structure, creating an association between them.
other parents. Yeah. And the kids get teased now, because as they get older, other kids are finding out their family situation. So, it's just, there is so much involved and so many	The focus again is on how the family creates this situation for itself, rather than the school's failure to create a space that is safe for nontraditional nonheterosexual families.
issues with these, with that particular family that people just kind of write it off as there is nothing I can do.	The particular family is seen as an exception. In this manner, each instance of a "problem" family can be explained as an exception to an otherwise equitable institution.

Implications for Teaching and Learning

Common sense, what even becomes salient to oneself in a context, enables and obscures perspectives on the world. This common sense exists in ideologies and in relationships of power. As evidenced by Stephanie, one can transform, without even necessarily being aware of it, a situation that threatens one's sense of self to a situation that preserves the status quo. This is precisely the function of common sense

Interview Segment		Comments
Interviewer:	So, do you consider that a problem, or do you consider that useful . . .	
Stephanie:	Oh, that's definitely a problem, because that gets those children to think that is all they expect of me. Nothing is ever going to happen. I might get in trouble, but really what is the outcome of that. Suspension, a couple of days at home? That's no big deal. They already do that anyways. The parents if it is not convenient for babysitting, they'll keep them at home, or picking them up is not convenient, so they keep them at home, or whatever reason, a lot of things going on. It is a problem. Someone needs to try to fix it. Because, you can't let that child, in the early stages of life think that that is your path in life. You have to kind of empower them to think that you know that I don't need to steal, fighting with people is bad, (laughs), you know, treating people, you know even the basic things of respect and socialization, they need to learn those things. So, for people write it off and think she fights all the time, she sees it at home, you know, no that's not, I don't think that's okay. I think you know as a staff you need to work on a family to try to change things. So that if it's not happening at home, it needs to happen at school where the kids are learning how to socialize with other people.	Initial focus on the problem of the school writing the students off.
		Shift toward the apparent lack of consequences for the child and the individual responses by the child.
		Focus is on the parents and their lack of appropriate choices for the child.
		It, with reference to the family, is now identified as the problem and "it" needs to be fixed by someone else. The teacher's responsibility is to undo the family's potential harm.
		Empowerment is equated to undoing the family's negative influence.
		Schools need to teach the basic morals that families fail to teach.
		The school's label for the family is no longer in question. The focus is now on how a staff can "work on a family" rather than addressing the label the staff has placed on the family.
		Reiteration that the school needs to fix what is happening at home.

given meaning in a hegemonic ideology. How does one bring about ideological change and promote a historical, social, economic, political, and institutional analysis in oneself and others? As in the case of Stephanie, naturalized primitives, or one's common sense operates to sidestep the uncontrollable feelings of "desire, fear, horror, pleasure, power, anxiety, fantasy and the unthinkable" that learning about difference such as racism evoke. It transforms potentially disturbing questions into situations that are no longer threatening and for which one's common sense that has served him or her before provides relatively simple answers. The preferred salience that naturalized primitives take on in a context limits the terms of argument, precluding the invocation of many of these feelings. It enables us to block out the gross injustices we see around us by shifting the focus to things more palatable and self-affirming.

There is a material reality to *naturalized primitives* and ignore-ance. Ideologies and material conditions exist reflexively, and categories of race and racism exist in this reflexivity. For instance, *natural primitives* employed by Stephanie within the context of a classroom may move between the ideological and material such that "youth of color accumulate deficits" and "white adolescents and young adults gather intelligence and merit" (Fine, 2004). Formed through power and difference, ignore-ance operates similarly to perpetuate oppressions such as class, gender, and sexuality, and the intersections of these identities as seen in Stephanie's reasoning about the "traditional" family.

"How we don't know can teach us something. There's a history to what we don't know, forget, ignore. At what moments in the dynamic interplay of power relations do we forget? At what locations within structures of address do we ignore?" (Ellsworth, 1997, p. 65). In my experience working with students at both the undergraduate and graduate level, one of the most troubling learning experiences is coming to the recognition that our thinking and reasoning is embedded in an ideology. The realization that what we think and what becomes salient in a situation is informed, in part, by our particular historical and cultural context, disconcerts our desire to preserve our sense of control. To accept that certain forms of analysis are obscured for the moment because of our ideology cuts at the foundation of our belief that we can always adequately contemplate multiple perspectives. These realizations, however, are essential if we are to seriously engage with Ellsworth's suggestion to examine the routes through which we arrive at our knowledge.

What do these routes have to do with power, history, and desire? Why and how is one route taken repeatedly and not others? Which are possible and intelligible, and what are the consequences of others remaining impossible and unintelligible? How have institutions, practices, and identities authorized some routes and deauthorized others? Where have they become stuck, fixed, silenced, or resisted? How have groups changed routes to produce challenges or disruptions? (p. 126).

Analyzing our reasoning for *naturalized primitives* and how these cognitive elements operate within the closed circle of ideology to constrain the terms of argument to spaces that reproduce inequities will enable us to interrupt "ignore-ances." While acknowledging the unpredictability, idiosyncrasy, and individuality of learning about oppressions such as racism, the expectedness, patterns, and social nature of *naturalized primitives* that are informed by hegemonic ideology enable us to pose Ellsworth's questions to ourselves and to place them before our students with a greater understanding of the mechanisms of "ignore-ance" and our opportunities to disrupt such "ignore-ance."

Note

1. Hegemony is used here in the Gramscian sense, where it does not signify a single dominant class, but a set of relations that favor certain groups and make concessions to others for their consent.

References

Bonilla-Silva, E. (2003). *Racism without racists: Color-blind racism and the persistence of racial inequality in the United States.* New York: Rowman and Littlefield Publishers.

diSessa, A. (1993). Towards an epistemology of physics. *Cognition and Instruction, 10*(2 and 3), 105–225.

diSessa, A. (2002). Why "conceptual ecology" is a good idea. In M. Limon and L. Mason (Eds.), *Reconsidering conceptual change. Issues in theory and practice,* 29–60. Boston: Kluwer Academic.

Ellsworth, E. (1997). *Teaching positions: Difference, pedagogy, and the power of address.* New York, NY: Teachers College Press.

Fine, M. (2004). Witnessing Whiteness/Gathering Intelligence. In M. Fine et al. (Eds.), *Off White: Readings on Power, Privilege and Resistance,* 245–256. New York, NY: Routledge.

Hall, S. (1982). The rediscovery of "ideology": return of the repressed in media studies. In M. Gurevitch, T. Bennett, J. Curran, & J. Woollacott (Eds.), *Culture, society and the media,* 56–90. London: Methuen.

Swadener, B. B. (1995). Children and families "at promise": Deconstructing the discourse of risk. In B. B. Swadener and S. Lubeck (Eds.), *Children and families "at promise": Deconstructing the discourse of risk,* 17–49. Albany, NY: State University of New York.

Valencia, R. R., and Solorzano, D. G. (1997). Contemporary deficit thinking. In R. R. Valencia (Ed.), *The evolution of deficit thinking: Educational thought and practice,* 160–210. Washington, DC: The Falmer Press.

van Dijk, T. A. (1992). Discourse and the denial of racism. *Discourse and Society, 3*(1), 87–118.

Conversation

Unpacking the Methodological Issues in Research for Social Justice

CONNIE NORTH & THOMAS M. PHILIP

Connie: Recently, I began my qualitative dissertation project, was studied by a peer dissertator while teaching a college-level course, and participated in a feminist research methodology seminar, all of which intensified my concerns about the intrusive, voyeuristic aspects of much educational research (including my own). Consequently, upon reading your insightful chapter on the subtle ways that commonsense ideas interrelate with and often perpetuate dominant ideological beliefs and practices, I was struck by the potential incongruence between your methodology and theoretical framework. I guess I want to ask you, if we are attempting to disrupt "business as usual" with our work, how beneficial is it to criticize someone else's practice without talking to her directly and explicitly about her underlying rationale?

I worry that we too rarely give the "human subjects" in our studies the opportunity to respond to our findings and perspectives and make known (in our publications and presentations) their viewpoints. I also worry that we do not provide these educators, on whose backs we build careers, the compensation they merit (e.g., material resources, professional development opportunities). My chapter assumed a very different form than yours largely because I was attempting to study my own practice—to relate my experiences and subjectivities to my teaching and the larger system of teacher education. (And I am curious what you think of this "starting from self" strategy, as I would not know from reading your chapter that you are a man of color.) But in several respects, the content of both chapters tackle the same problem: how commonsense beliefs can contribute to greater injustice.

I am left contemplating, then, the complicated dance between form and content and how we might undertake the processes of research and writing in ways that both reach and rouse as many readers as possible and humanize and involve the subjects in our research (since our critiques do not aim to paint them as bad people but to show that all of us are complicit—often unknowingly—in promoting an unjust social order and since we as researchers ought to position ourselves as learners).

I attempt to draw on participatory action research (PAR) approaches (e.g., Park, 1993; Fals Borda and Rahman, 1991) in my doctoral study to make the research process more practitioner-driven and less exploitative. However, like Patricia Maguire (1993), I think the founding "fathers" of PAR with their "emancipatory and extensive agenda for social transformation" do not acknowledge the constraints of trying to work within the very structures we seek to transform (p. 162). I am thus struggling to embrace Maguire's philosophy that university-based research, "no matter how flawed, small-scale, or less than ideal," can contribute to the "long-haul, collective struggle" for a more just distribution of power, particularly when we are "open to transforming ourselves and our relationships with others" (pp. 175–176).

Thomas: These are powerful objections that you raise concerning the nature of educational research and, in certain contexts, I agree with you wholeheartedly. Research has been so intertwined with the colonizing process and continues to be so. Research operates in a hegemony through means you write about—by not allowing the "researched" to respond, by researchers building their careers on the backs of the "other" and by creating arbitrary lines between the researched and the researcher. I share your concerns about the dominant research paradigm and feel that we need to be vigilant to see how it operates institutionally, societally, and individually. While I advocate "partial truths" and participatory research in many contexts, its appeal in academia raises some concerns for me. I'm reminded of the poet Nikki Giovanni's words, "Know who's playing the music before you dance." Historically, even the most progressive and "just" forms of education have been utilized against colonized peoples. To what extent has the notion that one cannot "research" the other gained currency because of the entrance of scholars from colonized groups into academia? In a world so structured by categories such as race, we cannot simply start off with inquiry or equal dialogue. To press people from colonized groups to "enter a dialogue" rather than "research" ensures that knowledge and research will remain the domain of Europeans. We must, as Patricia Hill Collins cautions, be weary when ideas such as decentering that grew out of critical scholarship is "appropriated by a class of intellectuals who keep the language of resistance, yet denude the theory of actual political effectiveness." The argument in the chapter is that Stephanie, teachers, society, in others words, all of us, reason to an extent within dominant ideologies that obscure certain ways of thinking and highlight others. I agree that it is problematic to pick apart another's practice without entering into a dialogue with her or him as researchers from colonizing groups have done historically. In our contemporary context, my intention is not to dissect Stephanie's practice, but to look for ideological trends that exist among us. This is part of a struggle for colonized peoples to understand relationships of power in order to change them. Our self-identifications in our research mean very different things. In my experience, it functions to lend validity to the work of white researchers, while it functions dissimilarly for scholars of color. There are contexts in which I feel less concerned than my white colleagues about voice and positionality, a position they often find surprising. To echo Patricia Hill Collins, words, "I remain less preoccupied with coming to voice because I know how quickly voice can be taken away. My concern now lies in finding effective ways to use the voice that I have claimed while I have it." Scholars from colonized groups must engage in strategic research and critique, similar to Spivak's notion of strategic essentialism. As Spivak cautions, this means we must accustom ourselves to starting from a particular situation and then to the ground shifting under our feet. We must be able to critique academia and research for all the flaws you've pointed out, and, as a part of our struggle, we need to engage in it strategically to subvert oppressions.

Connie: Thankfully, our different life histories render different perspectives, as the kind of "dialogue" that seems to evoke change involves both friction—a result of distinct perspectives and assumptions coming into contact—and mutual respect. Actually, respect lies at the heart of my concerns. In some of the philosophical debates about social justice (e.g., Fraser and Honneth, 2003), scholars claim that resistance to injustice often arises from a profound sense of disrespect—a disrespect that appears as institutionalized oppression and subordination in daily lives but is felt by individuals and social groups as injury.

Because I believe that every person longs for others to respect him, I worry about the symbolic violence to all research subjects wrought by critical scholarly approaches (and I mean small "c" critical here rather than solely Critical Theory, which, along with various feminisms, informs my work) that frequently "reinforce hierarchy by describing 'the ideal' and then detailing the inadequacies of those who do not compare favourably" (Ludema et al., 2001, p. 197). More specifically, I am thinking of a recent effort by an external consultant to educate local teachers about racism that began by calling all of the white teachers racist. I do not disagree with the "what" of this statement, but the "how" seems to ignore the fact that most of us do not wake up in the morning consciously wishing to promote oppression. Moreover, such an approach lends itself to being perceived by the teachers as further name-calling rather than productive engagement with complex issues and, more importantly, improving the well-being of students and teachers of color in "places of learning."

Nevertheless, as you point out, and as I emphasized in my chapter's conclusion, the access by people of color to leadership and professional positions in education at K-12 and post-secondary levels remains abysmal. Furthermore, I believe that power needs to be at the center of analyses and conversations about social justice. Accordingly, I am increasingly convinced that a "pedagogy of the oppressor" (see, e.g., Berlak and Moyenda, 2001), which ultimately teaches those with inordinate power in this society—because they have more resources and/or inhabit a dominant identity position (e.g., white, heterosexual, Christian, male)—to cede and redistribute some of their privileges, is an important strategy for anti-oppressive education.

And yet, if we are all implicated in a system where the dominant "common sense" involves deep-seated investments in, for example, the meritocratic ideal, then oppression is frequently internalized with the outcome being that everyone in this society needs to reevaluate what "we" mean by terms such as justice, equality, and democracy in the various settings where we live and work. I am continually drawn to Gloria Anzaldua's (1987) *Borderlands* in part because she emphasizes that even her Chicano roots and community require transformation. In her words, "I will not glorify those aspects of my culture which have injured me and which have injured me in the name of protecting me" (p. 22).

I guess I, a white graduate student who has always had a "room of my own" but still feels alienated and "crazy" as a woman in the university context, am troubled by what is required for *any* educational researcher committed to social transformation to obtain a foothold in the Academy. How can we resist "the taken-for-granted norms, rules, skills, and values" (Schon, cited in Anderson and Kerr, 1999, p. 17) that sustain rather than destabilize the status quo? Is it possible to become a participating member of the university with its specialized discourses of "expertise" and "professionalism" and simultaneously break down the dominating, exclusionary aspects of these institutionalized norms and accompanying practices?

Thomas: I completely agree with you that power needs to be at the center of analyses. Part of acknowledging this means understanding that we cannot prescribe an arbitrary method of research or understand the method outside of the context of current power relationships. I find writings such as Ludema et al.'s that you use to critique critical scholarship troublesome. They obscure analyses that focus on centers of power, whether they are institutional or ideological, and thereby, wittingly or unwittingly bolster the current hegemony. In the contemporary political and economic environment, it is essential that we understand, at some level, how oppression functions, whether it be through alliances between governments and corporations, or at the level of ideology and its tools of propagation in civil society. Ludema et al.'s model of Appreciative Inquiry and speaking about Positive Topic Choice or Appreciating "the best of what is" are the privilege of the dominant. Their research framework and its applications (such as the networking of members and funders in Bangladesh, initiating business entrepreneurs on a global level, or creating an East Africa NGO network that provides training, consultation, and funding) force open new markets in the Two-Thirds world under the guise of empowerment and innovation as they further the neoliberal free-market agenda. Such frames obfuscate lenses to study these global forces. They situate change in the ability of a group to *envision* their own change. This prioritizes the emotional well-being of privileged groups over addressing the nature of oppression, and implicitly situates culpability in oppressed communities for not visualizing a different reality. Critical scholarship must exist in these contexts as they shed understanding on how these putatively empowering research methods work within larger power relationships. For people from historically colonized groups, much of the conversations we have today around empowerment are refined ways of speaking about the white man's burden or the need to "kill the Indian, but save the Man." Returning to an example more related to education, Pauline Lipman's analysis of school restructuring through teacher participation shows how greater "participation" by dominant group members continues to marginalize students of color as long as these students' communities lack political power and resources. Critical theory enables colonized groups to create legitimate knowledge so that we can authentically engage in the dialogue that privileged groups constantly invite us to. I appreciate the questions you've raised, Connie, and would like to reiterate that I could see myself pose very similar objections to educational research in another context. I am cautious of these concerns about research in our current dialogue since it appears yet another way in which scholarship from the margins can never be centered. Your perspective has helped me realize that scholars working from a critical perspective need to articulate the nuances of context for it to continue to serve a productive role in social change.

References

Anderson, G. L., and Kerr, K. (1999). The new paradigm wars: Is there room for rigorous practitioner knowledge in schools and universities? *Educational Researcher, 28*(5), 12–21, 40.

Anzaldua, G. (1987). *Borderlands/la frontera: The new Mestiza*. San Francisco: Aunt Lute Books.

Berlak, A., and Moyenda, S. (2001). *Taking it personally: Racism in the classroom from kindergarten to college*. Philadelphia: Temple University Press.

Fals Borda, O., and Rahman, M. A. (1991). *Action and knowledge: Breaking the monopoly with participatory action-research*. New York: The Apex Press.

Fraser, N., and Honneth, A. (2003). *Redistribution or recognition?: A political-philsophical exchange*. New York: Verso.

Ludema, J. D., Cooperrider, D. L., and Barrett, F. J. (2001). Appreciative inquiry: The power of the unconditional positive question. In P. Reason and H. Bradbury (Eds.), *Handbook of action research: Participative inquiry and practice* (pp. 189–199). Thousand Oaks, CA: SAGE Publications.

Maguire, P. (1993). Challenges, contradictions, and celebrations: Attempting participatory research as a doctoral student. In P. Park, M. Brydon-Miller, B. Hall, and T. Jackson (Eds.), *Voices of change: Participatory research in the United States and Canada* (pp. 157–176). Wesport, CT: Bergin & Garvey.

Park, P. (1993). What is participatory research? A theoretical and methodological perspective. In P. Park, M. Brydon-Miller, B. Hall, and T. Jackson (Eds.), *Voices of change: Participatory research in the United States and Canada* (pp. 1–19). Westport, CT: Bergin & Garvey.

Part VI

Situating Anti-Oppressive Education

In Times of War and Globalization

11

Teaching in a Time of War and the Metaphor of Two Worlds

More than anything else, teaching is an act of faith in the future. The things that students learn in one class, one course, or one quarter have meaning largely as parts of a process designed to make them lifelong learners. Successful teachers seek to help their students become adults capable of careful, contemplative, and creative thinking; to become citizens skilled at seeing things for themselves and continuing to learn even when their teachers are no longer physically present to guide them. Successful students master the tools of evidence and argument. They learn to see through surface appearances, to avoid the path of least resistance, and to embrace complexity and contradiction.

The ways in which the Bush administration has waged war undermines all of these premises and presumptions. This has been a war waged without solemnity, sadness, or sorrow. Our leaders have not made the case for war on the basis of evidence, argument, and logic, but instead have performed the inevitability of war for us through sensationalism, spectacle, and sadism. Our leaders seek to inspire through fear what they cannot achieve by persuasion. This has been a war waged without solemnity, without sorrow, without sadness. It manifests a view of other humans as instruments for achieving our own ends. It substitutes the lust of the spectator for the responsibilities of the citizen.

The rationales given to us for the war come directly from the practices of some of the most antieducation elements in our society—advertising, entertainment, and public relations. In these realms, complex problems have simple solutions; quick fixes relieve us of our responsibilities to think things through. This is the world of masculinist fantasies about military heroism, where all the weapons work perfectly the first time they are fired, where civilians are never killed, and where violence solves problems once and for all. It is an imaginary domain, where revenge and retribution are both sweet and decisive; where resort to war brings lasting peace rather than endless cycles of retaliatory violence; an arena where combat purportedly confirms how different we are from our enemies even as it requires us to take actions that make us resemble them.

The war waged by the Bush administration in Iraq does not honor or avenge the victims of September 11. Instead, it exploits their suffering to advance a cruel, calculated, cynical, and self-serving campaign to exploit the tragedy for narrow economic ends and political purposes. The present war is part and parcel of a policy to transform the nation into an empire, to abrogate fundamental constitutional rights, to funnel public money to private firms whose executives preach the sanctity of competition but secure unearned profits for themselves because of their insider connections. Our leaders seek to win through fear what they cannot inspire through faith. They want national unanimity, not unity. Criticism of them becomes portrayed as criticism of the country. Yet in the process, they endanger the very nation they purport to protect.

Teachers know something about this nation. The national history, literature, and civic lore that we teach are permeated with a particular kind of nationalism that masquerades as patriotism. In his important book *The Death of a Nation*, David Noble (2002) identifies this way of thinking as the metaphor of two worlds—the idea of America as an island of innocence and virtue in a global sea of corruption and vice. The Puritans believed in the metaphor of two worlds even before they left Europe. They came to America seeking to build an exemplary "city on a hill" that could become a model for others largely because they hoped that the imagined purity of American space would provide an escape from the corruptions of European time. When the settlements that Europeans created in North America turned out to have many of the same problems that they thought they had left behind them, idealized images of "virgin land" and a redemptive national landscape led to westward expansion where the cycle was repeated all over again.

At its best, this ideal of earthly perfection encouraged subsequent generations of Americans to hold the United States to a high standard, to fight for the abolition of slavery, for equal protection of the law for all citizens, to honor the rights to free speech and assembly guaranteed in the Bill of Rights. Yet this same pursuit of perfection also created a discourse of counter-subversion and counterinsurgency. When U.S. society turned out to have the same kinds of problems that societies everywhere have, the metaphor of two worlds encouraged many Americans to deflect attention away from themselves and to attribute corruption, conflict, and vice to alien enemies or internal subversion. This rhetoric of counter-subversion has been directed against different groups at different times. It fueled discrimination against religious minorities (especially Catholics and Jews), restrictions against immigrants, and hatred of Indians, Blacks, Latinos, and Asians (Higham, 1981; Rogin, 1987). It provides the emotional subtext for homophobia, anticommunism, and misogyny. In the face of daunting tasks and difficult problems, it provides scapegoats rather than solutions. Instead of defining the U.S. nation positively, it makes the inclusion of some dependent upon the exclusion of others, encouraging passionate avowals of what the nation is not without doing the hard work of defining what the nation should be.

At one time, the metaphor of two worlds was invoked to justify the foreign policy that was called "isolationism"—the belief that the United States should remain pure by refusing to become involved in the affairs of other nations presumed to all be corrupt (Beard, 1946). Yet Noble (2002) shows that after World War II, when elites decided that the global market was even more sacred to them than the national landscape, this same metaphor justified policies of intervention all around the world. If America could not remain isolated from the rest of the world, the reasoning went, then the rest of the world must be made to be like America.

Yet elites such as the corporate executives and war profiteers who designed the Bush administration's policies toward Iraq do not really like the nation they rule— the multicultural society with diverse histories, religions, sexualities, and beliefs; the constitutional democracy rooted in guarantees of due process and equal rights; and the civil society that has believed resolutely in public education, public health, and public services and amenities. What they seek to build in Iraq is not a replica of the America that actually exists but another kind of city on a hill, a purified plutocratic free-market paradise where privatization and the profit motive stand at the center of social life. The massive contracts allocated (without competitive bids) to Halliburton and other firms close to the Bush administration; the hiring of thousands of mercenaries for combat and support roles; and the private prisons and communications systems introduced into Iraq by the Bush administration are not aimed at "defeating terrorism," but rather are efforts to use the fear of terrorism to implement in Iraq a model of free-market fundamentalism ultimately intended to transform the United States.

Teachers know a great deal about this kind of thinking too. The profitability crisis confronting global capitalism has led to desperate efforts everywhere to create new sites of private profit. Attacks on education have played a central role in this process, because schools are the most significant institutions in society that do not follow the profit motive, but instead seek to serve the needs of people. Teachers everywhere confront new regimes of high-stakes testing, not because these have been shown to be good ways of educating students but because they open up huge opportunities for profit-driven companies' marketing tests, testing aids, tutoring modules, and what they describe without a trace of irony as "teacher-proof" curricula. These are exercises in corporate synergy masquerading as pedagogical innovations. They directly contradict the experiences and knowledge of teachers, students, and parents about how pupils learn. In the name of setting "standards" they impose standardization on the infinitely plural and diverse activities of the classroom. They presume that one size fits all, that the ideal educational setting settles for an approach that suits only one kind of teacher, one kind of learner, one kind of pedagogy, one kind of curriculum. Instead of actually improving education by taking some of the $7 million per hour spent on the war in Iraq to create smaller classrooms, better-trained teachers, diverse educational aids, or better-nourished and healthier students, the Bush administration is content to cannibalize the classroom for the benefit of investors and entrepreneurs. It should not have surprised us, then, that when the National Education Association criticized the administration's failure to fund adequately its own "No Child Left Behind" program, Secretary of Education Rod Paige proclaimed that these teachers were "terrorists."

Teachers know that the most important bond we have with our students is their trust. Our slow, steady, and sustained efforts every day may not lead to sudden success and transcendent breakthroughs. But through teaching we act as witnesses for the value of creative, critical, and contemplative engagement with the world. We seek to earn our students' trust every day by showing them how dedication and determination pay off in the long run. One of our biggest enemies in that effort is the cynicism our students have developed from growing up in a society that does not practice what it preaches. The Bush administration preaches the sanctity of human life, but celebrates the sadism and savagery of war. They send troops into combat to fight for photo-ops rather than for freedom, for sound bites to be used in the next election, not for strategic aims and ends. They implement plans for posing the president on an aircraft carrier in front of a banner reading "Mission Accomplished," but devise no plan to deal with the brutality, violence, and chaos that their own military actions unleashed on Iraq.

President Bush and his representatives preach rugged individualism, but incite the mentality of the mob and foment the instincts of the herd. They preach the value of education, but sneer at educators. They promise war against evildoers, but ally themselves with drug lords, profiteers, and dictators. They preach democracy but practice plutocracy. They preach limited government, but pursue unlimited power for themselves. They preach the love of God, but practice the love of gain.

The faith in the future that comprises the essence of good teaching is always imperiled in a time of war. At the start of U.S. participation in World War I, a largely apolitical mathematics teacher and part-time piano tuner named Randolph

Bourne figured out that the equations offered in support of the war did not add up. In "War and the Intellectuals" he wrote that for the ruling elites in society war brings a kind of sanctity to the state, even though members of these groups routinely rail against the state as an impediment to their interests in peacetime. Reverence for the state in wartime for elite groups can easily be channeled into reverence for the ruling class "under the impression that in obeying and serving them, we are obeying and serving society, the nation, the great collectivity in all of us" (Bourne, 1964, p. 91). But this fidelity is not rewarded according to Bourne, because when the state's chief purpose is war "then the state must suck out of the nation a large part of its energy for its purely sterile purposes of defense and aggression. It devotes to waste or to actual destruction as much as it can of the vitality of the nation" (Bourne, 1964, p. 81).

In the midst of the Vietnam War, Dr. Martin Luther King, Jr., warned that the war on poverty at home would be lost on the killing fields of Vietnam overseas. He spoke out against the war because he felt it was indecent for a nation that could not seat Black and white children together in the same classroom in Southeast Georgia to send them to fight and die together in Southeast Asia. But beyond its cost to Blacks, Dr. King opposed the war in Vietnam because it put the United States on the wrong side of history, using its massive power for the destruction of human life when so many human needs went unmet.

Pronounced contradictions haunt the government's war. Their role as leaders obligates members of the administration to protect the bounded nation they rule, but they seem willing to dismantle that nation in pursuit of the boundless markets that mean more to them than the land they live in and lead. Their plan for perpetual war prevents the very peace and safety it seeks to secure. The perils that face any nation in a time of war have been compounded by the mendacity of an administration that seems incapable of telling the truth. People used to say that truth is the first casualty in a time of war, but this time the truth died even before the war began. The Bush administration could not lead us into war, so it lied us into it. It is not just a matter of the individual lies—the claim that Iraq had weapons of mass destruction; the charge that it had secured nuclear materials in the country of Niger; and the assertion that Saddam Hussein was responsible for the attacks of September 11, 2001. Behind and above all these individual lies stands a larger untruth. Vietnam veteran and novelist Tim O'Brien warns us against the ceremonial celebration of war, against the idea that war brings out the best in people. Any time we feel righteous or uplifted after reading an account of war, he advises, we should realize that we have been victimized by "a very old and terrible lie" (O'Brien, 1990, pp. 68–69).

If teachers are to retain our students' trust, we have to be truth tellers about war. Students must decide for themselves which policies they support and which policies they oppose, which candidates they vote for and which candidates they vote against. These decisions are not our business; they are decisions to be made by our students on their own. But talking openly, honestly, and realistically about the nature of war is up to us. In his extraordinary poem "Mother in Wartime," Langston Hughes zeroed in on the crucial question with characteristic moral and intellectual clarity. Describing the misguided assumptions of a reader of "the Daily News," he writes that "with no in between to choose," she was led to believe that in warfare "only one side won, not that both might lose" (Hughes, 1992, p. 53).

References

Beard, C. A. (1946). *Neutrality: American Foreign Policy in the making 1932–1940: A study of respon-sibilities*. New Haven: Yale University Press.

Bourne, R. S. (1964). *War and the intellectuals: Essays by Randolph S. Bourne, 1915–1919*. New York: Harper Torchbooks.

Higham, J. (1981). *Strangers in the land: Patterns of American nativism, 1860–1925*. Westport: Greenwood.

Hughes, L. (1992). *The panther and the lash*. New York: Vintage.

Noble, D. (2002). *The death of a nation: American culture and the end of exceptionalism*. Minneapolis: University of Minnesota Press.

O'Brien, T. (1990). *The things they carried*. New York: Houghton Mifflin.

Rogin, M. (1987). *Ronald Reagan, "The Movie": and other episodes in political demonology*. Berkeley: University of California Press.

12

Pedagogies of Presence

Resisting the Violence of Absenting

PROMA TAGORE & FAIRN HERISING

On the Saturday before the war starts, driving to the protest vigil in front of the White House, I begin to cry as I listen on the car radio to the Congressional roll call vote, the patriotic yesses. . . . Standing with a somber and angry crowd, I let the tears roll down my face, tears of despair, wordless prayers.

— MINNIE BRUCE PRATT, 1990

It is September 11, 2003, and for the second year in a row, here we are again chalking the walls and walkways of our University campus with antiwar, antiracist, and anti-imperial slogans. Again, like Pratt, we write and scream out "NO BLOOD FOR OIL" over the bleached white concrete. Pausing, we turn to each other and are compelled to ask: How do we make sense of this moment, and of the moment from which Pratt speaks? What does the word "again" represent in this moment? What shapes the understanding or the notion of "here we are again"? Between buildings and classrooms, in passageways, we hear it being said: "A war, another war, a new war." Certainly, in the world we occupy today, with the recent imperialist invasions of Afghanistan and Iraq, we are witness to different machineries of domination working to erode the civil liberties and rights of people through a skewed framework that calls itself "freedom." But is this "global war on terrorism" in fact a *new* war, *another* war? Or, is it the illusion of "peacefulness" that constructs a clear line between the end of one war and the beginning of another? In imagining war as belonging to exceptional times and discrete locations, what histories and lived realities are rendered invisible? This chapter examines ways in which we, as teachers, might move our practices beyond the naming of such absences, and toward pedagogies that strive for a reconfiguration of presences materialized through an understanding of the contiguities of colonial and anticolonial histories.

We are both teachers at a Canadian university teaching in two very different disciplines: English and Social Work. The University of Victoria, like most other Canadian universities, is a predominantly white institution situated in a city that fashions its self through narratives, histories, and practices of imperialist violence and violent imperial denial. The markings of British imperialism are everywhere visibilized in the structures, architecture, organization, and narrativization of this city at the same time that the violences upon which this city was "founded" and built—including the dispossession of Indigenous peoples, and the labor of various racialized groups—are simultaneously absented and invisibilized from its official history. It is within such a context that we have both worked hard, from our respective disciplines and classrooms, to centralize various social justice issues and practices. Our guiding frameworks, although interpreted and enacted differently, proceed within antiracist, anticolonial, and queer-positive theories and practices. We both arrive in our classrooms acutely aware of the dangers of teaching and learning and learning to teach, which separate the inner world of a classroom from the outer worlds of everyday living. We both remain committed to teaching for and with a sense of urgency that stretches and connects the flesh of words, bodies, and meanings beyond the flesh of a word, a body or a meaning—and into, instead, the intrasubjectivities of histories, geographies, and knowledges. It is within these unsettling, situated spaces that we would like to proceed in looking at and unraveling what it means to propose to teach in "times of war."

The formulation of present-day imperialist wars as "new" wars, we insist, supports hegemonic understandings of war that fail to recognize the historical consistencies, persistence and immediacy of imperial violences and occupations. Thus, we argue against the notion that we are teaching, only now, in a "time of war." We are not suggesting, however, that war within each historical moment and across times and places does not shift or take on different and complex meanings or deployments. On the contrary, we argue that by paying attention to the political mechanisms that construct and demarcate "times of war" from "times of peace," we can become more fully engaged with the differences, specificities, and connections between the meanings and complexities of war across relations, spaces, places, and times. In particular, this chapter encourages the formulation of what we are calling "pedagogies of presence"—namely, a political pedagogy that reads for and acts against the boundaries of foreclosure inherent in notions of exceptional times, exceptional places, and exceptional crises. In what follows, we hope to articulate, through particular examples and instances of our teaching and learning, what it has meant for us, individually, to teach in, about, and through war in this way.

The "Peaceful Violence" of the Canadian Classroom: Teaching Fanon's *The Wretched of the Earth*

My teaching takes place in the context of the very imperial discipline of English studies. There, I teach, as the only woman of color in my Department, under the rubric of postcolonial literatures and studies: a positioning that is wrought with its own peculiar contradictions. The rise and establishment of a discipline such as English is not at all coincidental to the historical trajectories of British imperialism. The setting up of universities by colonial administrations over the course of the nineteenth century, and the replacement of the use of Native languages with English in school curricula, were crucial strategies that colonial governments employed to gain power over subjugated populations. The study of English Literature took on an instructive role in perpetuating and enforcing British models of white and middle-class propriety, respectability, and decorum for the purpose of creating "good," patriotic citizens. The recent formulations of fields such as postcolonial and anticolonial literatures and studies within disciplines of English must, therefore, entail a thinking through of the links between colonialism and the institutional histories that have defined both the field and the discipline. On the one hand, postcolonial studies have grown out of anticolonial social and political movements such that this field is structured around an opposition to colonial domination. Yet, teaching to challenge imperialism in disciplines that depend so crucially on imperial and racist knowledges poses various tangible problems in classrooms, departments, institutions, as well as to pedagogy. For example, some of the problems I face in my role as a teacher of postcolonial studies includes the difficulty of establishing credibility and authority when speaking to a primarily white audience, who is not only unacquainted with the historical and political realities of the material being studied, but also unfamiliar and often uncomfortable with the very fact of a woman of color as instructor. At the same time, racist discourses of authenticity and various tokenizing practices also often serve to structure the woman-of-color instructor as representative of the "Other," thereby sometimes conferring on her an unquestionable sense of authority, which is equally uncomfortable, dismissive, and marginalizing. In challenging certain foundational truths of the discipline—such as Eurocentric aesthetic models of "good" writing and culture, notions of "objective" inquiry and interpretation, or the separation of literature from politics—I frequently risk backlash from students, other colleagues, as well as disciplinary and punitive action from departmental and institutional administrators. Backlash comes in many forms: student resistance, the monitoring of my curricula, threats to my job security, demands that I curtail my involvement in university activism, being told to "keep quiet," and other forms of silencing.

As Aruna Srivastava (1995) notes, many of the difficulties faced by teachers of postcolonial studies do not only have to do with the emotive and often controversial nature of bringing questions of violence, war, injustice, and racism into classroom discussion. Rather, a major challenge posed by our positionings involves working against the interests of our disciplines. Similarly, Bishnupriya Ghosh (1998) reminds us that in a neocolonial, global capitalist economy, one of the dangers of teaching postcolonial studies has to do with how such teaching often translates into a commodification of "others" in various models of cross-cultural exchange. What she means by this is that, too often, the study of postcolonial literatures and cultures ends up being a process whereby the art, knowledge, or cultural creations of non-Western or non-white peoples simply come to be seen as "objects" or "products" to be known, mastered, consumed, possessed, owned, and collected by the disciplinary machineries of the North American educational system. A whole host of questions thus arises: Who and what do our positionings work to embody and disembody in the classroom? Under capitalist imperialism, does such an education simply afford North American students a greater "ease" and fluency in a global economy? How is this different from earlier colonizing and missionizing projects? In teaching about histories and locations outside of Canada and the United States, how does one avoid the refocusing and remapping of specific issues along the lines of the concerns and interests of North American hegemonies? How does one avoid the recentralization of whiteness in such discussions, and go beyond the issues of white students unlearning their privilege? What happens to the bodies of the instructors and students of color in these conversations? How are our bodies used? What do they come to signify? As a woman of color, who am I teaching to and for? How do I resist certain sorts of disembodiment and teach in a way that centralizes not the absence, but the presence, of students of color in these discussions? What might such a pedagogical practice of presence look like?

I raise these questions and signal to some of the general contexts of my teaching, in order to suggest that the particular pedagogical challenges of my positioning complicates my understanding of what it means to "teach in times of war." Dominant understandings of war as singular and exceptional—for example, as bounded to moments of extraordinary crises, or to exceptional times and locations— collude with the sort of imperialist violences that seek to conceal the realities and details of ongoing wars waged against First Nations peoples, people of color, and the Third World. We must ask ourselves: Which wars are recognized? Which ones are not, and why? Colonial history, in general, may be described as a history of absences, disappearances, and genocidal violence. Colonial practices and policies of erasure, however, relate not only to a history of genocide, displacement, and dispossession, but also to the ways in which the regulatory processes of the colonial state, and institutions of the state, subsequently attempt to hide and deny their own inherent violences and racisms through an illusion of order, neutrality, and peacefulness. Against such violence, resistances to colonialism launched by Indigenous and Third World peoples have always insisted on a politics that involves an assertion of presence, despite imperialistic policies and practices of erasure. Similarly, anticolonial education must work to expose the violences that are rendered invisible—and thus normalized—through the processes of the colonial state. We are calling this method of pedagogy—teaching to make certain sorts of colonial absentings present and open to scrutiny—a pedagogy of presence. In teaching about colonial histories and wars, a pedagogy of presence means constantly working through and against absentings. In the context of the current global "war on terrorism," a commitment to anticolonial and antiracist pedagogies and politics thus entails teaching in a way that insists on locating this "new" war in a context of ongoing occupations and histories of imperial domination. By decentering the seamless version of history that imperialism presents to us, we can then also recenter alternate ways of imagining the flows and contiguities of history, and consequently, of lives that the state and the university renders as "elsewhere," or as "not here."

I would now like to move to a discussion of what such a pedagogy of presence might look like, by considering one particular example of my own teaching: namely, the process of teaching Frantz Fanon's *The Wretched of the Earth* (1963). Fanon's influential work on colonial violence and anticolonial resistance remains a crucial text in the curriculum of contemporary postcolonial studies, and it is a book that has been a pivotal text around which I have organized a variety of my classes in colonial discourse and postcolonial literature and studies. It is a book that is rooted—firmly and specifically, though not solely—in the context of the Algerian War of Independence. For many of my students, *The Wretched of the Earth* thus seems to be working within and out of a context that they find quite distanced from their own "Canadian" lives and contexts. Typically, my students first respond to the text by noting the "abstractness" or aloofness of its language, by remarking on the impersonality of the history and politics it relates, or by stating that the book feels remote and inaccessible. At the same time, students often feel viscerally jarred and affronted by the text. Fanon's opening suggestion that "decolonization is always a violent phenomena," along with his subsequent call for armed resistance in projects of anticolonial resistance, entails a position that most students often cannot understand, or will not consent to. It is important to note also, that even for those students who accede to the fact that perhaps in the situation of Algeria under French occupation, armed revolution might have been an important and necessary course of action, this thought is often qualified with an insistence on the exceptional nature and far-off locale of that history and that social space. Such a stance, however, I want to insist, suggests an implicit failure to recognize the violences and urgencies present "here." Himani Bannerji (1995) writes similarly about her experiences of teaching Fanon. "I soon realized," she says,

> how one text of Fanon's, *The Wretched of the Earth*, produced a terror, especially and invariably among white people. They who had to be wrestled with daily to learn to see the violences that structured their/our everyday lives . . . instantly branded Fanon's text as "terrorist" and irresponsible. . . . Reading Fanon often released in them fantasies of Black men with guns or Black rapists lurking in the alleys—all responses of an angry fear. (pp. 11–12)

Indeed, even as Fanon's discussions of violence are elaborate and far-ranging— from his critique of the logic of colonial manicheanism, to his discussion of the role of the nationalist elite in the struggle for independence, to the detailed account how colonial and nationalist violence marks itself on bodies and psyches in the "case studies" at the end—the only aspect of the text that many of my white students can focus on is the "violence" of armed struggle. Bannerji rightfully says, "They could not see the violence in their approach, or in the silent 'normal' culture of their society" (p. 11). I, too, want to argue that perhaps what affronts many of my white students is not simply Fanon's call for armed resistance. Rather, I would wager that their reactions also have much to do with their perception of their own distance and "difference" from the body of the text.

But what precisely shapes and constructs this feeling of distance and difference from the text for many students? Of course, it is important to note that Fanon's text, like any other text, is partial and limited. Readers, variably and differently positioned by their own social locations of race, gender, class, sexual orientation, religion, and nationality will relate to the text in different ways, and will derive multiple meanings, interpretations, and uses from his work. Many feminists, for example, have rightfully pointed out the absence of the voices and subjectivities of women of color in the text. Feminist critics have also highlighted the ways in which revolution is described by Fanon in highly masculinized terms; and women are figured, invariably throughout the text, as "betrayers" of the revolution and of nationalist aspirations (Mohanty, 2003). Fanon's idea of revolution thus employs notions that are not uncommon to various other nationalist projects, where the "purity" of the nation's women comes to stand for the "purity" of the nation itself. As such, *The Wretched of the Earth* does not adequately account for how either colonial or national violence and wars mark themselves out, routinely and specifically, on the bodies of women; nor does it leave open a concept of women as revolutionaries. The particular ways in which the text constructs and deconstructs the woman-of-color reader, or how such a reader constructs and deconstructs both the text and herself in relation to it, is an interesting question to pursue.

Part of what is at stake in such a reading of Fanon—and what is at stake in Fanon's own inquiry as well—is thus the question of to what extent his work is generalizable outside of the specificities in which the text is grounded. In many ways, a large part of *The Wretched of the Earth* is precisely concerned with the degree to which conditions of colonialism, and, therefore, also of anticolonial resistance, may be universalized. What does the Algerian example have to offer other projects of nationalism on the African subcontinent, or in Latin America? How do African nationalisms relate to issues of and movements for liberation in the African diaspora? Fanon's own multiple and contradictory subject positionings complicate his answers and his project. Born in Martinique and educated in France, the "home" that Fanon finds in the Algerian struggle for independence is never fixed, but always unstable and shifting. It is interesting to think about, for example, the "case studies" that Fanon records at the end of *The Wretched of the Earth*, which ostensibly are derived from his experience working as a psychiatrist in Algeria. In many of these narrative sketches, it is difficult to discern who Fanon is: doctor or patient? self or other? It is equally provocative to contemplate the profoundly mediated nature of these narrative accounts that present themselves, on the one hand, as simple "recordings" of events and encounters. Yet, as a French speaker, who is not versed in Arabic, Fanon often needed to have a translator present in order to carry out much of his work, and thus many of these "case studies" are in fact experiences in translation. What gets lost in the translation? What are the limits of translation? To what extent can we say that situations, contexts, experiences, or historical processes are translatable? What happens in the process of translation, transformation, change, revolution? What is obscured as we seek to bring into being the presence of something new? These are just some of the questions that fold over onto the pages of Fanon's text, and that are perhaps most evident in the middle sections of the book, where Fanon offers his important critique of nationalist movements. As formerly colonized countries achieve "Independence," Fanon asks, what and who becomes absented from the vision of the "nation"? Perhaps more than anything, Fanon demands that we continually ask ourselves: What is being rendered absent in any achievement of presence? What or whose presence do we overlook because the institution of state power sanction our unseeing? It is precisely such forms of absenting that Fanon means to elucidate when he speaks of "peaceful violence."

"Between the violence of the colonies and that peaceful violence that the world is steeped in," writes Fanon (1963), "there is a kind of complicit agreement, a sort of homogeneity" (p. 81). It is important to note that Fanon's discussion of "peaceful violence" occurs in the context of his larger discussion on the shifting forms of imperialist violence, namely, the global shift from older forms of European territorial colonialism to newer forms of violence engendered by a capitalist imperialism rooted in an ideology of liberal neutralism. Here, Fanon is specifically interested in what happens after formal independence, as nationalist dreams of liberation are co-opted into an emergent capitalist imperialism, in the context of the new hegemony of the United States in world politics and economy. Although the former colonial powers have supposedly "withdrawn" from the newly independent nation-states, they maintain their dominance through the "silent" exchanges of capital, commerce, trade, and international negotiations. In this new economy, imperialist and racist violence—although maintained through lines of force, coercion, and power—present themselves as natural and normal through the illusion of order, peacefulness, and reciprocity. Fanon asks us to consider whether or not such a moment consists, in fact, of something "new," or whether or not this historical shift simply involves the perpetuation of colonial violence, albeit in a different guise. Haunani Kay-Trask (2000) invokes Fanon's notion of a "peaceful violence" to emphasize that not only is imperial violence carried out through military invasions and occupations or physical warfare, but that it also consists of "the ordered realities of confinement, degradation, ill-health and early death" (p. 118) that result from imperial exploitation. The notion of "peaceful violence" thus points to the fact that the violences of an imperialist history might take different forms and shapes with relation to specific contexts and realities. However, forms of violence that are invisibilized by the state's regulatory and normalizing functions are not any more or less violent than those other forms of violence that we might have learned how to see.

What are the implications for politics and pedagogy, then, in considering Fanon's notion of a peaceful violence? "The distinctive *force* of Fanon's vision," Homi Bhabha writes (borrowing from Walter Benjamin), derives from "a revolutionary awareness that the 'state of emergency in which we live is not the exception, but the rule'" (1994, p. 114). Similarly, I am trying to argue, through Fanon, that conditions of war and crisis cannot simply be imagined as "elsewhere" or "outside," but they must also be acknowledged right "here." In a book that offers a painstakingly systematic, and yet also a deeply personal and experiential, examination of Canadian racism and the Canadian state, Bannerji writes of Fanon's immense influence, and further elucidates Fanon's relevance to thinking about the North American context. "Fanon was the first thinker who helped me to understand my big and trivial Canadian experiences as those of violence," she says, "he gave me a way of rethinking violence, including much which appeared benign and involved no blood or blow" (p. 11). Likewise, I want to suggest that Fanon's *The Wretched of the Earth*, and indeed even the situation of the Algerian struggle against French colonialism itself, offer an important lens for thinking through a variety of colonial contexts, including a view of Canadian and U.S. racisms *as* particular sites of a larger imperial project. Indeed, in reflecting back on many of my students' sense of distance from the text, it seems that that their feelings of "difference" have little to do with their unfamiliarity with the situation in Algeria in the 1950s, but rather more to do with a certain refusal to familiarize themselves with present-day racism and colonialism within the Canadian state. I urge my students to consider, for example, Fanon's description of what happens after the 1957 UN appeal to French authorities to find a peaceful and democratic solution in Algeria. He writes of how the French government, after the UN appeal, decides to create "civil militias" through new discourses of terrorism, heightened anti-Arab propaganda and suspicion, and by arming the European civilian population with new powers of surveillance, detection, investigation, and the arrest of suspects. In a North American classroom in the year 2003, when we contemplate the sorts of racial profiling, suspicion, detentions, and violences that this current "war on terrorism" has prompted, suddenly Fanon's Algeria of 1957 no longer sounds so distant. The classroom is far from neutral now. As we begin to work through the contiguities of colonial history, of anticolonial resistance, and our own differential positionings and implicatedness in these histories, we also begin to imagine, differently, what it means to teach, to learn, to act, and to live with a sense of urgency.

The Peace and Justice Statement: Enacting Principles of Social Justice

The School of Social Work is committed to principles and ideals that support and cultivate social justice, and as such we are compelled morally, politically and socially to speak up and against the war on Iraq. We stand in solidarity with the millions of voices globally calling for an end to the US and British invasion on Iraq. We call for the immediate end of this violent and illegal aggression in the name of a "pre-emptive war," which is threatening global and international peace and security. We fundamentally believe that military action cannot be the answer to global crises and firmly denounce the US and British rhetoric that this war is about liberating the Iraqi people. Military action always and automatically increases and puts at risk all human rights and none more fundamentally as the right to life. We firmly believe that human rights can only be sustained and realized through just and peaceful means and as such we urge the United Nations and all peoples and governments to speak up and out against the present invasion of Iraq.

We denounce the occupations of people by imperialist states wherever they exist—in Palestine, Iraq or Aboriginal Nations of Canada. We also denounce the illegal and unjust military aggressions against the Palestinian people and the settlements and continued occupation of their territory, in defiance of United Nations resolutions by the state of Israel, with the complicit support of the US. We are appalled by the continued and ongoing slaughter of Iraqi and Palestinian people and call for an immediate cessation of all military aggression and state repression waged against Iraqi and Palestinian civilians.

We stand in solidarity with the many peace and anti-racist activists at home and abroad calling for an end to the increased racial profiling and human rights violations against Arab, Muslim, Palestinian and South Asian peoples. We deplore and stand against all forms of hatred that arise out of conditions of war, oppression, repression and genocide at home and abroad. We call for and stand for a world and everyday relationships that are invested in cultivating solidarity amongst each other, encouraging diverse and dynamic ways of knowing and living, fostering of individual and collective involvement, and respecting the rights of individuals, peoples, and nations to self-determine their lives and futures.

My inquiry into the ways in which various shapes of absences are at work within pedagogy will be informed by the complex relations, actions, and discourses that occurred as a consequence of the Peace and Justice Statement created in my department. Specifically, I want to look at the spaces that disrupted, hampered, and betrayed (absented) enactments for social justice by centralizing (making present) dominant ways of knowing and relating. It is crucial, I think, to attend to various forms of absences. Absences shape and define what is present and foregrounds the limits and possibilities of practicing radical pedagogies. I argue that these forms of absenting that occurred "outside" a classroom, in fact exist outside/in teaching and learning. In other words, I want to challenge the borders between what is viewed as legitimate curriculum and where we believe "proper" teaching and learning takes place. These absences that occurred should not be seen as separate from pedagogy. Instead, they need to be read as spaces that intersect with how we engage with the (im)possibilities of radical pedagogies, how we construct and define "times of crises," and how we navigate the tensions and contradictions of the radical (im)possibilities of social justice.

Before I move into the substance of my inquiry I want to contextualize some general elements of the department within which I work, study, and teach. The School of Social Work that I am affiliated with positions itself within a number of emancipatory aims, foundationally reflected within the School's Mission Statement. The School attempts to situate itself within critical dialogues that simultaneously attempt to address social work's complicity within human suffering, demonstrated by its normalizing and regulatory practice frameworks, as well as its commitment to social, economic, and political change.

For approximately five years I have worked and continue to work within this department performing a number of different and connected "roles," as coordinator of student community based practicums, teacher, graduate student, and curriculum developer. I entered both the academy and my department grounded within a commitment to and for political activism. I felt that activist politics was not only possible within the academe and my department, but also imperative to disrupting "business as usual" approaches to various relations, teaching, curriculum, and research. Additionally, I have grown suspicious and concerned over the years as a community activist and as a student of teaching and research that segregated and abstracted my own and others' lives to research objects. Within social work, this form of abstraction takes place predominantly within the supremacy and expansion of professionalism and standardizations, consolidating its power through expert knowledges, exclusions, universal skills-based interventions, and positivist interpretations and definitions of "problems" and "solutions." Speaking about social work, Houston (2001) states that it "embrace[s] overly instrumentalized responses governed by procedures, competencies and managerialism" (p. 853). This abstracting repeats and reproduces the modernist project where difference and marginality must be labeled, treated, fixed, controlled, surveilled, and managed.

Prior to speaking to the context of, and response to, the Peace and Justice Statement, I should state that I was one of three people that created the Peace and Justice Statement. I am one of many involved in the various conversations that flowed from the Statement. As such, the diverse meanings I will engage with and convey are *my own.*

Within my department there were a few of us actively involved in organizing and participating in antiwar and anticolonial protests. As time passed, I felt a growing sense of unease regarding the silence I perceived within my department toward the heightened Canadian and American forms of racism and racial profiling, and the ensuing American invasion of Iraq. A couple of us within the department requested that the School take a more vocal and public stand against racism, war, colonialism, and imperialism. We brought forward our request, which was unanimously agreed to by "School Council" (comprised of staff, faculty, and student representatives); and a small group of us composed and submitted a Peace and Justice Statement that was posted on the School's website early April 2003. In a general climate of hostility and suspicion, at a time of heightened tensions across North American campuses, and at a university predominantly organized around imperial denials, the Statement served as a powerful moment of dissent. Colleagues at other universities remarked how difficult or impossible it might be for such a statement to be officially sanctioned and posted on their campuses. Indeed, the presence of the Statement provided critical interventions within hegemonic articulations of history and power. The Statement also served as a pedagogical text that made present and visible some networks of local and global power, elucidating the vicissitudes of counter-epistemic standpoints, crucial to critical pedagogies. Henry Giroux (2003) describes this project of critical education:

> Educational work, at best, represents a response to questions and issues posed by the tensions and contradictions of public life and such work, when critical, also attempts to understand and intervene in specific problems that emanate from the material contexts of everyday existence. (p. 11)

However, two months later the director of the School, under public pressure, chose to remove the Statement from the School's website and, in its place, posted a conciliatory letter. Public backlash to the Peace and Justice Statement was framed primarily by charges that the Statement was anti-Semitic, anti-American, and one-sided. Furthermore, the charges included that the School of Social Work and the university-owned website were inappropriate places for expressing these particular values and politics.

I think it is crucial to note that the Peace and Justice Statement as a document cannot be read or engaged with as a text that represents a pure idea or infallible incitement of/for social justice. The Statement, like any other text, cannot be fully representational of ideas or relations, for meanings always slip, readings are always multiple, and our environments are always incomplete. For example, the Peace and Justice Statement highlights and denounces specific global imperialisms by naming geographical and ideological violences. In doing so, it necessarily omits other and potentially intersecting forms and realities of violence. In this vein, the Peace and Justice Statement could have included a denouncement of anti-Semitism—not because there was a concern for a balanced viewpoint—but rather a concern for ideas and actions that directly contribute to the marginalization and subjugation of Jewish peoples.

Additionally, the Peace and Justice Statement were both produced and sanctioned "by the school" and took up an assumed speaking position that became representative of "the school." Thus, contradictions, dissent, and tensions were hidden within a monolithic framing of ideas and positions of social justice. How do we as social justice educators and activists take up social justice imperatives without foreclosing on the breadth of different speaking positions? How might we engage and transform the contradictions of our own texts and discussions while remaining deeply committed to principles of peace and justice? And possibly most importantly, we need remind ourselves that our visions and investments in social justice are never innocent or outside of social, historical, and political power relations. Our visions and investments of social justice are always partial and incomplete, and therefore, we must be attentive to our ideas and actions for social justice. If we are not attentive and critical of our ideas and how ideas affect the specificities of lives, we may become that which we resist. We may in other words "achieve" social justice at the cost of another and others. We must be careful not to propose a fixed or fully transparent idea of social justice or, for that matter, a truly or wholly pedagogy of presence. We need instead to continuously revisit, rework, regenerate, and transform our ideas and actions of and for social justice.

Balanced Viewpoints and Appropriate Spaces: Liberalism Made Present/the Absenting of Critical Differences

> Liberalism is committed to individualism for it takes as basic the moral, political, and legal claims of the individual over and against those of the collective. It seeks foundations in universal principles applicable to all human beings or rational agents in virtue of their humanity or rationality. In this liberalism seeks to transcend particular historical, social, and cultural differences: it is concerned with broad identities which it insists unite persons on moral grounds, rather than with those identities which divide politically, culturally, geographically, or temporally. (Goldberg, 1993, p. 5)

In this section, I want to pay attention to two forms of presence-ing that were made visible in the exchanges between the backlash to the statement and the responses to the backlash. The two primary public conversations called for *a balanced viewpoint*, and that *the academy was not a site for such texts as the Peace and Justice Statement.* I wish to read these comments within the liberalist framework that generates such ideas, and to discuss the critical forms of absenting that occurred within these conversations—namely, the absenting of power relations, the absenting of dissenting voices, the absenting of critical pedagogy and epistemology, the necessity of intervening in the political, and the absenting of ongoing urgencies and crises.

Within Western liberal democratic theories, a need for a balanced viewpoint is anchored within claims for objectivity and reason. Objectivity and reason serve as the cornerstone of legitimate liberalist thought and action. Liberal discussions of the nature of justice formulate objectivity and reason as the normative ground for balanced and fair political dialogue. Within this normative framework, no citizen is denied their individual right to express or speak about the demands of justice in society. However, while objectivity and reason, with requisites of intellectualized distance and emotional detachment, may be possible as an abstract idea, it fails to capture the epistemic difference in various social standpoints to understand the material and concrete realities of living and life. Within liberal thought, justice is procured without abandoning the ideal that any demand for justice must be designed and voiced objectively in order to sufficiently meet the standards to be admitted into public or political dialogue. Within pedagogy, liberalism demands that educators present knowledges outside of a political project, where the political nature of education, curricula, knowledge production, and relations of power remain absented from the classroom. Within liberal thought, the educational project provides knowledges of "both sides of a conflict," which in turn enables students to form their own conclusions. This liberal framework, I argue, is inadequate for creating an ethical ground from which to understand the various contradictions and possibilities of our lives, of creating counterhegemonic pedagogies, of nurturing dissenting voices, and sustaining epistemic inquiry that is both critical and engaging.

Within the backlash to the Peace and Justice Statement, the discursive responses were implicitly tied to forging a middle ground. This was evident by comments that the Statement was "one-sided," by the swift removal of the Statement from the school's website, and replaced by a conciliatory letter that stated, in part, "We are deeply committed to balancing freedom of expression with respectful work and learning environments" (Brown, 2003) on the website.

I am left asking the following questions: What specific moments and anxieties produce a desire for a balanced viewpoint? What is desired from a balanced viewpoint? What are the effects and consequences of objectivity and reason for crucial political debates for social justice in education? It is not unusual for citing balanced viewpoints as a strategy for silencing dissenting voices, and simultaneously constructing dissenting voices as irrational, emotional, and illogical. I would suggest that the desire for a balanced viewpoint within the debate called for objectivity and reason, signaling that the Statement and discussions that preceded the formulation of the Statement were not grounded in objectivity and reason. Rather, the Statement was constituted within the subjective, passion, and desire and, therefore, was in some way distorted, limiting, or unreasonable.

The need for a balanced viewpoint also proposes that there is a truth that we seek. In its current manifestation, the Statement is not inclusive of "the truth," and that a balanced viewpoint will help us all to arrive at "a truth" that is fair. Balanced viewpoints are often strategies for assuming equality and harmony in relationships. This strategy can also result in the neutralization and/or refusal of responsibility because it fails to account for inequalities and asymmetrical relations of power, status, and privilege that already exist in specific contexts. A balanced viewpoint would suggest that there was a need to neutralize the Statement, and in the process of neutralization, absenting the very conditions of lives and voices that the Statement supports. How are change, transformation, and regeneration made possible in pedagogies for social justice if interventions that question the social and political are neutralized? Neutralizing ideas and voices would consequently (re)inscribe and (re)naturalize dominance, while abstracting and excluding marginal subjects.

For educators deeply committed to pedagogies of social justice, whose lives have been profoundly marked by various forms of subjugation and who are critically aware of the tensions, contradictions, and paradoxes of the (im)possibilities of social justice, we know that speaking the political is always a risk and always poses certain dangers. In my own teaching career I have become quite aware of the risks and dangers of "choosing the margins as a space of radical openness" (hooks, 1990, p. 145). The risks range from explicit accusations of favoritism in the classroom to implicit accusations of being a troublemaker, resulting in isolation, alienation, and mini-mizing of my own political stances and desires. Over the years, I have come to engage and challenge the paradoxes of a radical or emancipatory pedagogy quite cognizant that there is no innocent speaking position, and what and how I teach is never neutral. Henry Giroux (2003) explains that

> any viable notion of pedagogy and resistance should illustrate how knowledge, values, desire, and social relations are always implicated in relations of power, and how such an understanding can be used pedagogically and politically by students. (p. 11)

Thus, to intervene in the historical and collective spaces of silences and absences is a commitment to enacting a pedagogy for both teachers and students that names and makes present sociopolitical relations of power, and rejuvenates a presence of those narratives that are absented within academic institutions.

I wish to further explore how the notion of a balanced viewpoint defines and understands peacefulness, and how in its attempts to neutralize and obfuscate rela-tions of power, reproduces and supports a repetition of singular dominant view of peacefulness. This view of peacefulness is largely constructed and framed as if we are *now* confronted by a sense of urgency. The problem, and my contestation, is not that we are confronted by urgent demands. Instead, I wish to challenge how our sense of urgency is repeatedly juxtaposed against a nostalgia for peacefulness, peace-ful times, quiet times, better times, good times, prosperous times, and so on. Who defines urgency? How do we measure urgency? And perhaps more importantly, what and who is lost in the processes of asserting that we are *now* in a time of crisis?

There is a poster on my door of four Indigenous peoples with a caption that reads: "Fighting Terrorism Since 1492." Who indeed is allowed to name meanings and speak to times of war, crisis, terrorism, and urgency? How is it that we do not confer the language of war and terrorism, or act from a space of urgency to the var-ious injustices occurring right now and long before September 11? As Paula Gunn Allen (1998) reminds us:

> [T]he cops beating African American men is a media sound bite, and the merciless destruction of Native people is largely ignored by all factions in the brawling American polity. Many are glad that "the war has ended," but I am compelled to object: it has not ended; it goes on and on. (p. 164)

The events of September 11 is read in North American public discourse as a narrative of beginnings, where all foreign and domestic concerns are couched in the language of a discrete, chronological history and location that began on September 11. This dominant discourse is made possible because we have naturalized and nor-malized racial and colonial violences. We have cast colonial conquest on this continent to the past, "a done deal." Therefore, it is crucial that we not only resist the dominant liberal discourse of a balanced viewpoint but we disrupt such aggressive discourses by actively rupturing our notions of linear narratives of times of crisis or war. I would suggest that we need to make present and visible how we carry out our racial interests. We need to question our assumption that times of war and times of crisis are disconnected events by naming and invoking the intersections of everyday racism, colonialism, subjugation, and oppression. We need to ask ourselves and each other: What wars, crises, and terrorism have we simply accepted and under what terms?

In questioning balanced viewpoint, and by unmapping the ways in which this discourse attempts to recover itself, we may be able to open up pedagogical possibilities to explore the ways in which we are deeply invested in ensuring tidy classroom relations, tidy learning, and tidy teaching. We might then be able to ask and explore how the need for the dominant position that calls for a peaceful, neat, and tidy pedagogy is already predicated upon a crisis of learning and living for some. Within classrooms and curricula, who is asked to carry the crisis and urgency of everyday bigotry, racism, and oppressive hierarchies? I believe we must foster and create spaces and places within our respective pedagogies that account for and work within everyday crisis of what and who is unsaid, unthought, and unimagined.

Within the backlash to the Statement, criticisms were also directed at the School for using the academy and institutionally owned websites as a site of pedagogical dissent and activism. Recognizing that the academy is not outside of community spaces or public discourses requires eschewing notions of the "rightful place" for pedagogical dissent and discarding the notion that institutions and education are somehow excluded from the larger questions of culture, power, politics, and authority. How does the assertion of "rightful spaces" for dissent discipline and manage pedagogical imperatives of belonging and exclusions, silences and disappearances, sanctioned proprieties and management of differences? What becomes the purpose or services of academic institutions if it is not expected to be a site that fosters and creates a climate conducive to critical thinking and engagements? Giroux (1997) argues:

> Institutions of higher education must be seen as deeply moral and political spaces in which intellectuals assert themselves not merely as professional academics but as citizens, whose knowledge and actions presuppose specific visions of public life, community, and moral accountability. (p. 263)

Some might argue (and some have) that the University is a place that produces decent, compliant, capitalist citizens. The academy becomes a site where lines are well formed ensuring that particular cultural and ideological values are nurtured, thus naturalizing the imperatives of individualistic global empires. Students are then prepared to accept standardized and universalized truths in order to comply with the bidding and desires of the nation. Accepting this model means that being "successful," "model" citizens (or "good" social workers) requires our acceptance of dominant narratives as universal truisms.

Universities need to work harder to utilize democratic processes to produce and disseminate knowledges that are not controlled by outside or hegemonic forces. Universities have to exercise autonomy and create a space for intellectual inquiry and dialogue. Closing the door on debate precludes such dialogue and thus decreases the possibility of moving toward justice and social equality. Revoking (and censoring) the School's Statement on Peace and Justice, the University chose to legitimate one voice and to consolidate a singular (and dominant) version of knowledge. In retracting their Statement, the School (and University) shut down a dissenting voice, and absented to memory the powerful moment of dissent present at the School of Social Work.

I believe that the university should be a place where we critically challenge, discuss, and debate a wide range of ideas and perspectives, where activism is imperative to shift the historical legacy and grounds of social work, which is bound up in collusion with imperialist nation-building projects. Chandra Mohanty (2003) offers a vision for open and democratic pedagogy:

> The struggle to transform our institutional practices fundamentally also involves the grounding of the analysis of exploitation and oppression in accurate history and theory, seeing ourselves as activists in the academy, drawing links between movements for social justice and our pedagogical and scholarly endeavours and expecting and demanding action from ourselves, our colleagues, and our students at numerous levels. (p. 216)

Moreover, the call to pay attention to issues of human rights and the imperative to voice demands for peace and social justice cannot be practices that are merely "reserved" for particular places or occasions. Censoring and expelling voices of dissent reengages and re-invokes the denial of history, collective memory, and situated experiences, and reasserts the presence of everyday relations of dominance.

Conclusions

Through our different and specific examples, we have hoped to articulate our attempts to engage a political pedagogy that not only politicizes what it means to teach, learn, and learn to teach but also make present the fact that our respective lives are collectively and dialectically implicated within various histories of authority, power, and privilege. For us, a pedagogy of presence arises out of a concern of and for absence. As such, we have tried to imagine a pedagogy whereby we can map out not only absence, but also the manner in which absences are made. Toni Morrison (1988/2000) describes, in many ways, what such a process might look like:

> We can agree, I think, that invisible things are not necessarily "not-there"; that a void may be empty, but it is not a vacuum. In addition, certain absences are so stressed, so ornate, so planned, they call attention to themselves; arrest us with intentionality and purpose, like neighbourhoods that are defined by the population held away from them. Looking at the scope of American literature, I can't help thinking that the question should never have been "Why am I, an Afro-American, absent from it?" It is not a particularly interesting query anyway. The spectacularly interesting question is "What intellectual feats had to be performed by the author or his critic to erase me from a society seething with my presence, and what effect has that performance had on the work?" What are the strategies of escape from knowledge? Of willful oblivion? (p. 34)

Morrison urges us to consider: How is it that we continue to repeat the notion that absences are innocent or unintentional? A pedagogy of presence believes that the project of education and of living is about moving with crisis and a sense of urgency. Such a pedagogy means being wary of our desires for harmony. As Deborah Britzman (1998) reminds us, "There is a problem with narratives that promise the normalcy of life, that presume a life without difference, without a divided self." A pedagogy of presence involves bringing certain sorts of colonial absentings into view, so that they may be scrutinized, and so that something new can come into being. However, it also means engaging our own resistances to critically interrogate how our presence-ing of our own selves and pedagogies might foreclose on other possibilities. What we propose, then, is not any sort of "model" or "blueprint" for anti-oppressive teaching. Rather, a pedagogy of presence requires sitting with discomfort, but it also requires that we prepare for spontaneity.

References

Allen, P. G. (1998). *Off the reservation: Reflections on boundary-busting, border-crossing, loose canons.* Boston: Beacon Press.

Bannerji, H. (1995). *Thinking through: Essays on feminism, Marxism, and anti-racism.* Toronto: Women's Press.

Bhabha, H. (1994). Remembering Fanon: Self, psyche and the colonial condition. In P. Williams and L. Chrisman (Eds.), *Colonial discourse and post-colonial theory: A reader*, 112–125. New York: Columbia UP.

Britzman, D. (1998). Lost subjects, contested objects: Toward a psychoanalytic inquiry of learning. Albany: State University of New York Press.

Brown, L. (2003). Open letter. University of Victoria. Retrieved January 15, 2006, from http://web.uvic.ca/socw/

Fanon, F. (1963). *The wretched of the earth* (C. Farlington, Trans.). New York: Grove P.

Ghosh, B. (1998). The postcolonial bazaar: Thoughts on teaching the market in postcolonial objects. *Postmodern Culture, 9*(1) (September).

Giroux, H. (1997). *Pedagogy and the politics of hope: Theory, culture and schooling.* Boulder, CO: Westview Press.

Giroux, H. (2003). Public pedagogy and the politics of resistance: Notes on a critical theory of educational struggle. *Educational Philosophy and Theory*, 35(1), 5–16.

Goldberg, D. T. (1993). *Racist culture: Philosophy and the politics of meaning.* Oxford: Blackwell Publishers Ltd.

hooks, b. (1990). *Yearning: Race, gender, and cultural politics.* Toronto: Between the Lines.

Houston, S. (2001). Beyond social constructionism: Critical realism and social work. *British Journal of Social Work*, 31, 845–861.

Kay-Trask, H. (2000). Keynote lecture [Video]. Violence Against Women of Colour Conference: Vol. 13.

Mohanty, C. (2003). *Feminism without borders: Decolonizing theory, practicing solidarity.* Durham and London: Duke University Press.

Morrison, T. (1988/2000). Unspeakable things unspoken: The Afro-American presence in American literature. In J. James and T. Denean (Eds.), *The Black feminist reader*, 24–56. Sharpley-Whitig: Blackwell.

Pratt, M. B. (1991). *Rebellion: Essays 1980–1991.* New York: Firebrand Books.

Srivastava, A. (1995). Editorial introduction. "Postcolonialism and its Discontents." *Ariel* (Jan/Aug).

University of Victoria, School of Social Work. 2003. Statement on Peace and Justice. www.social-work.uvic.ca/announce.htm. Website accessed October 2nd, 2003.

Conversation

Situating Anti-Oppressive Education in Our Times

PROMA TAGORE, FAIRN HERISING, JOCELYN ANNE GLAZIER, & GEORGE LIPSITZ

Undoing ingrained racial and sexual mythologies within feminist communities requires in Jacqui Alexander's words, that we "become fluent in each other's histories." It also requires seeking "unlikely coalitions" (Davis 1998, 299) and, I would add, clarifying the ethics and meaning of dialogue. What are the conditions, knowledges, and the attitudes that make a noncolonized dialogue possible? How can we craft a dialogue anchored in equality, respect, and dignity for all peoples? ... [H]ow to engage in ethical and caring dialogues (and revolutionary struggles) across the divisions, conflicts, and individualistic identity formations?

—CHANDRA MOHANTY (2003, P. 125)

Fairn: Proma, George, and Jocelyn—first, let me say thank you to each of you for your words, visions, and desires of what might be as we move into and across various thresholds in thought, living, loving, and hope. George and Jocelyn, we have not met face-to-face or spoken voice-to-voice, and yet I find myself folded and opened up upon new landscapes of what it means to teach *in* and *with* the world. Thank you for this and these moments.

Proma: Yes, hello, Fairn, George, and Jocelyn. Thank you, George and Jocelyn, for the work and thinking that you do in your chapter, and also for your responses. Your ideas encourage me to think more deeply about the relationship between teaching and politics, and raise important questions about *where* we imagine teaching and learning to happen. Fairn, I am honored, once again, to have the opportunity to think alongside and beside you in this conversation. As I sit down to write today, I am reminded of how every new conversation is often already situated and participating in a multitude of other conversations—ones from the past, ones taking place in the present, and possibly even future conversations.

Fairn: Here *we* are, brought together via many different means and routes. *We* have been asked to speak to/with each other, to read each others' various pieces of work, and to make connections with each other from our various pieces of writing.

Proma: Perhaps, then, as a start, we might think about the process of creating conversations, itself, and ask, as Mohanty does, what are the conditions and possibilities of a noncolonizing conversation?

Fairn: How do we converse without colonizing? Proma, I know I have a lot more questions than answers—which may, paradoxically, move me closer to enacting the question you have posed.

In this moment of writing to and with each of you I am reminded of the enormous creative potential that can exist in thinking and doing education as "a practice of freedom" (hooks, 1994). At the same time, I hold these words of Michel Foucault (1989): "Liberty is a practice. So there may, in fact, always be, a number of projects whose aim is to modify some constraints, to loosen, or even to break them, but none of these projects can, simply by its nature, assure that people will have liberty automatically: that will be established by the project itself" (pp. 335–347).

Proma: It seems to me that each of us, although in different ways, touch on the question of how certain sorts of foreclosures are enacted in the process of asserting a homogenized collectivity. George, for example, you evoke the processes of "othering" that occurs in the U.S. proclamations of a unified, singular national identity. Of course, this identity that understands itself as "free," "democratic," and based on the principle of "liberty" is an illusion that can only be maintained if one chooses not to see the various histories of colonization, war, and unfreedom that it has been built on. This process of "choosing not to see" is, I would argue, a process of willful denial, or what Gayatri Spivak (1994) describes as "sanctioned ignorance." Similarly, Jocelyn, you speak of various process of silencing and invisibilization that occur in the classroom and in schools that regulate who/what is seen and who/what is not. Fairn, you remind us that even what we see of our-selves and of our own projects is never fully transparent, fully evident.

The question—who is "we"?—is one that I often find myself ask-ing, coming back to. What sort of "we" is or is not being evoked at dif-ferent moments? The invoking of "we"—that is, the call for certain sorts of collective or shared frameworks of referencing, understanding, and belonging—is not in itself what I find myself questioning. But, rather, in invoking a particular "we," what other possibilities for we/me/you/I/us may be either advertently or inadvertently being left out this moment? What sort of disappearances are enacted for both myself and my students (who cannot come into view) when conver-sations assume a certain, homogenized sense of "we"? So, who is "we" and how does how this is imagined matter?

Fairn: So, who is "we," and how do we converse without colonizing? To begin, I am at any given moment unsure of the multitude of "Wes" that emerge from and with any given moment—like now, this very moment I am unsure of all the Wes, Yous and Is and Mes that are written across and in between each word, sentence, phrase, and paragraph. Yet, I know that how I come to understand, write, and work with these spaces and places matters.

I can see the dangers and poisons of a constituted "we" that George addresses—the Us and Them of Nationalism. I know this mat-ters—who lives, dies, and thrives.

I can see myself similarly encouraging, as Jocelyn does in her classroom, students to critically engage with the partiality and com-plexities of I and the fictions that can lie within any unity of I and We. I know this matters—why, who, and what lives, dies, and thrives.

I can see as I weave between each of your chapters the powerful ways in which I, you, we, us attempt to resist the various narratives (Nationhood/Belonging), techniques (Standards/Truth), and repeti-tions (Outcomes) of a foreclosed Sameness and Oneness. I know this matters—who and how we live, die, and thrive.

And yet, here I am watching, waiting, and wondering about the effects, possibilities, and impossibilities of our connections, cross cur-rents, eddies, and underflows of I, we, you, us. I know this matters—that "there is a problem with narrative that promise the normalcy of life that presume life without difference" (Britzman, 1998). And yet, is it possible to ask, what are these differences? What happens in the process of asking? And dare I ask in these postmodern times, which differences matter and why? And as I move through and with each of you I am aware of being caught like many of my students between and with the double thought of knowing and not knowing: between capture and becoming (Deleuze & Gauttari, 1987).

Yes, George, I too think teaching is hard work. As I read and reread all of your words I feel the tensions, excitements, loss, and grief of what it means to teach, to learn, and to write. I realize that I cannot simply hope for a better world, that I cannot simply through an act of will wish a better, more just world into existence—that, indeed, like all of your words, "liberty is a practice" and "hope is a practice" crafted from and emerging out of our relations (both real and imaginary) of everyday urgencies, necessities, possibilities, and impossibilities. Thank you all for these lessons.

Proma: Faith. Trust. Hope. The place of these in teaching, learning, and life. The relationship of these to political and everyday struggles and urgencies. Faith. Trust. Hope. Urgency. In reading and rereading our chapters and conversations, these are the words that keep resonating in my mind—these words at once, sit and unsettle. I know I am not willing to let go of these words. I also know that I do not have any blueprint of how these may be understood and enacted. Indeed, that I do not yet have language through which I am able to adequately "capture" their meanings and practices—nor, I suppose, do I want to. Speaking somewhat similarly, of concepts of hope, love, desire/wish, being, becoming, and belonging, Himani Bannerji (1995) reminds me that "there is not much point" in saying that one does not desire spaces of faith, trust, home, and belonging. Rather that the problem lies in thinking that these things only mean a "happy positivity" (Bannerji, 1995, p. 186). I imagine, too, that all of our own words, dreams, and practices take on certain shared, yet also very different and singular meanings, shapes, textures, and contours in the context of each of our lives. I appreciate this opportunity to be able to speak and write alongside all of you through these conversations, through these moments that are, at once, shared and yet highly distinct and singular.

Jocelyn: I enter into this conversation humbled by your convictions and your commitments. You rage eloquently about teaching and living in a time of war. Where is the discussion of war in my own teaching? I am inclined here to reference Proma and Fairn's idea of absenting in reference to my own work.

George: I agree—with all that you declare. The war the United States has waged on Iraq is a war built directly on a foundation of falsehood. While teachers might recognize that reality, they are left shackled in ways that resemble the silencing felt by you, Proma and, in particular, Fairn. I remember well after September 11, the stories my teachers exchanged about being told by their administrators not to share any information with their students. Teachers huddled around televisions in teachers' lounges, watching in disbelief as the World Trade Towers burned, and then had to walk back into classrooms as though the day was like any other. The same silencing occurred later that year when two snipers left those of us in the neighborhoods in and around Washington, DC, paralyzed by fear. Like Proma, my preservice teachers step into schools and classrooms in which they are "being told to 'keep quiet.'" And yet, ironically, they are at times in progressive classroom spaces; engaging their students in inquiry and discursive models of learning, asking their students to ask questions and to talk with one another. The question remains, however, as to *what* they ask and talk about.

Today in October 2004, as I write this letter to you, I can't help but think about the genocide in Sudan. More than 50,000 people killed, a million homeless. And I think too about all of the injustices you mention, George, ranging from the 30,000 children dying every day in Asia, Africa, and Latin America, to the thousands of victims of misogyny and pedophelia. Here in my hometown of Washington, DC, I mourn for the 21 juvenile victims of violence who have died between January and September 2004. Some—many—are constantly living at war, in a time of crisis. Our teachers are always, I would argue, "teaching in a time of war." Like you, Fairn, I ask "What and who is lost in the process of asserting that we are *now* in a time of crisis?" Weren't we—standing in solidarity with the oppressed—there yesterday, last week, last month?

As we delve into the sometimes oppressive messages imbedded in children's books in my critical literacy course, I often hear my students comment, "Why ruin the book? Kids shouldn't be thinking that deeply about this stuff. It's just a story! They'll have plenty of time to learn harsh realities when they get older." I sympathize with their concern. The world can be—and is for many—a devastating place. When and how do we share those realities with our students? I, alongside others, would argue that the reality is far from hidden to those who live crises on a daily basis. In contrast, as Beverly Tatum (1997) suggests: "Dominants do not really know what the experience of the subordinates is" (p. 24). Or, as Proma describes, refuse to acknowledge the existence of inequality, of racism, homophobia, etc. One responsibility educators have, as you express, Proma, is to "expose the violences that are rendered invisible," particularly to those who have been privileged enough to be removed from those violences.

What does this mean for anti-oppressive education, anti-oppressive educators? Is it then always about pain? Always about suffering? Always, ironically, about fighting? I am heartened, George, by the first line of your chapter: "More than anything else, teaching is an act of faith in the future." I am reminded here of Paulo Freire's (1996) work and the necessity of hope. Anti-oppressive education must be a "pedagogy of hope." If it is not, it is doomed to drive its proponents, its advocates, its messengers, its warriors to an early death. He describes peasants in Brazil coming to understand "not only that they could speak, but that their critical discourse upon the world, their world, was a way of remaking that world. It was as if they had begun to perceive that the development of their language, which occurred in the course of their analysis of their reality, finally showed them that the lovelier world to which they aspired was being announced, somehow anticipated, in their imagination" (Freire, 1996, p. 39). Thus, we need to break open silences, have frequent "one-minute on the mike rallies" in our classrooms, rendering visible those who have been invisible, naming crises that have been absent from classroom and community conversations. Pedagogies of presence such as this can lead ultimately to "the lovelier world." This needs to be our daily and collective work of teaching in a time of all crises.

I take the three of you inside with me into my teacher education classroom, fortunate in the sense that I do not have to hide you within a Trojan Horse. There, I will let you and your stories come out in conversation with my students and the stories of those living in and out of crisis. Thanks for the opportunity.

George (to reader): In their critical, thoughtful, and self-reflexive discussions, Proma Tagore, Fairin Herising, and Jocelyn Glazier enact the cultures of learning that their arguments envision. They present us with a profound dilemma—that classroom practices cannot change unless we identify and challenge the unstated assumptions, premises, and ideological commitments of the broader social pedagogy that permeates society. Yet we will not meaningfully contest that broader social pedagogy unless and until classroom educators produce new cultures of curiosity, critical thinking, work, achievement, and aspiration. Both pieces indicate that teachers have hard work ahead of us, that arming students with the skills they need to be lifelong learners and critical thinkers in this society goes against the grain of the dominant class-room and social pedagogies.

Tagore and Herising's "Pedagogies of Presence" focuses on how normative notions of pedagogy, curriculum, and epistemology work to isolate, marginalize, and devalue nonnormative identities, imaginaries, and epistemologies. Glazier's "Anti-Oppressive Pedagogy and Curriculum" emphasizes the necessary link between knowing and doing, that it is not enough for students to identify problems in their world; but that they also have to think of themselves as people able and willing to work with others to solve those problems. In my response, I will comment briefly on the original and generative contributions that Tagore, Herising, and Glazier make to our work, and then I will argue for the pedagogical, epistemological, and curricular value of the knowledge forged in struggle by social movement organizations.

Tagore and Herising point out that even our sense of urgency about teaching in a time of war betrays an unconscious privilege. The war in Iraq and its related political and ideological consequences threaten to destroy many of the things that citizens of the United States value—our constitutional rights, our social infrastructure, and our reputation in the world. But the state of war that strikes us as emergency is a perpetual reality for many people, from Palestine to Colombia to Okinawa. Even worse, if all wars in the world somehow ended tomorrow morning, more than 30,000 children under the age of five in Asia, Africa, and Latin America would still die every day from completely curable illnesses or malnutrition. One million children in Africa live homeless, orphaned, or abandoned as a direct result of the dictates of Western financial institutions that mandated the dismantling of state-sponsored education, health care, housing, and employment. Sixty percent of the 4.5 billion people living in the poorest countries in the world lack basic sanitation facilities and 1 billion do not have access to safe and uncontaminated water, 828 million people in the world do not have enough to eat; nearly a third of them will die before their fortieth birthday (Maxted, 2003; Schoepf et al., 2000). Global inequality combined with sexism, misogyny, and pedophilia creates profit-making opportunities in sex tourism whereby wealthy European and American predators buy sex from desperately poor adults, teens, and children in Asia and the Caribbean. Our problem is not that the war is such a departure from "business as usual" that it challenges our moral and intellectual resources; but rather that the war is such a logical consequence of "business as usual" that it forces us to look at the invisible commonplace and everyday "normality" against which the emergency of war is constructed.

In this context, it is difficult to imagine how imparting new knowledge to our students could make a difference. Tagore and Herising delineate how the dominant social pedagogy inhibits honest encounters with the depths, dimensions, and duration of unequal power. When *The Wretched of the Earth* (Fanon, 1968) speaks about the routine terror of colonial rule, about the hate, hurt, and fear imbued in individuals by colonialism and racism, some students defend themselves by dismissing Fanon as hateful and hurtful, missing entirely his critique of what these inequalities do to both dominator and oppressor. Even students who embrace Fanon's ideas from the safety of contemporary North America often miss his wrenching discussion of the costs the oppressed pay for the violence they feel they must use. They do not notice his prescient analysis of the limits of revolutionary violence and the betrayal of the masses built into the concept of anti-colonial nationalism. Yet uncomfortable as they are, these discussions of Fanon—like the fight over the School of Social Work's antiwar resolution—can be valuable tools for making the absent present, and for building what Walter Benjamin (1969) called "presence of mind"—a fully interrogated relationship to the past, present, and future.

Yet despite the fact that what constitutes an emergency for us may be someone else's routine expectation, our sense that the war poses an emergency for us is not entirely wrong. By making visible what was previously invisible, it can spur us on to new and better ways of knowing and being. Homi Bhabha (1994) writes that out of every emergency there is an emergence. A society that properly expresses anguish over 3,000 deaths at the World Trade Center in New York City in 2001 and over 1,000 deaths of U.S. military personnel in Iraq since 2003 but which forbids even mention—much less grief or mourning—over the thousands of Iraqis killed by the war (and by bombings and sanctions for nearly a decade before it) is a society that desperately needs new educational methods and practices. Some of those techniques come into clear relief in Jocelyn Glazier's discussion of critical literacy and anti-oppressive pedagogy.

Glazier argues for techniques that arm students with skills for critical thinking and problem solving so that they can succeed long after they leave our classrooms. Unlike the skills taught by the regimes of high-stakes testing that now dominate U.S. classrooms, the critical literacy pedagogy recognizes that learning does not take place in discrete isolatable moments, but rather as an ongoing organic process. Glazier notes the importance of connecting the unit plan to the broader curriculum, to encourage students to see their knowledge as cumulative and continuing rather than as atomized and isolated. Facts remain important in this pedagogy and curriculum, but they acquire their value through analysis, in relation to and in comparison with other equally true facts. Most important for Glazier is to make learning an active process, both in its immediate experiences and in its ultimate aims.

The new ways of knowing that we need to face the perilous present and the foreboding future will not be generated solely in classrooms. Social movement struggles produce more than material victories and defeats. They also generate patterns of organizational learning that contain new evidence, ideas, archives, imaginaries, epistemologies, and ontologies. The Okinawan Women Act Against Military Violence, for example, challenges the notion of security that lies at the heart of the U.S.-declared "war on terror" (Fukumura and Matsuoka, 2002). They charge that massive diversion of resources and labor to warfare serves to contain and control people like themselves who oppose the global economic system, who challenge neoliberal policies designed to privatize state assets, lower barriers to trade, and limit the power of local entities to regulate the environment. Perhaps most important, they call for a new definition of "security," one that places the security of women, children, and ordinary people before the security of the state and financial institutions. They "queer" the nation— not because they take an explicit position on the rights of gays and lesbians, but because they interrupt and contest the narrative of patriarchal protection upon which the nation-state so often rests.

The political position of the Okinawan Women Act Against Military Violence (OWAAMV) (Fukumura and Matsuoka, 2002) appears absurd to many people educated by the dominant social and classroom pedagogies in North America. It draws deeply, however, on the situated knowledge that emerges from struggles against inequality that make complete sense if one views the world from the perspective of Okinawan women. Coming from a country that has been serially colonized since the seventeenth century and occupied military by both the United States and Japan, OWAAMV activists cannot solve their problems within a single national context. Disadvantaged by colonial status, race, and gender they cannot turn to national liberation, antiracism, or feminism as their sole context for struggle. Coming from a small island with a limited population in a corner of the world far removed from metropolitan centers of power, they must forge alliances with outsiders based on political affinities and identifications, rather than counting on the solidarities of sameness that sustain most social movements. As eyewitnesses to brutal combat on the island in 1945 that killed more than 130,000 Okinawan civilians (one-third of the local population) and tens of thousands of Japanese and U.S. military personnel, they find it impossible to celebrate organized violence and masculinist militarism. As women confronted with the pervasive presence of commercial sex establishments, sex tourism, and rapes of civilian women and girls by military personnel, they see gender as a central axis of power and struggle.

The OWAAMV also advances a particular pedagogy. One of their techniques is the "one minute on the mike" rally, in which women speak in succession with no speaker allowed more than 60 seconds on the microphone. This enacts the democratic and egalitarian philosophy that the group envisions, resting authority in the cumulative testimony of the collectivity rather than in the eloquence of a charismatic leader. It also exposes the diversity and plurality of the group, resisting premature closures based on the solidarities of sameness to instead fashion a collective project that takes full advantage of the dynamics of difference, of the ways in which women all suffer from militarism, but not in the same ways.

The complicated history that brought the OWAAMV into existence, and which vexes them in so many ways, has produced new ways of being and new ways of knowing that contain enormous generative power. They seek allies and propose global solutions, but they do so as particular subjects formed by historically specific relationships to empire, war, and sexism. They are only one of many groups being thrown forward as a result of the inequalities, injustices, and indecencies of our time. They are not teachers or students in the formal meaning of those terms, but they are engaged in teaching and learning that speaks powerfully to our present moment.

Michael Eric Dyson (2003) argues that socially conscious teachers can function much as the Trojan Horse did in Greek mythology. He explains that we go through life and meet many serious people whom no one takes seriously, people with profound things to say and no place to say it. Most of the time, we cannot take those people with us to our college classrooms, our professional meetings, or our lecture halls. But we can carry them inside us like a Trojan Horse, and when we get to the microphones, lecterns, television cameras, or especially the word processors to which we sometimes have access, we can open ourselves up and let all those other people out. This can never be our only way of teaching, but it can be an important component of what we do. Learning from social movements can be a way to bring the classroom and the community closer together, one additional means for implementing the emancipatory agendas articulated so elegantly by Tagore, Herising, and Glazier.

References

Bannerji, H. (1995). *Thinking through: Essays on feminism, Marxism, and anti-racism.* Toronto: Women's Press.

Benjamin, W. (1969). *One way street.* London: New Left Books.

Bhabha, H. (1994). *The location of culture.* London, New York: Routledge.

Britzman, D. P. (1998). *Lost subjects, contested objects: Toward a psychoanalytic inquiry of learning.* Albany, NY: State University of New York Press.

Deleuze, G., and Gauttari, F. (1987). *A thousand plateaus capitalism and schizophrenia.* Minneapolis: University of Minnesota Press.

Dyson, M. E. (2003). "Be a Trojan horse." Author's notes, CNN Broadcast, December 12.

Fanon, F. (1968). *The wretched of the earth.* New York: Grove Press.

Foucault, M. (1989). Space, knowledge and power. In Lotringer, S. (Ed.), *Foucault live: Collected Interviews, 1961–1984* (pp. 335–347). Semiotext(e). Columbia University. New York

Freire, P. (1996). *Pedagogy of hope.* New York: Continuum.

Fukumura, Y., and Matsuoka, M. (2002). Redefining security: Okinawa women's resistance to U.S. militarism. In N. A. Naples and M. Desai (Eds.), *Women's activism and globalization: Linking local struggles and transnational politics* (pp. 239–263). New York and London: Routledge.

hooks, b. (1994). *Teaching to transgress. Education as the practice of freedom.* London: Routledge.

Maxted, J. (2003). Children and armed conflict in Africa. *Social Identities, 9*(3), 51, 56.

Mohanty, C. (2003). *Feminism without borders: Decolonizing theory, practicing solidarity.* Durham: Duke UP.

Schoepf, B. G., Schoepf, C., and Millen, J. V. (2000). Theoretical therapies, remote remedies: SAPs and the political ecology of poverty and health in Africa. In J. Y. Kim, J. V. Millen, A. Irwin, and J. Gershman (Eds.), *Dying for growth: Global inequality and the health of the poor* (pp. 120–121). Monroe, ME: Common Courage Press.

Spivak, G. (1994). Can the subaltern speak? In Patrick Williams and Laura Chrisman (Eds.), *Colonial discourse and postcolonial theory: A reader* (p. 86). New York: Columbia UP.

Tatum, B. (1997). *Why are all the Black kids sitting together in the cafeteria?* New York: Basic Books.

Contributors

Ann Berlak has been teaching for critical thinking, social justice and empowerment for over forty years. Her research focuses on promoting teachers' passionate concern for the survival of democracy. Presently she is adjunct professor in the department of elementary education at San Francisco State University. She is co-author with Sekani Moyenda of *Taking It Personally: Racism in the Classroom from Kindergarten to College.*

Mary Curran is an Assistant Professor of Language Education at Rutgers, The State University of New Jersey. She has taught ESL, EFL, and Spanish as a world language to children and adults. She is interested in the important role language educators can play in the quest for social justice. Her research focuses on pedagogical tools and assessments designed to help future teachers work effectively with linguistically and culturally diverse students. Some of her publications include articles published in *TESOL Quarterly*, *The Journal of Teacher Education*, and *Theory into Practice*.

Mark R. Davies is an Assistant Professor of Education at Hartwick College in Oneonta, New York. He was a New Jersey public high school teacher of social studies for eight years in Howell Township a culturally and economically diverse community. His position at Hartwick College is his first in academia. His focus is in critical pedagogy, cultural analysis and peer mediation programs.

Linda Fernsten is a member of the Human Development and Learning Department of Dowling College in New York. She works primarily in the graduate program with teacher-candidates and practicing teachers. Her main research interest is in the teaching of writing, not only across the disciplines, but also as writing combines with social justice concerns in our society. She has presented nationally and internationally on these topics as well as on writer identity, alternative assessment, and multicultural issues.

Jocelyn Anne Glazier is an assistant professor of Teaching and Learning at the University of North Carolina at Chapel Hill. Her research and teaching interests include teacher education, critical pedagogy and social justice. Dr. Glazier's current research includes an ethnographic exploration of how new teachers teach in critical ways within uncritical and oppressive contexts. Of particular interest to Dr. Glazier is how critical teaching ultimately impacts the lives and communities of K-12 students when they step outside of the classroom context. Glazier's research has been published in such journals as *Harvard Educational Review*, *Teachers College Record* and *Teaching Education*.

Fairn Herising is a graduate student at the University of Victoria. She has taught and developed anti-oppressive curriculum for the School of Social Work at the University of Victoria. Fairn has been actively involved in various community politics for 20 years from AIDS activism, violence against women, anti-racism and anti-colonialism to queer and trans-activism. Fairn's quirks include queering up spaces, looking for love in all the delightfully wrong places, and perpetually coloring outside the lines.

Dr. Mary Beth Hines is associate professor and chair of the Language Education department at Indiana University. She teaches courses on the teaching of writing, as well as interdisciplinary courses on literacy and cultural politics. Her research focuses upon English teachers conducting social justice inquiry in the classroom and in the community, thereby contributing to social change. She has written articles, book chapters, and presented at conferences on these issues. She is currently collaborating on a book with members of the Indiana English Teachers Collaborative, a network of teacher-researchers working for social change.

Judi Hirsch has been teaching public schooling New York, Israel, and California for over 30 years. Her main focus has been getting middle and high school students to believe that they are brilliant despite having been qualified as having a Learning Disability. Many of her students have gone on to graduate from four-year colleges, including UC Berkeley. One is now in law school. She has a doctorate in Multicultural Education, and is frequently asked to speak at national and international conferences.

Gloria Holmes is an Associate Professor of Education and Chair of the Division of Education at Quinnipiac University in Hamden, CT. She has done research on African American literature and culture, and is a diversity consultant who works to promote cultural literacy.

Rita Kissen is Professor of Teacher Education at the University of Southern Maine, where she teachers courses in pre-service education and Women's Studies. She is the author of *The Last Closet: The Real Lives of Lesbian and Gay Teachers* and editor of *Getting Ready for Benjamin: Preparing Teachers for Sexual Diversity in the Classroom*.

Jane L. Lehr is a PhD candidate in Science & Technology Studies at Virginia Tech and post-doctoral research associate at the Center for Informal Learning and Schools at King's College London. Her research seeks to initiate a dialogue about non-science classrooms as possible sites of informal science education, offering unique opportunities for feminist, critical, and radical educators to intervene in normative relationships between science education and non-scientist citizenship. She was the 2003 recipient of the Outstanding Graduate Student Award in the College of Arts and Sciences at Virginia Tech in recognition of her commitment to social justice work as a teacher, researcher, and community organizer.

Charlotte Lichter received her M.A. from the Department of Education at Mount Saint Vincent University. Her research interests include the underachievement of boys in school. She has specifically focused on the "What about the boys?" debate as it relates to boys, masculinity, and literacy.

George Lipsitz is Professor and Chair of American Studies at the University of California, Santa Cruz. He is the author of seven books including *American Studies in a Moment of Danger* and *The Possessive Investment in Whiteness*. Lipsitz edits the Critical American Studies series for the University of Minnesota Press and co-edits the American Crossroads series for the University of California Press. His articles have appeared in *American Quarterly*, *Comparative American Studies*, *American Literary History*, and *Journal of American History*.

Sekani Moyenda is in her eleventh year of teaching at an Elementary School in San Francisco. She teaches first grade, lectures and provides workshops in social justice classroom management strategies and curriculum with Teachers for Social Justice and in the classroom with her students and their families. She is co-author of Taking It Personally: Racism in the Classroom from Kindergarten to College. She continues to resist oppression in education through her curriculum and challenging educators to adopt a social justice model and world view in their everyday practice and life as teachers and citizens.

Connie North is a doctoral student, Departments of Curriculum and Instruction and Educational Policy, University of Wisconsin-Madison. Her areas of specialization are teacher and anti-oppressive education. Connie's research has appeared in journals such as the *International Journal of Qualitative Studies in Education* and *Review of Educational Research*.

Thomas M. Philip is a doctoral candidate in the Graduate School of Education at the University of California-Berkeley. In his work and teaching, he is interested in progressive pedagogy, and how to translate intellectual pursuits into everyday practices that address equity and learning in society. In 2005 Philip won an Outstanding Graduate Instructor Award for his work in helping to teach a graduate course, The Philosophy of Education.

Carol Ricker-Wilson is an English/Literacy consultant with the Toronto District School Board, and a long-time teacher in the Canadian free school and alternative school movement. She received the Mary McEwan Award from York University's Centre for Feminist Research for her Ph. D in Women's Studies. Her research background is in critical pedagogy, critical literacy, and gender and literacy. She was previously seconded as a course director at the Faculty of Education, York University, and is a sessional instructor in adolescent literacy at O.I.S.E., University of Toronto.

Proma Tagore teaches in the areas of postcolonial, feminist, and queer studies and literature at the University of Victoria, Canada. Her poetry has been published in *Red Silk: An Anthology of South Asian Canadian Women Poets*, and she is currently working on editing an anthology, entitled *In Our Own Voices: Teaching and Learning Toward Decolonization*.

Studies in the Postmodern Theory of Education

General Editors
Joe L. Kincheloe & Shirley R. Steinberg

Counterpoints publishes the most compelling and imaginative books being written in education today. Grounded on the theoretical advances in criticalism, feminism, and postmodernism in the last two decades of the twentieth century, Counterpoints engages the meaning of these innovations in various forms of educational expression. Committed to the proposition that theoretical literature should be accessible to a variety of audiences, the series insists that its authors avoid esoteric and jargonistic languages that transform educational scholarship into an elite discourse for the initiated. Scholarly work matters only to the degree it affects consciousness and practice at multiple sites. Counterpoints' editorial policy is based on these principles and the ability of scholars to break new ground, to open new conversations, to go where educators have never gone before.

For additional information about this series or for the submission of manuscripts, please contact:

Joe L. Kincheloe & Shirley R. Steinberg
c/o Peter Lang Publishing, Inc.
29 Broadway, 18th floor
New York, New York 10006

To order other books in this series, please contact our Customer Service Department:

(800) 770-LANG (within the U.S.)
(212) 647-7706 (outside the U.S.)
(212) 647-7707 FAX

Or browse online by series:
www.peterlang.com